Fodor's 90

Yugoslavia

D1359260

Fodor's Travel Publications, Inc.
New York & London

Copyright © 1990 by Fodor's Travel Publications, Inc.

Fodor's is a trademark of Fodor's Travel Publications, Inc.

All rights reserved under International and Pan-American Copyright Conventions.
Published in the United States by Fodor's Travel Publications, Inc., a subsidiary of
Random House, Inc., New York, and simultaneously in Canada by Random House of
Canada Limited, Toronto. Distributed by Random House, Inc., New York.

*No maps, illustrations, or other portions of this book may be reproduced in any form without
written permission from the publisher.*

ISBN 0-679-01850-6

Fodor's Yugoslavia

Editor: Richard Moore
Area Editor: Sylvie Nickels
Contributor: Robert Brown
Drawings: Beryl Sanders
Maps: Alex Murphy, Swanston Graphics, Bryan Woodfield
Cover Photograph: Steve Vidler/Four by Five

Cover Design: Vignelli Associates

Special Sales

Fodor's Travel Publications are available at special discounts for bulk purchases
(100 copies or more) for sales promotions of premiums. Special editions,
including personalized covers, excerpts of existing guides, and corporate
imprints, can be created in large quantities for special needs. For more
information, write Special Marketing, Fodor's Travel Publications, 201 East
50th Street, New York, NY 10022. Inquiries from the United Kingdom should
be sent to Fodor's Travel Publications, 30-32 Bedford Square, London WC1B
3SG.

MANUFACTURED IN THE UNITED STATES OF AMERICA
10 9 8 7 6 5 4 3 2 1

CONTENTS

FOREWORD

One of the very first images that springs to mind at the mention of Yugoslavia, impelled no doubt by colorful illustrations in travel brochures, is that of the sunny Dalmatian coast with its innumerable islands. But there is much more to this fascinating country. It is a complex nation consisting of six autonomous republics (Slovenia, Croatia, Serbia Bosnia-Hercegovina, Montenegro and Macedonia) and two autonomous provinces within Serbia (Vovodina and Kosovo), and demonstrates the molding influences of different civilizations. Over the centuries, Yugoslavia absorbed the varying characteristics of successive waves of invaders.

Such complexities of history and cultural influence, however, can bring problems as well as rewards, as have recently been manifested in nationalist conflicts between Serbs and Albanians in Kosovo. These are discussed in the section on south Serbia and, if you are planning to visit that region, it would be sensible to check the current situation. Most other parts of the country are untouched by the unrest.

So, though the country at large seems to be a homogenous unit to the casual visitor, the closer one looks, the greater the differences that can be seen between the republics, with some areas vividly recalling bygone ways of life. To appreciate them, it is wise to have at least a nodding acquaintance with Yugoslavia's incredibly complex history. Slovenia, for example, retains many facets of the Austro-Hungarian Empire. Istria and Dalmatia still recall the Venetian Maritime Republic. Bosnia and southern Serbia preserve the slower rhythm of life and Islamic color of the days of the Ottoman Sultanate. This fascinating, sometimes anachronistic mélange is heavily overlaid, of course, by a social system that adds interesting features of contemporary origin. The resulting mixture of old and new, together with the wonderful variety of landscape, make a trip to Yugoslavia uniquely rewarding. The Federal Socialist Republic of Yugoslavia, an association of Communist states, is *not* behind the Iron Curtain, and has placed no needles restrictions of foreign visitors for well over 30 years.

Over the last couple of decades, Yugoslavia has made huge efforts to provide facilities that will make the visitor's stay more pleasant. Standards of hotels and restaurants have been vastly improved, roads and transportation in general have developed by leaps and bounds with modern highways now sweeping through countryside that used to be served only by simple, gravel roads. Standards of service may not have kept pace with the building program and, it has to be admitted, plumbing and electric wiring are not always all they might be. But, despite soaring inflation, Yugoslavia remains a bargain as far as the visitor is concerned, for rising prices are more than matched by constantly adjusting exchange rates. The trick is never to buy more dinars than you'll need for your immediate requirements.

The creation of the vast modern hotel complexes along the Dalmatian coast turned the country into one of the most popular goals for the package-tour operators of most of the European countries. Yearly, waves of tourists break on the coast, filling the huge interlinked hotels to capacity. If you are looking for a reasonably-priced holiday and do not mind being one of a multiligual crowd, then the benefits are considerable. If, however, you want atmosphere, like to find character and interest in your surroundings and enjoy uncluttered scenery, then keep away from the hurly-burly of the coast in the high season, and head for the mountains of Slovenia,

Bosnia-Hercegovina, Macedonia or Montenegro. There you will discover that traditional fascinations of Yugoslavia are still very much alive.

We would like to thank Sylvie Nickels for her considerable assistance in preparing this edition. Our gratitude goes to Mr. Selim Selim, Director of the Yugoslav National Tourist Office in London, and to the staff, for their constant help, advice and kindness; also to the Yugoslav National Tourist Office in Belgrade and the tourist associations of many individual Republics, regions and resorts for their assistance and cooperation.

While every care has been taken to assure the accuracy of the information in this guide, the passage of time will always bring change, and consequently the publisher cannot accept responsibility for errors that may occur.

All prices and opening times quoted in this guide are based on information available to us at press time. Hours and admission fees may change, however, and the prudent traveler will avoid inconvenience by calling ahead.

Fodor's wants to hear about your travel experiences, both pleasant and unpleasant. When a hotel or restaurant fails to live up to its billing, let us know and we will investigate the complaint and revise our entries where the facts warrant it.

Send your letters to the editors of Fodor's Travel Publications, 201 E. 50th Street, New York, NY 10022.

FACTS AT YOUR FINGERTIPS

Planning Your Trip

WHEN TO GO. July and August are the most popular months for holidays along the coast. They are also, of course, the most crowded and the hottest. In the majority of places the heat is tempered by the sea breezes, but one or two spots, notably the town of Split (not the surroundings), are sheltered by mountains and become rather airless. The coast is also subject to strong winds: the cold, dry *bura* and warm, humid *yugo* (mainly in winter but can be at other times), and the more frequent *maestral.* Summer storms can be fierce but are usually of short duration. Bathing is possible on the coast from early May or June (depending on latitude of resort) to early October. Winters are relatively mild, though it may rain a lot up to about May.

Summers can be very hot indeed inland, unless you contrive to spend at least part of your time in the mountains. Spring and fall are decidedly the best times for the interior. Winters there can be extremely cold. Winter sports in the inland mountain regions of all the Republics begin in December and last until April or May.

Average maximum daily temperatures in degrees Fahrenheit and centigrade:

Belgrade

	Jan.	Feb.	Mar.	Apr.	May	June	July	Aug.	Sept.	Oct.	Nov.	Dec.
F°	37	41	53	64	74	79	84	83	76	65	52	40
C°	3	5	12	18	23	26	29	28	24	18	11	4

Dubrovnik

	Jan.	Feb.	Mar.	Apr.	May	June	July	Aug.	Sept.	Oct.	Nov.	Dec.
F°	50	52	58	63	70	76	80	79	75	69	60	52
C°	10	11	14	17	21	24	27	26	24	21	16	11

Here is a simple conversion chart to help you change Fahrenheit into centigrade and vice versa—

°Centigrade	°C or °F	°Fahrenheit
−18	0	32
−15	5	41
−12	10	50
−9.5	15	59

1

°Centigrade	°C or °F	°Fahrenheit
–7	20	68
–4	25	77
–1	30	86
2	35	95
4.5	40	104
7	45	113
10	50	122

Off-Season Travel. This can be rewarding in Yugoslavia, not only for bypassing the crowds and higher prices, but for the opportunity to meet and know the people of the country. Spring is particularly delightful for nature-lovers, and the most comfortable season for almost every kind of sightseeing. Fall and winter are best for hunting. Winters are cold inland, but usually pleasant by the sea (though there are rainy periods). The average winter temperatures along the Dalmatian coast are higher than those on the French or Italian rivieras, but note the strong winds mentioned on page 1.

The winter sports season is at its height, from January until about the end of March.

WHERE TO GO. Regions and Cities. Yugoslavia, except for its coast, is a relatively unexplored area. Travelers today, however, encounter all of the comforts and facilities to which they are accustomed. Yet a journey to Yugoslavia remains an adventure; wherever you go, this is a land of bold bright contrasts. Scenically, the Alps of Slovenia and wild peaks of Montenegro contrast with the vast flat Danube plains of parts of Serbia and the rugged river gorges that rib much of the rest of the country. Ancient cultures, everywhere in evidence, contrast with rapid economic and industrial growth. Holiday-wise, the sun-soaked siesta of a Dalmatian beach contrasts with a motor trip over the mountain roads of Macedonia. The extremes of physical tourist comfort range from the luxury of major resorts to the more basic joys of village tourism, now developing in many areas.

Yugoslavia is a sizeable country: its 98,000 square miles make it slightly larger than Great Britain, or Oregon; it has a population of over 22 million. Distances are made longer by the country's many mountain ranges. Fully three-fourths of its area consists of mountains and highlands. Most tourists prefer to concentrate on one region at a time. These (and main centers) are:

Istria and the Kvarner Gulf: Poreč, Portorož, Pula, Opatija, Rijeka; island centers: Mali Lošinj (Lošinj); Baška, Malinska (Krk); Rab (Rab)

Central Dalmatia: Zadar, Split; island centers: Bol (Brać); Hvar, Jelsa (Hvar); Korčula (Korčula)

Southern Dalmatia and Montenegro: Dubrovnik, Herceg-Novi, Budva

Inland Slovenia: Ljubljana, Maribor, Bled

Inland Croatia: Zagreb, Varaždin, Plitvice Lakes

Serbia: Belgrade, Niš, Priština, Novi Sad

Bosnia-Hercegovina: Sarajevo, Mostar, Jajce, Banja Luka

Macedonia: Skopje, Ohrid

Inland Montenegro: Titograd, Cetinje, Žabljak

The Coast. If, like most tourists, you seek the sun, Yugoslavia offers one of the most deeply indented coastlines in Europe, 628 km. (400 miles) as the crow flies, but 6,116 km. (3,823 miles) of actual shoreline, including about 1,000 islands and 100s of attractive beaches set against a scenic background of blue skies, towering limestone mountains and a myriad of offshore islands, covered sometimes with pinewoods, sometimes with olive groves or vineyards, and sometimes with Mediterranean scrub and fragrant wild herbs. The lion's share of the coast is in the republic of Croatia, the northern extremity in Slovenia and the southern in Montenegro. From north to south, some of the principal towns or tourist centers are: Poreč, ancient town and center for several major modern tourist complexes; Opatija, a highly popular seaside resort with many fine hotels; Rijeka, Yugoslavia's main seaport; Zadar, noted for both Roman and medieval relics and ruins; Split, where the entire heart of the old city is formed by Diocletian's third-century Roman palace; peaceful Makarska; fabulous walled Dubrovnik with its ramparts, moat and drawbridges; Budva, a little walled Venetian town; Sveti Stefan, a one-time fishing village, now a luxury tourist complex; and Ulcinj, a Moslem town with a splendid beach, close to the Albanian frontier.

You can cruise this marvelous coast on a comfortable Jadrolinija cruise steamer, starting from Venice or Rijeka. If you visit the islands you have to use hydrofoil, car-and-passenger ferries, or the passenger services run by Jadrolinija. You can also use the Jadranska Magistrala (Adriatic Highway) to travel up and down the coast by comfortable bus or private car, using the now numerous car ferries to reach the nearer islands (one or two are also accessible by road bridge). Either way you can visit such wonderful places as Rab in the north; Brač, a short sea journey from Split; Hvar; magic Korčula, where some maintain Marco Polo was born; Mljet, which some claim to be the most beautiful of all Dalmatia's islands, and a host of other lovely places. Wherever you choose, even the smallest resorts present a crowded, animated scene at the height of summer, in sharp contrast to the sleepy calm of the off-season.

Inland Slovenia. If you prefer Alpine lakes and mountains, Slovenia is for you. Its capital, Ljubljana, is bright and mainly modern with a fascinating medieval citadel, built on the site of prehistoric and Roman settlements. Bled is beside a mountain lake reflecting the peaks of the Julian Alps, featuring fine hotels, water sports and mountain trails. Higher up you come to Bohinj, by a larger lake nestled at the base of Triglav, Yugoslavia's highest mountain. Western Yugoslavia is noted for limestone caverns and underground rivers, characteristic of the karst that covers much of the country. One of the loveliest limestone grottos in the world is in Slovenia at Postojna, halfway between Trieste and Ljubljana.

Bosnia-Hercegovina. Perhaps your taste runs to the exotic? Then explore Bosnia-Hercegovina, a land of beautiful bare mountains, cut by fertile green valleys and spectacular river gorges. This once-remote mountainous province has retained a distinct Oriental character from over 400 years of Ottoman rule. You can reach Sarajevo, its capital, by air, train, or comfortable coach services and good roads. Here you will discover Turkish-era mosques, minarets, and bazaars, finely set off by well-designed modern structures, among the latest of them created to cater for the 1984

Winter Olympics. The Bosnian hinterland is a wild region of mountains and valleys, waterfalls and Moslem communities. The last two are combined in the little town of Jajce, a medieval capital of Bosnia though it was also here that Tito's partisans proclaimed the modern republic of Yugoslavia in 1943. In the south of the region, attractive Mostar, with its famous single-span bridge (1566), is the capital of Hercegovina. An hour or so's drive away is one of Europe's newest pilgrimage centers, the village of Medjugorje.

Inland Montenegro. Even more remote is the former kingdom of Montenegro, of which Titograd is the modern capital. Here, atop Mount Lovćen, is one of the most startling panoramas in Europe: a real Sputnik-eye view of the lovely Gulf of Kotor on the one hand, and the high-rearing Black Mountains of inland Montenegro on the other. At Cetinje, you'll visit the modest palace of Montenegro's former king. Beyond are the awe-inspiring gorges of the Tara and Piva rivers, and the exciting road over the Čakor Pass to Peć, gateway to Serbia and Macedonia. Žabljak is the developing resort from which you can best experience the spectacular mountain massif of Durmitor.

Serbia. In Belgrade (Beograd, meaning "White City"), you are not only in the capital of Yugoslavia but in the heart of the Balkans. Destroyed time and again in countless conflicts, Belgrade's checkered past is summarized in the silent stones of Kalemegdan and its park where you can wander through an ancient Turkish fortress built on a still more ancient Roman one, throw coins down a well from which people were drinking 2,000 years ago, or gaze out over the cliffs to where the mighty Sava river pours its waters into the still mightier Danube. Beyond begin the endless plains of the Vojvodina. South of Belgrade you are soon in the mountains, ribbed by remote valleys that shelter some of the most remarkable examples of medieval art anywhere, in the form of monasteries embellished by exquisite frescoes.

Macedonia. Worth an expedition in itself, this sizeable republic is scenically magnificent and historically fascinating. Its monasteries and their frescoes, many pre-dating those of Serbia, are stunning, and so are many of their settings. Some can be visited from the capital Skopje, imaginatively reconstructed after the destructive earthquake of July 1963; others, including some of the best, are in Ohrid, also a gorgeous lake-side resort, in the far southwest of the republic. Much earlier still are Macedonia's many substantial remains of Hellenistic, Roman and early Byzantine cultures.

Inland Croatia. Between Belgrade and Ljubljana, on Yugoslavia's main inland highway, lies Zagreb, city of the Middle Ages and at the same time, as happens so often in Yugoslavia, a very up-to-date town. In many parts of Croatia, where ancient ruined castles and fortresses stand on steep hilltops, the Middle Ages and the 20th century seem very close together. This is an extremely prosperous industrial and agricultural region.

South of Zagreb toward the coast lie the famous Plitvička Jezera (Plitvice Lakes), a chain of cascading mountain lakes, now a national park.

Here, amid centuries-old forests, 16 jewel-like green-and-blue lakes spill mile after mile, one into the other, as down a flight of steps.

Spas, Hot Springs. These are found principally in Slovenia, Croatia, Serbia and Bosnia. Among the 100s of thermal stations are a number which are once more beginning to attract international clientele. Some have been or are being developed to international standards and are referred to in our regional chapters. Information about specific disorders treated by Yugoslavia's curative springs can be obtained from any Yugoslav National Tourist Office.

WHAT WILL IT COST. Yugoslavia is currently experiencing a runaway rate of inflation. For this reason, there is little sense in quoting dinar prices and in most cases the dollar equivalents are given. Where dinar prices are quoted, it is essential to remember that they may well have doubled or even quadrupled by the summer of 1990. However, this will also be reflected in the rate of exchange, so that, from the visitor's point of view, Yugoslavia can still be an excellent bargain, especially at the level of moderate and inexpensive accommodations and restaurants, or away from the more popular tourist haunts. Please take particular note of the comments in the "Money" section below.

You can make major economies by traveling out of season when hotel prices are lower. In a large tourist area such as Dubrovnik, for example, the cheaper rooms in a hotel may double in price for July, August and September, and the more expensive rooms will go up by 30–50%. Remember, too, that you have only to venture a little off the beaten track to find a sharp drop in prices. Private house accommodations, available in four categories, cost substantially less than hotels. Our sections on "Hotels" and other accommodations give guidance on standards and other potential savings.

The Yugoslav National Tourist Office quotes *all* hotel prices in dollars or deutschmarks, though the hotels themselves must be paid in dinars. Consequently, as the exchange rate fluctuates, you may well find a difference between the advertised dollar price of a hotel and the actual dinar price. Watch out for these potential discrepancies.

Sample Costs. With current inflation and constantly changing exchange rates, there is little sense in quoting dinar prices, so dollar equivalents are given for the following. Tram or bus tickets 25–30 cents; taxi a basic 45–50 cents, plus 20 cents per km.; men's haircut from $1.20, women's $2–3; –4; cinema 40–50 cents; theater 75 cents–$1 (more for special, e.g. festival performances); opera tickets in Belgrade $2–3; beer 50 cents; whiskey $1; *sljivovica* 30 cents; bottle of wine in moderate restaurant $2.50–3.50, in supermarket 75 cents–$2; coffee in a café 30 cents.

MONEY. The unit of currency in Yugoslavia is the dinar. The rate of exchange is constantly changing to match the soaring rate of inflation, so *never* exchange more than required to meet your immediate needs; a week later it could well have increased. At press time, the rate was about 25,000 dinars to the pound sterling, 16,500 dinars to the U.S. dollar, but it is quite likely to have changed immeasurably by the summer of 1990.

You may import or export up to 300,000 dinars.

There are coins of 1, 2, 5, 10, 20, 50 and 100 dinars, and bank notes of 50, 100, 500, 1,000, 5,000, 10,000, 20,000 and 50,000 dinars. Note that some of the newer coins are a different size and color from the older ones for the same values.

Helpful Tips About Cash. Always carry a few single dollar bills; they will save you from changing small travelers checks, and come in handy for last minute airport shopping.

Once inside Yugoslavia, you may exchange your travelers checks or foreign currency at the tourist rate at official exchange offices located in travel bureaux, hotels and railroad stations, as well as banks.

Travelers checks are the best way to safeguard your travel funds. In the U.S. Bank of America, First National City, Republic Bank of Dallas and Perera Co., issue checks only in U.S. dollars; Thomas Cook issues checks in U.S. dollars, British pounds and Australian dollars; Bank of Tokyo in U.S. dollars and Japanese yen; Barclay's Bank in dollars and pounds; and American Express in U.S. and Canadian dollars, French and Swiss francs, British pounds, German marks and Japanese yen.

Many British banks now operate the Eurocheque card which, together with Uniform Eurocheques, enable you to pay for goods and services in local currency. Each cheque is guaranteed up to the equivalent of approximately £100. Major credit cards are accepted at many establishments.

SOURCES OF INFORMATION. You have now decided *when* you want to visit Yugoslavia, and probably have a fair idea of *where* you wish to travel in the country. Next thing to do is to seek the advice of a travel agent—that is, if you haven't done so already. Even experienced travelers will find it advantageous to do so. A good agent can save you endless time. For package tour bookings and transportation reservations his charge to you will be the same as you would pay direct, as he receives a commission from carriers and tour operators. If he works out for you an individual itinerary, he will make a service charge on the total cost of your trip— usually 10%–15%, but it will more than likely *save* you money on balance. If you don't know of a reputable travel agent near your home, write:

In the United States: The American Society of Travel Agents, Box 23992, Washington, DC 20026.

In Britain: Association of British Travel Agents, 55–57 Newman St., London W1P 4AH.

If you want further details to plan your trip, here are the addresses of some of the Yugoslav government tourist offices abroad:

In the United States:

New York City: Yugoslav National Tourist Office, Rockefeller Center, 630 Fifth Ave., New York, NY 10111. Yugoslav Consulate, 767 Third Ave., 17th Flr., New York, NY 10017.

Chicago: Yugoslav Consulate, 307 N. Michigan Ave., Suite 1600, IL 60601.

Cleveland: Yugoslav Consulate, 1700 East 13th St., Suite 4R, OH 44114.

Pittsburgh: Yugoslav Consulate, 625 Stanwix St., Apt. 1605, PA 15222.

San Francisco: Yugoslav Consulate, 1375 Sutter St., Suite 406, CA
                 94709.
Washington: Yugoslav Embassy, 2410 California St. NW, Washing-
                 ton, DC 20008.

In Canada:
Toronto: Yugoslav Consulate, 377 Spadina Rd., Ontario M5P
                 2V7.
Ottawa: Yugoslav Embassy, 17 Blackburn Ave., Ontario K1N
                 8A2.
Vancouver: Yugoslav Consulate, 1237 Burrard St., Box 48359, BC
                 V7X 1A1.

In the U.K.:
London: Yugoslav National Tourist Office, 143 Regent St., Lon-
                 don W1R 8AE. Yugoslav Embassy, Consular Section,
                 5–7 Lexham Gdns., London W8 5JU.

TOUR OPERATORS. Suggested **American** tour operators:
Globus-Gateway/Cosmos, 95–25 Queens Blvd., Rego Park, NY 11374.
Hemphill/Harris, 16000 Ventura Blvd., Encino, CA 91436.
Kompas Yugoslavia, 630 Fifth Ave., Suite 219, New York, NY 10111.
Saga International Holidays Ltd., 120 Boylston St., Boston, MA 02116.
(Tours for senior citizens.)
   Trafalgar Tours, 21 East 26th St., New York, NY 10010.
   Yugotours, 350 Fifth Ave., New York, NY 10118.

Suggested **Canadian** tour operators:
Canadian Travel Abroad, 80 Richmond St. West, Suite 2007, Toronto,
Ontario M5H 2C6.
   Yugotours of Canada Ltd., 100 Adelaide St. West, Suite 1350, Toronto,
Ontario M5H 1S3.

Suggested **British** tour operators:
Inatours, 210 Shepherds Bush Rd., London W6 7NL.
   Island Sailing (flotilla sailing), The Port House, Port Solent, Hants PO6
4TH.
   Pan Adriatic Travel (tailor-made independent holidays), 49 Conduit
St., London W1R 9FB.
   Peng Travel (Naturist Holidays), 86 Station Rd., Gidea Park, Essex
RM2 6DB.
   Phoenix Holidays, 16 Bonny St., London NW1 9PG.
   Pilgrim Holidays, 21 Maddox St., London W1R 9LE.
   Ramblers Holidays (walking), Box 43, Welwyn Garden City, Herts
ALP 6PQ.
   Saga Holidays (for senior citizens), The Saga Building, Middelburg Sq.,
Folkestone, Kent CT20 1AZ.
   Thomson Holidays, Greater London House, Hampstead Rd., London
NW1 7SD.
   Yugotours, 150 Regent St., London W1R 6BB.

PACKAGE TOURS. Many tour operators feature Yugoslavia in their programs; some indeed have entire and extensive programs dedicated to that country. An up-dated list of them is available from the Yugoslav National Tourist Office overseas, indicating the variety of tours available each year. By far the majority are based on coastal resorts, sometimes featuring two centers such as a mainland and an island resort. An increasing number, however, are catering for those who wish to combine, say, a week on the coast with a week in the mountains, or touring the interior.

Sample costs for two weeks with half board and return flight ex-UK (depending on season and category of hotel) were as follows for 1989: Poreč (Istria), £210–£450; Dubrovnik (southern Dalmatia), £230–£700; one week Portorož (Istria), one week Bled (Slovenian Alps), £260–£424; one week coach tour (all meals), one week Dubrovnik (half board), £380–£490.

The Yugoslav coast also caters very well for naturists, with special hotel villages or camps, complete with their own beaches, restaurants, shops and sports facilities, such as at Punat (island of Krk), Poreč, Medulin, Rovinj, Koversada (near Vrsar in Istria), Rab, Srebreno (near Dubrovnik), Vrboska (on Hvar island), and Ada on an island on Montenegro's river border with Albania. In addition, there are many beaches along the coast for the exclusive use of naturist bathers, many of them signposted by the letters FKK.

Well-established, too, are cruises, yacht charter and flotilla sailing arrangements. The latter provide good opportunities for even the less experienced to sail in the company of like-minded souls and with expert guidance at hand. Sample costs for 14 days based on sailing from Split (Dalmatia) are £320–£570 (for each of four), including return flight and all equipment and fuel, but excluding food.

Other special interests catered for on packages marketed ex-UK include art treasures, monastery tours, horse riding, golf, walking, sailing or hunting in some of the country's excellent game reserves. Prices for such tours are naturally higher, but of course offer special opportunities to pursue your particular interest in the company of fellow enthusiasts.

Package or independent arrangements for all forms of travel and/or accommodations are also available.

A sampling of package tours to Yugoslavia include: *Globus-Gateway/Cosmos's* 233-day "The Balkans," with stops in Yugoslavia, Austria, Hungary, Greece, Turkey, Bulgaria and Romania. Land costs begin at $1, 488. "Vienna, Hungary and Yugoslavia," another *Globus-Gateway/Cosmos* offering, features the best of Austria, Hungary, and Yugoslavia. Tours begin in the U.S. with land costs starting at $1,028 for the 15-day trip.

Yugotours, 350 Fifth Ave., New York, NY 10118, also offers package tours to Yugoslavia, generally similar to those listed above. However, you may book directly with them, rather than going through a travel agent. They also offer independent and fly/drive packages. These plans all allow you some of the price advantages of package tours with the flexibility of independent travel.

The pay-as-you-go, go-where-you-please tourist is of course more difficult to budget for. His tastes may call for deluxe, comfortable, economy or rock-bottom roughing-it accommodations. "Deluxe" as here used, means staying in the best hotels; traveling by plane, car and first-class railroad sleepers; best seats at the opera, and paying reasonable attention to nightclubs. "Comfortable" travel involves staying at good hotels but not the palaces; eating in good restaurants, but not the most expensive ones, indulging in moderate amounts of nightlife and orchestra-seat entertainment; traveling by train or bus. "Economical" travel still lets you into clean comfortable hotels, but without style, and away from the larger resorts; you can eat good food, but in crowded restaurants, since places both cheap *and* good are bound to be crowded. You'll patronize more bars with jukeboxes rather than live entertainment. "Rock-bottom roughing-it" means picnicking, hitchhiking, cycling, or sticking with second-class rail travel, dining in cheap restaurants and staying in the least-expensive private houses or hostels.

On these four levels, daily expenses and hotel-plus-three-meals in high season, double occupancy per person, will come to approximately $80–$120 deluxe, $50–$80 comfortable, $30–$50 economical and $15–$30 roughing-it.

An important budgeting consideration is the *season*. Highest rates are in July and August, for which period it is also essential to make your reservations far ahead: many tours and hotels are completely booked up, with long waiting lists, months in advance. There are significant savings during the shoulder seasons (generally April to mid-June and again from mid-September through November), when many hotels reduce rates by 30%–40%. The weather is still good in these months and the major tourist sites are not as crowded as they are in July and August.

TOURIST OFFICES IN YUGOSLAVIA. It is possible to plan various types of holiday with the help of the Yugoslav National Tourist Offices (addresses above), and they can advise on special-interest tours. In addition, each republic and every resort has its own tourist organization. The main problem is that it is often extremely difficult to get information in one area about another. Yugoslavia, therefore, does not lend itself to very tightly planned schedules based on specific excursions, especially away from main resort areas. Be prepared to check and double check—and to exercise patience!

Your best bet is to get in touch with the head office of one or other of the big Yugoslav travel firms. Though each specializes in the area where it has its headquarters, each has offices throughout the country, and can handle itineraries on a national scale. On the whole you do best to make your arrangements with the company whose head office is situated in the town or region where you *start* your journey, in order to deal with problems and changes in advance. Names and headquarter-towns of some of these are as follows:

Atlas, Pile 1, 50000 Dubrovnik.
Dalmacijaturist, Titova Obala 5, 58000 Split.
Generalturist, Praška 5, 41000 Zagreb.
Globtour, Maximarket, Trg Revolucije 1, 61000 Ljubljana.
Inex, Trg Republike 5, 11000 Belgrade.
Interimpex, Ive Lola Ribara 10, 91000 Skopje.
Intours, Mitra Bakića 1, 81000 Titograd.
Karavan-Narom Travel (Youth), Moše Pijade 12, 11000 Belgrade.
Kompas, Pražakova 4, 61000 Ljubljana.
Kvarner Express, Maršala Tita 186, 51410 Opatija.

Montenegroturist, 81310 Budva.
Putnik, Dragoslava Jovanovića 1, 11000 Belgrade.
Srbija-Turist, Voždova 12, 18000 Niš.
Unis Turist, Vase Miskina 16, 71000 Sarajevo.
Vojvodinatours, Bul. Maršala Tita 19, 21000 Novi Sad.
Yugotours, Djure Djakovića 31, 11000 Belgrade.

In addition to the commercial travel agencies, many localities maintain a Turistički Ured (Tourist Promotion Office) or Turist Biro which specializes in helping travelers to find accommodations and to enjoy the attractions of the area. They can also, of course, put you in touch with commercial travel agencies which will either book excursions or arrange for specialized activities such as hunting.

Congresses. Though special congress centers are only just beginning to appear in Yugoslavia, there are many towns and cities that are able to cater for most needs. Full information can be obtained through Yugoslav National Tourist Offices or *Yugocongress,* Kaptol 5, 41000 Zagreb.

Youth Travel. There is a special office which organizes holidays and travel for students and young people in Yugoslavia; it is *Karavan-Narom Travel,* at Moše Pijade 12, 11000 Belgrade. It maintains a number of youth hostels as well as international youth centers in Dubrovnik, Rovinj and Bečići; and arranges holidays and educational trips throughout the country.

TRAVEL FOR THE HANDICAPPED. One publication giving valuable information about facilities for the handicapped is Louise Weiss's *Access to the World: A Travel Guide for the Handicapped.* Published by Henry Holt & Co., the book can be ordered from Facts on File, 460 Park Avenue South, New York, NY 10016 ($16.95). Also helpful is the Travel Information Service at Moss Rehabilitation Hospital, 12th St. and Tabor Rd., Philadelphia, PA 19141. For a complete list of tour operators who arrange such travel, send a SASE to the Society for the Advancement of Travel for the Handicapped (*SATH*), 26 Court St., Penthouse Suite, Brooklyn, NY 11242.

In the U.K., information on travel for the handicapped can be obtained from the Royal Association for Disability and Rehabilitation, 25 Mortimer St., London W1N 8AB. Package tours for the handicapped are arranged by Threshold Travel, Wrendal House, 2 Whitworth St. West, Manchester M1 5WX.

TRAVEL DOCUMENTS. To visit Yugoslavia, you should have a national passport, though tourist permits allowing you to enter the country and valid for 30 days can be issued on the strength of a national identity card.

Passports

U.S. residents must apply to the U.S. Passport Agency in Boston, Chicago, Honolulu, Houston, Los Angeles, Miami, New Orleans, New York, Philadelphia, San Francisco, Seattle, Stamford (Conn.) or Washington DC, or to the local Federal or County courthouse. In some areas selected post offices are also able to handle passport applications. Take along proof of citizenship, proof of identity (Social Security and credit cards are *not* acceptable), birth certificate, two recent photographs two inches square, full-face, black and white or color, on non-glossy paper, and taken within the past six months, and $35 plus a $7 processing fee when applying in person (no extra fee when renewing your passport by mail); passports for those under 18 are $20. If you still have your previous passport, issued within the past 12 years, you may use this to apply by mail, and the fee will again be $35. U.S. passports are valid for ten years and are not renewable. Apply several months in advance of your expected departure date. If you expect to travel extensively you may request a 48- or 96-page passport instead of the usual 24-page one at no extra charge. Record your passport number and date and place of issue in a separate, secure place. The loss of a valid passport should be reported immediately to the local police and to the U.S. Dept. of State, 1425 K. St. NW, Washington, DC 20524. If your passport is lost or stolen while abroad, report it to the local authorities and apply for a replacement at the nearest U.S. Embassy or consular office.

British subjects must apply for passports on special forms obtainable from travel agencies or any Head Post Office. The application should be sent to the Passport Office for your area (this is clearly indicated on the guidance form). Apply at least five weeks before the passport is required. The regional Passport Offices are located in London, Liverpool, Peterborough, Glasgow, Belfast and Newport (Mon.). Applications must be countersigned by your bank manager, or by a solicitor, barrister, doctor, clergyman, or Justice of the Peace who knows you personally. You will need two photos. The fee is £15 (£22.50 if including details of spouse) and the passport is valid for ten years.

The British Visitor's Passport, valid for one year, is accepted, but if it's not valid for at least a further three months, holders will need to get a Tourist Pass, valid for 30 days, that is free at entry points. If you plan to stay longer and are using a British Visitor's Passport, you should obtain a visa before departure.

Visas

Yugoslavia has abolished visas on a reciprocal basis. Nationals of most European countries, including the U.K. (who hold full passports), can enter Yugoslavia without formalities; U.S., Canadian and Australian citizens require a visa, but this is issued free without formality at Yugoslav Embassies or, for a small fee, at any frontier post or airport. The Yugoslav Embassy in New York suggests that you obtain your visa before departure.

Health Certificates

Not required for entry into Yugoslavia. Canada, United States and U.K. do not require a certificate of vaccination prior to reentry. However, as the law changes from time to time and country to country, we suggest that you take advice about the current status of the need for vaccination before you travel.

WHAT TO TAKE. More important is what *not* to take. Travel light: by packing only as much luggage as you can easily carry yourself, you simplify going through customs, avoid registering and checking baggage, and make it easier to arrive at hotels where there are no porters. Baggage restrictions vary, but most American and major European carriers allow two checked bags, one no larger than 62″ overall, the other no larger than 52″, and neither more than 70 lb. One piece of carry-on luggage is also allowed. For air travelers from other parts of the world the old 66 lb. (in 1st class) and 44 lb. (in Economy) still obtains.

Travel simply: Yugoslavia is an informal country, where a man not wearing a suit or tie will feel awkward in only the very best restaurants. Lightweight clothes are essential in summer, with a light raincoat in case of sudden storms.

Other "musts" for your Yugoslav trip include: your own sports equipment; your favorite photographic film; some English-language books and magazines (though many can now be bought in large towns and resorts); and your own favorite make-up. Pack a small first-aid kit and any medicines you may need and a reserve packet of toilet paper, of the flat type which is easy to pack or carry around. If you wear glasses, bring a spare pair. Sandy beaches are few, so an inflatable mattress will make for more relaxed sunbathing, though these can be hired locally. Likewise the tender-footed will need a pair of beach shoes or sandals. If you're a coffee or tea addict take your own supplies. A universal bath plug is recommended if you are traveling about.

VACATION INSURANCE. The first thing to do when considering your insurance needs for an upcoming trip is to look at the coverage you've already got. Most major insurers (Blue Cross-Blue Shield, Metropolitan Life, etc.) treat sickness, injury and death abroad no differently than they treat them at home. If, however, you find that your existing insurance comes up short in some significant way (most do not cover the costs of emergency evacuation, for example); or if you would like help finding medical aid abroad, as well as paying for it; or if you would like coverage against those most vexing travel bedevilments—baggage loss and cancellation of your trip—then you may want to consider buying travel insurance.

Your travel agent will be a good source of information. She or he should have an idea of the insurance demands of different destinations; moreover, several of the traveler's insurance companies retail exclusively through travel agents. The American Society of Travel Agents endorses the "Travel Guard" plan, issued by The Insurance Company of North America. Travel Guard offers an insurance package that includes coverage for sickness, injury or death, lost baggage, and interruption or cancellation of your trip. Lost baggage coverage will also cover unauthorized use of your credit cards, while trip cancellation or interruption coverage will reimburse you for additional costs incurred due to a sudden halt (or failed start) to your trip. The Travel Guard Gold program has three plans: advance purchase, for trips up to 30 days ($19); super advance purchase, for trips up to 45 days ($39); and comprehensive, for trips up to 180 days (8% of the cost of travel). Optional features with the Travel Guard Gold program include cancellation and supplemental CDW (collision damage waiver) coverage. For more information, talk to your travel agent, or Travel Guard, 1100 Center Point Dr., Stevens Point, WI 54481 (1–800–782–5151).

The Travelers Companies has a "Travel Insurance Pak," also sold through travel agents. It is broken down into three parts: Travel Accident

Coverage (sickness, injury, or death); Baggage Loss; and Trip Cancellation. Any one of the three parts can be bought separately. Cost of the Accident and Baggage loss coverage depends on the amount of coverage desired and the length of your stay. Two weeks of accident coverage can cost approximately $20; baggage coverage for the same length of time costs $25. The cost of Trip Cancellation coverage depends on the cost of your travel; the rate is $5.50 per $100 of travel expenses. Again, your travel agent should have full details, or you can get in touch with the Travelers Companies, Ticket and Travel, One Tower Square, Hartford, CT 06183 (1–800–243–3174).

If an accident occurs, paying for medical care may be a less urgent problem than finding it. Several companies offer emergency medical assistance along with insurance. Access America offers travel insurance and the assistance of a 24-hour hotline in Washington, DC, that can direct distressed travelers to a nearby source of aid. They maintain contact with a worldwide network of doctors, hospitals and pharmacies, offer medical evacuation services (a particular problem if you're hurt in an out-of-the-way spot), on-site cash provision services (if it's needed to pay for medical care), legal assistance, and help with lost documents and ticket replacement. Access America offers its services through travel agents and AAA. Cost ranges from $5–$10 per day. For more information, Access America, 600 Third Ave., Box 807, New York, NY 10163 (1–800–851–2800).

Other organizations that offer similar assistance are:

Travel Assistance International, the American arm of Europ Assistance, offers comprehensive medical and personal emergency services. Costs range from $40 for a single person for eight days to $200 for a family over a year. Europ Assistance Worldwide Services, Inc., 1133 15th St., N.W., Suite 400, Washington, DC 20006 (1–800–821–2828).

Carefree Travel Insurance, c/o ARM Coverage, Inc., 120 Mineola Blvd., Box 310, Mineola, NY 11501, underwritten by the Hartford Accident and Indemnity Co., offers a comprehensive benefits package that includes trip cancellation and interruption, medical, and accidental death/dismemberment coverage, as well as medical, legal, and economic assistance. Trip cancellation and interruption insurance can be purchased separately. Call 800–654–2424 for additional information.

International SOS Assistance, Inc., Box 11568, Philadelphia, PA 19126 (1–800–523–8930) charges from $15 a person for seven days to $195 for a year.

IAMAT (International Association for Medical Assistance to Travelers), 417 Center St., Lewiston, NY 14092 (716–754–4883), and 188 Nicklin Rd., Guelph, Ontario N1H 7L5 (519–836–0102), makes available a free list of English-speaking doctors who have agreed to a fixed fee schedule (office visit, $30; house or hotel call, $40; night and holiday call, $50).

Note that U.K. citizens, through reciprocal arrangements, qualify for free medical treatment in Yugoslavia (but must pay for any prescribed medicines). They will need to produce their passports.

Getting to Yugoslavia

FROM NORTH AMERICA BY AIR. There are direct flights to Belgrade and Zagreb from Chicago, Montreal and New York, and to Ljubljana from Chicago and New York; or you can fly via these or several European cities to Yugoslavia's other main airports at Dubrovnik, Pula, Rijeka, Sarajevo, Split, Tivat and Zadar. Inside the country, an inexpensive domestic network links the airports listed below. Airport charges for international flights are the equivalent of about $7. In North America, Yugoslav Airlines, JAT, has offices in Chicago, Cleveland, Detroit, Los Angeles, Montreal, New York, Toronto, and Washington, DC, plus regular charter flights to Yugoslavia from Cleveland and Detroit.

In addition to charter fares, there are four types of air fare: First Class, Business, Economy (or Excursion), and APEX. Each has its advantages and disadvantages. Charter is the least flexible, but it is far cheaper than the others; and on regularly scheduled airlines, charter-group passengers, while paying far less for it, receive the same Economy Class service as do their seat-neighbors who are flying as individuals. For most people who fly as individuals, the level of service and comfort in Economy Class will be quite adequate, and the luxuries of First Class will *not* be worth the considerable added expense. The cost and amenities of Business Class fall somewhere between Economy and First Class. On strictly charter-flight lines, the amenities may be more sparing, and the flying times may be longer. From Toronto, Yugoslav Airlines and Yugotours operate charter flights to Ljubljana, Maribor, Dubrovnik, Belgrade and Skopje, late April to mid-October.

In the last several years the rules for charter groups have been relaxed, and the scheduled carriers have entered the charter/package field so much that the range of possibilities now available is too great to list here. Only you can decide what kind of schedule you have and what kind of trip you want to fit into it; and the best deals. Unless you want stopovers (see below), you will save greatly by picking one of the various kinds of excursion or package fares. As of mid-1989, a roundtrip New York–Belgrade (or Zagreb or Ljubljana) First-Class air fare was $4,138; Business, $2,274; Economy, $1,308 (mid-week), $1,348 (weekend); APEX, $1,002. The Economy fare requires no advance purchase and is good for stays of 7 days to 4 months. It also includes two free stopovers in Yugoslavia. The APEX fare requires a 21-day advance purchase and is good for 14 to 45 days only.

Bonus Stopovers. If you go by charter or package-tour you can save money. However, you are locked into the schedule and/or itinerary of that particular flight or group. If you travel as an individual, it will cost you more, but you can take advantage of various stopovers along the way, time permitting, then return by a circle route that lets you see even more. This is because when you buy a ticket from, say, New York to Belgrade, essentially you have bought the right to use up to 8,060 km. (5,406 miles) of transportation each way. Since the actual air distance is only 6,448 km. (4,505 miles), you have an extra 20% to use as you please, at no extra charge.

For example, here are some of the combinations possible on this particular ticket: New York-Lisbon-Madrid-Geneva-Zürich-Munich-Zagreb-Belgrade. These are by no means the only European cities that can be included, and we suggest that you investigate all the available possibilities, if you have the time to indulge in a really fascinating whistle-stop tour.

FROM NORTH AMERICA BY SEA. During the summer you can take the *Queen Elizabeth 2* to Britain or France and carry on from there by any means you like—that being the only regular transatlantic liner left. To check on the availability of freighter service to Yugoslavia, contact Pearl's Freighter Tips, Box 188, 16307 Depot Rd., Flushing, NY 11358.

FROM GREAT BRITAIN BY AIR. Belgrade, Zagreb, Ljubljana, Dubrovnik, Pula and Split airports are equipped for the largest international jets. Direct scheduled services are operated in summer by JAT Yugoslav Airlines to all these destinations from London, and some from Birmingham, Manchester and Glasgow. In winter there are direct services from London to Belgrade, Ljubljana,Zegreb, Split and Dubrovnik. See below for the complete list of centers linked by domestic services. Airport charges for domestic flights are the equivalent of about $2. At presstime (mid-'89) an APEX return to Belgrade cost £179 in peak summer. For a charter flight to Yugoslav destinations, it was around £120–£130 return. Adria Airways also now operate from London to Ljubljana.

Consult with your travel agent before booking, as there are always price-cutting battles being waged and fares change almost from month to month. Also, more and more scheduled and charter carriers are offering seat-only arrangements. JAT office in London: Prince Frederick House, 37 Maddox St., London W1R 1AQ. *Pan Adriatic Travel,* 2nd floor, 49 Conduit St., London W1R 9FB, are specialists in do-it-yourself Yugoslavian holidays. They advise on flights and car hire, and will make accommodation bookings, all at competitive prices.

Stopovers. Travelers from Britain holding full-fare tickets (and *very* few budget-conscious people will travel full-fare) can use stopovers en route to Yugoslavia. Here are just a few examples. Leaving the British capital, you may fly first to Paris and then into Switzerland (Basel). Then you can continue to Zürich or Munich and Zagreb before arrival in Belgrade.

Another possibility is to fly to Brussels and then via Frankfurt and Vienna, or Frankfurt, Stuttgart and Munich, to Zagreb.

FROM GREAT BRITAIN BY TRAIN. From London to Yugoslavia there is only one through service available. Now that the *Tauern Express* has been withdrawn there are no longer any through services from London to Yugoslavia.

The easiest way to reach Belgrade is first to travel from London Victoria using one of the City Link rail/hovercraft/rail services to Paris Gare du Nord. Then board the *Simplon Express* which leaves the Gare de Lyon at 6.50 P.M. and reaches Venice at 6.45 the following morning. It then runs via Trieste, arriving in Ljubljana at 1.10 the following afternoon, and in Belgrade at 9.45 P.M. Light refreshments are available from Paris to Dijon, and a buffet car from Zagreb to Belgrade. However stock up well for the daytime portion of the journey from Venice to Zagreb! There are sleeping cars from Paris to Zagreb, and second class couchettes to Belgrade. Advance reservation is obligatory. There are connecting trains (leave a good margin for delays) to Split from Zagreb.

Alternatively in summer travel from London Victoria via Ostend to Cologne or Stuttgart from where there are through trains to Ljubljana, Zagreb, Split and Belgrade.

In all cases reservation of seats is recommended. The *Thomas Cook Continental Timetable* has an excellent coverage of mainline services throughout Europe and contains a section on Yugoslavia. It is published monthly—but be sure to buy the latest edition as train services change between summer and winter. Available in the U.S. from Forsyth Travel Library, 9154 West 57th St., PO Box 2975, Shawnee Mission, Kansas 66201. In Britain order from: Thomas Cook Ltd., Timetable Publishing Office, PO Box 36, Peterborough, PE3 6SB. Or buy one over the counter at any branch of Thomas Cook.

For those under 26, one of the cheapest ways of getting to Yugoslavia, as well as around it once there, is the Inter Rail card. Valid for one month, it gives unlimited rail travel in 21 European countries, including Yugoslavia. If you buy the ticket in the U.K., you also get half price travel on all British Rail trains and substantial discounts on cross-Channel services. Cost around £140. To be eligible for an Inter Rail card you must have been resident in the U.K. for at least 6 months.

For direct travel—for those under 26—*Eurotrain,* 52 Grosvenor Gardens, London SW1W 0AG, and *Transalpino,* 71/5 Buckingham Palace Rd., London SW1W 0RE, issue reduced-fare round-trip tickets to several Yugoslavian destinations. Both companies offer a choice of routes and stopovers.

In addition for the modest outlay of £5, families or holders of British Rail Senior Citizens Railcards may respectively purchase a Rail Europ Family Card or Rail Europ Senior Card entitling them to very substantial reductions in most European countries including Yugoslavia, and on many cross-Channel services.

Note that Eurailpass does *not* cover Yugoslavia.

FROM GREAT BRITAIN BY CAR. Your destination inside Yugoslavia may determine the highway-route that you choose from England at the outset. To reach the Dalmatian coast your best bet is to cross the frontier at Trieste in Italy. (The most enjoyable way to reach Trieste is to drive across France to Basel in Switzerland and then take the new St. Gotthard road tunnel into Italy. Count on two nights en route.) But if you are making for Yugoslavia's main *autoput* (which leads to Zagreb, Belgrade and the south) you would be better advised to take one of the mountain passes from Austria. There are nearly a dozen of these; the three principal ones are the Würzen, Ljubelj, and Šentilj. A new road tunnel is under construction, entering Yugoslavia near Jesenice from Austria.

Car-Sleeper Expresses. Many hundreds of miles of tiring driving and hours of time can be saved by utilizing one of these summer express trains for transporting your car and your party. While the car-sleeper cost is apparently expensive, it is fairly reasonable when compared with the cost of hotels and meals en route by road. It is obviously more advantageous for a party of four than two.

Useful services for Yugoslavia-bound motorists include: Brussels/'s Hertogenbosch (Holland) to Villach, Brussels/'s Hertogenbosch to Ljubljana. Also Dusseldorf/Köln to Ljubljana, and Munich to Split on the Dalmatian coast. From Ljubljana there is an overnight motorail service to Belgrade. Internal Yugoslav services also carry cars and passengers on rail routes between main cities and the coast.

ARRIVING BY SEA. Jadrolinija, Yugoslavia's main shipping company, operates regular services linking several Adriatic ports with Corfu/Igoumenitsa in Greece; Split with Ancona and Venice in Italy, Zadar with Ancona, and Dubrovnik with Bari. In addition, Adriatica Line operates a number of car ferries between Italian and Yugoslav ports, and Strintzis Line between Italian or Greek and Yugoslav ports. (See also Traveling in Yugoslavia by Boat).

CUSTOMS. Frontier formalities for foreign tourists entering Yugoslavia are not at all irksome and take little time. Yugoslavian customs authorities observe the international customs convention and and are generally lenient toward tourists. At the present time, you may bring into the country duty-free:

1. **Personal effects** (clothes, luggage, etc.) in reasonable quantities.

2. **Supplies** for personal consumption (tourists over 15 years of age): 200 cigarets or 50 cigars or 250 grams of tobacco; one liter of wine, 1 liter of spirits (though one liter usually is allowed); ¼ liter of eau de cologne and small amounts of other perfumes; and reasonable quantities of foodstuffs for the journey.

3. **Equipment** for personal use: two cameras with 12 plates or five rolls of film; a small cine camera with two rolls of film; and a pair of binoculars. Portable equipment: one each, tape recorder, record player (ten records), radio, TV set, musical instrument, typewriter, pocket calculator; camping equipment, bicycle and sports boat with or without motor; sports equipment—e.g. fishing tackle, pair of skis, two tennis racquets, scuba diving equipment, a hunting weapon with 50 rounds of ammunition (but you must have permission from either the Yugoslav consular or the diplomatic office in your country of residence).

If you bring in more items than the above (e.g. full range of professional camera gear), you must declare them on entry and present the Customs document on departure.

Staying in Yugoslavia

GUIDES. Once past the customs inspection, your first contact with Yugoslavia is likely to be the man or woman representing one of the numerous Yugoslav travel organizations such as Kompas, Generalturist, Kvarner Express, Putnik, Dalmacijaturist, Montenegroturist, etc. Their service covers not only the usual hotel and transport reservations, but the thousand other needs of a stranger in a strange land, especially when he cannot speak the local language. All have accredited agents in the U.S., Britain and other countries, whose addresses can be obtained from Yugoslav Tourist Information Offices.

TRAVELING IN YUGOSLAVIA. By Boat. As mentioned above, a number of comfortable Yugoslav routes serve the main points on the country's Adriatic coast from Venice (in Italy) and Rijeka to as far south as Dubrovnik and Bar, some continuing to ports in Greece and including car ferries with drive-on facilities. Smaller vessels ply from main ports out to the islands and back. All of these are operated by Jadrolinija, with head offices, Obala Jugoslavenske Mornarice 16, in Rijeka. Cable address: Jadrolinija, Rijeka. The Yugoslav National Tourist Offices overseas should have the latest details.

The fast coastal routes are operated as pleasure cruises as well as passenger routes, calling at Rijeka, Rab, Zadar, Split, Hvar, Korčula, Dubrovnik and, once weekly, Bar. There are also many coastal and inter-island services, though on the remoter islands the boats set off very early in the morning, returning in mid-afternoon, so that if you start from the mainland you are obliged to spend at least one night away. You can also travel on the numerous hydrofoils or car ferries, whether you have a car or not. Basic schedules are given in the Thomas Cook Continental Timetable and further guidance is given in our regional chapters.

Cruises along the Danube from Passau (Germany) or Vienna (Austria) to the Black Sea, pass through Yugoslavia, including one of the river's most spectacular sections between Belgrade and the Iron Gates. This stretch can also be traveled by hydrofoil on excursions from the capital.

By Air. Yugoslavia is a country chopped up by innumerable mountains. Air travel is a very practical means of transport, and among the most scenic as well. On the flight from Belgrade to Dubrovnik, for example, the plane spans in 45 minutes the flat, level plain of the Danube, the rugged uplands of western Serbia and Bosnia, the lunar escarpment of the Dalmatian *karst,* and finally the island-studded Adriatic.

JAT, Yugoslavia's internationally-accredited airline, serves the country's principal cities several times daily. In the summer months, the main Adriatic resorts are well connected by air with Ljubljana, Belgrade, Zagreb and beyond, with the principal air traffic centers of Western Europe. Dubrovnik, Pula and Split have all-year-round daily services to Belgrade, Zagreb, etc., and seasonal services to many towns in Europe. The complete list of centers served by the domestic network is: Belgrade, Dubrovnik, Ljubljana, Maribor, Mostar, Niš, Ohrid, Osijek, Portorož, Priština, Pula, Rijeka (Krk island), Sarajevo, Skopje, Split, Titograd, Tivat, Zadar, Zagreb.

As part of the government's overall transport policy, the cost of flying internally in Yugoslavia is among the lowest in Europe and is well below that in western Europe.

The free baggage allowance is 15 kilo. (33 lb.) per passenger on internal flights.

By Train. Yugoslavia's railway system has been extended and improved by electrification and the introduction of diesel express trains, many of which connect the chief cities almost non-stop. Such expresses, for instance, link Ljubljana – Zagreb – Belgrade; Belgrade – Split; Belgrade – Rijeka; Belgrade – Skopje – Bitola; Belgrade – Sarajevo – Ploče; Zagreb – Rijeka; Zagreb – Split; Zagreb – Zadar; Zagreb – Šibenik and Zagreb – Sarajevo. Most have restaurant or buffet cars, and there are sleeping cars or couchettes on the night trains. Overall speeds, however, are not high, because of the nature of the terrain, but the fastest expresses cover the flat 420 km. (260 miles) between Belgrade and Zagreb in just under five hours. The railway from Belgrade to Bar, which opened in 1976, is a major engineering feat. It crosses Yugoslavia's once remote mountainous center via Titovo Užice, Bijelo Polje and Titograd; its 514 km. (319 miles) include scores of tunnels and some spectacular scenery. However, much of it is single track, so it is a slow journey.

Branch lines run to other principal cities. Thus, Ljubljana is linked to Rijeka, Belgrade (via Vrpolje) to Sarajevo and Kardeljevo (this line following the gorge of the turbulent, though scenic, Neretva River via Mostar).

Four kinds of passenger trains ply the Yugoslav network: "ordinary" (i.e. slow, stopping at all stations), "fast," "express," and "rapide." On most of these though not all, there are both first and second class. A special supplement is charged on express and rapide trains.

The publication *Red Voznje* contains all rail timetables and some ferry and bus services. If you can't get it anywhere else, try the Belgrade railway station.

Note that the Eurailpass and Eurail Youthpass are not valid in Yugoslavia; Inter Rail, Rail Europ Family and Rail Europ Senior cards, however, are good for Yugoslavia.

By Bus. Coach travel is not only cheaper than travel by train, but often faster and more comfortable as well. Regular schedules operate along the Adriatic highway and all principal coastal centers are connected with inland centers by overland bus routes. Wherever you may find yourself, you will probably be able to get by bus to any other point in Yugoslavia within 24 hours.

It is very advisable to have a seat reservation, though this may not be possible unless you are boarding the vehicle at the start of its itinerary. As there is often more than one company operating on the same route, be quite sure which bus you are traveling on and get to the terminus in good time.

Besides the principal long-distance luxury lines, there are of course any number of local services running out of the big cities to the small surrounding towns and villages.

By Car. Foreign tourists driving to Yugoslavia by motorcar or motorcycle may cross the frontier at numerous customs points. No special international documents are required for tourists entering Yugoslavia with a private car (up to nine seats) or motorcycle. Drivers from the U.S., Great Britain and most European countries need only their national driving licence and car registration document. These should be in English, French or German, or should be translated into one of these languages or into Serbo-Croat.

Drivers who are not owners of the vehicle they are using should carry the owner's permit; this document must be certified by a competent national automobile or touring club.

Trailer and motor caravans and small boats on trailers are admitted without special formalities.

Automobile Associations. The National Yugoslav Automobile and Motorcycle Federation (headquarters at Belgrade, Ruzveltova 16, tel. 011–980 or 419–555) supplies information to motorists on road conditions, etc.

Yellow-painted patrol cars provide free help on all the main routes. You will be asked to pay only for spare parts supplied. If towing is needed, this is provided at fixed rates for members of foreign motoring organizations. In addition, help can be summoned by calling the number 987. Yugoslavia has roadside telephone kiosks on main roads; elsewhere you can ask a passing motorist to summon help for you.

Car Rental. Fly-drive can be arranged from many countries including the U.K. International car rental firms have offices in most Yugoslav cities, and cars can also be hired through travel agents and some hotels. Addresses are easily available from local tourist offices.

Insurance. Third-party insurance is compulsory, and the green card is recommended. The Yugoslav insurance companies offer short-term coverage at moderate premiums, with a seven-day minimum. They are members of the International Automobile Insurance group, and can act for your home insurers. Main address in Belgrade is 6 Kneza Mihaila; also offices in principal cities and at most frontier points. Apart from ordinary car insurance, it is advisable to have extra cover for the costs that may arise in the case of illness or accident. This can be arranged in Britain through Lloyd's, several of the large insurance companies, the motoring organizations, Thomas Cook Ltd., and also through Europ Assistance. (See also Vacation Insurance, page 11).

Rules of the Road. International signs are in use throughout Yugoslavia. You drive on the right, pass on the left, and yield right of way to all vehicles approaching from the right (except on posted main highways). Park on the right; overnight parking is prohibited on main thoroughfares. In and around built-up areas the speed limit is 60 k.p.h. (37 m.p.h.), elsewhere 80, 100 or 120 k.p.h. as indicated. On the Adriatic Highway, because of the sharp bends, it is advisable to keep below 80 k.p.h. (50 m.p.h.). On-the-spot fines are imposed for parking on the wrong side, entering any main road without stopping, crossing a solid white line when overtaking, etc. Penalties for driving under the influence of drink are very severe. Parking in cities at all times, and in resort centers during the high season, is a major problem for facilities are sparse. Many Yugoslavs solve this by illegally parking on sidewalks; however, illegally parked cars are likely to be removed by a machine known as a "spider," and retrieving them is costly as well as time consuming. Drivers should note that in Yugoslavia a driver involved in an accident tends to be considered blameworthy until he is proved innocent, rather than vice versa. The moral is: take a lot more care than usual and drive more slowly than you might do at home. In case of accident you are legally obliged to call the police (tel. 92) and, in case of injury, ambulance (tel. 94). Drivers and passengers in the front seat must wear seat belts; motorcyclists must wear crash helmets.

Fuel. Visitors can buy gasoline coupons offering a 5% discount either abroad or at Yugoslav border crossing points, though with the frequently changing exchange rates, it really isn't worth the hassle. They are also available for lead-free gasoline which can be obtained at a growing number of gas stations (list from the Yugoslav National Tourist Office). Three grades of fuel are available: 86 and 98 octane, and 95 octane lead-free.

Road Conditions. Yugoslavia's road network is gradually improving and there are now substantial stretches of toll motorway, as indicated on the annually revised map of the Yugoslav National Tourist Office, and the more detailed maps published by the Yugoslav motoring organizations which are on sale in local bookshops. Nevertheless, there remain long stretches which, though often well surfaced, are too narrow for the weight of traffic they must carry at the height of the season when hordes of visiting motorists join the heavy long-distance trucks and more-local traffic. The Adriatic Highway is a case in point, and so is the country's main artery, the *autoput* E70/E75 linking Zagreb–Belgrade–Niš–Skopje and Greece. This road is gradually being widened and improved, but its narrower sections require particular care and patience to contend with some often quite hair-raising examples of overtaking. The number of road-side memorials marking accident spots on this and other roads is a sobering reminder of what can result. Further guidance is given in the regional chapters.

Some excellent lateral routes link this highway across the mountains to the coast, but they are still often relatively narrow. The network is best-maintained in the north and center of the country. Further advice on recommended routes is given in the regional chapters, but the best advice is to drive with special care and patience at all times—and enjoy the usually marvelous scenery. If you're of a nervous disposition avoid the roads indicated in green on the tourist map—but if you're not, they are often spectacular.

As already mentioned, the main roads throughout the country are patrolled by an aid and information service (look for yellow cars bearing the word Pomoć-Informacije).

Signposting. This is improving, but in remoter parts of the country, signposting, even of important historical monuments and ancient sites, can be rather poor.

The Coast by Car. If you do not want to drive either up or down the coast you can put your car aboard one of the comfortable fast vessels at very moderate prices. The ships have drive-on facilities.

From the Adriatic Highway it is easy to visit the islands by regular ferries. Krk and Pag are linked to the mainland by bridges.

Spare Parts. Service stations and workshops for repairs exist in most towns and tourist centers. Spare parts for many European-made cars should be available from appointed dealers, but the process may be time-consuming. Your best bet is to hire a pack of spares from your car dealer or motoring association on the normal sale or return basis.

Kilometers into Miles. This simple chart enables you to convert from either miles into kilometers (read from center column to the right) or kilometers into miles (from center column to the left). For example, five miles = eight kilometers, and five kilometers = 3.1 miles.

Miles		Kilometers	Miles		Kilometers
0.6	1	1.6	37.3	60	96.6
1.2	2	3.2	43.5	70	112.3
1.9	3	4.8	49.7	80	128.7
2.5	4	6.3	55.9	90	144.8
3.1	5	8.0	62.1	100	160.9
3.7	6	9.6	124.3	200	321.9

Miles		Kilometers	Miles		Kilometers
4.3	7	11.3	186.4	300	482.8
5.0	8	12.9	248.5	400	643.7
5.6	9	14.5	310.7	500	804.7
6.2	10	16.1	372.8	600	965.6
12.4	20	32.2	434.9	700	1,126.5
18.6	30	48.3	497.1	800	1,287.5
24.8	40	64.4	559.2	900	1,448.4
31.0	50	80.5	621.4	1,000	1,609.3

HOTELS. Yugoslav hotels are officially graded as L, A, B, C and D, meaning deluxe, first, second, third and fourth class respectively. Deluxe hotels are somewhat thin on the ground, but hotels in all other categories are numerous and As and Bs have generally good standards. An important anomaly, however, is the variation in standard and price that can arise between hotels of the same category. This can be quite marked when comparing, say, a category A hotel in a main city or popular resort with one in lesser-known centers, especially in the interior. The price lists quoted below indicate these discrepancies; as a guide, those in the second column apply to inland regions in the center and south of the country, or some small resorts with fewer facilities on the coast. On the other hand, in popular resorts, you may well find that B or second class hotels, especially more recent ones, qualify in practically all respects as A hotels and are downgraded only through lack of the likes of a swimming pool, for example. Hotels in the C and D groups cater adequately to those traveling on a tighter budget, but at the bottom end of the scale are strictly for those roughing it.

The Yugoslav National Tourist Office publishes an annually revised booklet listing most hotels, though there are sometimes some surprising gaps. Because of the instability of the dinar, prices are quoted in U.S. dollars or German deutschmarks, but on-the-spot payment must be made in dinars at the prevailing rate of exchange. If you have not pre-booked, local tourist offices or travel agencies will help you find accommodations on arrival, but in large towns and on the coast in high season advance booking is essential. In resorts, tourists are charged a Visitor's Tax, but this is modest.

Note that in many resorts most hotels are closed during the winter, though you will probably find that at least one remains open all year round. But where resorts do generally close for the winter we have given the months when they are *open* in our listings. It's also important to remember that many of the more modern tourist complexes are actually some distance from the town or resort they purport to be in. Though they are normally well-provided with facilities, they will be largely self-contained and will not provide much in the way of local color or contact with the natives.

Prices. We have divided the hotels in our listings into four groups: Deluxe, or (L); Expensive, or (E); Moderate, or (M); and Inexpensive, or (I). These gradings are determined solely by price but correspond largely with the official Yugoslav gradings. Thus, our Deluxe equals the Yugoslav Deluxe, our Expensive equals the Yugoslav A, our Moderate equals the Yugoslav B, and our Inexpensive equals the Yugoslav C and D.

Prices (in dollars) for two people in a double room with breakfast are approximately:

	Main cities and resorts	Smaller resorts and inland regions
Deluxe (L)	$120–160	$80–100
Expensive (E)	$70–120	$50–80
Moderate (M)	$45–70	$30–50
Inexpensive (I)	$30–45	$20–30

Prices at the lower end of the scale apply to the low season, except in the cities where they remain much the same year-round.

General Information. A number of Moderate establishments have fewer rooms with private bath or shower than many modern Inexpensive hotels. In this respect, the point to note, at least in the cheaper establishments, is the hotel's age. Those that were built in the last two decades have been designed with full modern equipment. Similarly, international investment is being encouraged, and some of the international chains have invested in Yugoslavian hotels.

Service in better hotels in the main towns is usually good though receptionists are often badly overworked because separate hall porters are lacking—and there is a shortage of good reception staff anyway. In the coastal resorts service is rather more variable, especially in summer, when many part-time hotel staff are engaged. The main faults of many Yugoslav hotels are poor maintenance and shoddiness in the actual construction, usually increasing in degree as you progress inland and south, though the situation has improved a lot in recent years, especially in coastal and mountain resort areas where there are some very fine hotels indeed. Except in the better hotels plumbing can still be erratic, and bath and wash basin plugs frequently missing (take one with you if you are traveling about to any extent). And if anything in your room, such as a light or a tap needs attention, tell the receptionist—and continue to badger until it is put right.

If you value peace, make certain to get a room which is not above the hotel disco or overlooking the terrace, otherwise you may have the noise of pop groups or general chatter running into the arrival time of the first delivery trucks.

Hotels, like nearly all commercial enterprises in Yugoslavia, are managed by all those working in them, with managers and management committees selected by the employees. If you want the personal family touch you would do well to take rooms in a guest house or private house—which are also, of course, a great deal less expensive.

Guest Houses. Usually privately run, these have increased considerably in number in recent years. They are often charming and particularly prevalent in Slovenia and Croatia, though increasingly in evidence elsewhere.

Private Homes. Such accommodations are well organized through local tourist offices or travel agencies, and are divided into four categories, the top one providing private bath or shower. The Yugoslav National

Tourist Office publish a price list, with addresses, but count on $12–$30 in the high season, depending on the popularity of the center, for a double room in the top category. In many places you will see the sign *Sobe,* meaning "rooms," indicating these are available. In resort areas you may well be approached by individuals with rooms to let.

Village Tourism. An extension of private accommodations are the increasing possibilities of staying in village households in attractive rural communities that are not developed as resorts. The Yugoslav National Tourist Office have a booklet about this.

Self-catering. A lot of private accommodations (see above) offer self-catering possibilities. Otherwise, there is a growing number of self-catering complexes, apartments and bungalows, especially along the coast. Chalets are also available for hire at many camp sites.

Farmhouse Accommodations. This growing facility is especially available in Slovenia.

Camping. A directory of campsites, with detailed listing of facilities, services and prices along with a map and general information on regulations and requirements is available from Yugoslav tourist offices.

There are about 200 camping-areas, more than half of them along the Adriatic coast and most of the others conveniently along main highways. Modern washing facilities, sanitation, electricity, shops and restaurants, organized entertainment, sports and recreational facilities, are standard for most of them, and medical and automotive services are usually available. In some there are bungalows and chalets for rent. In general, camping is allowed only on the official camp sites; anywhere else you must have permission from the local authorities or tourist bureau.

Camping equipment brought into Yugoslavia is free of customs duty provided that it is taken out again when you leave.

Youth Hostels. Youth hostels in Yugoslavia are now affiliated to the International Youth Hostel movement. The Yugoslav Youth Hostel Federation head office is at Moše Pijade 12/1, Belgrade. In addition to their network of hostels, there are the International Youth Centers at Rovinj, Dubrovnik and Bečići operated by Karavan-Narom Travel, the youth travel organization. Student hostels, without age restrictions, are very low-priced in all main cities and towns (summer only). Tourist offices can advise.

RESTAURANTS. In restaurants frequented by tourists, the 1989 prices for a three-course meal without drinks were the equivalent of: Deluxe (L) $13–15; Expensive (E) $10–13; Moderate (M) $7–10; Inexpensive (I) under $7; less for fixed-price meals. Devaluation and rising rates of exchange account for these low dollar prices, but anything can happen in the coming months.

There are very many small restaurants, most of them privately run, often with attractive décor and specializing in regional or national dishes. If the name includes the word *riblji,* the restaurant specializes in fish. Self-service restaurants, coffee shops *(kafana)* and ice-cream parlors also abound in most resorts.

Our chapter on *Food and Drink* gives guidance on national and regional specialties.

TIPPING. In restaurants, add up to ten percent to your bill according to standard of service and the total involved. There is usually a specific charge quoted for the use of cloakrooms and the like. As is also the case with most people who do odd jobs for you, taxi drivers appreciate a little bit extra. But in no case is this obligatory.

REST ROOMS. Except in better establishments, rest rooms or public conveniences are prone to erratic plumbing and doors that don't lock—again tourist areas fare the best. It's wise to carry tissues for drying your hands and a small supply of toilet paper.

SPECIAL EVENTS. Among events that attract foreign visitors to Yugoslavia is a full program of music, drama, film, and folklore festivals, as well as trade fairs and international sports events. The famous Dubrovnik Festival is described separately below. Other festivals of music and drama include the Split Summer (mid-Jul.–mid-Aug.) and the Ohrid Summer (12 Jul.–20 Aug.), both containing a little bit of everything, as do Opatija's Summer Festival (Jun.–Sept.) and Ljubljana's Cultural Summer (Jul.–Aug.). In similar vein are the Zagreb Summer (Jun.–Sept.) and Belgrade's fairly extensive Bemus Musical Festival (mid-Oct.).

More specialized are: the International Jazz Festival at Ljubljana (mid-Jun.); the Yugoslav Children's Festival at Šibenik (second half of Jun.); Adriatic Melodies at Split (early Jul.); musical evenings in the 1,000-year-old church of St. Donat, Zadar (Jul.–Aug.); International Poetry Evenings at Struga (late Aug.); and varied cultural events and musical entertainments in Belgrade's Skadarlijske Večeri in the city's 19th-century quarter (May–Dec.). Pop and rock music can be heard at the Belgrade Spring in May and in many other places.

Folklore festivals include the Kmečka Ohcet (Peasant Wedding), in which large numbers of couples, including non-Yugoslavs, get married with the whole town *en fête*; you will find this at Plitvice (late May), Galičnik (about 10 Jul.), Bohinj (late Jul.) and Bled (mid-Aug.). Melodies from Istria take place in many Istrian and Kvarner resorts in June. Late July is the International Review of Original Folklore in the streets and squares of Zagreb. At Sokobanja there is the final round of the Yugoslav accordion competition (early Aug.). The Vojvodina Festival is held at Vršac (late Sept.).

The Moreška sword-dance mime has been enacted in Korčula for centuries on 27 July. Performances now take place every Thursday from May to Sept. Outstandingly spectacular, it is still danced by the ordinary townspeople. The colorful centuries-old horseback spear-throwing contest at Sinj, near Split, commemorating a victory over the Turks in 1715, is in early Aug.

The highly recommended Yugoslav Feature Film Festival is held in the Roman amphitheater at Pula in late July, and there is also a film competition at Niš—this one in late August. The well-known Fest Film Festival of Belgrade occurs every February, while in March—again in Belgrade—

there is a Documentary Festival. Theater-wise, September sees Belgrade's celebrated BITEF Festival, an annual event featuring avant-garde companies from many parts of the world.

Of the numerous trade fairs in Yugoslavia, Ljubljana Alp–Adria Fair is in late March; the same venue sees a Winter Sports Fair in November. Biggest of all are the Zagreb Spring Fair in April and the Autumn Fair in September, with specialized fairs at other times of the year. Belgrade has an International Car Fair beginning late May. Then there's the Agricultural Fair at Novi Sad in May. There are many other fairs held in various towns—the Yugoslav National Tourist Office or Embassy can supply full details.

In addition, there are local events in all larger resorts during the tourist season, as we have indicated in the regional chapters.

DUBROVNIK SUMMER FESTIVAL. The ancient ceremonial marking the opening of Dubrovnik's annual Summer Festival takes place on 10 July in front of the Sponza Palace. The festival itself runs until around 25 August. A detailed description of planned events is published in the spring and can be obtained from Yugoslav Tourist Offices abroad, but each year the program includes about 100 performances of great plays and operas—by both foreign and Yugoslav dramatists and composers—as well as numerous presentations by Yugoslav folk-dance ensembles.

Most of the festival is staged out-of-doors, with the medieval palaces, fortresses and courtyards of Dubrovnik's Old City providing the perfect (and authentic) period setting.

ARCHEOLOGICAL SITES. For 5,000 years or more Yugoslavia has been at the crossroads of history: the evidence is clearly and beautifully visible today. Prehistoric cultures abound, especially in the Danube area. Traces of Greek, Roman and early Byzantine cities and individual monuments are strewn liberally throughout the country. Particularly striking are the archeological sites of Stobi and Heraclea Lyncestis in Macedonia, the Roman amphitheater of Pula, Split's Diocletian Palace, and Roman mausoleums in Celje; but there are many others. South Slav Christianity began building a mighty network of monasteries about 1,000 years ago. Years of study could easily be devoted to the frescos that have survived in the churches in southern Serbia and Macedonia, since many of these show the characteristics of Renaissance paintings up to two centuries before the Italian Renaissance began. For five centuries, the Turks occupied much of Yugoslavia and more than three million Yugoslavs are still Moslems. They, too, have left their mark on Yugoslavia's architecture and town planning. In Sarajevo, Mostar, Tetovo, and many other towns, you can visit fine mosques, Turkish palaces, and *hammams* (baths). Check that a mosque is open to non-Moslems and remember that, unless it has been prepared specially for visitors, you need to remove your shoes before entering.

Dalmatia's stone architecture is something apart, exemplified in magnificent walled towns and churches that date back in some cases to the ninth century. The influence of Venice is strong along this coast in many a slender bell tower and ancient palace. Elsewhere, in the north and west, Habsburg times have left their unmistakable mark in the Gothic and especially exuberant Baroque of churches, castles and many other buildings.

Guidance on all major monuments and the best museums is given in our regional chapters. Entrance varies from the free or nominal charge to the quite expensive (in Yugoslav terms) in the case of some well known monuments. Remoter churches or monasteries will not be open at set hours and, in these cases, a very useful word to know is *kluč* (key), usually available from a nearby householder.

FISHING. A fairly wide range of sport fishing can be enjoyed in Yugoslavia's lakes, streams and rivers, as well as in the Adriatic Sea. While the variety of fish waiting to be caught is great, so are the detailed regulations for obtaining licenses. Information can be had by writing to *Sportski ribolovni savez Jugoslavije,* Slobodana Penezića Krcuna 35/V, 11000 Belgrade. A leaflet obtainable from most Tourist Information Offices or from the Sport Fishing Association, above, outlines the principal sea fishing areas of the Adriatic, lists the main species of fish to be caught and summarizes the rather complex Yugoslav laws relating to sea fishing. Note especially that you are in all circumstances forbidden to sell the catch.

Sea fishing is possible and enjoyable from many points on the coast. Gamefishing, however, is not very highly developed, though fishing expeditions are organized by a number of Yugoslav travel firms. The area round Zadar and the Kornat Archipelago is especially popular, and Zadar is a good base.

Freshwater anglers have discovered that Yugoslavia's streams and lakes are well supplied with sizeable specimens of many kinds of fish. The choicest freshwater game belong to the salmon family: trout, huck and salmon parr. Huck often reach a weight of 20 kilo. (55 lb.). Salmon parr go up as high as four kilo. (about eight lb.). Fishing permits are issued by district fishermen's unions, and can be obtained at some hotels and most tourist agencies.

You will find huck mostly in the Neretva, Soča, Zeta, Morača, and Beli Drim rivers, and in Lake Skadar. Salmon parr are numerous in the Drina River. The rivers of Bosnia-Hercegovina contain large numbers of salmonoids, while Croatian waters abound in trout. Visitors wishing to undertake any serious fishing should make early contact with one of the large Yugoslav travel agencies, most of whom are well equipped to organize trips of this kind.

SWIMMING. There are no private beaches in Yugoslavia; applied to a hotel, the term "own beach" means that it is by a beach and, in some cases, access to it may only be from that hotel. The Adriatic coast provides superb bathing in beautiful surroundings in waters that are, almost everywhere, kept crystal clear by the pattern of currents. There is some misunderstanding, however, over what constitutes a sandy beach; in the Yugoslav's mind a beach does not end where the sea begins so there is, indeed, often sand underfoot once you reach the water, but the beach itself as we know it is frequently stoney or pebbly—very hard on tender feet, so take along a pair of beach shoes or sandals. That said, some hotels and resorts have attractively "landscaped" bathing areas, cementing over rough stretches between rocks to provide suitable sunbathing and diving platforms, linked by paths and steps to make pleasant shore-side walks. Some resorts do have small areas of sandy beach, but the only really long one is south of Ulcinj, close to the Albanian frontier. In certain areas where bathing is off rocks, you need to look out for sea urchins.

The Yugoslav coast is particularly well provided with beaches reserved for nudist bathing and there is a wide range of naturist holidays marketed by U.K. tour operators. Topless bathing is also becoming rather common in some places.

Bathing is best from June until mid-October, and is even possible from early May in the south. Lake swimming may be enjoyed in many inland waters, notably at Bled and Bohinj in Slovenia, Ohrid in Macedonia, and elsewhere.

BOATING. Salt-water sailors, whether of yachts or motorboats, will find snug harbors at all the islands and coastal ports of the Adriatic. Ask for the excellent "Nautics" leaflet from the Yugoslav National Tourist Office, which outlines regulations, facilities and weather hazards. There are now many marinas along the coast, and at the larger seaside resorts sailboats or motorboats may be hired. Among them is the expanding chain of marinas operated by Adriatic Club Yugoslavia (ACY), offering excellent mooring and dry-dock facilities at very reasonable rates. ACY membership entitles you to berth at any of their marinas without extra charge. Flotilla sailing is being marketed by an increasing number of tour operators ex-U.K. based on harbors in Istria and Dalmatia from which itineraries of varying duration are arranged along the coast and through the archipelagoes. They provide excellent opportunities for sampling these magnificent waters in the company of others of similar disposition, with expert help and guidance available if required.

The rivers provide some splendid canoeing and kayaking, though as yet organized facilities are very limited and your best bet is to get in touch with local clubs especially in Slovenia and Croatia. Rafting trips of varying duration, some including overnight camps, are arranged on some very exciting waters in Bosnia and Montenegro, notably the rivers Drina and Tara.

Wind surfing, water skiing and other water sports are widely catered for in both lake and coastal resorts.

HUNTING. If you like hunting, large and small game of all kinds await you in abundance in Yugoslavia, including such fine prizes as the hart, brown bear, wild boar, ibex, and chamois. The hart, specimens of which run as high as 300 kilo. (660 lb.), with horns weighing over ten kilo. (20–25 lb.), lives in the brushwood by the rivers Drava, Sava, and Danube. The chamois keeps to the high rocky mountains of Slovenia, Hercegovina, western Macedonia, Serbia, and Montenegro. In addition to the fairly high cost of a hunting tour, a tax of varying proportions has to be paid on all animals shot. Hare, fox, wolf, marten, and other animals also abound, as well as many species of wildfowl. In the numerous hunting preserves there are well-equipped lodges which afford comfortable accommodations and food. Further information is available through Yugoslav National Tourist Offices.

MOUNTAIN CLIMBING. Hikers and mountain climbers will find that in a normal year most of the snow has disappeared from the passes by the beginning of June, even in the Julian Alps and the other ranges along the northern frontier. The Dinaric Alps, lying parallel with the coast of Dalmatia, and inland ranges like the Durmitor of Montenegro and the Macedonian Šar Planina, are very hot in summer, even at high altitudes. The day's hike should start at dawn and finish by noon if you want it to be enjoyable and not an endurance test. Triglav, the highest peak in the Julian Alps at 2,863 m. (9,393 ft), was first climbed in 1778. Other worthwhile peaks are in the Durmitor range, where altitudes reach up to 2,650 m. (8,301 ft.), in Montenegro, the Gorski Kotar region of Croatia, the Velbit mountains of Dalmatia, Treskavica near Sarajevo, and the Šar Planina of Macedonia. There is a splendid walking region around Maribor in the Pohorje Mountains, 1,150–1,400 m. (3,500–4,500 ft.). Even major cities such as Zagreb and Belgrade have good access to fine walking country. A number of walking holidays are arranged ex-U.K.; the Yugoslav National Tourist Office can give details.

WINTER SPORTS. Some fine skiing awaits you in Yugoslavia, with the thrills enhanced by a rugged setting, less crowded and less expensive than better-known tourist areas of Europe. The northern resorts of Slovenia are the more developed, Bohinj and Kranjska Gora especially. A 160-m. (525-ft.) ski jump draws the world's leading competitors to Planica. In Delnice (Croatia) a ski center has been developed in the mountains of Gorski Kotar. The vast bare plateau of Jahorina, near Sarajevo, offers perhaps the finest and most varied all-round ski terrain in Yugoslavia, and this area underwent major development for the 1984 Winter Olympics, making it one of Europe's top winter sports centers. In South Serbia there are major developments at Kopaonik and at the far end of Yugoslavia rises the majestic Šar Planina of Macedonia, 2,100 m. (6,560 ft.) high, with the resort of Popova Šapka.

OTHER SPORTS. There are growing facilities for tennis and horse riding. The only golf course is the excellent one at Bled in Slovenia and the most famous horse riding center, Lipica, is also in Slovenia. Details are given in our regional chapters.

THE LANGUAGE. Luckily for the English-speaking tourists, English is now the most popular foreign-language study in Yugoslav schools. German is widely understood and used for basic needs. Older folk in many areas still speak good German, and on some parts of the coast, Italian.

Beside various dialects of Serbo-Croat, Slovenian is spoken in Slovenia, and Macedonian in Macedonia. All are Slav languages and bear a general family resemblance to each other, as well as to Russian, Polish, Czech, etc. (roughly as French resembles Italian or Spanish). In Slovenia and Croatia they are written in the Latin alphabet; in Bosnia-Hercegovina, Serbia, Montenegro, and Macedonia in Cyrillic, both being official alphabets.

You will find the Latin and Cyrillic alphabets and a tourist vocabulary at the end of this guide. Main signs are always in the Latin alphabet, but a working knowledge of the Cyrillic alphabet is highly recommended if you're wandering off the beaten track in more southerly regions.

We can also recommend the *Language/30* cassette tapes: there is one for Serbo-Croat. As a handy, compact way of getting both expert tuition and a good command of a tourist vocabulary, the series is hard to beat.

HOLIDAYS AND CLOSING TIMES. On the following national holidays, banks, shops, travel agencies and Government agencies are closed: 1–2 January; 1–2 May (Labor Day); 4 July (Partisan Day); 29–30 November (Republic Day). Additional regional holidays are: in Serbia 7 July; in Montenegro 13 July; in Slovenia 22–3 July; in Bosnia-Hercegovina and Croatia 27 July; in Macedonia 2 August and 11 October.

Business hours in Yugoslavia vary from season to season and from district to district; thus, Belgrade summer hours are as follows:

Banks: 7 A.M. to 7 P.M., Sat. 7 to 1 P.M.

Post offices: 7 A.M. to 7 P.M. in larger towns; 7 A.M. to midday and 4 P.M. to 7 P.M. in smaller places

Stores: 8 A.M. to 8 P.M., Sat. 8 to 3 P.M. (self-service stores open earlier and some operate on Sun., from 7 to 11 A.M.)

Shops: either non-stop as above, or 8 A.M. to midday and 5 P.M. to 8, Sat. 8 A.M. to 3

Food Shops: 6 A.M. to 7 P.M.; some open Sun. 7 A.M. to 11 A.M.

Markets: 5.30 A.M. to 12.30 P.M., Sun. 6 A.M. to midday

Offices: 8 A.M. to 3 P.M.

Restaurants: 7 A.M. to midnight

Cafés: 6 A.M. to 11 P.M. (later for those with music)

Nightclubs: 10 P.M. to 3 A.M.

Cinemas: 3 P.M. to 11 P.M. and from 10 A.M. in city centers

Travel Agencies: 8 A.M. to 8 P.M.

Theater curtains rise at 7 or 8 P.M., depending on the show

SHOPPING. Peasant and Oriental handicrafts still survive in present-day Yugoslavia, and you will find many beautiful and useful items available in the shops and markets, including costumed dolls, embroidered blouses, tablecloths, dinner mats, fine lace work, ceramics, woolen goods, carved wooden objects, filigree jewelry, leather items. Carpets, of fine brilliantly dyed wool, vary from small prayer rugs to huge floor coverings. Each region has its own carpet-weaving design. Gold, silver and copper metalwork, including items set with precious stones, are offered in the lively bazaars of Sarajevo and elsewhere (strike your own bargain), and good filigree work is found in many places.

In the large towns and resorts shops bearing the names Narodna Radinost, Jugoexport, Dom, Bosna Folklore, Rukotvorine and Minceta are reliable. A discount of 10% is granted in some stores on articles paid for by travelers checks or foreign currency. Prices are fixed in all shops and there is no haggling except in some open-air markets. Export of craft and souvenir items is not limited; you may take out any amount, unless they are of historical or cultural value, when you'll need a special permit. Note that prices for similar items are often lower in the markets of big cities than in tourist resorts. At the height of the season, small shops specializing in handicrafts stay open late into the evening—in even the smallest resorts—the local color often being added to by the activities of street artists.

Duty-free shops (hard currency only) now abound, selling tobacco, liquor, perfumes, cameras, souvenirs etc. You'll find them in many hotels, at frontier crossings and along main highways, and also in very remote places nowadays.

MAIL AND TELEPHONES. Because of inflation, mail rates are changing so frequently there is little point in quoting the current charges. Post
offices and most other places selling stamps have up-to-date lists of mail
rates to all major foreign destinations.

Much of Yugoslavia's telephone network is now on the automatic system and most calls within the country and to much of Europe can be dialed
direct, though in the peak season or in the south insufficient lines can cause
long delays.

Yugoslavia is one hour ahead of Greenwich Mean Time (GMT). From
late March to late September it is five hours ahead of U.S. Eastern Day-
light Time: in fall and winter it is six hours ahead of U.S. Eastern Standard
Time.

ELECTRICITY. 220 volts AC; sockets are of the two-pin Continental
variety, so take an adaptor.

RELIGIOUS SERVICES. The Serbian Orthodox faith prevails in Serbia, Macedonia and Montenegro. The Roman Catholic religion is predom-
inant in Slovenia and Croatia, including Dalmatia. Religion in Bosnia divides three ways: Orthodox, Catholic and Moslem. There are many
Moslem communities in Macedonia and southwest Serbia. Protestant
churches may be found only in major towns and cities.

PHOTOGRAPHY. Yugoslavia is very photogenic. Plan on bringing
along your own film rather than buying the locally available products.
Films imported to Yugoslavia are more expensive than in their countries
of origin.

Black-and-white film can be developed and printed everywhere in Yugoslavia. However, if you are a camera enthusiast, you will probably prefer
to keep your undeveloped films for processing at home. Color film and
motion-picture footage are also better taken home for processing.

There are some restrictions on photography in Yugoslavia. In a few
areas near military installations, roadside notices in several languages request foreign motorists not to stop. Elsewhere, places where photograph-
ing is forbidden are indicated with signs showing a camera crossed out
in red. As these signs are not always obviously placed, we seriously suggest
that you always have a good look round before clicking the shutter. This
applies also to the use of binoculars—so birdwatchers beware! Though incidents have been few, there have been misunderstandings.

USEFUL ADDRESSES. Belgrade: American Embassy, Kneza Miloša
50; British Embassy, Generala Ždanova 46; Canadian, Kneza Miloša 75.
Zagreb: American Consulate, Braće Kavurića 2; British Consulate, Ilica
12.

NEWSPAPERS. In the large cities and most resorts, you'll find English-language newspapers.

Leaving Yugoslavia

CUSTOMS—RETURNING HOME. If you propose to take on your holiday any *foreign-made* articles, such as cameras, binoculars, expensive time-pieces and the like, it is wise to put with your travel documents the receipt from the retailer or some other evidence that the item was bought in your home country. If you bought the article on a previous holiday abroad and have already paid duty on it, carry with you the receipt for this. Otherwise, on returning home, you may be charged duty.

Americans who are out of the United States at least 48 hours and have claimed no exemption during the previous 30 days are entitled to bring $400 worth of purchases duty-free. For the next $1,000 worth of goods, a flat 10% rate applies. Above $1,400, duties vary according to the merchandise. The value of each item is determined by the price actually paid (so keep your receipts). All items purchased must accompany the passenger on his return; it will therefore simplify matters at customs control if you can pack all purchases in one carry-on bag. Every member of the family is entitled to this same exemption, regardless of age, and the allowance can be pooled.

The $400 figures if based on the fair retail value of the goods in the country where acquired. Included for travelers over the age of 21 are one liter of alcohol, 100 cigars (non-Cuban), and 200 cigarettes. Any amount in excess of those limits will be taxed at the port of entry, and may additionally be taxed in the traveler's home state.

Antiques are defined, for customs purposes, as articles 100 years old and over, and are admitted duty-free. If there's any question of age, you may be asked to supply proof. Gifts valued at under $50 may be mailed to friends or relatives at home duty-free, but not more than one per day (of receipt) to any one addressee. These gifts must not include perfumes costing more than $5, tobacco, or liquor.

If your purchases exceed your exemption, list the most expensive items that are subject to duty under your exemption and pay duty on the cheaper items. Any article you fail to declare cannot later be claimed under your exemption.

Do not bring home foreign meats, fruits or plants, or soil or other agricultural items when you return to the United States. To do so will delay you at the port of entry. It is illegal to bring in foreign agricultural items without permission, because they can spread destructive plant or animal pests and diseases. For more information, read the pamphlet *Customs Hints,* or write to: "Quarantines," U.S. Department of Agriculture, Federal Building, Hyattsville, Md. 20782 for Program Aid No. 1083, *Travelers' Tips.*

Residents of Canada may, after seven days out of the country, and upon written declaration, claim an exemption of $300 a year plus an allowance of 40 ounces of liquor, 50 cigars, 200 cigarettes, and 2 pounds of tobacco. Personal gifts should be mailed as "Unsolicited Gift—Value Under $40." Canadian Customs regulations are strictly enforced; you are recommended to check what your allowances are and to make sure you have bought abroad. For details ask for the Canada Customs brochure, "I Declare."

British Customs. There are two levels of duty-free allowance for people entering the U.K: one, for goods bought outside the EEC or for goods bought in a duty free shop within the EEC; two, for goods bought in an EEC country but not in a duty free shop.

In the first category you may import duty free: 200 cigarettes or 100 cigarillos or 50 cigars or 250 grammes of tobacco (*Note* if you live outside Europe, these allowances are doubled); plus one liter of alcoholic drinks over 22% vol. (38.8% proof) or two liters of alcoholic drinks not over 22% vol. or fortified or sparkling or still table wine; plus two liters of still table wine; plus 50 grammes of perfume; plus nine fluid ounces of toilet water; plus other goods to the value of £32.

In the second category you may import duty free: 300 cigarettes or 150 cigarillos or 75 cigars or 400 grammes of tobacco; plus 1½ liters of alcoholic drinks over 22% vol. (38.8% proof) or three liters of alcoholic drinks not over 22% vol. or fortified or sparkling or still table wine; plus five liters of still table wine; plus 75 grammes of perfume; plus 13 fluid ounces of toilet water; plus other goods to the value of £250. (*Note* though it is not classified as an alcoholic drink by EEC countries for Customs' purposes and is thus considered part of the "other goods" allowance, you may not import more than 50 liters of beer).

In addition, no animals or pets of any kind may be brought into the U.K. The penalties for doing so are severe and are strictly enforced; there are *no* exceptions. Similarly, fresh meats, plants and vegetables, controlled drugs and firearms and ammunition may not be brought into the U.K. There are no restrictions on the import or export of British and foreign currencies.

DUTY FREE is not what it once was. You may not be paying tax on your bottle of whiskey or perfume, but you are certainly contributing to somebody's profits. Duty-free shops are big business these days and mark ups are often around 100 to 200%. So don't be seduced by the idea that because it's duty free it's a bargain. Very often prices are not much different from your local discount store and in the case of perfume or jewelry they can be even higher.

Motorists should note that there are duty-free shops at most frontier crossing points.

THE
YUGOSLAV
SCENE

THE COUNTRY AND THE
PEOPLE

A Panoply of Paradoxes

by
SYLVIE NICKELS

Yugoslavia is a superb, colorful mixture which makes fascinating fare for the visitor; but it is a good idea to know at least a little of what that mixture comprises. Underlying it is a unity that reveals itself whenever the Yugoslavs find themselves with their backs to the wall or in times of national sadness. It's something you don't learn from sitting on a beach or in the comfortable insulation of a modern tourist hotel. You learn it from staying with the Yugoslavs, from traveling in the same buses and trains as they do, from eating in the same restaurants and taking part in the same activities—especially in that most favorite pastime, conversation.

All these things are open to anyone. Some of my most pleasant memories are of incidents that not even the best travel agent could ever have organized. One was of an early spring bus journey that should have taken seven hours and took 17. Crossing Čakor Pass between south Serbia and Montenegro, we got caught in an unseasonable blizzard which turned the landscape into one of Arctic grandeur. The entire busload, mainly Shiptars

(Albanians), adopted me, as the only and very unsuitably-dressed foreigner, and entertained me and each other with traditional songs led by the conductor. On another occasion, I found myself spending Easter alone with a family in Belgrade as a paying guest. We had no common language, yet any possible loneliness was dispelled on Easter Sunday morning when a tray of special delicacies was brought in to me, despite the fact that the family was Orthodox and their Easter on a quite different date from mine that year. It was also in Belgrade that I was "picked up" in a most proper fashion by a young man who wanted to practise his English, and spent the next two days showing me round.

In a Roman Catholic monastery on an island off the Dalmatian coast, I became involved in an amicable argument between one of the priests and a local official, which ended, as a good argument should, with agreement to differ. The monastery had a fine collection of Roman and other treasures taken from the sea, a small (and I hasten to add imperfect) sample of which was slipped, quite unofficially, into my pocket, and which adorns a bookcase today. I left my scarf in the monastery on that occasion, and it was handed back to me by another young priest on the early morning boat to the mainland the following day. This monastic order had its headquarters on the mainland, and it subsequently became a regular bolthole whenever I was passing that way, for a cup of coffee and pleasant conversation in halting French.

It was in Ohrid, Macedonia, that I was sitting on a wall by a monastery one morning when a lady from a nearby first floor flat leant out to invite me up for coffee (the word *kava* is not too difficult to distinguish). She worked in the local post office and she, too, with her family and friends adopted me for the next two or three days, with only a few words of French and my two tiny Serbo-Croat dictionaries to help us along. We still correspond, each getting the other's letters translated in order to be able to answer them. In Montenegro, chance acquaintances have become old friends; and the same is true of a dozen or more Croats and Bosnians from all walks of life. Through them, I have had the privilege of joining in family events and outings in a way that has never quite happened to me anywhere else.

In a Nutshell

So how did the marvelous mix come about? It may be an old truism to say that Yugoslavia is one country with two alphabets, three religions, four (main) languages, five (principal) nationalities, six republics and a border with seven countries; but I know of no mnemonic that better summarizes a complex and fascinating situation. The fact that within about 70 years, interrupted by a world war and a total political upheaval, Yugoslavia has made for herself some kind of unity is one of the greater miracles in nation-making of the 20th century—even if that unity is currently being sorely tested by ethnic conflict in parts of Serbia, in addition to dire economic problems throughout the country. The fact that she has grown into a respected small non-aligned power out of the utter disruption of that war is another miracle. The fact that she survived politically her unequivocal opting out of the Cominform in 1948 further compounds these miracles.

All of this does not mean of course that the Yugoslavs are saints. They have done terrible things to each other in the past, and intermittent dissent between Serbs and Croats, and recent nationalist tensions in the Albanian-majority region of Kosovo can make more impression on world headlines than the achievements that lie behind the country's growth into maturity. The Slovenes continue to object from time to time to helping to foot the bill for the less affluent Macedonians, and the Montenegrins still talk nostalgically of their tough and not always so romantic past. I doubt however whether many would choose to depart their homeland, except for a few years in order to make more money somewhere else; and that goes for most of the minorities, of whom there are many.

Let's begin with the seven national frontiers which, starting in the north and working round clockwise, are with Italy, Austria, Hungary, Romania, Bulgaria, Greece and Albania. You don't need to know much about European history to imagine what effect such an assortment of neighbors might have had on the Yugoslavs. Their history is described in another chapter of this volume, but certain facts are crucial to any attempt to begin to understand the kaleidoscopic nature of the Yugoslav way of life. The fundamental fact is that for centuries the country was split, in fluctuating proportions, between the Ottoman Turkish Empire and that of the Habsburgs, with the Venetians putting their spoke in along the coast for much of the time.

Topography too has a considerable influence. In the north you have the towering splendors of the Julian and Karavanke Alps, in the south and southwest the Transylvanian Alps, and running parallel with the Adriatic coast, more or less linking these ranges, you have the Dinaric chain. Cutting through these mountains are rivers that often become glorious, raging torrents hemmed in between soaring rock faces. Because of the curious nature of some of the limestone formations, known as *karst,* some of these rivers disappear underground for considerable distances, carving out fantastic subterranean worlds like the Postojna caves, which are among the sightseeing wonders of the country.

Not many of these capricious and dramatic waterways flow into Yugoslavia's own sea, the Adriatic. Most of them head inland, eventually joining the mighty Sava, which in turn pours itself into the Danube in Belgrade. The mighty plains fed by these great rivers are simply an extension of the Hungarian *Puszta,* across which the Mongol hordes thundered toward Western Europe and the Turks advanced toward the very gates of Vienna.

A Look at the Yugoslavs

Take as an example an office or factory worker earning his daily bread in a city like Ljubljana, capital of Slovenia in the north of the country. Many of the more tangible aspects of his life have been influenced—architecturally, religiously, culturally—by centuries of association with neighboring Austria. Or take a shepherd grazing his flocks above some Bosnian or south-Serbian village in the mountainous center of the country. Here a dominant feature of the community is likely to be the slender minaret of a mosque, and the bazaar will resound to the hammering of copper or plaintive music that has more than a hint of the East in it. Or take Macedonia in the deep south, where the costumes change from one village to another. Here the architectural and spiritual essence is in the medieval Orthodox monastery echoing long-ago Byzantine strength and later Macedonian tenacity. Or consider a fisherman or a market gardener or a hotel waiter on the long, languid Adriatic coast. His ancestors were for centuries effectively barred from their fellow South Slavs by a mountain barrier and the politics that lay beyond. Multiply these examples some scores of times and you will see why it is impossible to generalize about the Yugoslavs.

But they have one important common heritage. Yugoslavia means "land of the South Slavs." The six republics into which it is divided are Slovenia, Croatia, Serbia, Bosnia-Hercegovina, Montenegro and Macedonia. Within the boundaries of Serbia, two autonomous provinces minister to the special needs imposed by history and the presence in them of large national minorities. Kosovo in the mountainous south has a majority population of Albanians. In Vojvodina in the Danube plains, Hungarians predominate, but there are other substantial minorities. For all these, Yugoslavia has done probably more than most other countries in a similar position in terms of safeguarding the language and culture of each group. It has not been without its less fortunate repercussions as in the case of Kosovo, where nationalist tensions between Albanians and Serbs continue to cause unrest and alarm as we go to press.

The South Slavs who first appeared in the area of present-day Yugoslavia in the sixth century brought with them certain social and cultural conventions and absorbed others from the indigenous Romanized Illyrians and Celts, which have survived many subsequent strains. The fundamental native feature was the *zadruga,* the tight-knit organization of a family unit, in which everyone had his place. This as much as anything perpetuated the strength of South Slav unity, and it survived as a legal entity right up to 1868. Remnants of its influence exist even today, though the demands of the later 20th century have probably put more pressure on it than all the horrific turmoils of the past ever did. Nevertheless, despite all the rapid changes that have swept the Yugoslavs from a predominantly rural society to an industrial economy in a few decades, and in spite of the resulting strains that have been imposed on a slower, simpler way of life, there is still a feeling for family that has, alas, become much rarer farther west. People are concerned about each other, the old are not so readily left to the care of others, and you don't hear much about battered babies.

The five main nationalities are the Slovenes, Croats, Serbs, Macedonians and Montenegrins. The four principal languages (Slovene, Croat, Serb and Macedonian) are really three, since Croat and Serb—known to the rest of the world as Serbo-Croat—are very similar.

Three Religions, Two Alphabets

And so we come to the three religions. With the splitting of the Roman Empire into the Catholic West under the aegis of Rome and the Orthodox East under Byzantium, came the first major division of the future land of the South Slavs, before they even arrived on the scene. With the coming of the Turks, the division became dramatically incised across the map of Yugoslavia as the Orthodox regions were absorbed into the Ottoman Empire, some of them for over five centuries—indeed, right up to World War I. Contact between the South Slav inhabitants on either side of this political and cultural barrier was almost nonexistent. Orthodox churches and monasteries, with few exceptions, were turned into mosques or fell into disrepair. With a degree of coercion that varied in different parts of the region, the Moslem faith was adopted by many—but by no means by all. The fine novel *The Bridge on the Drina* by the Nobel prizewinner Ivo Andrić tells graphically of life over a 400-year span in a small Bosnian town under the Turks.

The use of the Roman and Cyrillic alphabets follows the divisions imposed by the splitting of the Roman Empire, the Roman or Latin alphabet being used as one would expect in the northern and western Catholic areas and the Cyrillic in the southern and eastern Orthodox regions. Cyrillic, based on the alphabet developed by two brothers, the monks Cyril and Methodius, in the ninth century, was taught by their followers in a monastery in Ohrid, Macedonia, whence it spread across the rest of the Slav world, including, of course, Russia. In fact, today, the Roman alphabet has substantially infiltrated the Cyrillic areas of Yugoslavia.

Nowadays, the street names and other useful signs are usually printed in both alphabets, though it is well worth the effort of learning the Cyrillic letters, so that at least you can recognize a *PECTOPAH* for what it is: a restaurant. The knowledge of foreign languages has increased enormously of recent years, the older generation still tending to speak more German, but the younger ones English. Still, it has never done anyone any harm to learn a few words like "good morning" and "thank you" in the language of the country, nor the correct pronunciation of the names of people and places; the effort is often well rewarded.

So it should be clear by now why it is impossible to make any generalizations whatsoever, either about Yugoslavia or the Yugoslavs. It is one of the very good reasons why it would be a sad waste to confine your visit to one resort hotel (which tends anyway—in Yugoslavia as anywhere else—to be much like another). The small amount of energy needed to travel only a few kilometers can bring you into a totally different world. Combine this with a little planning, and you can participate in some of the rich folk traditions which here retain their authenticity, and have not yet grown tired and stale.

Events Great and Small

One custom which you can hardly avoid in coastal resorts and smaller inland towns is the *korzo.* You hear it before you see it: a faint hum in the distance, growing in intensity as you approach until it sounds like the buzzing of a million angry bees. In fact, it is nothing more than the local people taking their evening stroll. The tradition goes back for generations, and is kept up in many places with much enthusiasm today. Usually it takes place at dusk, somewhere between 6 and 8 P.M., the scene rapidly filling and, later on, equally rapidly emptying, as if at an unseen signal. Don't be surprised if you chance upon a group of men along the Dalmatian coast, suddenly bursting into well-harmonized song. Such a group is known as a *klapa,* and there are many of them—some formed at work places, or just as often friends who arrange to meet to practise their talents. Songs of a traditional nature are usually preferred.

At the other end of the scale, each republic has its special day, commemorating its integration into the Federal Republic; and the whole country celebrates 29th November as the day on which in the small town of Jajce in Bosnia, Yugoslavia was born as a Federal People's Republic in 1943 (today, Federal Socialist Republic). Labor Day, celebrated on May 1st and 2nd, is another national event, in this case with the emphasis on activities and entertainment with family appeal. There'll be plenty of open-air concerts, folk dance performances, sports events, and trips into the country or to the sea—so don't expect to find your Yugoslav friends at home unless you've advised them in advance of your visit.

Many of the more local celebrations are associated with the rhythm of the seasons or with some dramatic, historical or legendary event. One of the best known in the latter category is the *Moreška* of Korčula island, a most vivid dance pageant depicting the struggle between the Black and the Red King for a beautiful princess. The kings may represent the Moors and Turks, and the princess the town of Korčula, but it is in any event a highly skilful (and exhausting) display, for which the local men and boys participating have to train rigorously. The traditional date for the event is 27th July but, because of its popularity, weekly performances are arranged throughout the season. *Alka,* a spectacular tournament of costumed knights tilting at the ring, commemorates a victory over the Turks in 1715 at Sinj, on the Dalmatian coast near Split; this is in early August.

In August or September, some of the mountain villages of Slovenia have special festivities—in the tradition of many other mountain areas—connected with the return of the cattle or sheep from the high summer pastures. In Macedonia, where weddings can still be very colorful, an enchanting multiple marriage ceremony takes place at Galičnik, a small place in the heart of the mountains not far from the Albanian border.

In most of these festivities traditional dancing plays a major part, and the Yugoslavs excel at it. Here folk dancing lives on not simply as a tourist attraction—though it is that, too—but because both young and old enjoy it. Thus many different kinds have survived, of which the *kolo,* a group dance reminiscent of a reel, is the most common, varying from region to region and even from village to village. Dance bands in restaurants, incidentally, will quite often break into a *kolo* at some stage in the evening, and pretty well every Yugoslav customer is likely to get up and participate. If you do the same, it will certainly be appreciated. Internationally, Yugoslav folk groups are quite outstanding, carrying off first prize in many a contest. Performances demonstrating dances from different parts of the country can be seen in numerous towns and resorts throughout summer, sometimes in beautiful natural or historic settings. But the small, spontaneous local celebration can be even more fun, and away from the beaten track you may find yourself the only foreigner there. Quite often there'll be a whole sheep roasting on a spit, and as the wine flows you might be surprised to find how much Serbo-Croat you can suddenly understand!

Of the more sophisticated summer cultural festivals, the most famous is Dubrovnik's, not only because of the quality of the performances (many international guest stars participate), but also because of some of the unsurpassed settings in this beautiful walled city. Medieval and Renaissance Dubrovnik produced its own fine artists and writers, among them Marin Držić whose play *Dundo Maroje* (Uncle Maroje) is often performed at the festival, and whose style has been likened to that of Molière. Other Yugoslav cities also make good use of their architectural heritage. The Ljubljana Festival, for example, centers upon Križanke, a fine complex combining a 16th-century monastery with remains dating from medieval and Roman times. In Split, various parts of the Emperor Diocletian's Palace provide wonderful settings for summer festival performances. In Pula, the great Roman arena is the annual scene of the Yugoslav Film Festival.

Communism and Private Enterprise

But now let's take a look at Yugoslavia's own brand of Communism, which they prefer to call Socialism. You have probably already heard that it is rather different from anyone else's. Indeed, the Yugoslavs might claim with quite a lot of justification that they are the only ones who are really putting Communism into practise. So what's so special about it?

You won't travel very far in Yugoslavia without hearing someone mention the term "workers' self-management," and therein lies the clue to the whole business. State ownership does not exist in Yugoslavia. Most enterprises and services are owned and managed by the people who work for them, under the system of workers' self-management. To these can be added a rapidly escalating number of private businesses (see below) and even, following recent changes in the Constitution, enterprises financed by foreign investment.

"Workers", in the context of workers' self-management, means all who work, whether they are medical specialists, university professors, hotel managers or waiters, skilled artisans or the people who sweep factory floors. Ownership in this sense does not mean that workers contribute hard cash, but that in return for their time and their labor they get not only wages, but the right to participate in decisions affecting every level of the organization of the enterprise. Basically, the organization works from the lower echelons upward like the building of a pyramid, rather than the other way round. Workers' councils are elected by secret ballot of all workers in each department and sub-department of an enterprise, each of these representing what is known as a basic organization of associated labor—more simply, a self-contained unit responsible for and to itself. Each council must report back to the workers' assembly it represents on major decisions before they are finally acted upon. In a large factory or group of factories these units can number as many as 50. Workers' councils take care of the general running of their unit, but major decisions are arrived at by a referendum of all the workers. In larger organizations, there are at progressive levels additional workers' councils representing groups of units, and so on, until one reaches the apex, the management workers' council for the whole enterprise.

The system works a little differently where there is no actual end product, such as in a school or hospital. Contributions to all these kinds of social services are made by every working member of the community from his or her gross salary, and in exchange he and his family benefit from the product—in this case the skills—of each service. The fundamental organization of a school, hospital, etc., however, is on the same lines as those of a commercial enterprise, each self-contained department or unit fulfilling its own specific function, and governed by the same system of workers' councils.

The philosophy of workers' self-management has been the aim of Yugoslavia's form of socialism right from the beginning. It did not appear overnight, and its progress has been one of gradual expansion, consolidation and decentralization, culminating in 1974 in a new constitution. Developing economic problems have since caused some re-thinking resulting in revisions to the Constitution enacted in 1988, while others are still under discussion as we go to press. The main aims of the changes are to resolve the shaky economy by encouraging foreign investments and developing the private sector further. The new law also allows shareholder companies to take their place for the first time on the Yugoslav economic scene.

As a working philosophy, I find it quite fascinating but you may wonder in what way it is likely to affect the visitor to Yugoslavia. The answer is that it depends on what your preconceived ideas of Communism, or your previous experience of a Communist country, might be. The degree of competition comes as a surprise to most people when they find, for example, two or three different bus companies operating similar services at different times and at slightly different prices. The same applies to all kinds of products and services.

From the tourist's point of view, the process of decentralization and the competitive nature of the system have their pros and cons. Healthy competition makes it well worth shopping around, whether it's for meals or mementos. On the other hand, things are sometimes so decentralized that it is not always easy to find out in one place what is going on in another!

One final example of the possible side effects of workers' self-management on the community at large might be of interest. This example occurred in a big industrial works near the town of Split, where a good deal of thought and discussion has been going on of recent years on the subject of pollution. The Yugoslav coast, so far, has been more fortunate than many, but the relatively heavy concentration of industry round Split makes it a higher-risk area. Programs of public education on the problem have been organized at different levels to increase awareness, and their effects had filtered through to the workers' councils of the enterprise concerned. Thus a decision was reached to invest a considerable sum into a plant for processing their industrial waste, certainly to the benefit of the city (and its visitors) as a whole.

And what of private enterprise? Anyone can run his own business, the maximum number of people employed, however, being limited by law. Thus far, among the most successful adherents of the private approach are restaurants, guest houses, and repair and handicraft workshops, but there is also a move to encourage small light industries, involving private investment repaid with interest over a limited period. Such enterprises have already proved very successful in progressive Slovenia, and are now being taken up in less developed regions. Of agriculture there will be more to say later.

The Economic Recovery

As far as economic development is concerned, the change in Yugoslavia since World War II has been dramatic—notwithstanding the serious difficulties encountered since the death of Tito in 1980. As time goes on, that war for a rapidly increasing number of us is becoming an historical event rather than a remembered personal experience. But it is impossible really to grasp Yugoslavia's achievements without knowing something of the devastation she suffered. A few stark figures will serve to illustrate the point. By the end of World War II, Yugoslavia had lost ten percent of her population, *i.e.* 1,700,000 dead. Over 820,000 homes had been destroyed and 3½ million people were without a roof over their heads; two-thirds of the hospitals had been totally or almost totally razed; two-fifths of industrial installations were in ruins and the remainder seriously damaged; over half the railway lines were devastated and the rest unfit for use; thousands of road and railway bridges had been bombed out of existence and many thousands of kilometers of the roads themselves rendered useless. One can, indeed, use the word "holocaust" with justification.

These facts, of which little evidence remains in Yugoslavia today, help us to realize what amazing feats of recovery were achieved in a comparatively short time. For the phoenix did not merely rise out of the ashes, it emerged into a world that itself was undergoing great changes as it entered the era of technology. At the outbreak of war, three-quarters of the Yugoslav population were dependent on agriculture for their livelihood; today the proportion is less than a fifth.

It is important to remember too that especially during the earlier part of this period industry had to be totally reorganized, communications almost entirely rebuilt, the homeless rehoused and the production and distribution of practically every basic commodity arranged to fill empty shops and meet the needs of interminable queues. The foundations of the new Yugoslavia were laid by hundreds of thousands of her people rolling up their sleeves and working on short rations. This is worth remembering from time to time as we bowl along one of the new highways or gaze out of the window of our modern hotel at some idyllic holiday scene.

In Terms of Technology

Yugoslavia is fortunate in possessing rich resources of such useful raw materials as coal, iron ore, crude petroleum and chemicals, as well as great and fertile plains and river valleys for her now highly-developed agriculture. 84 percent of the latter is in private hands, but as landownership is limited by law to ten hectares/about 25 acres (this is about to be tripled), the result is rather unwieldy—many 1000s of small parcels of land. For this reason, there are continuing moves to revive the cooperative movement, by which private owners can benefit from modern technology, credit schemes and efficient marketing.

The skills and technology needed to turn raw materials and unworked products into semi-manufactured and finished goods had to be learned and developed, and it is in this field that the transformation has been most startling. Nowadays over 60 percent of Yugoslav exports are finished goods, compared with 5.4 percent pre-war, and these include an enormous range of items, from heavy machinery to furniture and footwear. The increase in exports of such capital goods as ships and complete power-generating and industrial plants, especially to developing countries, was another success of the 1970s. While the Soviet Union remains the country's most important single customer, the EEC is the biggest economic group trading with Yugoslavia, with Italy and West Germany at the head of the list. There is also quite substantial trade with the United States.

But alas economic miracles have their converse aspects. The recession which has affected the rest of the world has had a profound impact on the Yugoslavs too, who have had to face the fact that they have diversified too much and borrowed for too long. Soaring inflation, a shortage of imported raw materials that need to be paid for in precious hard currency, and declining productivity have resulted in an economic uncertainty unknown a few years ago.

The Yugoslavs seem to be facing the facts with a sense of realism, though it is difficult to see how they will stem their spiralling inflation. Nevertheless, a constant devaluation of the dinar helps Yugoslav exports to remain fairly competitive and, from the visitor's point of view, makes the purchase of local goods and services extremely reasonable (though it's wise not to exchange more than your immediate needs since the rate may well increase overnight). Imports have been rationalized, so take note that such items are expensive. A careful look is being taken at all investments with new laws to encourage those from abroad. One wishes them well. But whatever the troubles of the present, there is no doubt that technology has made its ineradicable marks on the Yugoslav landscapes, transforming whole regions or bringing ease of access to hitherto isolated areas. One example is the remarkable railway completed a few years ago to link Belgrade with the south Adriatic port of Bar. To achieve this, a way had to be cut through formidable mountain barriers, necessitating over 100 tunnels and 230 bridges. Thus, in addition to its economic value, it is today one of the most beautiful scenic railway routes of Europe. Another example is the Danube–Tisa–Danube hydroengineering scheme in the autonomous province of Vojvodina, resulting in a network of 930 km. (580 miles) of canals between these two great rivers. This network not only irrigates 50,000 hectares (over 120,000 acres) of productive land but, even more importantly, removes excess flood waters from 700,000 hectares (over 1,700,000 acres). The increase in average yields of this "granary" of Yugoslavia has effectively made each field as productive as four were formerly. Yet another Danube project completed a few years ago, this time involving cooperation with Romania, was the remarkable Djerdap (Iron Gates) power plant and navigational system harnessing the river's turbulent waters to provide hydroelectric power for both countries. A second plant, Djerdap II, has now been completed 80 km. (50 miles) downstream.

But in the end, especially in this materially-minded last quarter of the 20th century, a country's affluence (though sometimes more *apparent* than real) is perhaps most easily gauged by the proliferation of luxury goods. Thus the enormous increase in private traffic on the roads (with attendant parking problems in the cities!) becomes significant, as does the fact that almost every family now possesses a television set. But perhaps the most striking feature of all is the phenomenal rash of private building. Practically everywhere you go in Yugoslavia, you will see private homes in varying stages of construction. If some of these strike you as unusually large, you can be sure that they have been built with the intention of renting rooms to tourists.

The countryside also shows signs of change. The boom years left their mark as people abandoned the country for the cities. But now there is evidence of a small-scale return to the land with areas of recently cleared terrain, freshly tilled soil, and newly planted vines and vegetables.

Accent on Youth

There has indeed been an educational explosion. Nearly 95 percent of all children of school age now have at least elementary schooling and, at the upper end of the educational scale, there are at least 20 times as many students (about 375,000) as there were before the war. Thus the sons and daughters of peasant farmers, fisherfolk and factory workers have become teachers and lawyers, doctors and scientists, politicians and journalists. It is significant that few of them forget their origins; going home to some small island community or remote mountain village is not simply the fulfillment of a duty: South Slav family ties are strong. It will be interesting to see what happens in the future.

One other special feature of the Yugoslav educational system is the way in which it caters for ethnic minorities. There are schools teaching in the Albanian (by far the biggest group), Bulgarian, Italian, Hungarian, Romanian, Ruthenian, Slovak, Turkish and Czech languages. In regions with substantial minorities, additional means of education and amenities for national expression exist, such as the Albanian-language University in Kosovo, the cultural center ministering to Albanian and Turkish speakers in Skopje, Macedonia, and similar facilities for Hungarians in Novi Sad, Vojvodina. Similarly, newspapers and journals are available in most of the minority national languages, which also have their own television programs. The degree to which national forms of music, dancing, costume and customs have survived is quite remarkable and is one of the bonuses for the visitor to enjoy. And more recent forms of expression have been found. The splendid canvases of the naïve painters in the villages of the Danubian and Sava plains, whether they be Serb, Croat, Slovak or Hungarian, illustrate a whole folk-culture with a vividness that has won acclaim in international salons all over the world.

Sports fans will need no reminding of the Yugoslav enthusiasm for their two great loves: football and basketball. Recent failures in international football have indeed caused national dismay, but this has been more than compensated for by basketball successes. Athletics, tennis, and boxing are other sports in which the Yugoslavs do well, and they have had a number of triumphs in a wide range of competitive activities ranging from bowling and table tennis to Graeco-Roman wrestling and judo. Chess has always been a popular pastime, and Yugoslavia holds the record for the number of international tournaments held in the country each year. When it comes to sporting activities for which visitors can expect ideal conditions, the most important include hunting, fishing, canoeing along the splendid rivers, sailing in the magnificent coastal waters, and winter sports. Amenities for all sports are continually expanding, with a periodical additional boost provided by preparations for such international events as the Winter Olympic Games in Sarajevo in 1984, and Universiade, the World University Games, in Zagreb in 1987.

You, the Tourist

But what of tourism in general? It is certainly no exception in illustrating the country's phenomenal growth. From 62,000 foreign visitors in 1948, the figure soared to nearly 9 million in 1988, and with rising affluence the increase in domestic tourism has been just as dramatic. Rapid growth can bring its dangers, and Yugoslavia, like many other countries suddenly projected into popular tourism, made its share of mistakes in indiscriminate building to standards that were not always as high as they should have been. The mass overdevelopment of stretches of coast suffered by some countries, however, has been avoided, and the sensible calling in of United Nations experts for advice on planning some years ago has been effective. Similarly, there is a lively and growing awareness of potential pollution dangers. Yugoslavia is a very active participant of the International Blue Plan for cleaning up the Mediterranean, and a number of conferences (in which most of the countries bordering the Mediterranean have participated) have already taken place on Yugoslav soil. For the moment, her Adriatic coast compares very favorably with many others; industry is limited to a few places like Rijeka and Split, and the currents weaving through the labyrinthine sea passages between 100s of islands act as a good cleanser. The treatment of industrial waste and of vastly greater amounts of sewage—one of the by-products of a healthy growth in tourism—is the subject of much discussion and more importantly of action, an example of which has already been mentioned.

For a short period in recent years, there was a tendency for the number of foreign tourists to remain static. Perhaps the success story had come too easily and too rapidly, and human nature being what it is, an infiltration of lower standards of service or higher prices for "extras" was becoming apparent. Whatever the cause, it gave the Yugoslavs pause for thought, resulting in the preparation of new laws on catering and tourism, both to ensure a higher standard of tourist services and to protect the consumer. Some resorts have even most laudably arranged meetings between visitors and local tourist agencies to exchange ideas and to resolve problems.

That said, the main flaws in Yugoslav tourism, in some areas, have long been shoddy construction and insufficient maintenance. This is much less in evidence in resort areas along the coast or in the mountains, where there are some very fine hotels indeed. But in inland areas, even in some of the major towns, faulty plasterwork, loose light fittings and especially erratic plumbing are still far too prevalent. There is also the repeated mystery of the missing bath plug. A Yugoslav hotelier friend told me "We keep replacing them and they keep disappearing, so we've just given up!" As honesty is a particularly strong Yugoslav characteristic (in a dozen extensive visits over a quarter of a century I have never had anything stolen), I can only assume that these treasured items are collected for the innumerable private homes that are under construction . . . In any case, it is a good idea to take one with you if you plan to travel around.

Spreading the Benefits

Much consideration has been given to the fact that over 80 percent of visitors stay at resorts along the Adriatic coast. This is obviously serious neglect of the magnificent landscapes and cultural wealth of the rest of the country, especially when 75 percent of visitors come by their own transport, and therefore have the mobility to enjoy these attractions. To broaden the scope of tourism more amenities are needed, and the process is now under way. Some inland regions, such as the Slovenian Alps, the magnificent Plitvice Lakes of Croatia, the culturally mixed Sarajevo and other centers of Bosnia-Hercegovina, are already popular inland destinations, though often on a fairly short-term basis. Others, such as the mountain regions of Macedonia, South Serbia and Montenegro, have only recently begun to acquire such tourist accessories as first-class hotels, and some have yet to develop the standard of service normally expected.

The main point is that awareness of the needs exists, with regard not only to the standard but also to the variety of amenities required. Thus the outstanding cultural attractions of the medieval monasteries of Macedonia and South Serbia provide a theme for an increasing number of tours. So-called "village" tourism is being developed in a number of regions, whereby visitors can stay in village households in rural communities, usually very attractive and in beautiful surroundings but not otherwise developed as resorts. There is no better way of experiencing the "real" Yugoslavia. Other forms of village tourism include visits to shepherds' cottages, barbecue picnics, and participation in local folk events. In these various ways, a proportion at least of the devotees of sun-and-sea should be lured away from the beaches to see something of the rest of Yugoslavia. I'll wager they won't regret it.

THE PAST

The Ancient Story of a Young Nation

Yugoslavia officially became a single state only in 1918, after the 1917 Pact of Corfu. When Slav tribes entered the Balkans during the Dark Ages, at the time of the Wandering of the Peoples, they came in waves, with differing aims and under separate leaders. Having settled in the Balkans, they were at once subject to diverse influences, for they had settled across the dividing line of the Eastern and Western Roman Empires, Byzantium and Rome. Even more important for them was that the Balkan peninsula was a disputed territory between the Roman and Orthodox churches. The Serbs, Macedonians and Montenegrins adopted the Orthodox creed from Byzantium, the Croats and Slovenes the Catholic faith of Rome. The Bosnians had for a time a heretical religion of their own, Bogomilism, but after the Ottoman conquest in the 15th century they accepted Islam in large numbers.

Thus any attempt to summarize the history of the Yugoslavs is like the construction of a complex cable. Many strands of various colors are interwoven to form, in the end, a single unit.

Multicolored Mosaic

There are at least half-a-dozen such strands. Among the Yugoslav peoples themselves, there are the Serbians, the Croats, the Slovenes, the Bosnians, the Montenegrins and the Macedonians. Almost as varied at different periods are the peoples who have at one time or another been the overlords of the South Slav lands—the Byzantines, the Bulgarians, the Turks, the Venetians, the Hungarians and the Austrians. A most brilliantly colored thread, interwoven in the pattern for more than 1,000 years, traces the independent existence of the Republic of Ragusa, later Dubrovnik.

The large majority of these Slav peoples were hostile to one another for most of their history. They fought fiercely and frequently. They differed in social and cultural background, in historical traditions, in religion and in alphabet. They resembled one another in language, in racial memory and in the folk traditions of the common people. But the differences still exist. The ancient frontiers can still be roughly traced by those of the Socialist Republics. Nor have the years of unity always been years of internal peace. But deep-rooted racial tradition, tempered and annealed by years of war, has brought unity at last to the Yugoslavs. They are now a single people, albeit with marked provincial variations.

Until 1918, the Yugoslav lands were but once united under a single rule. The only time in history that this happened was before the coming of the Slav tribes, under the later Roman Empire. Then, for a time, the Balkan peninsula was a vital overland link with the rich eastern provinces, and supplied huge quantities of much-needed grain from the fertile Sava and Danube plains. Many of the great Emperors were of Balkan origin. The most impressive memorials of that time are the Palace of Diocletian at Split and the nearby ruined city of Salona. To British visitors the palace may seem strangely familiar. It was studied and sketched by the English architect, Robert Adam, in 1757. What he saw there became the model for London's original Adelphi buildings.

After the coming of the Slavs, these lands were once again almost united under the rule of the Ottoman Turks. But Turkish dominion, though at one time it stretched almost to the gates of Vienna, was not complete. Quite large areas of Croatia were unconquered military frontiers, and Slovenia was subject only to occasional forays. Also, two pockets of South Slav independence remained, in fact if not always in theory: the Republic of Ragusa-Dubrovnik and the State of Zeta (modern Montenegro or Crna Gora). Many of the Dalmatian cities remained subject to another foreign rule, that of Venice.

Until the end of the Middle Ages, nationality as we know it today did not exist, not even in some of the more centralized countries of Western Europe. Its place was taken by loyalty to a leader or to a creed.

The South Slavs were divided not only by tribal differences and history, but even more by the existence of three major religions, Catholic and Orthodox Christianity, rivals as much of one another as of Islam. These forces of division were stronger than any tending toward cohesion.

The idea of nationality began to emerge at about the beginning of the 19th century. At that time it had many names, for example, the Illyrian Movement, but for the sake of simplicity it may be called the "Yugoslav Idea." It was built at first upon shallow foundations.

Awakening of National Consciousness

In Slovenia the invasion of Napoleon's armies, the first major invasion of the Yugoslav lands from the west since that of Charlemagne's Franks, was hailed as a deliverance. The Slovenes, hitherto considered the boorish peasantry of an outlying Austrian province, had preserved their Slav language and little else. In fact, their continued existence as a racial group was largely due to their complex and archaic Slav tongue, and was little short of a miracle. Napoleon formed of Slovenia the short-lived Illyrian Province. The Slovene language was recognized as equal in administrative affairs with French and German, and Ljubljana became an administrative center.

National consciousness awoke, and there was a vigorous and patriotic outburst of Slovene literature. The great Slovene poet, Fran Prešern, hymned the Napoleonic armies (which had just crushed forever the political independence of Dubrovnik farther down the coast) as harbingers of a new kind of liberty. The Slovene Church (the Slovenes are devout Catholics) took up the cause of national liberty. When Slovenia reverted to being an Austrian province, the seed had already been sown. The Slovenes felt themselves to be a nation, and it was but one step further to feel themselves one with the other Yugoslav peoples. Attempts to "Germanize" the country failed. In 1870, the Croats and Slovenes made common cause of their Yugoslav aims, and after World War I, under their leader Father Antun Korošec, voted for union with the Serbs and Croats.

With the Croats the position was somewhat different. Memories of their early independence had died out among the peasantry and only a few scholars knew anything of the Croat kings of Dalmatia. Remembrance of the Military Frontiers had consolidated into a military tradition, but the Croat soldiers were almost always mercenaries. There was still, however, a strong tradition of separateness within the Habsburg Empire, as a sort of third force distinct from the dominant Austrians and Hungarians.

But in Bosnia and the Vojvodina, Orthodox Serb and Catholic Croat peasants lived and worked together, and despite religious rivalry still felt a community of race in their struggles with foreign overlords, which developed into active cooperation in the unrest of 1848 and at the time of the annexation of Bosnia by Austria-Hungary.

Bishop Štrosmajer of Djakovo, one of the great churchmen who preached the Yugoslav ideal, dreamed of a union of the South Slav peoples based on religious tolerance. But he was before his time. Another strong current of political consciousness demanded Croat independence within the framework of the Habsburg Empire. These nationalists hated the Serbs, whom they considered unlettered and schismatic barbarians.

These two main ideologies among the Croats bedeviled the whole of their later history, and led to the tragic fiasco of the Independent State of Croatia set up by the Axis during World War II.

The Montenegrins lived in their mountain stronghold in a state of almost continuous guerilla warfare against the Turks. Later a kingdom, they founded a theocratic state under prince-bishops, whose successors were chosen from collateral branches of the episcopal family of Petrović-Njegoš.

Of Traditions and Language

One of these prince-bishops, Petar Petrović-Njegoš, was the greatest poet of the Yugoslav peoples. His works were read far outside the boundaries of his petty state, and a quotation from one of them, "He is my brother, of whatever creed he be," became a rallying cry of Yugoslav patriots. The Montenegrins, incidentally, never considered themselves a separate people. The founder of the great Nemanja dynasty of medieval Serbian emperors was born in Montenegro, and the Montenegrins saw themselves as the élite, the free unconquered remnant of the Serbian people.

The Serb, Vuk Štefan Karadžić (1787–1864), worked unremittingly during the Serbian insurrections against the Turks, and his success was to make dreams of Yugoslav unity politically possible. Vuk wandered through the Yugoslav countryside collecting and publishing the rich store of peasant oral literature—ballads, songs, proverbs and folk-tales. He also compiled the first modern Serbian dictionary. The publication of these works had an immediate and startling effect, hard to understand in lands where there has been a long tradition of patriotic literacy. All the Yugoslav peoples remembered the past of which they had every reason to be proud. The beautiful and tragic cycle of the Kosovo ballads is filled with hope for the future, a future which many felt was about to dawn. The songs of the *haiduks* (patriotic outlaws who kept alive resistance to the Turks) reminded men that opposition to tyranny is glorious, while the cycle of Karageorge's revolt against the *dahis* (Turkish feudal warlords) showed them that it could also be successful.

A huge mass of national traditions, mainly but not exclusively Serbian in origin, was made the heritage of all Yugoslavs. Though not always true to history (the arch-figure of resistance, Marko Kraljević, a sort of Yugoslav Robin Hood, was less impressive in fact than in legend), these "traditions" were true to the spirit of the people, something more potent than literal accuracy.

An immediate and incalculably valuable effect of Karadžić's work was his simplification of the language, which for the first time in nearly 1,000 years made the spoken and written languages the same. As a result, all the Yugoslav peoples of that time (save the Slovenes) adopted a single literary dialect. The Croats, in particular, made a great and magnanimous gesture in abandoning their local idioms, though retaining their Latin alphabet. Thus, from the time of Karadžić onward, Serb and Croat have become almost the same language, though with minor dialect differences. The parallel of British and American English is evident and pertinent.

Serbia Independent

The writers and the dreamers created the pan-Yugoslav idea. The soldiers and the politicians were to make it viable. Their difficulties were even greater and their setbacks more serious. Yet they too succeeded. The first and greatest achievement was the liberation of Serbia. By the beginning of the 19th century, the highly-centralized structure of the Ottoman Empire had broken down.

Local warlords usurped power in the provinces and held it by force, cruelty and corruption. Four such men seized power in Serbia and began systematically to murder the Serbian leaders. The people, driven to desperation, rose in revolt under Karageorge, a peasant leader of military genius rather in the tradition of the medieval *haiduks*. He succeeded in liberating Serbia, but had to withdraw with most of his supporters when the Turks returned in force. One of his generals remained, Miloš Obrenović, who again raised the standard of revolt. Almost as great a soldier as Karageorge, Miloš was a better statesman. He knew the art of the possible. Under his rule, Serbia became a more or less independent principality, the

Turks merely keeping garrisons in five fortresses. Karageorge tried to return, but was murdered by Miloš and his head sent to Istanbul, an act of political wisdom at the time, but which led to nearly a century of dynastic quarrels between the families of the two men. In 1867, the Turks were forced to leave their fortresses. Serbia became a free and independent kingdom.

As such she became the focus of Yugoslav hopes. Many of her greatest statesmen openly proclaimed federal ideals. Free Serbs cooperated with the Croats and with their countrymen under Hungarian rule in the troubles of 1848. Free Serbs, too, tried to help the patriots of Bosnia when that country was annexed by Austria-Hungary.

World War I

As a result, Serbia was regarded with ever-growing hostility by the Habsburg Empire, which ruled over many millions of discontented Slavs—Bosnians, Slovenes, Croats, Dalmatians, Serbs, Czechs and Poles. In Bosnia itself, hopes ran high. The "Young Bosnia" group was openly pan-Yugoslav in its ideas. The whole country was in a ferment of unrest which culminated in the assassination in 1914 of the Habsburg heir, Archduke Franz Ferdinand, at Sarajevo by a Bosnian student called Gavrilo Princip. That Princip had been supported and encouraged by the Serbian government is very doubtful and has never been proved; that his group had the sympathy, and perhaps the support, of patriotic Yugoslav groups on Serbian territory is most probable.

Austria-Hungary affected to believe in the involvement of the Serbian government, and sent an ultimatum so severe that its rejection was a foregone conclusion. Serbia, though recently victorious in the Balkan Wars, first against Turkey and then against Bulgaria, was so much weakened that she seemed an easy morsel to swallow. But the first Austro-Hungarian invasion was thrown back and the war spread. Austria-Hungary, instead of being faced with a localized conflict in which she expected rapid victory, was embroiled in a European war which brought about the downfall of her Empire.

In the last years of World War I, Serbia had indeed been defeated. Her country was occupied and her armies forced to retreat through Albania in conditions so hard that the Central Powers were ready to regard the Serbs as a force with which they need no longer reckon. But while the Serb armies, reformed and reequipped by Britain and France, were regrouping on the Salonica front, all was not well with the Habsburg Empire. Her Slav soldiers were unwilling to fight against their fellow-Slavs for the benefit of the Habsburgs, and deserted in considerable numbers when faced with Serbian or Russian troops. Her politicians continued to press for the eventual independence of the minority peoples. The South Slav deputies of the *Reichsrat* formed a Yugoslav Committee and demanded the unification of all the Serbs, Croats and Slovenes of the Empire in a single state. Later they signed a common declaration with the Serbian government, one of whose avowed war-aims was the liberation of all the Yugoslavs, and openly expressed their desire for a single, independent, democratic Yugoslav state under the Karageorgević dynasty. This was the declaration of Corfu, the basis of the creation of modern Yugoslavia.

Yugoslavia a Kingdom

The end of the war found the Yugoslav peoples in a state of hopeless confusion. The popular will had declared its desire for a unified state. The figure of President Wilson dominated the Peace Conference; his Fourteen Points had stressed the principle of self-determination. But there was much bitter argument about whether this principle should apply to the Yugoslav peoples individually or collectively; and if the latter, what form the new state should take—federal or centralized.

Events forced a degree of centralization. In 1915 the Italians had been promised large areas of ethnically Croat and Slovene lands in Istria and Dalmatia as a price for their entry into the war on the side of the allies. The promise was made before the collapse of the Habsburg Monarchy was foreseen and before America had entered the war. But President Wilson refused to recognize the treaty, as its terms were contrary to the principle of self-determination of peoples. The Italian armies entered the Yugoslav lands to take by force what they claimed was theirs by treaty. There were no Yugoslav forces to oppose them save the Serbian armies. Furthermore, there was no organized administrative body to restore order in the post-war chaos except the Serbian civil secretariat. When the new Kingdom of the Serbs, Croats and Slovenes (S.H.S.) was created on 4th December 1918, its administrative and military forces were predominantly Serb. This was to be a cause of friction and discontent right up to very recent times, in fact up to the creation of Marshal Tito's Federal People's Republic of Yugoslavia on 29th November 1945.

The period between the wars may be summarized as a continual strain between the forces of centralism and those of separatism, culminating in the assassination of King Alexander at Marseilles in 1934, during a State Visit to France. The country was then in a most unstable political condition. Parliamentary democracy had failed, owing to racial tension, inexperience and intolerance. King Alexander suspended parliament and ruled mainly by decree. The centralist faction had success after success, even in its breaking down of the old tribal and traditional frontiers by the creation of new administrative units—the *banovinas*. The Croats had almost withdrawn from the central administration and created a sort of state within a state under the powerful Croat Peasant Party. The governments in Belgrade were becoming less and less representative of the people—finally, they did not represent even the majority of Serbs.

In this atmosphere of smothered political discontent, two extremist groups became very powerful. One was the Macedonian Revolutionary Organization and the other the Croat Ustaše. Both were originally extremist patriotic organizations, but both sought external aid, each finally becoming mere executive organs of its own foreign sponsor.

Finally, as was inevitable, the two groups came to an understanding. King Alexander was killed by a professional M.R.O. gunman supported by Ustaše accomplices. Foreseeing the possibility of his assassination, King Alexander had appointed a Regency Council to rule the country in the name of his young son Peter. The only important member of this council was the young king's uncle, Prince Paul.

A former Oxford student and a distinguished esthete, Prince Paul was neither eager nor able to rule a divided and turbulent people at a time when the fate of Yugoslavia, and indeed of all Europe, was in the hands of two dictators, Hitler and Mussolini. Successive Yugoslav governments tried a policy of appeasement toward Germany and Italy, to which Yugoslav economic, and finally foreign, policy was closely linked. Under the Premier Milan Stojadinović, the government became openly fascist, with the artificial and somewhat comic Yugoslav Radical Union (J.R.Z.) assuming the rôle of the "single party." But a majority of the Serbs was hostile, the Croats were in open opposition and the other peoples largely non-cooperative. The experiment failed and Stojadinović was dismissed in 1938.

His successor, Dragiša Cvetković, tried to stop the rot by concluding an agreement, the *sporazum*, with the Croat leader, Vlatko Maček, but, though any slackening of tension within the country was welcome, it was soon clear that this was too little and came too late.

World War II

Thus Yugoslavia faced the outbreak of World War II in almost as dis-united a state as it was at the close of the first, but with greater disillusion and less hope. Prince Paul, hoping to spare his country the fate of Poland, declared Yugoslavia neutral, but was forced to make greater and greater concessions to the Axis Powers. In March 1941 he paid a secret visit to Hitler at Berchtesgaden, and on the 25th of that month the Yugoslav Premier and Foreign Minister signed a treaty with Germany placing Yugoslavia in the Axis camp.

Events then moved with extraordinary rapidity. Cvetković had scarcely returned from Germany when the Serbs, ashamed and disgusted, rose against the government in the 27th March *coup d'état,* largely engineered by airforce officers and supported by the Serbian Orthodox Church. Prince Paul abdicated and fled, and the young Peter was proclaimed king. Yugoslavia reaffirmed her neutrality and repudiated her signature of the Axis Treaty. Though attempts were at once made by the new Prime Minister, Dušan Šimovič, to maintain Yugoslav neutrality, it was clear that Germany would attack very soon. Mobilization was ordered. In the early morning of 6th April 1941, German airplanes bombed Belgrade, and German mechanized forces crossed the frontier. The Italians also attacked from the west.

The king, the government and most of the service chiefs left Belgrade the same day. Plans were drawn up for a defense of the central mountain bastion of Serbia and Bosnia, and there was sharp fighting in Macedonia against German forces which had entered the country from Bulgaria in the east. But the Yugoslav mobilization had been too slow and too late. There had not been time to reorganize the cadres and remove the pro-Germans and separatists. There was much confusion and not a little treachery. Within ten days the Yugoslav armies had capitulated. The country was occupied and the "new European order" of Hitler and Mussolini established. The king and many political and military leaders escaped by plane. A government in exile was set up in London.

All Yugoslavia's external and internal enemies took advantage of the collapse. Slovenia and parts of Dalmatia were divided between Italy and Germany. Bulgaria annexed a large part of Macedonia. The rich farm lands of the north had a special German-Hungarian administration. Albania annexed certain frontier provinces with Albanian minorities. Montenegro, after an abortive attempt to restore the Petrović-Njegoš dynasty, found itself under Italian military government. In Serbia, a quisling government was formed under General Milan Nedić. In Croatia the extremists seized power and Ante Pavelić, the Ustaše leader who had been involved in the murder of King Alexander, returned from exile. An independent Croatian state was proclaimed and the worst features of Axis rule introduced.

The Resistance

Almost at once, however, resistance movements sprang up. Two of these became nationwide and of great importance. One, the Četniks, was commanded by Draža Mihailović; this was mainly Serb nationalist in spirit, and was regarded with suspicion and distrust by the other Yugoslav peoples. The other, the Partisans, was led by Josip Broz (Tito), and was under the control of the Communist Party. Attempts to found a common front soon foundered on mutual distrust, and Yugoslavia experienced the unhappy fate of having two mutually hostile resistance movements facing four enemy armies—the Germans, the Italians, the Bulgarians, and the Ustaše-Croatians.

The Četniks had the backing of the Yugoslav government in exile, which appointed Mihailović their minister of war and a general. He had also the support of the Western allies at first, which was often considerable. The activities of the Partisans, however, were little known in Western Europe, and their dependence on Communist leadership was regarded with some suspicion. But as conditions in the resistance movements became clearer, it was evident that the Četnik movement was inconsistent, without inner cohesion and above all ineffective. Some of the Četnik groups collaborated with the enemy, and despite the undoubted courage and patriotism of many individual Četniks, it was obvious that the movement was a spent force of little military value. The Partisans, on the other hand, were rapidly developing their military forces, already had effective control of large areas of the country and above all were actively and continuously fighting the enemy. Allied assistance was transferred from the Četniks to the Partisans, and a military mission sent to Tito's headquarters.

The efficient organization and continued military success of Tito's Partisans drew to his support a large number of patriotic Yugoslavs whose opinions were not necessarily Communist, among them a number of former Četniks. Furthermore, his movement was successful in overriding regional jealousies (President Tito himself was, incidentally, a Croat), whereas the Četnik movement had been too predominantly Serbian nationalist. The formation of the new Yugoslavia was presaged at the meetings at Jajce in 1943 of the A.V.N.O.J. (Antifascist Council of the National Liberation of Yugoslavia).

The New Yugoslavia

There is no space here to enter in the complicated details of the Partisan campaigns. Suffice it to say that they were characterized by unimaginable acts of endurance and bravery, sparking off in the Nazis (including, tragically, fellow Yugoslavs) appalling reprisals. In effect they held down large numbers of Axis troops in the Balkans, and thus contributed greatly both to Western and to Soviet victories on other fronts. The Partisans liquidated Axis puppet-states in the Balkans, including Ustaše-Croatia, and finally, after linking up with Soviet armies advancing from the east, liberated the whole country. After prolonged and rather acrimonious discussions with the exile government in London, the Communist Party won the day, the king not being permitted to return to the country. The new Yugoslavia was proclaimed the Federal Democratic People's Republic of Yugoslavia (renamed in 1963 Socialist Federal Republic of Yugoslavia).

From the mid-60s on, Yugoslavia made rapid progress toward becoming a modern industrial state. The standard of living soared, but so eventually did unemployment and prices. Roads have spun a network of communication across the face of the land, opening up the more remote regions. Under the leadership of President Tito, who remained amazingly alert and active almost up to his death in May 1980, the country maintained its precarious position between the Eastern and Western blocs, and became a founder and leading exponent of non-alignment policies.

Tito's death was mourned not only by the Yugoslav nation, but by many millions across the world. The array of heads of state and other notables that attended his funeral was indeed a tribute to the high regard in which he was held. Whether the system of revolving collective leadership devised by Tito himself to succeed him provides the right solution remains to be seen. Few Yugoslavs today will be able to tell you the name of their President, now elected from a rotating Presidency for a term of only one year.

The new leadership currently is contending with two major problems: unrest arising from growing conflict of nationalist interest, especially in Serbia; and a disasterous economy. As we go to press, the results of many months debate on changes to the constitution are being implemented and more are under discussion. Among these are amended laws which are notably edging Yugoslavia towards a market economy, as mentioned in the previous chapter. Others have restored to Serbia certain rights that had been truncated by the 1974 Constitution, giving her more say than, in the eyes of her minority nationalities, might seem desirable. The rest of us can only hope that the final result will be that this admirable country will find a way through these political and economic quicksands.

CREATIVE YUGOSLAVIA

From Phidias to Meštrović

Before the United Nations Plaza in New York stands Antun Augustinčić's magnificent statue, *Messenger of Peace*. A gift from the Yugoslav government, it represents a figure reminiscent of the Italian *condottieri* of the Renaissance; it is a work of tremendous power and virility.

Another contemporary Yugoslav sculptor, whose vigorous, lyrical works you will come across all over the country is Meštrović, and it comes as something of a surprise to visitors from Western Europe to discover these budding Michelangelos in what they believed to be a backward Balkan country. But Augustinčić and Meštrović are only two of the best among the many who are carrying on an ancient artistic tradition, European in its origin, which is the common heritage of countless artists and artisans in every corner of the land.

That heritage is manifested in a thousand different ways: ninth-century Croat ecclesiastical architecture; the Orthodox churches of Serbia and Macedonia; the metalwork of Kadar, belonging to the same period; the Bogomil tombs of Bosnia; the Renaissance buildings of the Dalmatian coast. Surely these alone are enough to prove the artistic genius of the southern Slavs. Upon these foundations their art evolved according to its own laws, and its refusal entirely to succumb to the influences of the country's Turkish and other rulers was a sure proof of its dynamism.

The earliest examples of the art of the inhabitants of what today is Yugoslavia belong to the Stone Age, sandstone vessels and crudely carved idols. The *situle* urn of Vače is one of the numerous relics of the Iron Age, and may be seen in Ljubljana Museum. The intensively vivid figures depicted upon it epitomize the civilization of Illyria, as rich in diverse ways as was the Etruscan in Italy.

The Greek occupation of Macedonia and the many Greek colonies founded along the shores of the Adriatic cut short the evolution of Illyrian art, and by the sixth century B.C. had transformed it into the Archaic Greek style, some of the best surviving examples of which may be seen in Belgrade, having been sent there from Macedonia. Classical Greek sculpture is represented by a copy of the statue of Athene, worked by the great Athenian sculptor Phidias in the fifth century B.C., which was found at the ruins of Heraclea, near Bitola. Two superb bronze statuettes of dancing satyrs came from the same site. Finally, there are various fine examples of ancient Greek workmanship from Ohrid, Trebenište, and other places. Of the Greek colonies on the Adriatic, little survives beyond the necropolis at Budva.

Roman art and architecture completely dominated not only the coastal regions but the interior also. Roman penetration began as early as the third century B.C., although it was not until the beginning of the Christian era that Yugoslavia was incorporated into the Empire. Soon good roads and beautiful cities made their appearance, and the campaigns of Tiberius and Trajan in the first and second centuries were celebrated in impressive public works that may still be seen today, notably along the Danube.

Other Roman buildings include the theater at Stobi in Macedonia; the temple and amphitheater at Pula; the majestic Palace of Diocletian at Split and the Roman town of Salona nearby. Roman sculpture is at its best in the statues at Stobi and Zadar, the reliefs of Šempeter, and the altars to Mithras at Ptuj. In a way Yugoslavia was a meeting-place of Hellenic and Roman art, and exemplifies a partial blending of the best in both.

The migratory waves of savage tribes from the northeast which followed the collapse of Rome brought the Huns, the Avars, and in the sixth and seventh centuries, the Slavs, from whom the present population of Yugoslavia is descended. Byzantium clung on for a while to the remnants of Imperial power, and the Emperor Justinian (A.D. 527–568) built the fortified town of Caričingrad in Serbia. This imposing site, which lies not far off the main Niš–Skopje road, reveals features of public building of the period, notably cisterns and water-conduits. It was while this descendant of Illyrian peasants was emperor that the Basilica of Poreč was built and decorated with precious mosaics.

The newly arrived Slavs were influenced by these Roman and Byzantine buildings in the design of their own simple churches, and produced a sometimes crude but nonetheless sincere imitation of their predecessors. These first examples of a native architecture are all to be found on the Dalmatian coast—St. Donat at Zadar, St. Barbara at Trogir, St. Michael at Ston, and the Holy Cross at Nin. Though some are small they perfectly exemplify pre-medieval monumental architecture, as is proved by the way the walls rise above the tetrastyle foundations.

The only church in Serbia possessing the same characteristics is that of St. Peter at Novi Pazar, which dates from the ninth or tenth century and was designed in the form of a Greek cross, topped by circular walls. In Macedonia there is the interesting church of St. Sofia at Ohrid, where beautiful frescos have recently been uncovered. It is a perfect example of

Byzantine architecture, a forerunner of the blending of the Roman and Byzantine, which later became the native style of the country.

Serbo-Byzantine School

The most impressive examples of the architecture of the medieval Serb state are the monasteries of Serbia and Macedonia, built by their kings or high dignitaries as evidence of their piety.

During the second half of the 12th century, under the Nemanja dynasty, there was an exceptional upsurge of artistic activity among the Serbs, which found expression in the works of the Raška school in the neighborhood of the River Ibar, and spread to the Dalmatian coast and the nearer Byzantine provinces. Their typical combination of the Roman and Byzantine styles is obvious in the monasteries of Studenica, Žiča, Sopočani, Mileševo and others.

As their rule expanded southward the Serb kings introduced modifications in the monastic architecture of Macedonia, as a result of which the interior space is broken up by a complex system of supports for the slender cupolas. The Macedonian school is also distinguished by its preference for Byzantine-style decoration, the polychrome façade of various different materials being the principal form of external ornamentation. With the sole exception of the church at Dečani—the work of Vid of Kotor, a native of the coast—the Roman influence now disappears. Other examples of the Macedonian school are to be seen at Gračanica; in the little church of Panteleimon near Skopje; and at Staro Nagoričano, Lesnovo and Prizren, all of which possess the typical multiplicity of cupolas.

A further Serbian school grew up during the 15th or 16th century in the Morava valley, then far removed from the Turkish threat. Its originators built the base in a clover-leaf configuration, and relied upon the skilful use of stone and brick for external decoration. The delightfully vigorous results have led most experts to agree that they represent the most original achievement of early Serb architecture.

The paintings in the earliest religious foundations of the Nemanja are in the aulic Byzantine style introduced into Serbia during the 11th century. However, the frescos at Studenica include (in addition to inscriptions in Cyrillic characters) other indications of a new national style, which developed rapidly during the course of the 13th century.

Serb mural painting reached its apogee during the 14th century, declining at the time of the Italian Renaissance, which also coincided with the disappearance of the last remaining traces of Serbian independence. At its height, however, Serbian mural painting was further advanced than any other of the same date.

In 1881, A. Ewans, the well-known art historian, published a series of articles in various British magazines and reviews on the subject of Serbian religious painting—a subject which seemed to fascinate him. In one of these he wrote, "It is almost incredible that the Byzantine form of art should have been able to find a place for its final flowering upon Slav soil, yet it is precisely there, and in Italy, that the cold forms of Byzantium acquired a special warmth. I will go even further, and state that if we had never known the buildings hidden away in the Balkan peninsula we should never have fully understood the significance of the great Italian Renaissance. To me nothing painted by Michelangelo surpasses the beauty of the image of the Angel of the Resurrection on the walls of Mileševo, founded by the Serbian kings."

Mural painting continued to develop at the same rate as architecture, the first native period of which began in the 12th century in the Ibar and Lim valley areas, and reached its greatest moment with the creation of the huge frescos in the Monastery of Sopoćani. Neo-Hellenistic work somehow seems even more striking when discovered among simple mountaineers, and becomes at the same time less formal and more human in such a setting. Mileševo, Ziča, Peć, Morača and the church at Gradac mark stages of a vigorous architectural development, into which a number of lay elements have now been introduced.

At the southern limits of the medieval Serb state a new style of mural painting appeared. Its subjects are of an epic character, richly-colored. A notable example is the narrative calendar in the Monastery of Dečani, which contains a separate illustration for every day of the year. Other examples of this school of art may be seen in the Church of the Holy Virgin of Leviška at Prizren; at St. Nicetas near Skopje; at Gračanica and elsewhere.

Later, in the 15th century, new developments of the fresco were being used in the region of the River Morava. Brighter colored, and in a more original style than its predecessors, wholly independent of all foreign influences, this technique is exemplified in the monasteries of Manasija, Ravanica, and Ljubostinja. With the total eclipse of medieval Serbia, distinctive architecture also ceased to develop. Under the Turks, almost the only artistic achievement was in the painting of icons on wood, and in the illustration of manuscripts. If you are interested in icons, you should make a point of seeing those at Ohrid, Skopje and Sarajevo, or if in graphic art, the manuscripts at Peć.

Romanesque and Gothic Art

Under Turkish rule, Romanesque art in all its forms took refuge on the shores of the Adriatic, and survives in the churches of St. Krševan at Zadar; St. Tryphon at Kotor; the cathedrals of Trogir and Rab and the many lovely 13th-century spires of the Dalmatian coast. The plastic arts found two masters in Radovan and Buvina, whose finest works are respectively the carved portal of Trogir Cathedral, and the great wooden door of Split Cathedral.

The *ciborium,* the carved stone baldachin or canopy supported by columns, which disappeared from the rest of Europe with the appearance of Romanesque, survived on the Adriatic coast of Italy, and appeared soon after in such Dalmatian churches as those of Zadar, Rab, Kotor and Korčula.

Zadar became the center for gold- and silverware, the collections of church treasure that exist there being among the finest in the world, the silver sarcophagus of St. Simeon (Sveti Šimun) especially being an absolute masterpiece.

The members of an heretical religious sect in Bosnia, the Bogomils, produced a unique kind of sculptured tomb for their dead and many of these strange memorials are to be seen, the stones ornamented with geometric designs, or figures of huntsmen, mounted soldiers or groups of dancers. The artists are unknown, and the reason for these elaborate gravestones is a mystery, but those at Radimlje, near Stolac, at Borotnice and Ubosko, are of great artistic merit. A few of the best examples are on view in the State Museum at Sarajevo.

This brief outline would be incomplete without mention of Turkish architecture, introduced into Macedonia, Serbia and Bosnia-Hercegovina during the 15th century. The most notable mosques are those of Sarajevo, Banja Luka and Tetovo. The graceful bridges at Mostar and Višegrad are also of Turkish workmanship.

Gothic architecture as we know it developed only in Slovenia and Croatia. There, every town built its Gothic church, sometimes in open country or upon some steep hill, and they were more sanctuaries and places of pilgrimage than for daily use—a proof, perhaps, of the greater spirituality of those times. Good examples are Sveti Primož in the Kamnik Alps and Ptujska Gora in Slovenia, both being decorated with touchingly naïve frescos. In Beram, Istria, the murals by Vincent of Kastav, painted in 1474, presage Renaissance art.

Šibenik Cathedral is a delightful blend of Gothic and Renaissance styles, while the Rector's Palace and the old Customs House in Dubrovnik are typical of the Dalmatian, inspired by Venice, of which there are countless lesser examples everywhere along the coast. The great architects of this period were the native George of Dalmatia; the Andrijić brothers; and the Italians Michelozzi, Sammicheli, and Nicholas of Florence. The city of Dubrovnik is an architectural entity almost unequaled throughout Europe.

Two great painters from Dalmatia contributed to the Italian Renaissance, Juraj Čulinović (Giorgio Schiavoni) and Andrija Medulić (Andrea Medolla). The late architectural flowering which is to be seen in Kotor is entirely indigenous, and reached its zenith at the beginning of the 18th century. The dead city of Perast and the noble buildings of Prčanj and Dobrota recall the period of fame and prosperity ushered in by the renowned navigators making their homes here.

Advent of the Baroque

Italy was responsible for the advent of the baroque in Croatia and Slovenia, and of the Venetian style in Dalmatia. The so-called Vojvodina baroque found north of Belgrade is little more than a variation of the form found in Austria.

The principal monuments of the period are the *iconostases,* huge screens covered with the images of saints, worked in the traditional way, with precious wood carving framing richly-colored paintings on panel. Baroque painting is at its best in Slovenia in the works of Cebej, Jelovšek, Bergant and Layer.

During the 19th century all European artistic movements had their followers in Yugoslavia, the greatest figures of the period being Konstantin Danil, Duro Jakšić, Vlaho Bukovac and Anton Azbe. Sculpture flourished later, and it was not until the start of the present century that Ivan Meštrović, the "Yugoslav Rodin," became known. He was born in 1883 and has achieved world renown, his brilliant virtuosity inspiring a school of gifted disciples, such as Antun Augustinčić, Frano Kršinić, Toma Rosandić and Petar Palavičini. Insofar as painting is concerned, the influence of Parisian schools is apparent in the works of, for instance, Petar Dobrović, Milo Milunović, Petar Lubarda and Milan Konjević.

We should also make mention of the naïve, or "primitive" painters of Yugoslavia. The Hlebine Group has become particularly well known beyond the confines of the country (Hlebine is a village in Northern Croatia). Krsto Hegedušić influenced these primitive painters most, among whom Ivan Generalić, Mirko Virius and Franjo Mraz are the most celebrated. Naïve painting first attracted critical attention in the 1930s. There are similar "schools" elsewhere, notably in Serbia.

Literature

The earliest Yugoslav literature dates from the times of Cyril and Methodius, two Greek monks familiar with the Slav dialect of Macedonia. They were sent to Bohemia and Moravia by the Emperor Michael of Byzantium, at the request of Prince Rastislav, to preach Christianity to the inhabitants in the vernacular tongue. The two missionaries set to work to translate the Scriptures and prayer books, but to do so they had first to invent the Glagolitic alphabet so as to be able to reproduce the sounds of the Slav language. They were accused of heresy on this account by the German clergy, so carried their case to Rome, where the Pope ruled in their favor and approved their employment of the old Slav language for their missionary work.

When Cyril retired to a monastery in Rome to die in 869, his disciples Kliment and Naum, both from Ohrid in Macedonia, replaced the Glagolitic with the far more commonly used Cyrillic, named in honor of their master. The Cyrillic alphabet was rapidly adopted wherever the Christian Slav-Orthodox rites were followed and, today, is almost universally used in the Soviet Union.

The Catholics forbade the use of the national language in their Slav churches, but the Croats, who by this time had created their own independent kingdom, continued to use Glagolitic characters in various parishes, and even in modern times the Slav Liturgy was used on the island of Krk, and in churches along the Adriatic coast.

A relic of that period is the "Text of Freising" discovered in the Bavarian town of that name, which is a Confession written in Latin and Slovene. "The Annals of Father Dukljan" belong to the 12th century, and are of greater literary than historic worth. The "Vinodol Code" of 1288 is the earliest collection of Croatian laws in existence.

First Expressions of National Consciousness

Literature was encouraged at the court of the medieval Nemanja kings of Serbia. Popular literature then included many cycles of epic chants, recited by wandering minstrels, the communications medium of their day. The best known are *The Marriage of Tsar Dušan* and the *Maiden of Kosovo,* both of which movingly relate the brave struggle of a small people against the mighty Turks. Those that tell of the heroic exploits of the *haiduks* (outlaws) are vivid with the yearning of a whole nation to be free of foreign domination.

At the same time the literature of philosophy developed in the city-state of Ragusa (Dubrovnik), at first only reflecting the Humanist ideas of the Renaissance, but later achieving a native individuality.

Drama reached its golden age in the comedies of Marin Držić. The epic poetry of Ivan Gundulić, *Osman,* covers the period of the first Christian victories over the Turks at the beginning of the 17th century. Two patrician contemporaries were the moralist Marko Marulić of Split and Hanibal Lucić, the poet of the island of Hvar.

For Primož Trubar, son of a Slovenian serf, the Reformation was not so much a question of differing dogmas as a chance to bring spiritual help to an oppressed people. He was forced to escape to Germany where, in 1551, he published the first two books written in his mother tongue, a catechism and an elementary reading manual. The first liturgies in old Slav were printed in Montenegro in 1493.

The Romantic period saw a radical reformation of the Serb language brought about by Vuk Karadžić, and the appearance of such writers as Petar Petrović-Njegoš in Montenegro. The epic *Gorski Vijenac* ("The Laurels of the Mountain") of Petrović-Njegoš appeared in 1847, a kind of hymn to liberty of a lyric beauty unequaled in Yugoslav letters. The Illyrian Movement was not only militantly political in its efforts to form a Southern Slav Union, but was also literary in character, bringing into prominence such writers as Ljudevit Gaj in Croatia and Fran Prešern in Slovenia, second only to the movement's great leader Karadžić.

Most of the writers of the 19th century found their inspiration in Russian and French literature, notably the dramatists Nušić and Vojnović, and the novelists Lazarević, Cankar and Čipiko.

Among modern writers we should mention the poets Oton Župančić and Vladimir Nazor, the essayist Miroslav Krleža and the novelist Ivo Andrić, who most brilliantly uses the tragic history of his native Bosnia as the background of his work. Ivo Andrić received the Nobel Prize for Literature in 1961.

The Theater

Before World War II there were probably not more than a dozen theaters in the whole of Yugoslavia while, today, this country of only 22 million possesses over 70, including several opera houses. The many new companies of actors necessary to supply so greatly increased a public began as amateurs after the war, but even so the theater would have continued to languish had it not been for the fact that the state covers up to 75 percent of the deficit of each theatrical run. The result, as far as theatergoers are concerned, is that you can buy tickets for a price that is only a fraction of what you would be charged if each company had to pay its way without state assistance. Similarly, the charge for a seat at a performance of grand opera is less than the price of a cinema ticket in London or New York.

Yugoslavia has reason to be proud of her theatrical past. The little theater on the island of Hvar was opened in 1612, and is still in business, occasionally as a concert room. Dubrovnik today runs an annual Summer Festival from about the beginning of July until the end of August every year. Ballet and music of every sort are included along with drama, and foreign artists from all over the world are invited to take part. Belgrade's September Theater Festival, BITEF, is already world-famous. Smaller but similar open-air festivals take place each summer at Split, Ljubljana and in the Roman amphitheater of Pula.

Sophisticated theatergoers from the great Western capitals of Europe and America will find the staging and acting of modern plays very exciting, and the quality of performances in classical works particularly, notably good. Similarly, a single visit to the opera in Zagreb, Belgrade or Ljubljana will convince you that the Yugoslavs are born singers, and you will hear performances that will bear comparison anywhere. Where the Yugoslavs excel is in the singing of their own magnificent folk songs. In Dalmatia especially, everyone sings: a man or woman without a good voice seems unthinkable here.

Music and Science

It is a curious fact that, unlike the northern Slav peoples, such as the Russians, the Czechs and the Poles, the Yugoslavs have never produced any world-famous composers. However, they are highly gifted performers, and their massed choirs are outstandingly good.

The four centuries of Turkish occupation seriously hindered the development of formal music in Yugoslavia. However, in Dalmatia, under the more benign Italian influence, a truly inspired musician appeared in the person of Ivan Lukačić (1574–1648), composer of motets that were sung in the cathedrals of Split and Šibenik. The Slovene Jakub Petelin (1550–1592) was a great master of the polyphonic, and in the 19th century Stevan Mokranjac became a recognized composer for massed choirs. The neo-Romantic style of music found expression in the now classic ballet of Stevan Hristić, entitled *The Legend of Ohrid,* and in the works of Krešimir Baranovič and Josip Slavenski.

The incessant struggle of the Yugoslav people to achieve their independence left them with little time or opportunity for scientific work, although the eminent philosopher, mathematician and astronomer Roger Bošković (1711–1789) was Yugoslav born. He lived for many years in London, and was elected a member of the Royal Society. His greatest work, *Theory of Natural Philosophy,* was published in Venice. In this he based his beliefs on the universal understanding of natural science. The book appeared in seven editions in Vienna, Paris and London during the course of the next seven years, and was instrumental in Diderot's formulation of the Materialist philosophy of the period.

Nicola Tesla (1858–1943) is acknowledged as one of the leading figures in the development of wireless communications. Pavle Savić was one of the principal assistants of Mme. Joliot-Curie in the years between the two world wars. Today Yugoslavia's universities provide an eager new army of young investigators, and three institutes train specialists in nuclear engineering. The country is determined to make up for all the years lost in war and enforced idleness.

YUGOSLAV FOLKLORE

Somber Beauty—Bright Patterns

Yugoslav folk culture is a complex and fascinating tapestry in which it is often easy to recognize the threads of many influences from different directions imposed on or absorbed by the native artistic skills of the south Slavs themselves in the course of their checkered history. Much of it survives to a remarkable degree, either as an integral part of everyday life in the remoter areas of the country, or enthusiastically kept alive by groups or societies or cooperatives in the towns and resorts of what has developed in a few decades into a thoroughly modern state.

For the visitor this means that performances of folkloric music and dance are very much part of the Yugoslav holiday scene, and often of an unusually high standard; also that the availability of attractive handicrafts abounds in markets, bazaars and specialist shops. Among them are examples of popular art that are relevant to the day to day life of at least some of the people, such as the shepherd's goblets and the engagement distaff, which a woman will often carry with her to her grave; also beautiful handwoven carpets, blankets and bags, and superb embroidery that lasts for generations. Such artifacts are made without haste and with loving care, for permanent use by the persons to whom they are given, and it is perhaps just this intimate quality that goes into the making which accounts for the inimitable warmth and charm they seem to possess, qualities that are missing in commercial goods.

There are many traces of the Illyrian tradition within the Byzantine, just as Slav characteristics appear in the Turkish-Oriental work, as though the people had always sought to retain something essentially their own through the long centuries of foreign occupation.

Handicrafts and Costumes

Craftsmanship of high quality is common in Yugoslavia, and in the mountain districts, many ancient trades still thrive—weaving, for instance—the women being the only producers of textiles in their villages, as was universally so in medieval times. The beautiful embroidery decorating the cloth woven by the peasants is wholly typical of their life, revealing all the natural, vigorous joys and sorrows of a simple people.

Though you will have to go well off the beaten track in most areas to see peasant costume in everyday use, it is clearly in evidence at folkloric performances. The costume is essential to good folk dancing, for the music as well as the spirited movements is incomplete without its display, the costume of each district being entirely different from that of its neighbors.

In the Alpine province of Slovenia, the native costumes are similar to those in neighboring Austria, and are worn only occasionally, at folk festivals, pageants and parades. The men usually wear short trousers and large-brimmed hats, the women, a dirndl-type dress, richer in color and embroidery than their other Alpine counterparts, and special styles of headdress. Descending into the rich plain of central Croatia and the Serbian Vojvodina you will immediately notice many women wearing multiple skirts that flare out from the hips, and richly embroidered blouses with wide sleeves, while the men's hats are small, round and brimless. The men also wear linen trousers over Russian-style boots.

In the mountains inland from the Dalmatian coast, where the winters are hard, costumes are of embroidered wool. Both men and women wear round forage caps, and aprons, those essential additions to feminine attire being delicately embroidered. The embossed leather belts give the men a virile air, and the older men still wear *opanci* (pumps), or slipper-like shoes worn with brightly-colored knitted stockings.

The baggy trousers clasped at the ankles, the small shawls and embroidered blouses of Bosnia-Hercegovina clearly reveal Turkish influence. South of Belgrade the men wear dark brown suits ornamented with black lace, and military-style forage caps. Here the leather *opanci* with turned-up toes, found throughout the Balkans, are held in place by highly ornamented leather thongs.

Farther south the costumes become increasingly Turkish in appearance, filigree jewelry and hand-embroidered shirts being generally worn. In Macedonia Greek influence appears, the men wearing short kilts, and in the mountains to the west the clothes are of heavy wool, admirably made. Sometimes leather is used instead of cloth, and is decorated with rich and many-colored appliqué-work.

In Zagorje, Dalmatia, and also in Montenegro, you can still see old, finely-chiseled guns, swords and knives, which are purely decorative, adding interest and distinction to the regional costumes. Bronze and silver are much employed in the chasing, gold rarely. The metal itself is inset with many fragments of colored glass or precious stones or, occasionally, pearls or coral.

In Bosnia and Macedonia the women continue to wear necklace-crowns composed of coins to "draw men's eyes away from their faces," and there is a further reminder of the Orient in the remarkable gold and silver filigree work.

Lacemaking is Italian in its form in the coastal regions and oriental in Macedonia. It is easy to distinguish between lace made by the Moslem Yugoslavs and that produced by their Christian compatriots. In either case, you can still acquire the most exquisite handmade lace at moderate prices.

In old times the principal wood carvers were the shepherds, but today it has become a domestic handicraft. The remarkable gourds and drinking cups decorated with both Turkish and Slav motifs make excellent, though not inexpensive souvenirs, as does the pottery work, which is at its best in northwest Croatia. If you can find paintings on glass with a religious motif you may have discovered collectors' pieces of some value, as many of these go into folk-museums.

A specialty of Slovenia are the famous beehives, whose entrances are decorated with historic scenes painted on wood.

Handmade pottery is giving way to factory-made products. The best surviving hand-thrown examples come from Croatia and Macedonia.

Wall Carpets

The often beautiful wall carpets, still found in old farm houses, are made with ewes' wool. In the Lika, carpets are long-haired and shaggy, and dyed all one color. In the east, on the other hand, they are close-cropped, and ornamented with geometric patterns or stylized forms of animals and vegetables, the colors being very varied. The Lika also produces carpets made of feathers sewn together with hemp. The best centers for carpets are Pirot in Serbia, Lazaropolje and Kruševo, both in Macedonia. Kelim carpets are made in Sarajevo.

Folk Dances

The popular dances of Yugoslavia can be divided into groups according to the role of the women-dancers. In Serbia and Croatia the women play a part equal to the men's in the dancing of the *kolo*. In Bosnia, Macedonia and Montenegro, on the other hand, the influence of Oriental tradition requires them to keep in the background.

Serb dances are vigorous and exuberant, reflecting the intense vitality of the people. Generally the dance is led by the acknowledged best male dancer in the village accompanied by his fiancée. The round dance is a kind of *farandole* accompanied by flute and violin, and more recently, by accordion.

The *kolo slavon* is danced in the parts of Croatia between the Sava and the Drava. This is the most prosperous and fertile region in the country, which probably accounts for the dance's robust optimism. With backing provided by violin or accordion, a young girl sings certain couplets, which are then picked up by both men and women and sung by them together in a kind of chorus.

The Dalmatian *kolo* is a round dance to the music of a single-stringed violin at a rapid rhythm, comprising a number of original and often difficult figures set by the lead dancer. There may be an accompaniment of recited verses.

The Bosnian *kolo* is danced in silence, perhaps because under the Turkish occupation these men of the hills had no wish to attract attention to themselves, and so danced in the forests without music.

The people of Macedonia are particularly devoted to music, and in addition possess an innate sense of timing and rhythm, which probably explains why Macedonia is choreographically the most interesting part of the whole country. In the mountainous region of Galičnik and Lazaropolje you will find not only the *kolo,* but also the *lesnoto* and the *teskoto,* danced at marriage feasts, which incidentally often continue for three whole days and nights. These dances begin at a slow and solemn pace, and gradually accelerate to a wild finish.

Montenegrin dances are performed by couples, and include a number of enormous leaps by the man toward his partner. In moments of amorous enthusiasm the male partner may pull a pistol from his belt or sash and fire into the air. It is perhaps as well, therefore, that such performances usually take place out of doors.

At the end of September, when the cattle return from summer pasture on the high Alpine meadows, there are always great celebrations by the mountaineers of Slovenia, and there are a number of dances special to the occasion. Slovenian dances usually have a 3/4 beat, similar to the Austrian-Bavarian *Ländler* (country dances) and are accompanied by a peasant band comprising accordion, trumpet and bass. In the Bela Krajina or "White Borderland" region (so called because the people there wear white costumes similar to those of the Croats) of the southeastern part of Slovenia, the only existing Slovenian type of *kolo* is danced during the festival of Zeleni Jurij ("Green George"), which celebrates the coming of spring, and dates back to pre-Christian times.

The war dances of Macedonia which feature large groups of "contestants" armed with long swords, are tremendously impressive and are known as *Rusali.* In spite of their geographic proximity these bear no resemblance to the Albanian dances from the Rugovo district, not far from Peć, which are violently aggressive.

One of the most important features of Serbian folklore is becoming increasingly rare. The *guslari,* or wandering minstrel, is now found only very occasionally. He is a direct heritage of the Middle Ages, and chants the heroic exploits in the struggle against the Turks. The long, romantic tales are accompanied by a single-stringed violin, known as a *gusle.* These epic ballads often have tens of thousands of verses, pathetic in telling of defeat, exultant in victory and tender in love, and are beyond all price as revealing life as it was lived in those harsh and distant days of oppression. During the 19th century a collection of these ancient oral epics was made, so that the message of the fast-disappearing itinerant minstrel has not wholly been lost.

Folklore Shows and Discs

Yugoslavia is in many ways in a happy position. The old order has changed very suddenly. Little more than two generations ago millions of Yugoslavs had never been outside their own villages and were still so poor that even a radio set was an unattainable luxury. Today they have television—and take it for granted. At the same time they remember very clearly all the old songs and the old dances and the old ways. Neither they nor their children, the new generation, have had to be taught their own folklore by ardent revivalists. No one has had to roam their country collecting the old songs as Cecil Sharp did in England, so that younger folk could learn to sing them. They've been in the family (the same family) for generations, and with a little care, won't be lost.

The old ways emerge at the oddest moments. A Yugoslav pop group from Dubrovnik, for instance, represented their country at a Eurovision Song Contest in London. At a party on the following night an English friend struck up a traditional Dalmatian song. The boys from Dubrovnik took it up, and for the next two hours these apostles of pop regaled those present with a magnificently-sung impromptu concert of Dalmatian folk songs. The same thing happens frequently with folk dances. Strike up the music, and any and every Yugoslav present will be up and ready to take part. No one has taught them these traditional ways. It's in their blood.

So, if you find that a display of folk dancing is billed for the following evening, you can be quite sure it will be authentic. The performers may all be young people who are now attending technical colleges and universities and as up-to-date and technologically contemporary as the most ardent modernists could wish. Nevertheless, the old dances are still as real and as meaningful for them as anything else in their world.

The same applies in most respects to folk music, except that there are far fewer musical performers than there are dancers. You can hear some staggeringly lovely performances. But, alas, these occur far more rarely than good dancing. Some quite wonderful recordings have been made by various Yugoslav record companies. They are worth hunting out, if you have the time. Many of the songs, in particular, have inexpressibly moving melodies that affect you deeply, even though you don't understand a single word of the text.

The "Slava"

The populations of Serbia, Macedonia (mostly) and Montenegro belong to the Orthodox Church, and attach great importance to the family celebration known as the *slava*. This is half-pagan, dating from the time of the conversion to Christianity of the Slavs. Each family has its own patron saint, and celebrates the saint's day with great pomp and hospitality, sometimes in a style that they can only achieve as the result of many personal sacrifices.

On the morning of the great day the whole family goes to church to attend a special ceremony. Then accompanied by all their friends, who wish them good luck and good health—for their cattle—they return home and the celebrations begin.

FOOD AND DRINK

Both Full of Zest

Cooking in Yugoslavia admirably illustrates the effects of history and geography. The already varied local dishes of Bosnia and Macedonia show additional influences from Turkish cuisine, while food from northern Croatia and the Serbian Vojvodina has an unmistakable Hungarian flavor, and that of Slovenia an undeniable touch of old Vienna. Italian pasta and risotto (*rizoto* in Serbo-Croat) have both crossed the Adriatic.

In Bosnia-Hercegovina, south Serbia and Macedonia there are a considerable number of Oriental-style restaurants, echoing the centuries of Turkish occupation. Some may look shabby by any standard, but nevertheless serve the most succulent food. The preparation of each dish is carried out before the eyes of the client in enormous cooking kettles. If you do decide to try one of these establishments (and you should do so at least once) then ask for an * aščinica.*

Serbian cooking is unquestionably the richest in regional dishes, with highly seasoned meats prepared in lard—not, as in so many countries, in butter or oil. Lunches tend to be more interesting than dinners, as Yugoslavs generally take their main meal at midday, before their siesta. However, main towns and resorts have plenty of attractive restaurants, many privately run, where you can eat well at any time. There has also been a marked improvement in the variety of dishes, including specialties, available in quite a few tourist hotels.

Restaurants serving the specialties of other parts of the country are to be found in many resorts and towns, and you can usually distinguish these by their names. For example, if it's called *Dalmacija, Split* or *Korčula* it's likely to be serving Dalmatian dishes; or if it is named *Sarajevo* or *Bosna,* the fare will probably be Bosnian. If the word *riblji* appears, it will be a fish restaurant.

Soups and Entrées

Let us observe the accepted order of dishes and begin with soups. The clear soups are prepared with chicken *(pileća supa),* beef *(govedja supa),* or a kind of bouillabaisse or fish soup *(brodet* or, in Serbia *alaska čorba).* The paste-like *Kacamak, palenta* or *mamaljuga* is ground maize cooked in salt water and eaten either with milk and sugar or with cream and cheese and usually accompanied by maize bread cooked without yeast. It is first-cousin to the Italian *polenta* and the Romanian national dish of *mamaliga.*

Hors d'oeuvres *(meze)* are served both hot and cold. The most familiar item is *gibanica,* which is simply a hot pâté of vermicelli cooked with the cream taken from boiled milk and eggs and cream.

We recommend the *piktije,* jellied pork or duck, and the *pogačice sa čvarcima,* which is a kind of oven-browned cake containing a great deal of pepper, that is supposed to arouse the appetite, and quite certainly makes it essential to drink. Do not miss the *dalmatinski pršut,* which is lightly smoked ham, or *užička pršuta,* beef smoked until it is hard, but be sure to leave room for the *salama Gavrilović,* certainly the equal of the very best Hungarian or Italian salami.

Now come a variety of dishes that are really neither hors d'oeuvres nor the main course, though they may be made to serve as either. Most popular of these is *ražnjici,* small squares of pork grilled on a skewer and eaten on a slice of bread. *Ćevapčići* is similar, except that the meat (pork, beef or lamb) is minced before grilling, and shaped into sausages. If you are not afraid of the consequences of an enormous thirst (or of social downfall if anyone should come within range), follow the uninhibited Yugoslav custom and eat this dish with finely chopped raw onion. The *ćevap* is not unlike *ćevapčići* but is of thick slices of heavily spiced pork.

In central and southern Yugoslavia, a variety of savory items make excellent snacks, for example *burek,* flaky pastry with layers of cheese, spinach or minced meat; *pita* or *banica,* again a flaky pastry filled with a combination of spinach, cheese and egg.

Conservative eaters may decide to play safe and ask for a steak, in which case they should keep their fingers crossed and ask for a *čulbastija*— though they may not recognize it as steak when they see it.

Try *pljeskavica,* which consists of a dozen small morsels of *ćevapčići,* already described, mixed with a similar amount of lamb and strips of sweet pepper, all grilled together.

A variation of this, known as *pljeskavica sa kajmakom,* differs only in that it is cooked in *kajmak*—a kind of cheesy butter made of the salted cream from boiled milk, which replaces ordinary butter in summer in country districts.

All the dishes described above are accompanied by salads, such as *srpska salata,* which consists of slices of red and green peppers, cucumber and lettuce leaves. *Ajvar* is a spicy mixture of sweet peppers and egg plant, chopped up together with garlic.

Main Dishes

One of the most delightful things to be found on a Yugoslav menu is *punjene tikvice,* zucchini (or vegetable marrow) stuffed with minced beef and pork mixed together with rice. In Bosnia the same dish is served with a fresh cream sauce called *sogan dolma*—this you should be sure not to miss. A variation is *punjena paprika,* in which a sweet pepper replaces the zucchini, tomato mixed with the rice stuffing, and a thick, fresh tomato sauce added.

An excellent Serb dish is *djuveč,* a mixture of egg plant, carrot, potato, rice and meat, roasted with grated cheese. *Musaka* is entirely Turkish, and is made of alternate slices of meat and potato, though often egg plant and zucchini replace the potato. At the moment of putting the dish into the oven the cook pours over it a mixture of beaten eggs and sour cream. Yugoslav experts insist that the musaka made with egg plant is the finest, not only to eat, but also because the blend of colors pleases the eye as well as the palate.

You may have heard the Arabic word *pilav.* It is the almost universal name throughout the Near East for any meat dish prepared with rice. In Yugoslavia the meat is either minced or cut into small squares, and mixed with variously seasoned rice before being grilled. In the days of the Turkish occupation the outlaws produced *hajdučki ćevap* (the haiduk was the maquis of the period), which was easy to make and tasty. It consists of pieces of meat, potatoes and smoked lard stuck on a skewer and roasted over a roaring fire. If you like oriental delicacies, then try *kapama,* squares of lamb, the stalks of green onions and spinach stewed together.

The savory stews of Yugoslavia nearly always contain a touch of cream and the yolk of an egg. The veal *râgout* is called *teleća čorba,* the chicken *pileća čorba.* In all cases the meat is stewed very slowly with sausage, red and green peppers and tomatoes, the yolk of an egg being added at the last moment. The result is a *lešo.*

In the same family as the *râgouts,* though with the emphasis on vegetables, are the *podvarak,* which is a kind of sauerkraut, combined with various different meats, and also the *kalja,* a subtle combination of cabbage with saddle of mutton. There is also *lonac,* which has a whiff of garlic—a dish that is found outside the frontiers of Yugoslavia under the name of *papazjanija,* a *râgout* of vegetables in season.

An attractive and nourishing dish in Slovenia is *bržola,* pork meat stuffed with capers and mushrooms. Somewhat similar to an item of other perhaps less imaginative cuisines is breaded fried chicken under the name of *pohovano pile* in Croatia and *pohana piška* in Slovenia.

Fish and Shellfish

In both Istria and Dalmatia fish and crustacea are excellent and plentiful, and many of them difficult to translate! We can recommend such grilled fish as red mullet *(barbuni),* mackerel *(skuše),* sea bream *(komarča),* and sea bass *(lubin).* Ink-fish and squid *(lignje)* are delicious fried, and also feature in *crni rižoto* (black risotto) in which the rice is cooked in the "ink" of the squid.

Lobster *à la dalmatienne (jastog)* is simply cold boiled, and most people prefer the crayfish *(sufle od rakova).* In Serbia, however, there is considerably more interest in freshwater fish, and there is a delicious dish consisting of a mixture of two Danube fish, sturgeon *(jesetra)* and the boneless sterlet *(kečiga)*. There is a great deal of trout *(pastrmka)* to be had from Yugoslavia's turbulent mountain rivers, the most delicious probably being those caught in Lake Ohrid in Macedonia, a special variety of salmon-trout found nowhere else in Europe. Prepared in the Ohrid way, in a sauce of onions, tomato juice and parsley, it's really delicious.

Incidentally, lumpfish from Lake Ohrid also provide a red caviar, as do the Danube fish.

Desserts—Heavy and Sweet

Various rich fillings are included with desserts in Yugoslavia. A blend of pastry and fruit produces the superlative *štrudla,* with apples *(sa jabukama)* or cherries *(sa trešnjama).* Served warm these are delightful, but hardly to be recommended for those with delicate digestions.

A popular Slovene dessert is ribbon noodles *(rezanci)* with fresh cheese and grated nuts or poppy seeds, heavily sugared. Another is *štruklji,* white cheese folded into a very thin dough, boiled and served with toasted or fried breadcrumbs.

Fortunately there are a number of cakes and tarts which make less serious demands upon your digestive powers, and we strongly recommend to you the local light cakes sprinkled with nuts or poppy seeds. The style of cakes in Croatia is more familiar to Western eyes and palates, while those of Slovenia reveal the beneficent influence of Vienna. A Slovenian specialty is *potica,* a kind of cake made with several layers of nut filling. Many visitors fall to the temptations of *doboš,* which is of Hungarian origin, and is garnished with coffee and caramel. In the areas of the country longest under Turkish rule you will find plenty of *lokum* or Turkish delight, *kadaif, baklava* and *gurabije*—none of them recommended to anyone not possessed of a very sweet tooth. Macedonia produces *alva* which is made of egg whites, sugar and nuts, and *ćeten-alva,* which consists of sesame crushed in honey.

Wines

Yugoslavia is a great wine-growing country, and there are several areas almost wholly dedicated to the cultivation of the vine. You will come across local wines that change name according to their color, namely *crno,* which is dark red; *belo,* white; and *ružica,* which is rosé. These wines are obtainable everywhere, are drunk by the local people in great quantities, and are extremely cheap. In Dalmatia particularly, most families own their own vineyards, and until the recent emergence of large wine-shipping firms there was nothing they could do with their own wine except drink it.

The ordinary table wines are both cheap and agreeable, and can be ordered in jugs of various sizes, according to requirements.

Probably Yugoslavia's best-known wines are those grown in Slovenia, the white *Traminer* and *Riesling* being particularly good. A well known village in the northeast of this region is Jeruzalem, so called, legend has it, by fainthearted Crusaders, who hoped that they would thereby have completed their oath "to reach Jerusalem"!

From the vineyards of the Slovenian coast come the red *Teran* and *Merlot,* each having an excellent bouquet. In Istria there is an admirable strong red wine known as *refošk. Malvazija,* a malmsey, is also made in Istria, and elsewhere on the Croatian coast you will come across a sparkling, fruity wine, "the little water of Bakar" *(Bakarska Vodica).* In Split you will find the light red *opal* and the sweet muscatel called *Omiš.*

Nearly all the Dalmatian islands grow wine. The red varieties are often called *Dingač,* though strictly speaking this is produced only on the peninsula of Pelješac. Of the white wines, the best in our opinion are the *Vugava* grown in Vis, and *Grk,* which means "Greek." This is produced on the island of Korčula and is of a particularly clear amber color.

From the vineyards of Hercegovina, near Mostar, comes the international-award-winning dry, white *Žilavka.*

Everywhere in Serbia you will meet the faintly effervescent *fruškogorski biser,* which is good when drunk iced. *Smederevka* is made from grapes grown on the banks of the Danube. *Prokupac* and *Negotin* are equally Serb, and resemble light Burgundies. Excellent products of the Tikves area of Macedonia include the full bodied red *T'ga za jug* and the dry white *Temjanuga.* The list could be extended indefinitely, as there are literally 100s of local vintages.

As sometimes happens in wine-growing countries, beer is relatively expensive, not very good and apt to be tepid. A possible alternative is *špricer,* one-third white wine and two-thirds soda water, well-known in the States as a *spritzer.*

Numerous non-alcoholic fruit syrups are available, which can be mixed either with tap water or with one or other of the bottled mineral waters, of which there is a profusion in Yugoslavia. Even better are the small bottles or cans of pure fruit juices—cherry, strawberry, raspberry, blackberry and many others. Ask for *gusti sok* (meaning concentrated juice); if you just ask for juice you may get orangeade or even Pepsi or Coca Cola, which are also widely available and, in our opinion, not nearly as good!

Tap water in all main towns and resort areas is perfectly safe—better, in fact, than in many more affluent countries. But beware of well water in remote districts.

Coffee and Rakija

This is the land of *turska kava,* the authentic Turkish coffee, which improves in quality the nearer you get to the center of the country. In Croatia and Slovenia, Italian-style (black) *espreso* and (white) *cappuccino* are more prevalent. Turkish coffee is made of finely ground beans, rapidly boiled and very sweet—in fact it accords with the classic definition of perfect coffee. "Hot as hell, sweet as sin, and black as a woman's heart." If you don't like sugar you must ask for it *bez šećera.* Except when you are in Slovenia or Croatia, avoid the local *café au lait* with your breakfast *(doručak);* it is nearly always poor, and you will do better to stick to Turkish coffee at all times, or take your own supplies. Tea is regarded as some kind of witches' brew for anyone suffering from stomach disorders, so if your cup of tea means something in your life, then take along a tea-making outfit with you.

All Yugoslav spirits are extremely strong, but a glass is often taken together with the first Turkish coffee of the day, whatever the hour. The generic name for most of these distilled drinks is *rakija,* though what you will most usually be given will be *šljivovica.* Nearly all *rakija* drinks are taken before eating, the cocktail habit being more or less unknown outside luxury hotels.

The best distilleries in Yugoslavia are at Zadar, where every kind of liqueur is manufactured in more or less successful imitation of all the well-known French brands. However, in our opinion, originals are always better than imitations, so you should try the liqueur of the country, which is called *maraškino.* Its special bouquet comes from the stones of the morello cherries from which it is made. "Maraškino" is better known in Western Europe under its Italian name of *maraschino.* It was invented in the still flourishing Maraska distillery in Zadar. Other well-known liqueurs are *vinjak,* a sort of cognac, and *pelinkovac* (very bitter) and *mastika* (aniseed). Take a bottle home with you: it will make an inexpensive, unusual and much appreciated gift.

EXPLORING
YUGOSLAVIA

ISTRIA AND THE KVARNER GULF

An Introduction to the Coast

We start our detailed description of Yugoslavia with the coast. It is justly regarded as being one of Europe's most beautiful holiday areas. However, there's a great deal of it. If you drive your car from the Italian frontier just south of Trieste to the Albanian border south of Ulcinj you will have covered all of 1,125 km. (700 miles), and this despite the road's not taking you out to the tip of every headland nor closely round the shore of every bay. Still less does this overall distance include side trips to any of the 1,000 or so islands off the coast, over a dozen of which are highly developed holiday areas in their own right, and not all of them specially close to the mainland. Over recent years, there has been a great rash of new building along many stretches of this coast, sometimes forming a ribbon development linking one small resort with another. Much of it is in the form of private accommodations, guest houses, restaurants and autocamps, so there's no shortage of choice. Even then, during the peak season it's wise to start looking early for a place to rest your head.

Finding a satisfactory way of covering this long and lovely vacation strip is almost impossible. When we come to deal with inland Yugoslavia things are simple enough. We follow the boundaries of the Republics that make up the Yugoslav federation, because they are based on understandable geographical limits. The River Sava, for instance, is the dividing line for many kilometers between Croatia and Bosnia-Hercegovina. Slovenia ends and Croatia begins where the northern Alpine ranges give way to less rugged country. Many of these boundaries are not, however, immediately obvious. For instance, you will certainly have little impression of passing from one Republic to another as you drive from the plain of Slavonia in Croatia on to the Vojvodina plain forming part of Serbia. Nevertheless, these demarcations are practical and easy to understand. Along the coast the situation is different.

The first 30 km. (20 miles or so) of coast that you see after leaving Trieste form part of Slovenia. The next 965 km. (600 miles) are part of Croatia, with the exception of a 16 km. (ten miles) stretch just east of the port of Kardeljevo; this corridor was ceded to Bosnia-Hercegovina in the 18th century to allow it an outlet to the sea. Subsequent overlords Austria-Hungary, and, since 1918, Yugoslavia, have confirmed the arrangement. The final 110 km. (70 miles) or so of coast, to the Albanian frontier, are Montenegro's. If you look at an ordinary map, you will think this arrangement very strange.

The answer to the conundrum lies partly in geography and partly in geopolitics. Take a map on which the contours are clearly marked, and you will see that high mountain ranges run all along the coast from the Gulf of Kvarner's eastern coast to a little north of Albania. The islands are simply the peaks of largely submerged parallel ranges. Until the 1960s only a few difficult tracks crossed those mountains, and only a military cart-track built by Napoleon's troops ran along the coast. Almost till 1965 the coast was a place apart, completely different from the inland areas and where the best form of travel was by boat. In this same period it was not unusual for country folk to travel 30 km. (about 20 miles) or more down the coast in the little passenger steamer to see the doctor and to be quite content to stay overnight in his waiting room till morning surgery began. It is hardly surprising that the history of the coastlands and islands is markedly different from the interior's.

The earliest coastdwellers of whom we know anything were Illyrian, Liburnian and Dalmatian tribes whose civilization is only now being revealed by excavation. From the sixth century B.C. onward, trader-colonists from Greek city-states settled at points on the coast and islands such as Cavtat, Korčula, and Trogir. In the second century B.C. Rome expanded across the Adriatic and in time colonized the interior as well as the coast. When Roman power waned some 600 years later Slav invaders moved in overland from the north. Gradually their tribal organization developed into feudal kingdoms, the Croat kings ruling most of the coast. In time their territory was merged with Hungary's, and it was a Hungarian king who sold the whole of Dalmatia to Venice in 1410. By this time the Turks were establishing their rule through modern Yugoslavia's interior except for Croatia and Slovenia. A treaty between Turkey and Venice defined their common frontier as the line of mountain crests nearest the coast, except at the southern end, where the Turks held Bar and Ulcinj. Dubrovnik, then called Ragusa, contrived to remain independent. Venice mostly controlled the rest of the coast, including all the major seaboard towns in Istria.

In the early 19th century Napoleon overthrew Dubrovnik as well as Venice. When Napoleon in his turn was defeated Austria-Hungary claimed its former territories of Slovenia and Croatia—including all the coast. Just as the preceding 400 years of Venetian occupation left its mark on what were then the region's main ports and towns (each with its main square like a miniature Piazza San Marco, a tiny clock tower modeled on the Campanile, an open-air loggia which acted as law courts—several have survived—and plentiful reliefs of the Lion of St. Mark, Venice's patron saint) so the Austrian occupation left its own traces. In the latter part of the 19th century the Austrians began to develop "watering-places" along the coast (better health was the objective in those days, rather than rest and recuperation, as now). They built hotels at selected points as far south as Herceg-Novi. Some are still in use—in Pula, Opatija, Crikvenica, Split, Hvar and Dubrovnik, for instance, as well as Herceg-Novi.

When Austria-Hungary went the way of Napoleon and Venice in 1918, the entire Istrian peninsula was ceded to Italy as part-payment for joining the Allies. She later seized Zadar and some of the islands. The rest were returned to the now independent former provinces, with Montenegro extending its control northward to embrace the whole of the Gulf of Kotor. In 1944, the whole of the coast and all the islands became Yugoslav.

So—to return to the original question—how can we divide our description of the coast into manageable parts? The answer is that we have disregarded all the administrative and political divisions, and taken as separate entities those areas which tourists and Yugoslavs connected with tourism feel belong together. We consider first the coast of the whole Istrian peninsula and the Kvarner Gulf, together with the islands in the gulf and off the Istrian coast. We call our second "Central Dalmatia": it runs from just north of Zadar to the River Neretva and a line produced due west from the river's mouth, to include a large number of offshore islands. Our third section is called "Southern Dalmatia." It includes the coast and the islands that belonged to independent Dubrovnik as far as the Bay of Kotor and the border with Montenegro. The Montenegrin coast is covered in a separate chapter.

Thus we have Central and Southern Dalmatia, "Northern" has apparently got lost. This isn't the case. Strictly, our first chapter does not include any of Dalmatia, though the term Dalmatian is as often applied to this part of the Yugoslav coast as to all the rest. Northern Dalmatia begins (or used to begin) at the Velebit mountain's southern end: Zadar was its capital, with Split and the region round it comprising Central Dalmatia. Southern Dalmatia was in reality the area once governed from Dubrovnik. However, words change, like everything else. It seemed sensible to accept the new meaning assigned to Dalmatia. At least it spares us the presence of long and cumbrous chapter-titles.

Istria and the Kvarner Gulf

We have already given a brief historical summary of this area—Venetian till the early 19th century, Austro-Hungarian till 1918, partly Italian and partly Yugoslav between the wars, and wholly Yugoslav since 1944. Now we must describe it. Briefly, the coast has limestone hills, sometimes covered with woods, sloping down to a very blue sea. The islands are simply the tops of part-submerged mountains like those on the mainland. The coast has been worn into attractive coves and bays, with picturesque old fishing towns and ports in some of them and very modern holiday resorts in others: sometimes ancient town and modern resort are pleasantly combined. Olives and vines and other Mediterranean crops grow inland and on the slopes above the sea.

In appearance, the coastal and island towns range from almost pure medieval-Venetian (Rab, for example, with its fine stone buildings, church belfries and solid fortifications) to Austrian-Venetian (for example Piran), 19th-century Austrian (the older parts of Opatija) and pure 20th-century modern holiday Mediterranean (Medulin, Veruda, etc.). Each has its appeal, the new as well as the old, and each includes the timeless joy of flowers and fine trees. There are not many sandy beaches, but the bathing is excellent, as hundreds of thousands of visitors from Europe and beyond discover each year.

Poreč, with its huge nearby tourist complexes providing some 25,000 beds as well as private accommodations and camping sites, has replaced Opatija as tourist capital, at least in summer, followed by Portorož and Rovinj. Pula is the cultural center, and Rijeka is both an industrial and a communications center, as well as being Yugoslavia's main port.

The Istrian Interior

Most holidaymakers will no doubt want to head as quickly as possible for the coast, but they will make a grave error if they do not allow some part of their stay for exploring Istria's hilly and unspoilt interior. A major feature are the truly exquisite medieval hill villages, most of them built and fortified during Venetian rule and adding immeasurable charm to the landscape. Among them is Motovun, where folklore performances are held six evenings a week in summer, and Grožnjan which has become an international center for artists, especially musicians. Others include Buzet, the furthest inland, and Buje, Bale and Vodnjan, all three by the main Koper–Pula road. Some of the villages have exceptional treasures, such as the 15th-century frescos in the tiny church below the little hill village of Beram, near Pazin. The latter was for centuries the boundary between Venetian and Frankish (later Austrian) territory and is an interesting town in a dramatic setting.

Excursions are arranged from many of the coastal resorts to some of the hill villages and other places of interest, but if you have a car, a good map and local advice, you can have an unforgettable day or two exploring aspects of Istria undreamt of by the majority of the sunworshippers crowding the coast.

Istria's Western Coast

Koper has a fine 15th-century Town Hall, a Gothic-Venetian style loggia and a cathedral, all of them to be found in the main square. The narrow and tortuous streets and venerable palaces of the old town are in striking contrast to the adjoining modern port, sprawling suburbs and beach resort area.

Koper was the Roman Capis, and in Italian, Capodistria. Like Trieste, Koper was once a warm sea port at the service of landlocked central Europe, but with the passing of sail, she was soon eclipsed by her larger rival. Today, though there are modern port installations, the old town itself is a pleasant and quiet little backwater. A few miles from Koper at Ankaran is one of the most perfect bathing beaches on the northern shore of the bay. It's now a well-equipped resort and also a lovely spot for a camping or self-catering holiday.

From Koper a coast road leads to Izola, a former fishing village now completely changed by modern building and industrial developments. Between Izola and Piran, you pass salt pans and two small bays, Strunjan and Fijeso, the latter remarkable for the fact that only 20 m. (65 ft.) from the sea there is a lake of perfectly fresh water.

Piran is really charming: it is centered on a tiny medieval city perched on a rocky headland, birthplace of the Italian violinist and composer Tartini in 1692. The Municipal Theater is named after him. The two basins of the harbor are filled with many brightly painted sailboats, and the pure Venetian-Gothic buildings seem almost untouched by the hand of time. An odd reminder of long dead lovers is in the form of an inscription over one of these old houses which reads *Lasa pur dir*— "Let them talk." The story behind this is that a passionate love was poisoned by the scandalmongering neighbors.

Piran Cathedral has a Venetian campanile from which there is a wonderful view of the whole of the Gulf of Trieste, and an octagonal baptistery. If you walk for a few minutes through this strange little town you will come across remains of its medieval walls and numerous noble mansions in Venetian-Gothic or Austrian baroque. Here, too, you can see works by such masters as Carpaccio and Tintoretto, though to most visitors it is primarily a specially attractive resort for swimming and sunbathing, and enjoying the Mediterranean summer.

Nowadays, the bathing areas of Piran virtually merge into the outskirts of Portorož, one of Yugoslavia's longest-established and most popular watering places. Because the town is completely sheltered by hills from the north winds the many parks of Portorož are filled with subtropical plants and flowers. There are good sport and entertainment facilities, and the atmosphere is generally more sophisticated (and more expensive!) than in other resorts, with a fine selection of new and traditional-style hotels in the grand style. It is not a town that has notable historical associations, but the open-air exhibition of modern stone sculpture—a collection of the works of sculptors who have participated in the annual International "Forma Viva" Symposium—is well worth a visit. Portorož offers a great range of excursions along the coast (including Venice), to the islands, or inland, with a local airport from which panoramic flights are also arranged.

South of Portorož you soon reach Umag, until as recently as the 1960s an undistinguished and decaying little fishing village but now a flourishing sea resort, though overlooked by an industrial complex. The main tourist settlement is a couple of miles from the town, set in vineyards. The next town to the south is Novigrad which, like Umag, was an almost totally decayed fishing village, with very few remaining inhabitants, till new hotels were built there. It had some importance, under Venetian rule, however, as well as in Roman times—as a museum of Roman carvings and inscriptions, some fine old houses and a Venetian loggia testify.

The road to Poreč turns inland skirting the River Mirna's estuary. Founded in the 1st century A.D. and called Parentium, Poreč still has the ruins of Roman temples of Mars and Neptune, as well as traces of its pentagonal-plan city walls, and a labyrinth of charming narrow streets. Its most imposing monument, however, is the magnificent basilica built in about A.D. 550 by Bishop Euphrasius, one of the most remarkable buildings of the entire coast. The basilica, now a museum, features Roman columns topped by Byzantine capitals and the interior glows with superb shimmering wall mosaics and inlay. Immediately north of it a huge and fine floor mosaic dates from an even earlier church (third to fourth century). Today the whole of the area round this once-tiny town is studded with what the Yugoslavs call "tourist complexes"—concentrations of hotel blocks, restaurants, bars, swimming pools, chalets, nightclubs, etc., all under the same management. If you don't mind that the crowds throng here the summer through, this is one of the liveliest places on the coast with excellent facilities.

Beyond Poreč the road turns inland again to go round the long, V-shaped Limski fjord, famed for its oysters. On its northern bank is Vrsar (near one of the country's largest naturist colonies), another gorgeous little place. Back again on the coast is the lovely old town of Rovinj, piled up on a promontory. Its center is a maze of shadowed, crooked streets beneath the baroque cathedral and the delicate silhouette of a Venetian campanile. The bright colors of houses and boats are reflected in the little harbor that was once the center of its life and livelihood. Most of the tourist hotels are a short stroll away round the bay to the south, or on the two islands of Sveta Katarina and Crveni Otok, reached by motor launch.

Yet once more, on the way to Pula, the rocky coast forces us inland past the village of Bale and the ancient town of Vodnjan. Away out to sea we can pick out the Brioni islands, where the late President Tito had a secluded summer home. Here many major conferences were held and heads of state entertained, including Queen Elizabeth II. Now proclaimed a National Park, this has also become Yugoslavia's newest resort area, featuring several archeological sites and great open spaces where herds of deer roam free. It's a particularly peaceful spot as it's still a military zone and access is limited to day-excursionists and those who have pre-booked accommodations. No motorized transport is allowed, but you have the choice of bicycle, horse-drawn carriage, electric buggy, motorized "train" or, of course, your own two feet.

And so we come to Pula, a port and industrial center with a very long history indeed, called Pietas Julia in the 1st century A.D. There is plenty of evidence of Roman occupation in this bustling and fascinating town, of which the most remarkable is undoubtedly the relatively-intact oval amphitheater, designed to seat at least 23,000 people anxious to watch such spectacles as gladiatorial combat. Some time ago its acoustics were discovered to be excellent, and it has for many years provided a spectacular setting for an annual International Song Competition and an annual Film Festival as well as performances of opera.

Though the amphitheater must take pride-of-place, the Temple of Augustus, built a few years before the Crucifixion, is also of great interest. It stands next to the medieval Town Hall, which incorporates the remains of a Temple of Diana. The 15th-century Cathedral, just off the main quay of Obala Maršala Tita, has many interesting features—columns, stonework, mosaics from Roman or Byzantine times. From here a short street leads to the Kaštel, with its fortress rebuilt by the Venetians on a hill in the heart of the old town. East of this, on the hillside, is a small Roman theater and beyond it the fine Archeological Museum. Nearby are more

Roman remains—the Twin Gates and Hercules Gate, the latter on a corner of Pula's busy modern main square (Trg Bratstva i Jedinstva).

Despite her great heritage from the past, Pula is also a flourishing industrial and shipbuilding city, as well as a port and the center of a modern tourist area, with excellent hotels and several charming beaches. These are on the Verudela peninsula a mile or so south and further afield at Medulin, also at Premantura, near Istria's southern tip.

Opatija and Istria's East Coast

Our tour of Istria's east coast is centered on Opatija, the oldest resort on the whole peninsula, boasting all that is most loved by the poster artist. Across the long, deep bay the islands of Cres and Krk emerge from the intensely blue sea. Behind the town the leafy heights of Mount Učka rise to a majestic 1,396 m. (4,580 ft.). Moreover, Opatija has preserved some old-world comfort and elegance amid the brash modernity of the coast.

Just over a century ago there was little here but a modest fishing village—still intact as the northern suberb of Volosko. Then, about 1880, doctors began recommending its healthy climate. Luxury hotels were built, and within a few years Opatija was a fashionable holiday resort of the Austrian and Hungarian nobility. Its rapid growth toward the end of last century explains the rather Edwardian air of some of the hotels. Most are built close to the beach, and nearly all have their own beautifully kept gardens, with views of sea or mountain framed by trees.

This region has the supreme advantage of an extraordinarily equable climate, with a mean annual average temperature of 57°F. The lowest and highest mean monthly temperatures ever recorded here are 48°F. and 79°F. respectively. This is partly explained by the fact that the mountains to the north protect it in winter from cold winds, and regular sea breezes keep it from really oppressive heat. The sun shines for most of the year and fog, frost and snow are unknown. In winter rainy days are rare. There are actually quite heavy falls of rain in summer, but on relatively few days.

Naturally this privileged climate means that Opatija is a paradise of flowers, fruit and sweet-scented shrubs and plants—palms, lemon and orange groves, bamboo and yucca. A great variety of cacti lends a subtropical air to the many delightful little parks and gardens.

Tito Avenue, Opatija's main street, has fine shops and several luxury hotels, and not far away is Volosko, the picturesque small village of 18th-century houses, which is somewhat reminiscent of the French Riviera. Here begins the well-arranged coastal path that stretches for around 12 km. (7½ miles) along the Kvarner Riviera, through Opatija and via the fishing villages of Ika and Ičići to Lovran.

Opatija has a large, lively marina and several separate beaches, of which the most popular is the Kvarner Lido. In the evenings there are concerts or folk-dancing displays in the big open-air theater. In short, it affords every opportunity for the enjoyment of sun, peace, comfort and excellent sea bathing amid beautiful surroundings.

It is also a good center for excursions to the Kvarner islands or other parts of Istria. Highly recommended if you have a car is to take the old road to Mount Učka. To reach the top you'll need to walk an hour or two, but even if you don't there are simply stunning views over the Gulf of Kvarner on the road up or from the terrace of Učka pension on the roadside near the top. The main road to Koper now avoids this upper route by means of a new tunnel (toll payable).

South of Opatija, the 80-km. (50-mile) long eastern coast of Istria is punctuated by numerous attractive, flower-decked little seaside resorts that have grown up there because of the excellence of the climate and the bathing. Lovran, already mentioned, is the oldest, and has a 12th-century church and tower, but its greatest attraction lies in the luxuriant gardens that surround the hotels and villas, and the many laurel and chestnut groves on the outskirts. Two perfectly kept bathing beaches lead away north to Opatija, while southward lies Medveja, with another beach situated at the mouth of a ravine that pierces the flanks of Mount Učka. Next comes Mošćenička Draga and Mošćenice, both pleasant small resorts, and after them Plomin and Rabac. The latter, once a tiny fishing port and now a bustling modern resort, has a most dramatic approach down five km. (three miles) of steep, twisting road from the old mining town of Labin. The old part of Labin itself clusters on a hill and is very picturesque. From here it is only 57 km. (35 miles) to Pula, described earlier.

Rijeka and the Croatian Littoral

The Yugoslavs consider the "Croatian Littoral" to be limited to the 160 km. (100 miles) or so of Adriatic stretching from Rijeka (known before the end of World War II as Fiume, when it was part of either Italy or Austria-Hungary; both words mean "River") to just north of Zadar, where Dalmatia proper begins.

The coast is deeply indented, with delightful bays facing the intense blue of the open sea backed by steeply-rising mountains. Towns and villages are perched far above the water, but the dramatic element in the scene is softened by the warm beauty of the island-flecked sea. Since 1965, many modern tourist resorts have been built along this part of Yugoslavia's Adriatic coast, to join the much older (but now also modernized) watering place of Crikvenica.

The city of Rijeka was occupied in a daring raid by the poet D'Annunzio in 1919 and remained Italian until 1945, even though its Sušak district on the opposite side of the river was Yugoslav. Today the frontier no longer divides the city, and it has become Yugoslavia's most prosperous port.

Rijeka's tourist importance is as a major port from which to explore the coast, the islands, or take a trip to Venice. But it is more than just an industrial town and major seaport, for it can boast a pleasant medieval center, and there are other attractions too. From Titov Trg (Tito Square), for instance, 412 steps lead up to Trsat with its medieval castle and church (both rebuilt in the 19th century).

The fortress was built by the once powerful Counts of Frankopan, and the church was also erected at their orders to commemorate the Miracle of Trsat. The church was built in 1291 on the spot where angels were supposed to have deposited the humble house of the Virgin Mary from Nazareth. Traditionally, after an interval of three years, the angels continued their journey to Loreto in Italy, but Trsat has always remained a place of pilgrimage.

The *Jadranska Magistrala,* the well-surfaced but narrow Adriatic Highway, runs, often high above the sea but never very far from it, to Senj and Zadar. Between Rijeka and Senj, the road skirts a wide bay, with Bakar and Bakarac sited at opposite ends of it. Both have become holiday spots in recent years, though the scene is rather dominated by the big industrial installations on Rijeka's outskirts. Bakar is perched on a rock and largely medieval in character, despite its modern buildings. Here there is a remarkable 12th-century church and also one of the many castles of the Counts of Frankopan.

Next comes the little seaside resort of Kraljevica at the mouth of a narrow bay, sheltered by the mountains that almost encircle it. Beyond it a new bridge crosses to Rijeka's airport on Krk Island.

Crikvenica and Senj

Crikvenica's pebble beach, bounded at one end by the last outlying foothills of the Kapela range, can be unpleasantly crowded in summer. But at other times, the bathing is very acceptable here, and the sun decidedly warm. There are many pleasant walks and well-kept little parks, which combine to make Crikvenica a good holiday resort. It has all the usual seaside amusements. The once-unnoticed little fishing port of Selce nearby is now a busy resort with a number of hotels.

Novi Vinodolski, 11 km. (seven miles) south, is also pleasant and popular. It has a medieval castle of the ubiquitous Counts of Frankopan. It was here that the earliest Croat Constitution, known as the Vinodol Code, was drawn up in 1266. Novi also has a remarkable 14th-century church, which was designed to recall the earliest kind of Christian basilica found occasionally in Asia Minor. It is only half-an-hour's drive from Novi to Senj, whose Gothic Renaissance palaces, remains of fortifications and labyrinth of little streets leading to the Baroque square of Marka Balena make it well worth a visit. In particular, don't miss Nehaj fortress, dominating the little town from a nearby hill; it now houses a museum and you can climb to the top of it for even greater views.

Senj has been important since ancient times because it stands at the foot of one of the few routes (the Vratnik Pass) over the gaunt Velebit Mountains which rise to over 1,500 m. (5,000 ft.) above the coast. It is also linked nowadays by car ferry with the islands of Krk and Rab.

The people of Senj proudly recall the heroic rôle that their town played during the Turkish occupation of the surrounding country. Late in the 15th century a band of Serbs, who rose to notoriety as the Uskoks, successfully defied the Ottoman armies. With the old fortress as their base, protected on one flank by the mountains and on the seaward side by the windswept narrows of Senjska Vrata, these bellicose patriot-pirates and their descendants not only held off the attacks of a powerful enemy, but were themselves for 200 years a scourge to all the shipping of the Adriatic. The Venetians used to say of them *"Che Dio vi guardi delle mani dei Segnani"* —"God preserve you from falling into the hands of the men of Senj"—and this almost superstitious dread of the Uskoks was more than justified. They were eventually quelled, but their deeds live on in stirring folk ballads.

The restful little seaside town of Jablanac, dominated by a medieval castle of (as you will have guessed) the Counts of Frankopan, lies in the lovely fjord of Zavratnica, at the foot of the mighty Velebit Mountains. From here there are ferry services to the islands of Rab and Pag. A few kilometers further south is Karlobag, with its Capuchin Convent and its ferry

services to Pag. South of Karlobag, there is a long stretch of almost undeveloped coastline backed by the stark drama of the Velebit Mountains.
Near Starigrad-Paklenica, a rough road leads for a couple of miles into
the Paklenica National Park where pine woods clamber toward the entrance of a dramatic cleft in the soaring limestone cliffs. A walking trail
leads for five km. (three miles) into this spectacular landscape.

Farther on, the main Adriatic Highway turns west and crosses a fine
bridge over the Maslenica Channel to reach Zadar 32 km. (20 miles) away
over flat coastal land and past the Novigrad Sea, described in our next
chapter on Central Dalmatia.

The Islands of the Kvarner Gulf

Several large islands are to be found in the Kvarner Gulf. All are linked
by ferries or hydrofoils to the mainland, and Krk, additionally, by road
bridge. Krk is the northernmost and the largest. The scenery is majestic,
the eastern part being arid and wild, the southern and western areas fertile
and for that reason more populated. In fact, both on the islands and along
many parts of the coast, even some of the most uncompromisingly arid
areas are often patterned with piles of stones and traces of stone walls
showing how earlier tiny fields of cultivation were created out of the most
unpromising terrain. Many have fallen into disuse, however, as young people have left to seek easier ways of earning a living, though there are now
signs of a return to the land.

Krk was colonized by the Romans, fought over by Caesar and Pompey
in 49 B.C. and subsequently changed its masters with each fluctuation of
the balance of power in the Adriatic. The charming seaside village of
Baška, which has one of the longest pebble beaches in the northern Adriatic, has right-of-place in Yugoslav history as the site where the famous
11th-century Baška Tablet engraved with Croat inscriptions in Glagolitic
characters was found.

Several of the little towns are enchanting. The capital, Krk, clusters
round the head of a bay: Roman baths supplied some of the building materials for the sixth-century basilica which preceded the 12th-century Cathedral, and you can see some of the original columns and stonework. A few
minutes' stroll along a shore path brings you to the coves and beaches of
Dražica and Krk's main hotel. In the middle ages Krk was a main seat
of the Counts of Frankopan from which they ruled their extensive territories on the islands and coast of Kvarner, and there are many traces of those
times.

Excursions can be made to the interesting old villages of Malinska (now
dominated by major tourist developments at adjoining Haludovo), Punat,
Vrbnik and Omišalj—this last particularly rich in folk traditions. Vrbnik
is becoming something of an artists' colony because of its picturesque situation on the summit of a rocky promontory, and because of the extraordinary beauty of the eastern coastline. Košljun islet, facing the sandy beach
of Punat, has a particularly fine Benedictine Monastery whose collections
include a copy of the Baška tablet. Punat itself is only a few miles from
Krk and is one of the quieter resorts, despite its very large marina. All
these villages have now been developed as resorts, and the island combines
the advantages of easy accessibility with the peace that comes from relative

remoteness. In addition to wind surfing and water skiing facilities, it has an unusual number of tennis courts.

The island of Rab is among the best-known of the Croatian islands and is famous, among other things, for its delicious lobster. The Phoenicians were the first to install themselves here and then as in so many places throughout the Mediterranean, the Greeks, Romans and Byzantines followed. Later it became part of Croatia and so lived under Venetian and, finally, Austro-Hungarian rule until Yugoslavia was born, in 1918. Most older buildings on the island in one way or another reflect these different influences.

Rab is in the same latitude as the French Riviera, and enjoys a similar climate. It is a perfect setting for the flowers and subtropical vegetation that grows in rich profusion away from the barren northeastern coast.

The capital town was founded in Roman times on a narrow tongue of land, so that, approaching by sea, the traveler sees it set at the head of the bay, its ancient ramparts above, and the sails of many ships at its feet. It is a town of rare charm with its fine old private houses built by noble Venetian families centuries ago, and its Romanesque-Gothic cathedral—one of the most remarkable on the Adriatic. Its bell-tower soars above every other building offering fabulous views.

The town is packed with other interesting buildings, including the 13th-century Prince's Palace, now housing the tourist office, and such handsome Gothic-Renaissance structures as the Velika (Big) Nimir-Dominis Palace, the Mala (Small) Palača Nimir, the Town Loggia and the Benedictine monastery and church of Sv. Andrija, founded in the 11th century. A short stroll out of town brings you to the Franciscan Monastery of St. Euphemia whose several interesting features include the Library and a 15th-century Madonna by Vivarini.

But Rab is not wholly given over to things of the past, for there are plenty of modern villas and even naturist camps set among umbrella pines; and there are also several well-appointed beaches. If bathing is one of the main objects of a visit to Rab, then a day spent in the idyllic bay in the north of the island is to be recommended. Here nestles the small, quiet summer resort of Lopar, according to legend the birthplace of the Dalmatian stonemason Marino, who founded the Italian Republic of San Marino. Rab can be reached by ship from Rijeka or by ferry from the island of Krk and from Senj and Jablanac on the mainland.

Also in the Gulf of Kvarner facing the east coast of Istria are the two islands of Cres and Lošinj, both of them Italian until 1945. The eastern side of Cres is bare, but its western slopes are covered with excellent vines and dark pine woods. Cres is also the name of a charming little fishing town with a beach, a 15th-century loggia and a fortified tower. Almost in the center of the widest part of this long, thin island there is a mysterious freshwater lake called Vrana, as much as 83 m. (273 ft.) in depth at one point—far deeper than the sea anywhere within kilometers of the island's coasts.

A road runs the length of the island from Porozina in the north, connected by ferries to Brestova and Rijeka, to Osor in the south. In Roman times Osor was an important port-of-call for ships on the route from Aquileia, in the Bay of Trieste, to Split, Salona and Greece. It was attacked by the Genoese in the Middle Ages, and later became the base of a band of bloodthirsty pirates. For 1,000 years from the sixth century it was the seat of a bishop and from the end of that period date the Renaissance cathedral, the town hall, which also houses a museum, and several palaces. It is now something of a showplace, with modern sculptures dotted about among the old buildings, and is the venue for open-air performances in summer.

A bridge spans the shallow channel only some 12 m. (40 ft.) wide between Cres and the island of Lošinj, where orange and lemon groves descend to the edges of the many excellent bathing beaches.

The little town of Mali Lošinj is most attractive, built round the curve in a narrow bay, its gardens bright against the ancient buildings, and there are also 16th-century fortifications to hint at former greatness. It gets very crowded in summer when the harbor is also packed with foreign yachts. Most of the tourist hotels are scattered about among pine woods near the shore of Čikat, about 15 minutes' walk from town. Mali Lošinj began as a winter resort at the end of the 19th century, known for the beneficial effects of its climate on respiratory ailments. Nowadays, it's a bustling summer place with good facilities for bathing and wind surfing, but as proof of its balmy winters it still holds international underwater swimming contests every New Year.

Alternatively, cross the three km. (two miles) to the opposite side of the island—Lošinj though some 30 km. (20 miles) long is rarely more than a tenth of that distance in width—to Veli Lošinj, an ancient village with each of its houses in its own flower garden, by a beach.

There is an interesting excursion to be made from Lošinj to the neighboring, much smaller island of Susak, where some excellent wines are produced. This is said to be the only sandy island in the Adriatic. Another of its curiosities is the traditional local costume; on special occasions, the women in particular still wear this unusual dress: a kind of mini-skirt with many flared petticoats. There are no hotels, though accommodations can be arranged in private houses. Most famous of the excellent local wines is the sweet pink *prošek*.

Tours to several other islands are arranged from Mali Lošinj.

PRACTICAL INFORMATION FOR ISTRIA

WHEN TO GO. The tourist season in this region is from May until October. Because of the protection provided by Mount Učka against cold north winds the whole of Kvarner Bay, and in particular Opatija, also has a wonderfully mild winter climate. As a result, visitors come here in winter to avoid the cold, and in summer to escape the inland heat with the help of cool sea breezes. The mean summer temperature on the Istrian coast is 77°F. In spring it is made even more attractive by the mass of hazel, almond, and cherry trees in blossom. Mali Lošinj holds underwater swimming contests at New Year.

There are small casinos in several resorts. Opatija has almost every night during the high season, opera, concerts or folklore dancing and singing in an open-air theater. At Pula a Yugoslav Film Festival is held in late July, and performances by the Ljubljana and Zagreb Opera Companies alternate with concerts and folk music, songs and dancing throughout the summer. The Istrian Song Festival in June and the Yugoslav Folklore Festival in mid-July have offshoots in all the bigger resorts. The artistic and sports events at Portorož last from May through September. Nearly all the resorts have a busy summer program of entertainment.

HOTELS AND RESTAURANTS. The range of hotels has increased enormously in recent years, but it's still highly advisable to make advance reservations at the height of the season when all resorts are packed. Most resort hotels have some sports facilities or access to those of a well-equipped sports center.

Unless otherwise specified, resorts are open year-round and listed hotels have all or some rooms with private facilities. Smaller establishments or private homes are much less expensive. What they lack in comfort and facilities they often make up for in friendliness and personal contact. Tourist Information Offices (*Turistički Ured* or *Turistički Biro*), often indicated by the letter "i," are found in nearly all resorts, as are one or more travel agencies and these will take care of bookings and sometimes also of payments—though families prefer cash in hand.

Food and Drink. The region's cooking blends Italian and Austrian cuisine—not too heavy, and particularly good in its preparation of fish. The oysters of Vrsar are delicious, as also in their season are the locally caught crab—these are excellent and surprisingly inexpensive. Adriatic prawns (*škampa*) are also recommended, either boiled or fried and breadcrumbed. Most fish is grilled. However, mussels cooked in wine (*ostrige*) are a specialty. Fish soup (*brodet*) is somewhat similar to bouillabaisse, and is usually very good.

Cheese is not a particularly strong suit in Yugoslavia, but Istria produces one of the best in the country, a kind of gruyère. Another specialty is smoked ham (*pršut*), which goes very well with dark wines such as *Teran, Refošk, Vipava, Rebula,* and the delicious *Malvazija* from the island of Susak.

ISTRIA

Ankaran. Good beach in the Bay of Koper, with accommodations built round converted Benedictine monastery; season May–Oct. *Cedra* (M), 96 rooms, open-air pool. *Convent* (M), 30 rooms, open-air pool, plus annexes including *Week-End* (I), 104 rooms, and *Cipresa Bungalows.* Sports facilities.

Brioni Islands. One of the residences and conference centers of the late President Tito, on beautiful secluded islands, now National Park. Accommodations must be pre-booked. *Istra* (E), 50 rooms and *Neptun* (E), 55 rooms, share similar locations near the harbor, indoor pool, sports facilities. *Jurina, Franina* (M), 65 rooms, beach.

Koper. Picturesque old town with modern port. *Triglav* (M), 80 rooms. On quayside of old town. *Žusterna* (M), 153 rooms, pool. On shore across bay.

Restaurant. *Capris* (E), at lower end of price range. In the old town.

Lovran. Old-established beach resort in verdant setting near Opatija. *Excelsior* (E). New, shore-side, 170 rooms, pool, nightclub, sports facilities. *Beograd* (M), 102 rooms. Set in a fine garden on seafront. *Lovran* (M), 54 rooms. Central, in pleasant gardens, tennis. *Belvedere* (I), 30 rooms. On the seafront.

Mošćenička Draga. Pleasant, lively small resort. *Marina* (M), 192 rooms, indoor pool. Built round quadrangle near the sea. *Mediteran* (M), 80 rooms. More animated situation by the harbor and beach. *Pension Jadran-Rubin* (I), 27 rooms without bath. A short stroll along coastal path. **Restaurant.** *Montenegro* (I), small, good value.

Motovun. Glorious inland hill village. *Kaštel* (M), 26 rooms, at lower end of range. Adequate, but folklore performances make it noisy six evenings a week in summer.

Novigrad. Attractive small town, good for fishing; season Apr.–Oct. *Maestral* (E), 370 rooms, indoor pool, sports facilities, by beach, a little out of town. *Emonia* (M), 28 rooms, and annexes (I), 147 rooms. *Laguna* (M), 228 rooms; a little out of town. Pool, sports facilities.

Opatija. Long-established riviera-style resort with wide range of facilities. Newest is *Admiral* (E), 168 rooms. Shore-side position by large marina, open-air and indoor pools, sauna, disco, all amenities. *Ambassador* (E), 271 rooms, similar facilities. *Kvarner* (E), 83 rooms. Central, traditional style and spaciousness from the 1880s but modernized. In beautiful grounds, famous ballroom, open-air and indoor pools, seashore terrace.

All (M)s are: *Adriatic,* 333 rooms. Modern, eighth-floor pool and solarium, nightclub, disco. *Avala,* 62 rooms. Central, adjoining fine park. *Belvedere,* with annexes. On sea shore, indoor pool, tennis, gardens. *Brioni,* 98 rooms. Gardens, on the shore. *Continental,* 66 rooms. Central. *Dubrovnik,* 42 rooms. Near public beach. *Ičići,* 225 rooms. Modern, fine situation on sea shore on way to Ičići. *Imperial,* 129 rooms. Central, in comfortable traditional style, disco, bowling. *Jadran,* 90 rooms. Shore-side, garden, disco. *Kristal,* 135 rooms. Central, shore-side, indoor pool, sauna. *Paris-Garni,* 90 rooms. Central. *Residenz,* 49 rooms. On the shore. *Slavija-Bellevue,* 150 rooms. Traditional style, indoor pool, sauna, games rooms, nightclub, near sea. *Zagreb-Esplanade,* 110 rooms. In two near-neighboring buildings near sea with garden terraces. (I)s include *Palme,* 80 rooms. Central, disco. *Panorama,* 54 rooms. A little out of town.

Restaurants. Apart from those in the hotels, the following are especially recommended. *Bevanda* (E), Volosko, fish specialties. *Lido* (E), on Kvarner Beach, has a terrace with dance floor. *Pužev Breg* (E), at Matulj Dobri in the hills above town. *Ariston* (M), in Opatija. *Plavi Podrum* (M), Volosko. *Zelengaj* (M), in Opatija. *Korzo* (I), quick service, next to Imperial Hotel.

Poreč. Lovely old town, center of the largest beach-resort area; season Apr.–Oct. unless otherwise specified. On or near the waterfront of the old town are: *Neptun* (M), 145 rooms, and *Poreč* (M), 54 rooms (both open all year), and older *Riviera* (M), with annexes, 120 rooms, some (I).

On the islet of **Sv. Nikola** opposite the harbor: *Fortuna* (E), 174 rooms, pools. New. *Miramare* (M), 65 rooms. *Splendid,* bungalows.

The tourist complexes in the vicinity of Poreč are numerous and all modern, with water sports and tennis facilities and plenty of entertainment. A recommended selection is: *Pical* (E), (all year), 241 rooms plus apartments. About one km. (half a mile) north, pools, near beach, sports facilities. *Diamant* (M), (all year), 274 rooms plus apartments. About 1½ km. (one mile) south, pools, tennis. *Galijot* (M), 71 rooms plus bungalows and apartments. About four km. (2½ miles) south at **Plava Laguna,** lovely setting amidst pines on rocky headland, pool, disco. *Parentium* (E), 368 rooms. Five km. (three miles) south on wooded headland between Plava Laguna and **Zelena Laguna,** pools, sauna, nightclub, casino, plus facilities of big sports center.

Restaurants. *Riblji Restoran* (M), overlooking the quay, offers seafood specialties. In town are a number of small private restaurants. Some of the tourist complexes feature restaurants serving national specialties, such as *Pical*'s à la carte and the *Delfin* at Lanterna, 13 km. (eight miles) north.

Portorož. Fashionable resort on Slovenia's small stretch of coast, with good sports facilities. All (E) are: *Grand Hotel Emona,* 254 rooms. *Grand Hotel Palace,* 207 rooms. *Slovenija,* 160 rooms. These have private beaches and pools.

All (M), with pools, are: *Bernardin,* 273 rooms. Built round small harbor and marina of holiday village. *Mirna,* 89 rooms. *Neptun,* 89 rooms. *Palace,* 165 rooms. *Park Villas,* 240 rooms. *Riviera,* 204 rooms. *Vesna* (E), 174 rooms.

Restaurants. *Edvina Boarding House* (E), a few km. out of town, fish specialties. *Marina* (E), Lucija, by the yacht harbor. *Tri vdove* (E), on the old town shore at Piran. *Istra Inn* (E–M), in town, local specialties. *Trije lovci* (E–M), fish and game specialties at Šmarje, a few km. inland.

Pula. Commercial and historic city and port with notable Roman remains and nearby beach areas. Only centrally located hotel is old but renovated *Riviera* (M). Otherwise: *Brioni* (M), 223 rooms. About five km. (three miles) from town on pine-clad point; own beach, pool, sauna. *Park* (M), 141 rooms. Near Brioni, pool, near beach. *Splendid* (M), 364 rooms. On the outskirts above rocky shore, pool. In both cases, extensive sports facilities at nearby Verudela Center. Also in Verudela area, new *Histria* (E), 240 rooms, open-air and indoor pools, near rocky beach; *Palma* (M), 132 rooms, two open-air pools; and *Punta Verudela Village* (M), 400 rooms.

Restaurants. *Gorica* is in its own garden. *Zagreb,* serving local brown "stone" mussels, and *Jadran* are both good. *Ribarska Koliba,* at autocamp south of town, is also recommended.

At **Medulin,** about 11 km. (seven miles) south of Pula, is a major resort and sports area on a pine-covered promontory with three-km.-long (two-mile) beach. *Belvedere* (M), 460 rooms. Near beach, indoor pool, tennis. *Medulin* (M), with annex, 320 rooms, pool. *Mutila* (M), 172 rooms plus apartments, pool. Also naturist complex, *Kažela.*

Rabac. Small fishing port, now major resort; season Apr.–Oct. In town, *Apollo* (I), 54 rooms. A few minutes' walk on approach to town is the mammoth complex of *Mimosa-Hedera-Narcis* (M), with total of 600 rooms, sports facilities, indoor pool (in Mimosa), separated from beach by large *Oliva autocamp.* On wooded slopes close to town are *Fortuna* (I), 72 rooms, and *Istra* (I), 44 rooms. Near the sea shore beyond town are the newly constructed *Marina* (M), 100 rooms, pool, and the *Lanterna* (I), 155 rooms, with easy access to beaches of pebble and rock, and recreation facilities. A little further are the pavilions and villas of the *Girandella* complex (M), 580 rooms, with many sports facilities and disco, not far from beach.

Rovinj. Lovely old town crowning headland, and lively resort with good sports facilities. In town is *Rovinj* (M), 72 rooms. A little south of town is the *Park* (E), 188 rooms, pool and, in pinewoods beyond, *Eden* (E), 338 rooms, pool; *Montauro* (E), 285 rooms, pool; *Monte Mulin* (M), 180 rooms, all near rocky beach and with sports facilities. Nearby is the entertainments center *Monvi,* featuring restaurants, bars, disco, and open-air theater.

Opposite the harbor is the islet of **Sv. Katarina,** with *Katarina* (M). Further south is *Crveni Otok* (Red Island) with *Istra* (E), 310 rooms, pool, and *Park* (M), 100 rooms, sharing sports facilities.

Other tourist complexes within a few miles of Rovinj are at *Polari* to the south, and *Monsena* and *Valalta* to the north, all with naturist beaches.

Umag. Tiny fishing village on peninsula expanded into vast modern beach resort; season May–Oct. On headland of **Punta** across bay, with sports center, and all by or near rocky beach with concreted sunbathing areas are: *Adriatic* (E), 142 rooms, indoor pool; *Punta* (M), 250 rooms, landscaped gardens; *Umag* (M), 154 rooms, pools. A little further at **Katoro,** about 5 km. (3 miles) from town, with sports center, are: *Koral* (E), 250 rooms, pools; *Aurora* (M), 206 rooms; *Istra* (M), with annex, 550 rooms; *Polynesia apartments,* 686 rooms. Forming part of the Katoro resort complex is the Za-Za Entertainments Center with disco, restaurants and bars.

Savudrija, eight km. (five miles) from Umag, has *Savudrija* (I), 64 rooms, and *Savudrija bungalows* (M), 103 rooms, in delightful pinewood setting near beach.

Vrsar. Old fishing village at the mouth of Lim fjord, with modern resort and sports facilities in pinewoods 0.5–2 km. (¼–1 mile) away; season Apr.–Oct. *Belvedere Holiday Complex* (M), 204 rooms, plus apartments, open-air pool. *Panorama* (M), 188 rooms, pool. Recently renovated. *Pineta* (M), 100 rooms, pool. A few km. from Vrsar is the huge *Koversada Naturist Settlement,* with apartments, chalets, restaurants, etc., one of the largest in Europe.

EAST KVARNER COAST

Crikvenica. Small town and crowded beach resort facing Krk island. *Crikvenica* (M), 78 rooms. New; central. *Kaštel* (M), converted from old monastery and fully modernized, 98 rooms. *Mediteran* (M), 72 rooms. *Omorika* (M), 117 rooms, plus 162 in pavilions, a little out of town; sports facilities. *Therapia* (M), 117 rooms, at top end of price range. Restored pre-war building in gardens on hill; with pools. *Zagreb* (M), 72 rooms, some (I). Good value is the *Ad Turres* (I), 255 rooms, tourist settlement in pine forest with own beach.

At **Dramalj**, *Riviera Pavilions* (M), and annex, 100 rooms, some (I). On the Kačjak promontory, *Tourist Settlement* (I), 226 rooms.

Restaurant. *Jadran* is noted for its seafood.

Jablanac. On small fjord across from Krk island. *Jablanac* (I), with annex, 26 rooms, a few with shower.

Kraljevica. Road bridge to Krk island. *Oštro-Villas* (M), 40 rooms, at lower end of price range. Chalet-style. *Uvala Scott* (M), 338 rooms. *Almis* (I), 25 rooms.

Novi Vinodolski. Facing Krk island; season Apr.–Oct. *Lišanj,* with annex *Horizont* (M), 470 rooms, pools. On private beach. *Zagori* (M), 337 rooms, some (I), and *Povile* (I), 84 rooms, are tourist settlements north and south of the town respectively.

Rijeka. The country's main port and a partly industrial area. *Bonavia* (M), 154 rooms. In town center about 200 m. (220 yards) from quayside. With garden restaurant, café and dancing on roof terrace. Old-established and the best in town. *Jadran* (I), 81 rooms. By the sea in the Susak district, with pool and private beach. *Neboder* (I), 52 rooms. Good situation, but noisy. *Park* (I), 47 rooms. Outside town. *Motel Lucija* (I), 81 rooms. In Kostrena area east of town.

Restaurants. *Gradski Restoran* on the wharf near Narodni Trg (square). Nearby *Zlatna Školjika* specializes in seafood.

Selce. Almost a suburb of Crikvenica. *Varaždin* (E), 180 rooms, top-class, pool.

Senj. Historic little town and beach resort opposite Krk island. *Nehaj* (I), 43 rooms. On waterfront.

THE KVARNER ISLANDS

Cres

Cres. Picturesque port and capital of island; season Apr.–Oct. *Kimen* (M), 215 rooms. About a mile from town, adjoining camp site near stony beach.

Krk

Baška. Charming old village and port with extensive pebble beach; season Apr.–Oct. On outskirts, near sea, and linked by shore-side path are *Corinthia* (I), 130 rooms, and its annexes.

Krk. The island's attractive capital. *Dražica* (M), 530 rooms, including (M) and (I) annexes. A few minutes' walk by shore path from town, set in pine woods near extensive and well-arranged beach of rocks and cemented sunbathing areas. The complex includes open-air dancing.

Restaurant. *Marina* (M), by the harbor.

Malinska. Season Apr.–Oct., except *Tamaris* (all year). *Malin-Malin, Slavija* and *Triglav,* all with (M–I) annexes. A shore path leads to a major development at adjoining **Haludovo,** with *Palace* (E), 220 rooms, pools; *Tamaris* (M), 289 rooms, and self-catering villas of *Ribarsko Selo* (Fisherman's Village). Good sports facilities.

Njivice. *Jadran* (M), 220 rooms. On the waterfront. *Beli Kamik* (M) and annexes, some (I), totaling 620 rooms. A little away from village, near the sea, sports facilities, open-air dancing.

Omišalj. Lovely hill village. On the shore below is *Adriatic* (M), and annexes, 364 rooms, some (I).

Punat. Pleasant, quiet resort with large marina. *Park* (M), and annexes, 245 rooms, at lower end of price range; near sea.

Lošinj

Mali Lošinj. Lively little commercial and pleasure port. Only hotel in town is *Istra* (I), 23 rooms, none with bath. On the waterfront. The main tourist area is **Čikat,** 15 minutes' walk through pinewoods, where hotels include: *Alhambra* (M), 49 rooms, built in 1909 and the most charming, with annexes, some (I). *Aurora* (M), 404 rooms, pool; *Bellevue* (M), 226 rooms, pool; *Vespera* (M), 404 rooms. All in attractive pinewood setting, near rocky shore with good bathing, wind-surfing school and tennis.

Veli Lošinj. Smaller, quieter. *Punta* (M), 320 rooms, is close to village; pools, sports facilities.

Rab

Lopar. *San Marino* (M), 557 rooms. Situated outside the village. Sports facilities.

Rab. The island's lovely capital. *Imperial* (M), on slopes above old town, 127 rooms, traditional style. *International* (M), on old town waterfront, 130 rooms, indoor pool. Newest is *Padova* (M), across the harbor at Banjul with fine views of old town, 177 rooms, pools.

Restaurants. *Marijan* (M), facing the old town across the harbor, fish specialties. *Santa Maria* (M), in the courtyard of attractive patrician house in old town.

Five km. (three miles) northwest from town in wooded setting: *Suha Punta* (M) tourist settlement with 430 rooms. Somewhat more expensive are *Carolina,* 150 rooms, pool; and *Eva* (M), 196 rooms.

HOW TO GET AROUND. Krk and its international airport (for Rijeka) are linked by bridge to the mainland near Kraljevica. There are rail terminals at Koper, Pula and Rijeka. Frequent bus services run between the coastal towns. All major agencies organize trips in comfortable motorcoaches to the Postojna Caves, the Plitvice Lakes, or to beauty spots or places of interest within the area; also to Venice by launch, passenger steamer, or hydrofoil. Motorboat excursions are run from the coast towns, numerous car and passenger ferries operate between the mainland and the islands, notably Brestova and Rijeka to Porozine (Cres); Pula to Mali Lošinj (Lošinj); Crikvenica to Šilo (Krk); Senj to Baška (Krk); Senj to Lopar (Rab); Baška (Krk) to Lopar (Rab); Jablanac to Mišnjak (Rab); Prizna to Stara Novalja (Pag); Karlobag to Pag.

SPORTS. First and foremost—swimming. The Istrian beaches are nearly all gently sloping and shallow, and thus—though more often pebble than sand—absolutely safe for children. Among the best are those of Medulin 11 km. (seven miles) from Pula, also Savudrija, Lovran, Lošinj and Opatija. There is also excellent bathing off rocks, often attractively interspersed with paved or cemented sunbathing areas. There are heated fresh or salt water pools in some of the better hotels in winter.

The clear warm waters of the Adriatic in summer are ideal for underwater fishing, and there are plenty of fish to choose from. The best centers for this sport are on the islands of Cres and Lošinj. At Mali Lošinj there is an annual International Underwater Fishing Contest at the end of December. Fishing excursions are organized by travel agents.

Water skiing, wind surfing, and yachting can be arranged in many resorts, most of which possess fully-equipped marinas. The newest of these, under construction near Opatija, will be the largest of its kind in the northern Adriatic. Excellent flotilla sailing arrangements off the Istrian coast are marketed ex-U.K.

USEFUL ADDRESSES. Every town and resort has a tourist information office. Istria's largest travel agency is Kvarner Express, which also owns several of the better hotels. Head office is at Maršala Tita 186, 51410 Opatija, with branches in most resorts. These organize all kinds of activity and sightseeing excursions. Many other leading Yugoslav travel agencies also have branch offices in the resorts, a major one here being the Slovenian agency Kompas.

CENTRAL DALMATIA

The Heart of the Coast

The section of the coast which we cover in this chapter is not long, bare-ly 320 km. (200 miles), but it includes everything ever brought to mind by the name Dalmatia. Here you can see gaunt limestone mountains slop-ing sharply to the shore—sometimes direct into the sea. Here you have 100s of small, scrub-covered islands sharply etched against the intense blue of sea and sky, and colorful little villages tucked into bays and inlets, their red pantiled roofs glowing warmly. A number of lovely small stone-built towns, little larger than the villages but embodying high standards of civi-lized living and whose medieval and earlier remains blend harmoniously with predominantly Venetian architecture, are scattered along the coast, often perched picturesquely on small peninsulas. Private houses, many of-fering accommodations, small guest houses and restaurants grow in num-ber each year. And almost every few kilometers there are modern hotels or "tourist complexes," with chalets and restaurants to welcome the visi-tor and give him the opportunity of sampling the region's delights in mod-ern comfort. This coast is indisputably crowded in summer, but there are still quiet corners if you're prepared to try out the lesser-known resorts or to walk that bit further along the shore away from the established facili-ties.

Preeminent among the towns is Split, centered upon a vast fortified pal-ace built by the Roman Emperor Diocletian for his retirement. In the north the main town is Zadar, in plan still much the same as when it was designed by Roman civil engineers 20 centuries ago. Šibenik, south of

Zadar, has much of beauty still too little appreciated, including a magnificent cathedral. Medieval Trogir, though overshadowed by Split and its modern airport, remains beautiful. South of Split, Makarska and the lovely coast on either side of it have now deservedly recovered their former popularity as centers of tourism. On the islands, Hvar and Korčula are outstanding among the region's "Venetian" towns. The appeal of these ancient places is quite different from that of the more modern holiday resorts that have grown up beside or between them. In bygone centuries the tiny towns were the only places that offered comfort and civilization. Today you can find all the comfort you could wish for in the resorts and holiday-complexes which were once picturesque but primitive fishing villages.

Approaching Zadar

As we travel south toward Zadar, the character of the landscape changes. The mountains gradually recede, as you pass the inland waters of Novigrad Sea on your left and cross a flat and fertile plain. The actual shore is still for the most part rocky and stony. Separated from it only by a narrow channel, the myriad islands of the Zadar and Kornat (or Kornati) Archipelagos spread out from the coast for many kilometers, providing a sheltered stretch of sea where fish thrive and boating enthusiasts can enjoy themselves. Most of the coast can be seen easily enough from the Adriatic Coastal Road. But to enjoy the islands to the full you need to spend long days exploring them by boat. If you have the good fortune to approach them across the sea from the west on a course of your own choosing, sail up under the fantastic cliffs of Dugi Otok's western side.

Exploring Zadar

The old core of Zadar, the ancient capital of Dalmatia, is built on a small peninsula and this is where you will find the most interesting sights. Its origins date from a long way back, and it still has many monuments of its glorious past to show. As early as Roman times it was already important, called at that time Jadera; it later became for a while a Byzantine stronghold. Following eight years of Napoleonic occupation it became part of the Austrian Empire in 1814, until under the 1920 Treaty of Rapallo it was handed over to Italy. Only in 1944 did it finally become part of Yugoslavia.

Zadar was much damaged by air-raids during World War II, but has been pleasingly rebuilt. Some of the most interesting buildings are grouped round the substantial traces of the Roman forum, the most dominant being the remarkable ninth-century circular Church of St. Donat, one of the earliest surviving buildings in Dalmatia. Its foundations were laid upon part of the forum, and the outward effect is massively imposing, though its interior is austere. As might have been expected, the Croatian architects made good use of the already dressed Roman masonry they found on the spot, and on many of the columns you can still make out the original Latin inscriptions. If you climb the 55-m. (182-ft.) tower, you will be rewarded with a fine view of the Velebit Mountains and the nearer islands. The Archeological Museum with its excellent collections stands opposite, next to Sv. Marija housing an impressive display of Sacral Art.

Immediately behind St. Donat's is the Cathedral of Sv. Stošija with a magnificent Romanesque portal. There are no less than 14 churches in the old town in various stages of repair. Among them is that of St. Simon, the town's patron-saint whose bones are kept in a sarcophagus richly decorated with silver and copper bas-reliefs, presented by Elizabeth of Hungary in 1380. Don't miss this. Another is Sveti Krševan, built in 13th-century Romanesque style, with a richly-decorated 16th-century altar, also some interesting frescos belonging to the original building, only recently rediscovered.

Among the medieval remains are the ruined but still impressive fortifications, best seen above the pretty little harbor of Foša with its massive Town Gate still in use. In this part of town you'll also find the Five Wells built by the Venetians whose influence is everywhere to be seen; note especially the Loggia and Guard House (now Ethnographic Museum) on Narodni trg (square), a lively hub of the old town.

Zadar has quite a lot of industry, including the famous Maraska distillery. Its main tourist recreation area is at Borik, 3½ km. (two miles) away along the shore.

Around Zadar

The splendid archipelagos that can be visited from Zadar are described later in this chapter. On the mainland is the ancient village of Nin, 16 km. (ten miles) north, known to the Romans as Aenona. There are traces of a forum and other Roman remains, and the desolate ruins of medieval town walls still to be seen as they were left after being deliberately broken down by the Venetians in the 16th century so that they should not fall intact into Turkish hands. The tiny ninth-century Church of the Holy Cross is a perfect specimen of pre-medieval Croat architecture, and a splendid collection of gold and silver can be seen in the chapel adjoining rebuilt Sv. Anzelm. But it needs some imagination to visualize this sleepy little place as a one-time capital of Croatia in the 9th–11th centuries.

It was from here, too, that Bishop Gregory of Nin (commemorated in the impressive bronze statue by Yugoslavia's foremost sculptor, Městrović, near the Church of the Holy Cross) conducted his campaign against the abolition of the Slavic liturgy. Having decided that the use in celebrating mass of a "barbaric" language written in the difficult Glagolitic characters was tantamount to heresy, the Holy See suppressed the practise. Gregory however triumphed, and the Glagolitic mass remained in use for two centuries.

Another excursion from Zadar takes us 30 km. (19 miles) east along the main road to Novigradsko More, the so-called Sea of Novigrad. This is a wide, almost enclosed bay, linked with the Adriatic by a narrow, deep channel. On the shore of the bay is the charming little town of Novigrad. From here you can hire a boat to take you through the wild gorge of the River Zrmanja as far as Obrovac, where there is a splendid view from the old walls of a Turkish fort down the famous Zrmanja canyon.

From Obrovac you can continue inland, over the magnificent Alan Pass across the Velebit into the Lika. Or if you return to the main road near Posedarje, another village by Novigrad Sea, you can continue along it to the Starigrad-Paklenica National Park, already mentioned, or branch immediately north eventually to cross the road bridge to the island of Pag, known for its lace and its cheese. This lies parallel with the Velebit range on the mainland, and has a desolate moon-like beauty of its own. Close to extensive salt pans, the island's capital is also called Pag, and is a fascinating old town. Both the capital itself and Novalja to the north have been developed as modern resorts and are linked by ferry services to the mainland, but this is still a quiet and peaceful part of the coast.

South from Zadar

25 km. (16 miles) south of Zadar the coastal road passes the beach of Filip Jakov, near Biograd na Moru (the "White Town on the Sea"), a walled town where once the Croatian kings were crowned, now a crowded resort. Just beyond it are the tourist center of Crvena Luka and the village of Pakoštane. The coast in this area is unusually flat, and has quite extensive pinewoods, and other trees.

Continuing south the road follows a ridge between the sea and the wide lake Vransko. A branch left leads to the little town of Vrana, dominated by the impressive ruins of a crusader castle and boasting one of the best examples of a Turkish caravanserai to be found in Yugoslavia.

Crossing the narrow strip of land that separates Lake Vransko from the sea you glimpse rocky islands sunk in the rich blue of the Adriatic. Between the coast resorts of Pirovac and Vodice, a branch road crosses the promontory right (west) to Tijesno, a picturesque fishing port, and by road bridge over a narrow channel to the island of Murter. The shore of this rather off-beat area is now crowded with bathers in summer and the adjoining communities of Betina and Murter, about 15 km. (nine miles) from the main road, have become very popular family resorts. The latter is especially favored as a pleasure port for yachts.

Vodice is another attractive fishing village that has blossomed into a popular resort, engulfing it in holiday houses and apartments. A few miles further you approach Šibenik by a bridge over the twisting fjord-like estuary of the Krka, from which there are splendid views. The old town is built of a particularly attractive golden stone, and from the port it seems like a vast amphitheater crowned with formidable 17th- to 19th-century fortifications. Its narrow streets climb past the many ancient churches and medieval palaces.

Šibenik was founded in the 11th century and reached the height of its prosperity and power during the Middle Ages though, like nearly all the coastal towns of Dalmatia, it suffered during the protracted wars between the Turks and Venetians. The town was sold to the Venetians by Ladislas, King of Naples and Hungary, in 1410 but its citizens denounced the sale and resisted the Venetian troops sent to take possession.

Šibenik Cathedral was the work of four architects, and took a century to complete. The work was begun under the direction of the Italian di Giacomo, but he soon gave way to Orsini of Zadar, who completed the walls in Venetian Gothic. His successor, Nicholas of Florence, continued in Tuscan Renaissance style, and George of Dalmatia completed the task in Gothic.

The vault and great cupola are formed of stone tiles of a kind found nowhere else in Europe, and the body of the cathedral is built entirely of the beautiful local stone. The frieze outside the apse is particularly interesting because of the carved heads of contemporary workmen, masons, fishermen, and so on.

Excursions can be made from here to the Kornat archipelago, described below, or you can go either by road or by boat 18 km. (ten miles) north to the Krka waterfalls near Skradin, surrounded by vineyards. The water plunges sheer from a height of over 50 m. (160 ft.), and it is an unforgettable experience to look down through the iridescent spray to the basin of the falls far below. Modern hydroelectric works have somewhat reduced the force of the waterfalls. From here you can also do a boat trip to the Franciscan Monastery of Visovac, on an islet, famous for its manuscripts, incunabula and old paintings. Further south along the coast Primošten, originally an island village, is now connected to the mainland on whose shore are a number of modern hotels and a lot more houses and apartments. Despite the developments, the original village is still very charming. A heated sea-water pool under a glass dome makes this resort particularly suitable for a winter holiday. Rogoznica is flanked by excellent beaches on several inlets opposite a tiny wooded island.

The Island Route from Zadar to Split

Many day excursions are arranged to the islands that lie off this section of the Adriatic coast, but they also offer infinite possibilities for holidays ranging from the peaceful to the unreservedly off-beat. In addition to small hotels and restaurants in several of the villages, private accommodations are available in most centers. Even on some of the remotest islands you can rent a summer cottage and have supplies brought out to you by boat—a true desert island experience. Local tourist information offices can tell you where to apply. Opposite Zadar is the long narrow island of Ugljan which can be reached in half an hour by car ferry. You land at the little port of Preko (hotel), over which a ruined ancient fortress broods. From its walls there is a fine view across the straits to Zadar. The entrance to the port is almost blocked by the small island of Galovac, the thick woods that cover it encircling the ancient monastery. Near the southern tip of the island, there is the picturesque fishing hamlet of Kukljica, with a tourist complex nearby.

Between Ugljan and Dugi Otok are several inhabited islets. Iž (hotel at Iž Veli), the largest, is rich in olives, figs and vines.

Dugi Otok, literally "Long Island" (New Yorkers please note), supports seven small communities: Veli Rat, Soline, Božava (hotel), Luka (hotel), Žman, Zaglav and Sali (named after medieval saltpans; hotel). There's a car ferry from Zadar to Zaglav. From these you can explore the Kornat archipelago, now a national park area, made up of 125 islets, most of them uninhabited. Over the centuries, many of the islands have been eroded (by fire, over-grazing and wind) into fantastic shapes and offer endless fascinating opportunities for exploration. Some are still used for grazing, the sheep being delivered and collected by boat. There are hidden creeks, deep caverns, grottos and wild rocks abounding, remotely beautiful and providing superb fishing. The great cliffs at the southwestern end of Dugi Otok form one of the coast's most magnificent sights. Underwater fishing is forbidden, but the whole area is quite fabulous for underwater swimming and photography, though you will need to check the local regulations. The main centers from which fishing trips are organized are Zadar, Biograd, Murter, Vodice, Šibenik and Sali.

The island of Pašman is connected to Ugljan by a bridge at the northern end. Tkon faces the mainland town of Biograd, to which it's connected by car ferry. There are the ruins of a ninth-century monastery in which you may see many inscriptions in contemporary Glagolitic.

We have mentioned Murter island, accessible by road bridge, already. Further south still, another pleasant little bathing resort is Zlarin, situated on a small island in the group of 30 extending to Šibenik. This is one of the few places in Europe where you can still buy coral from fishermen who have won it from the sea.

The Historic Town of Trogir

Only 26 km. (16 miles) before you reach Split, the uniquely beautiful little medieval town of Trogir is set on an island about 400 m. (440 yards) long by 140 m. (150 yards) wide. A stone bridge makes it accessible from the mainland, a mobile bridge connects it with the Island of Čiovo, and there are small passenger ferries from Split.

Because of its relative isolation Trogir is largely unchanged, though modern hotels rise in the vicinity. Its tiny main square, in particular, still looks much as it must have done 300 years ago.

In the third century B.C. the Greeks founded a city here which they called Tragurion, perhaps because of the great herds of goats or *tragoi,* which are still a feature of the district, and both Strabo and Ptolemy refer to the importance it soon acquired. In the seventh century it somehow escaped the barbarian raids that sacked neighboring Salona. Before long, the newly arrived Croats colonized it, and with the erosion of the power of Constantinople between the ninth and 11th centuries, the Croatian kings granted Trogir municipal autonomy. After the death of King Zvonimir in 1089 the city developed rapidly under the Hungarian-Croat dynasties. In 1242 King Béla IV of Hungary, in flight from the Tartars, took refuge within its stout walls, and in gratitude for his escape confirmed it in all its rights and privileges. But Venice had long coveted Trogir and, in 1420, captured it after a desperate resistance. The Venetians remained until 1797, to be succeeded by the French under Napoleon's Marshal Marmont. This régime lasted until 1814, when the Congress of Vienna awarded Illyria to the Austrian Empire. Under Austrian rule it again rapidly declined and, when the Austrian régime ended in 1918, Trogir had lived through 1,000 years of foreign occupation.

This almost forgotten city possesses however one claim to fame long recognized by classical scholars. In the 17th century the fragment of the Latin poet Petronius' *Satyricon* known as "Trimalchio's Feast" was discovered. The *Satyricon,* written in Nero's time, is an earthy, riotously funny satire dealing with Rome of the first century, and is now in the Paris Bibliothèque Nationale. Again, in 1928, a magnificent bas-relief of Kairos, the God of Opportunity (or Luck) was found, face down, on the kitchen floor of an old house. This dates from the first century B.C. and is on view in the Benedictine Convent of St. Nicholas.

Exploring Trogir

Fortunately, cars are banned from the walled Dalmatian towns, so Trogir is entered on foot through the narrow Renaissance gate of St. Ivan. More picturesque still is the Porta Civitatis beside the little loggia (today the fish market) where, in former times, strangers had to wait until the City Magistrates had examined their papers. The gate itself is the same heavily nail-studded wooden one placed there 400 years ago. A few steps lead us to the main square, where the walls of the surrounding buildings have been weathered by the centuries; and there the Town Hall and its tower speak with the unmistakable accents of Venice and Florence. When long ago the open loggia was the center of the city's public life, it served alike as a Law Court, a provisional prison and as the site for public festivities. The Clock Tower was built by Donatello's brilliant pupil, Nicholas of Florence, in 1477. Trogir's oldest church is that of St. Barbara, dating from the ninth century and decorated in the now rarely found early Croat style.

Opposite the cathedral (of which more later) you will note the richly decorated Venetian Gothic façade of the 15th-century Ćipiko Palace. On a little covered platform there is the painted wooden head of a cockerel, taken from a Turkish ship at the battle of Lepanto by Alviz Ćipiko, commander of the Trogir squadron. Beside it is the wooden figurehead of the Goddess of Fortune, which ornamented Admiral Alviz's ship at the same battle.

Unquestionably the most remarkable building in Trogir is the 13th-century Cathedral of St. Lawrence. A Romanesque basilica with three naves, it is one of the most perfect examples of medieval architecture in the country. Enter by the Radovan portal, which is flanked by two lions surmounted by statues of Adam and Eve carved in 1240. The columns above bear representations of the apostles and various saints, and then there are carvings of animals and grotesques. The tympanum of the portal is decorated with the miracle of the Nativity, and while the outer side of the arch illustrates scenes from the New Testament, the inner illustrates the story of the Annunciation.

Probably the most remarkable part of the cathedral is the Chapel of St. John of Trogir, the masterpiece of Nicholas of Florence, built in 1480. The Sacristy contains a number of treasures, not the least among them being some of the works of the Venetian painter Bellini. Climb the clock tower for the view across the ancient roofs of the city, golden brown, but with the special patina of mellow old age.

Apart from St. Barbara and the cathedral, Trogir contains the 13th-century Romanesque Benedictine Abbey of St. John the Baptist, and a 14th-century Gothic Dominican church and convent, both housing notable art treasures. Domestic architecture is represented by the various palaces built by noble families in the Middle Ages, chief among them the Renaissance Lučić and Fanfogna palaces, both of which contain richly illustrated manuscripts. Lastly, the Kaštel-Kamerlengo fortress is a fine and well-preserved example of 15th-century military architecture from whence, in times of war, strong chains crossed to Čiovo and blocked the entrance to the harbor. A maritime power like Venice naturally preferred the familiar style of yet another island to the hazards of the mainland, thus Trogir extended across the wider channel to Čiovo. Čiovo features the fine 15th-century cloisters of Holy Cross Monastery.

Before abandoning Trogir, where the list of ancient buildings is necessarily rather formidable, we must just mention the temple-like gloriette built by Marmont during the Napoleonic occupation, which stands near the Venetian fort of Kamerlengo at the west end of this island city.

The Kaštela Riviera

The *Jadranska Magistrala* follows a wide curve through the plain round the Bay of Split, but a narrower road follows the coast more closely for 16 km. (ten miles) through the Kaštela Riviera ("Castle Riviera"), so called after the seven castles built by the nobility of Trogir to guard their islands against the Turks.

The charm of the fine churches, with their campaniles set among vineyards and orchards, is somewhat swamped now by Split's rapid industrial expansion and by the proximity of the airport.

On our way to Split we pass Solin, once the first-century Roman town of Salona. The original city was built by the Illyrians in the second century B.C., reaching its greatest importance after the Roman conquest in about 30 B.C., when it rapidly became a city of 60,000 inhabitants. Diocletian, the first of the great Illyrian commanders who tried to halt the barbarian incursions, was born nearby in about A.D. 245, son of a freedman. In 615 Salona was sacked by the Avars. Today there is a modern town—Solin—but scattered about the countryside to the north of it are the very substantial ruins of its Roman predecessor, including walls, gateways, baths, an immense amphitheater, cemetery and a massively impressive section of aqueduct, still in use; also the foundations of many important early Christian churches.

From Solin, a modern road leads up a defile to Klis and Sinj, described later.

Exploring Split

Split lies almost exactly halfway between Rijeka and Dubrovnik and is the official administrative capital of Dalmatia. The approach to it has changed beyond all recognition in recent years with the building of huge new residential high-rise districts and some very striking architecture, including the City Stadium and nearby Swimming Complex, and ultramodern shopping and entertainments centers such as Koteks. But this bustling city with its major industries and busy sea, rail and air communications, has spread from its historic, and still thriving, core contained in the remains of Diocletian's tremendous palace.

Diocletian became Emperor at the age of about 40, after a brilliant career as a soldier of Rome. His first task was to reorganize completely both the army and the civil administration, as a preliminary to undertaking the series of victorious campaigns which firmly reestablished even the remotest frontiers of the Empire. Though married to a Christian wife, he found it politically expedient to persecute the Christians.

Work on the palace was begun in A.D. 295 and it took ten years to complete. As soon as it was ready Diocletian abdicated, though still only 61, and spent the last eight years of his life in the peace of his native Dalmatia. His attempts to secure a stable succession failed, however.

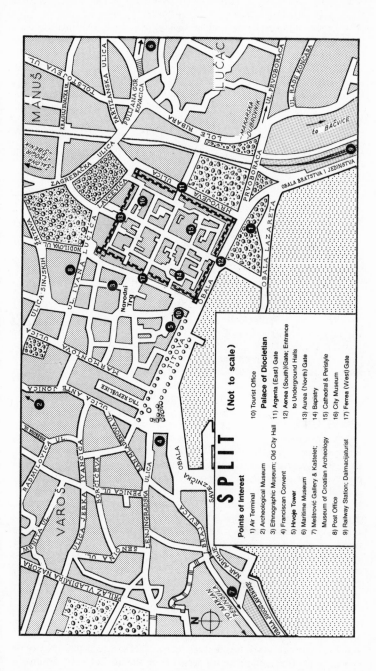

SPLIT (Not to scale)

Points of Interest

1) Air Terminal
2) Archeological Museum
3) Ethnographic Museum; Old City Hall
4) Franciscan Convent
5) Hrvoje Tower
6) Maritime Museum
7) Meštrović Gallery & Kaštelet;
   Museum of Croatian Archeology
8) Post Office
9) Railway Station; Dalmacijaturist
10) Tourist Office

Palace of Diocletian

11) Argenta (East) Gate
12) Aenea (South) Gate; Entrance
    to Underground Halls
13) Aurea (North) Gate
14) Bapistry
15) Cathedral & Peristyle
16) City Museum
17) Ferrea (West) Gate

After his death it was difficult to know how to make use of the great palace and it became successively a military camp, a market, and the shopping center of the city. The last reference to it in old chronicles relates how the Emperor Julius Nepos drove out these commercial tenants just before he himself was assassinated there in A.D. 480.

When Solin was sacked by the Avars in A.D. 615, such of the inhabitants as managed to escape fled first to the neighboring islands, and then when the raiders had gone, sought more permanent shelter within the walls of Diocletian's Palace, eventually building houses in the spacious courtyards, with any kind of material that came to hand. The Roman Palatium became medieval Spalato, and in 1918, the modern town of Split.

The enormous palace rectangle covers approximately 30,000 square yards. It is in a surprisingly good state of repair. In the 18th century it was visited by, and proved a potent influence upon, many artists and antiquarians, including the Scottish neo-Classicists John and Robert Adam.

The south front of the palace faces the sea, and it was here that the imperial apartments were placed so that for visitors arriving by sea, the first sight is of the outside of the main hall. The thickness of the walls makes it clear that the palace was originally designed to serve at all times as a fortified castle. The east and west walls are each some 188 m. (618 ft.) long, the north wall measuring 150 m. (491 ft.), and the south some 155 m. (510 ft.). The four corners were capped with high square towers, of which three are still standing, and each of the four walls is pierced with a central gate. The largest of these is the Golden Gate (Porta Aurea), which faces Meštrović's statue of Bishop Gregory of Nin, defender against Rome of the Slavic Liturgy during the tenth century. The entrance through the western wall is the Iron Gate (Porta Ferrea), that through the east wall the Silver Gate (Porta Argenta), while the Bronze Gate (Porta Aenea) is in the south wall. The area is laid out somewhat after the model of a Roman military encampment.

The underground halls in the southern part of the palace, built as vast storerooms on ground sloping to the sea, now house exhibitions and souvenir shops. They correspond in plan to the upper halls, later destroyed.

The northern wing was the quarters of the Palace Guard, and also housed the permanent staff of 100s of slaves and servants needed to run the vast establishment. Medieval buildings flank one side of the central courtyard, or peristyle, but the original columns have been reerected on the other side. A stone stairway leads from here past a 3,500-year-old Egyptian sphinx of black granite to what was designed as the Emperor's grandiose octagonal mausoleum. It was later encircled by a colonnade, underwent further changes when the crypt was turned into an Early Christian church, and finally—in the 13th–14th centuries—the mausoleum was incorporated into the present fine Cathedral. The interior of the mausoleum is circular, with square or semicircular niches designed to hold the illustrious dead. Massive granite pillars with Corinthian capitals carry the dome, with the added support of slender columns of red porphyry. Beyond these is the original antique frieze of an exceptional beauty.

The choir is a masterpiece of eighth-century Romanesque workmanship, and you should be sure not to miss the magnificent carved wooden reliefs in the main door. These were the work of the 13th-century Dalmatian sculptor Buvina, and depict scenes from the life of Christ. One of the best ways of appreciating the original plan and design of the palace is to climb to the belfry where, from a height of close on 60 m. (200 ft.), the great enterprise lies plainly revealed below.

A short distance away in the west part of the palace, the so-called Jupiter Temple was converted into the baptistery by the first Bishop of Spalato, John of Ravenna, in the 7th–8th centuries. Much of it is well preserved, including a beautiful coffered barrel vault, decorated columns and door lintel. The font is probably from the 12th century. Indeed, the old core of Split is packed with treasures from every era of its long history. Under the Venetians, humble refugee dwellings gave way to stately mansions, many of which survive. An outstanding one is the Gothic-Renaissance Papalić Palace housing the Split Museum, which should by now have reopened after lengthy restoration.

Inevitably, the city spread beyond the palace walls, and the surrounding districts are just as interesting. Immediately beyond the West Gate, for example, is Narodni trg (square) with its Venetian Gothic Town Hall, now the Ethnographic Museum. A short distance to the south is the octagonal Hrvoje Tower, once part of the 15th-century defenses. In the little square in front of it is a statue of the poet Marko Marulić by Meštrović.

There are innumerable churches, from small and humble ones to the larger and more ornate. One not to miss is the Franciscan Convent with beautiful cloisters and fine Stations of the Cross.

Some distance north of the old town toward the City Stadium is the Archeological Museum with good Roman and early Christian collections. Two more museums that should not be missed are on the road leading along the southern side of the Marjan peninsula, a protected recreation area pierced by a road tunnel to the west of the old city. Here, almost next door to each other, are the modern and very fine Museum of Croat Archeology, and the Meštrović Gallery housing many of the works of this great sculptor in his beautiful former home and gardens. A little further on is Kaštellet where other works of Meštrović, including magnificent wooden reliefs of New Testament scenes, are contained in the little Church of St. Cross. On the way, you will pass Split's splendid marina.

Only a few kilometers inland is the hill-top fortress of Klis, for centuries a Turkish stronghold. From its towers you can look across open country all the way from Trogir in the north to beyond Split and the islands of Šolta and Brač. Continue along this road and in 30 km. (20 miles) you reach Sinj, where a great folklore festival known as *Alka* is held every year in early August in commemoration of the great victory in 1715 of a peasant army over a Turkish force of 60,000. In this colorful and exciting equestrian tourney, the men are dressed and the horses caparisoned in early 18th-century fashion.

The Makarska Riviera

The *Magistrala* south from Split leads through the port of Omiš, at the mouth of the River Cetina, after which there is a road that follows the river upstream for six km. (four miles) through a tremendous gorge. Once a pirate lair, the bay is hidden between cliffs rising steeply to a height of nearly 300 m. (1,000 ft.), presided over by an old fortress. On the right bank, at Priko, stands the Old-Croat Church of St. Peter, and in the town itself are the Renaissance Church of the Holy Spirit and the Baroque parish church.

The coastal region beyond is known as the Makarska Riviera, with modest little fishing villages, some of which have burgeoned into major holiday resorts, backed by thick pinewoods, olive groves, and vineyards. The narrow coastal plain ends abruptly at the foot of the impressive *karst* wall of the Biokovo mountains, 1,400-1,700 m. (4,590-5,576 ft.), served by a network of marked trails. The highest point is Sveti Jure at 1,745 m. (5,726 ft.) accessible by road, but the full length of the range can be explored on foot following the Partisan Path, with a number of lateral tracks down to the coast.

Strung out along Biokovo's lower slopes is a series of old villages surrounded by stoney fields from which the inhabitants once scratched a hard-won living. For a time, the simple houses were semi-abandoned, but many of them are now being restored. This is good territory for rambling through the vineyards and olive groves, along the rocky paths that link them, with fine views down to the lovely Makarska Riviera.

The first coastal resort is Brela, followed by Baška Voda, both surrounded by pines beside long pebble beaches, with sizeable hotels. A few miles further on is Makarska, the region's "capital", once a favorite summer playground of the Croatian aristocracy. It has grown rapidly in recent years, but the old part of town still clusters attractively round a bay between two headlands, while most of the newer hotels stand in a line near the adjoining pebble beach. One of the town's sights is the Franciscan Monastery, part of which houses an unusual shell museum.

This is a lively area, with plenty going on in the tourist season; there's a regular car ferry across to Sumartin on the island of Brač, excursions to the islands, up and down the coast, or by the new road over the mountains to such historic centers as Čapljina, Mostar, and Sarajevo. If you are a walker, there is a shore path running most of the length of the Makarska Riviera.

South of Makarska, the two main resorts—with more hotels and pebble beaches—are Tučepi and Podgora. The latter is the most picturesque of the two, and still has an active fishing fleet. A large monument here commemorates the founding of the Partisan Navy.

From here the appearance of the surrounding country changes abruptly to become no less beautiful, but far wilder and rougher. Fishing villages, clinging to the steep foothills of the Biokovo, like Igrane, Živogošće, and Zaostrog (where the Makarska Riviera officially ends) are all exploiting their holiday potential. With magnificently sheltered water off their shores, these are delightful places in which to spend a quiet vacation, and in all of them there are plenty of guest houses and private accommodations. After bypassing the large port of Kardeljevo the *Magistrala* crosses the River Neretva by way of a fine new bridge, and crosses the vast marshy estuary that is a fisherman's and wildfowler's paradise. Various small villages border on the delta, and the people often use boats to travel around on the channels threading through the marsh. Extensive areas of these marshes, however, have been drained in recent years to provide fertile land for excellent crops of fruit and vegetables; in summer you'll pass any number of stalls selling fresh produce and cold drinks. A railway runs inland from Kardeljevo to Sarajevo, Zagreb and Belgrade.

The Islands

The Central Dalmatian islands form a little world apart from the rest of the coast. Korčula and Hvar always were, and still are, ports-of-call for long-distance ships sailing the coast. And attachment to the sea rather than to the land has given the islands a distinctive atmosphere, which they still keep intact—although now linked by many regular services to the mainland, or the subject of numerous day trips. To spend a few days in Korčula or Hvar is a special experience, particularly if you can avoid the inevitable crowds of the high season. Even Orebić, the charming small resort on the peninsula of Pelješac opposite Korčula town, exudes the same feeling of peace. This was, in fact, the chosen home of large numbers of sea captains till steam put sail out of business, and we will return to it after we have described the islands.

Šolta, Brač, Vis and Biševo

Opposite the Bay of Split lies the island of Šolta, famous for its wines, and to the south its far larger and much more visited neighbor of Brač. The pace of life on these islands is particularly conducive to a restful holiday, and among the charms of their pretty little ports and fishing villages is the survival of such traditional occupations as boat building.

The quarries on Brač were once renowned throughout Europe and can still be visited. Marble from here has been provided for buildings as varied and famous as Diocletian's Palace at Split, the White House in Washington and the United Nations Building in New York, as well as for the construction of many local towns. Brač is touristically developed, Supetar on the north coast (regular ferry to Split) and Bol in the south being the main centers. Bol is approached by a steep winding road and has a marvelous spit of coarse sand and stones—Zlatni Rat—one of the best beaches of the islands. The lovely Dominican Monastery has a particularly well-planned museum including Graeco-Roman items dredged out of the sea, incunabula, and a painting by Tintoretto.

Remotest of all is Vis, though it has witnessed naval battles which profoundly affected the destiny of the coast. Today, the islands of Vis, neighboring Biševo (which has fabulous sea grottoes), and Lastovo (south of Korčula) are military areas and can only be visited by British war veterans or official visitors by prior arrangement. However, there's talk of opening the islands up, so it's worth checking.

Hvar

Hvar—the ancient Greek *pharos,* or lighthouse, of which there is today no trace—is also the name of the "capital" near the island's western tip. From Vira, a few kilometers away, there's a regular car ferry link with Split. Hvar conforms to the general shape of these islands, long and narrow, and it has probably been inhabited for some 7,000 years. A Greek merchant colony founded Pharos in 4 B.C., but Illyrians, Romans, Croats, Hungarians, Byzantines, Venetians, French, and Austrians have all had their turn as its masters.

In every respect the little town of Hvar is entrancing. It lies at the heart of a bay backed by green hills and protected from the open sea by a scatter of small islets known as Pakleni Otoci. High above its red roofs looms the 16th-century Town Fortress (later enlarged), now housing a restaurant and a splendid collection of ancient amphoras, mostly dredged from the sea. It is still linked to the town by ancient defensive walls. Higher still, another fortress, built during Napoleonic rule, dominates the skyline and is now an observatory.

Rosemary and lavender grow in profusion, a pleasing foil for Hvar's stone buildings, so much of whose architecture is unmistakably Venetian in inspiration. The town was largely destroyed by the Turks in 1571, so the principal buildings are mainly late 16th and early 17th century. Most of the major ones are on or near the main square leading off the waterfront, and include the Renaissance-Baroque Cathedral with its attractive campanile, and the works of many Venetian artists. Also bordering the square is the Arsenal which encloses one of Europe's oldest theaters (1612), still sometimes used for concerts. More or less opposite, the splendid Renaissance-style loggia and a clock tower form part of the Palace Hotel.

From the main square, a maze of little streets lead up through the old town beneath the fortress. There are interesting architectural details to be discovered, such as the well dating from 1475 bearing the Lion of St. Mark, its paw on a closed book indicating that Venice was then at war. If you have an interest in unusual crafts, pause at the Benedictine Monastery to see the delicate lacework woven by the nuns from the fibers of local cacti. You'll find some of the best art treasures in the Renaissance Franciscan Monastery on the small bay a little south of the town center. The cloisters and gardens are lovely, and the monastery museum and church house some very fine paintings, among them a *Last Supper* from the Venetian school of Palma the Younger, and *The Crucifixion* by Leandro Bassano.

From Hvar there are regular motor boat links with the islets of Pakleni Otoci. The bay of Palmizana on Sv. Kliment (St. Clement), with its marina and fine beach, is particularly popular. Of the many delightful places within easy bus-distance of the old town, the most interesting is Stari Grad, 20 km. (12 miles) away, on the site of the original Greek colony of Pharos. Here you should visit the 16th-century fortified mansion of the poet Hektorović with its charming fishpool; also the fortified Dominican monastery whose church contains fine paintings, and Baroque St. Stephen whose tower incorporates Greek and Roman stonework. Stari Grad, which is linked by ferry with Split, is now a popular resort as are Jelsa (attractive old quarter) and nearby picturesque Vrboska (massive fortified church), both a few miles further along the north coast. At the furthest eastern tip of the island, Sućuraj has frequent ferry connections with mainland Drvenik.

Korčula

Korčula is the last island port called at by most coastal steamers before Dubrovnik, and has frequent ferry links with Orebić on the Pelješac peninsula. The island has been continuously occupied since prehistoric times, largely because the thick woods that covered it provided the raw material for shipbuilding. Greeks from Cnidos settled here, as is proved by an inscription dating from the fourth century B.C., calling it Korkyra Melaina (Corcyra the Black) in allusion to its dark forests, and to distinguish it from the better-known island they called Korkyra, now Corfu.

The "capital" is situated on a headland which commands the strait that separates Korčula from Pelješac and is set within still-formidable defensive walls. Most of the hotels are along the rocky shoreline to the east of these. It is one of the most picturesque towns of any on the entire Dalmatian coast. Crooked and narrow medieval streets open out suddenly into little squares where nobles' palaces glow golden-brown in the sun. The layout of these streets forms a sort of herring-bone pattern on either side of the main street-central axis, to prevent the north and south winds that blow up and down the strait from whistling unimpeded through the town. A Greek inscription of the fourth century B.C. makes reference to Korčula as a "stone town." It is at least possible that Korčula's layout is another example of the Ancient Greeks' townplanning skill. Much later, like so many other places, Korčula was under frequent threat from the Turks and there are particularly graphic contemporary accounts of how one such attack was fought off in 1571.

One of the palaces may have been the birthplace of Marco Polo, who commanded a Venetian fleet of ten galleys which fought a battle against the Genoese within sight of Korčula in 1298. He was beaten and taken prisoner, together with the Doge of Venice, Andrea Dandolo. Once he had regained his liberty, Marco set out on his travels across a still-unknown world. Polos still live on the island, and one of the old palaces, debatably known as Marco Polo's house, is a museum.

Korčula's 14th- to 16th-century Cathedral of St. Mark is an interesting example of the transition from the Romanesque to the Gothic style of architecture. Its greatest treasures are one possible and one definite Tintoretto and a Bassano. In addition, there is a beautifully-carved stone door, the work of a wandering French artist, Antoine de Vienne (about 1500). Near the cathedral, the 11th–12th-century Church of St. Peter (Sv. Petar) has a collection of Baroque wooden statues of the Apostles.

Among other notable churches in Korčula, All Saints is remarkable for its collection of 14th–17th-century Greek icons brought back after the Candia war in the 17th century.

There are also the 17th-century Triumphal Arch by the 16th-century Town Hall (still in use), a quayside loggia, the old fortifications, any number of narrow streets between lovely stone-built houses, and glorious views across the strait of Pelješac. Of two small museums in the little square where the cathedral stands, one has the rich Cathedral treasury housed in the former Bishop's Palace, and the other, the Town Museum in a 16th-century mansion, contains local relics. On the same square is one of Korčula's finest buildings, the Arneri Palace, in Gothic-Renaissance style (under restoration).

It is hardly surprising to find the island, with so long and remarkable a history, has kept alive many ancestral customs and costumes. One of the most colorful of these is the procession by three religious brotherhoods which takes place every Good Friday.

But the most colorful of all is the symbolic sword dance of the *Moreška*, originally held on 27th July, and now every Thursday in summer—the Korčulani in dance and mime recall the incidents of a great battle between the kings of the Moors and the Sultan of Turkey for possession of a beautiful princess. The dancers wear magnificent costumes and are armed, each with two swords. One represents attack, and the other defense. Though nothing certain is known of its origins, it is supposed that the Moreška was introduced into their folklore early in the Middle Ages by sailors returning from Spain. Another similar, though less colorful, event is the *Kumpanija,* the commemoration of the island's successful defeat of a pirate raid, which takes place in Blato every 23rd of April.

A popular excursion from Korčula is to cross to the islet of Vrnik, less than 3½ km. (two miles) away, where the Romans built an important stone quarry still in use today, from the highest point of which you can see no less than 12 neighboring islands, on one of which there are ruins of an ancient monastery.

Korčula island possesses several first-rate bathing beaches, one of them near the village of Vela Luka at the western tip of the island (car ferry to Split), where the deep bay provides excellent fishing and curative baths as well. Another attractive little fishing-village on the island is Lumbarda, only a few kilometers from Korčula town, where there is one of the finest sand beaches of the entire coast. It also produces the potent amber-colored *Grk* wine; beware, it goes straight to your knees! The fishermen of Korčula occasionally take out tourists who wish to join an expedition into deep waters.

From Korčula you can also visit the glorious island of Mljet, described in the next chapter.

Pelješac

Separated from Korčula by a narrow channel, Pelješac possesses all the climatic and geographic characteristics of a Dalmatian island. A road branches off the *Magistrala* to run the entire length of the peninsula through most of the 40 villages. Increasingly popular are the bathing resorts of Orebić and, 15 minutes away, Trpanj, facing Kardeljevo on the mainland, to which it is linked by car-ferry. Both have pleasant beaches in attractive settings. Some of the houses in Orebić date back to the 15th century, and because of its great seafaring tradition, quite a few of them were owned by retired sea captains. You can find out more about this side of Orebić's past in the entertaining small Maritime Museum. The backbone of the peninsula is formed by a rocky mountain range which rises to well over 900 m. (3,152 ft.). Enthusiasts tackle the steep climb very early in the morning to watch dawn rise over Dalmatia and to refresh themselves afterwards with the famous *Dingač* wine, produced at Potomje some 20 km. (about 12 miles) away. If you're not quite that energetic, we recommend the much shorter but steepish slog up through the pinewoods to the Franciscan monastery above Orebić. It's an idyllic spot. Other expeditions can be made by motorboat. Many people like the way in which Orebić combines all the charms of Dalmatia (including a magnificent view across the sea to the lovely medieval town of Korčula, and entertaining excursions) with almost perfect peace. The hotels have been beautifully placed on the beach so as not to interfere with or even to be visible from the old village.

PRACTICAL INFORMATION FOR
CENTRAL DALMATIA

WHEN TO GO. The Dalmatian season now lasts throughout the year. Winters are relatively mild, though rainy, summers rarely unpleasantly hot; but note the comments on page 1 of *Facts At Your Fingertips.*

Throughout the summer, a full program of entertainment and sports events is arranged at many resorts. The most important are as follows. In Split, "Melodies of the Adriatic," a festival of light music, takes place in early July, followed by the Split Summer Festival of drama, concerts, opera and ballet from mid-July to mid-August. *"Splitske Lude Noči"* (Split Crazy Nights) occur on about one Saturday a month in summer, with street festivities lasting most of the night. In the second half of June Šibenik hosts the Yugoslav Festival for Children, while from mid-July to mid-August concerts are held in Zadar's St. Donat church. Makarska's Biokovo Nights, from early July through mid-August, offer a nightly program of music or drama. In Omiš, there is an annual festival of *klapa* singers (see page 41).

On 27 July and each Thursday from May through September, the *Moreška* is danced in Korčula town. It is an extremely spectacular mimed sword dance. On the first week-end in August, the "Sinjska Alka," an equestrian festival commemorating a battle against the Turks in 1715, is held in Sinj.

HOTELS AND RESTAURANTS. This is one of the major tourist regions of Yugoslavia, with a great concentration of hotels and some of the country's better restaurants. There is also a wide choice of private accommodations. Demand in season is, of course, great, and you will find that booking in advance is wise. Local tourist offices and travel agencies can advise if you haven't a reservation. Unless otherwise specified, resorts are open year-round and listed hotels have all or some rooms with private facilities.

Food and Drink. Fish and all shellfish are plentiful in Dalmatia, and there is a fish soup called *brodet.* As an hors d'oeuvre try *dalmatinski pršut,* which is a delicious smoked ham, or the unbeautiful, but delicious fried ink-fish (*lignji*). Local restaurants are at their best preparing a mixed grill of fish known as *ribe pržene na ulju.* We recommend red mullet (*barbuni*) and mackerel (*skuše*); Dalmatian lobster (*jastog*) is simply plain cold-boiled, as is the crayfish (*rak*). Try cheese after dinner: Primorški sir, Krčki sir or Paški sir. In Hvar, a specialty is *sir u maslinovo ulje* (cheese in olive oil).

Do not overlook the wines of the district, most of which are bottled commercially. There are no vintage years, but expert supervision ensures that wines from the big firms maintain the same character and quality each year. The best red wines include *Postup, Plavac* (which has a unique bluish tinge) and, the best of all, *Dingač* (but make sure it's the genuine article from the Pelješac Peninsula as the name is applied fairly indiscriminately to any heavy red wine). *Grk* is a strong amber-colored wine from Korčula. Lighter white wines include *Pošip* and *Vugava*. A rosé (*ružica*) is also available. A popular dessert wine is *Prošek*, though knowledgeable visitors prefer *Maraština*, an excellent local dessert wine.

ZADAR AND NEARBY ISLANDS

Biograd Na Moru. *Adriatic* (M), 110 rooms, pool, disco, and *Ilirija* (M), 180 rooms, stand side-by-side in a seaside park near the village. *Kornati* (M), 88 rooms, pool. *Crvena Luka* (I), 240 rooms. Tourist settlement three km. (two miles) to the south.

Božava (Dugi Otok Island). Season May–Oct. *Kadulja* (M), 50 rooms, by rocky shore. *Lavanda* (M), 87 rooms.

Iž Veli. Fishing village on Island of Iž; season Jun.–Sept. *Korinjak* (I), 78 rooms, none with shower. Simple. Near beach.

Luka (Dugi Otok Island). Season Jun.–Sept. *Luka* (I), 62 rooms, none with shower. Basic facilities. Just above shore.

Novalja (Pag Island). Season May–Oct. *Liburnija* (M), 136 rooms. *Loža* (M), 41 rooms.

Pag (Pag Island). Apr.–Oct. *Bellevue* (I), 166 rooms.

Petrčane. See Zadar below.

Preko (Ugljan Island). Facing Zadar across strait. *Preko* (I).

Primošten. Charming fishing village on islet with causeway to mainland. Facing it on wooded peninsula, *Adriatic* complex with *Slava,* 161 rooms, and *Zora,* 145 rooms. *Raduča,* 90 rooms. All (M), near rock and pebble beach, with sports facilities, including circular indoor pool open year-round except July 1 to mid-Aug.
Restaurant. *Villa Fenč,* in old Primošten, is recommended for fish.

Sali (Dugi Otok Island). Season May–Sept. *Pavilion Sirena* (M), 12 rooms. *Sali* (I), 36 rooms without bath.

Šibenik. Naval base (be careful what you photograph!) and beautiful old town on Krka estuary. In town is the *Jadran* (M), 65 rooms. The modern resort complex of *Solaris* (M) is six km. (3½ miles) from town, set in gardens with beaches of rock and gravel and cemented sunbathing areas. Extensive sports facilities. Hydrotherapy treatment. Best is *Ivan* (E), 317 rooms, indoor pool (closed July–Aug.). Also *Andrija, Jure, Niko. Motel Medveščak* (M) is on coastal highway six km. (four miles) north of town at Krka river bridge.

Starigrad-Paklenica. Near Paklenica National Park, on slopes of gaunt Velebit Mountains. *Alan* (M), 217 rooms.

Vodice. Little fishing town and resort with sports center. A short stroll from town are: *Gloriette* (M), 24 family villas, pool. *Imperial* (M), 110 rooms, at top end of price range; pool. By pebble beach. *Olympia* (M), 261 rooms, also at upper end of range. In pine forest above beach, with pool (closed in high season). *Punta* (M), 300 rooms, nearer center.

Zadar. Historic city and port. In the old town and on the waterfront is the *Zagreb* (M), 120 rooms. About one km. (half a mile) south, *Kolovare* (M), 237 rooms, at upper end of price range; pool, sports facilities, across the road from bathing area.

The best choice is on the Borik peninsula, $3\frac{1}{2}$ km. (two miles) north of old town, with a total of 795 rooms in the *Barbara* (E), or (M) range *Adriana, Donat, Novi Park, Slavija* and *Zadar*. The complex features open-air and indoor pools, nightclub, several restaurants and a camp site, all set in gardens or pine woods beside or near the extensive sandy or man-made beach.

Restaurants. In the old town are *Balkan* and *Primošten,* both (M) and privately run, offering good value and choice. The latter is mainly a fish restaurant. *Samoposluživanje* (Self-Service) (I).

Near **Petrčane,** 12 km. (eight miles) northwest, *Pinija* (M), 302 rooms, outdoor pool. On wooded promontory. Also *Punta Skala Tourist Settlement* (M), 665 rooms.

At **Zaton,** 16 km. (ten miles) northwest, near Nin, a modern tourist settlement includes self-catering accommodations, camp site, marina, restaurants and sports facilities.

SPLIT AND NEARBY COASTAL REGIONS

Baška Voda. Bathing resort north of Makarska. Season Apr.–Oct. *Horizon* (M), 200 rooms, upper end of range; nightclub, indoor pool, sports facilities. Above pebble beach, a short stroll from village. *Slavija* (M), 76 rooms, at upper end of price range. Across road from pebble beach, close to village.

Restaurant. *Bacchus* (M), in village.

Brela. Seaside village north of Makarska, with long pebble beach backed by woods. Season Apr.–Oct. *Maestral* (E), with annex. *Marina* (M), 132 rooms, top-class; nightclub, open-air pool, tennis, sports facilities. Above pebble beach, 15 minutes' walk from resort center. *Soline* (E), 230 rooms; indoor pool, sports hall. Other sports facilities at nearby *Maestral.* By pebble beach, ten minutes' walk from resort center. *Berulia* (M), 220 rooms, at upper end of price range; open-air pool, above pebble beach. Closest to resort.

Restaurant. *Punta* (E–M), in pine woods near beach.

Gradac. Good beach. *Laguna* (M), 220 rooms plus chalets. Own beach.

Igrane. Unspoilt village near Makarska. Season Apr.–Oct. *Punta* (M), 130 rooms, by pebble beach in the village.

Makarska. Port and major resort at foot of Mount Biokovo. *Meteor* (E), 280 rooms; nightclub, open-air and indoor pools, sports hall, tennis.

By pebble beach, close to resort center. *Biokovo* (M), 56 rooms, on waterfront in resort center. *Biokovka* (M), 220 rooms; two indoor pools, medical facilities. Near pebble beach beyond *Meteor. Dalmacija* (M), 200 rooms; nightclub, open-air pool. By pebble beach and small harbor, a short walk from center.

Restaurants. *Susvid* (E–M), steak house, good atmosphere, near Cathedral. Private. *Riva* (M), pleasant, near waterfront. Private.

Omiš. Season May–Oct. *Brzet* (I), 85 rooms. Just south of the town. *Plaža* (I), 35 rooms, none with shower. Adjoins the sandy public beach in the town.

At **Ruskamen,** on the coast six km. (four miles) south, *Ruskamen* (M), 171 rooms.

Restaurant. Pleasant excursions from both Omiš and Ruskamen up the Cetina gorge lead to the old mill-restaurant at *Radmanove Mlinice.*

Podgora. Pleasant old fishing port and modern summer resort. Season Apr.–Oct. The hotels are clustered together in the east of the resort above or by pebble beaches, a short stroll from center. *Minerva* (E), 200 rooms; indoor pool. *Aurora* (M), 150 rooms; disco. *Mediteran* (M), 150 rooms. *Podgorka* (M), with annexes (I), 250 rooms.

Restaurant. *Paradizo* (M), fish specialties, private, at Čaklija in east of resort.

Split. Major historic city and port. Excellent base for island-hopping. *Bellevue* (E), 50 rooms, some (M); close to old town. Traditional style, but can be noisy. *Marjan* (E), 331 rooms, some (M); *Park* (M), 60 rooms; nightclub. Gracious building in garden setting above Bay of Bačvice, the city's main public beach, a short walk from center. Nearby tennis courts. Due for major expansion. *Slavija* (M), 32 rooms, some (I); splendid historic buildings in heart of old city. No restaurant, but cellar tavern planned.

Three km. (two miles) east is *Split* (M), 320 rooms; disco, 100 meters from beach. On secluded promontory eight km. (five miles) southeast of city is *Lav* (M), 375 rooms. Beautiful situation, small harbor, disco, sports facilities.

Restaurants. *Adriatic* (E), in elegant new ACY Marina; you get the same marvelous views from the adjoining (M) pizza restaurant. All in (M) range and mostly private: *Adriana,* pavement terrace on waterfront, Serbian specialties. *Arkina,* Radmilovićeva 2, near *Bellevue* hotel. Good atmosphere, fish specialties. *Ero,* Marmontova, by old town. National specialties. *Kod Joze,* Sredmanuška 4, northeast of old town. Typical Dalmatian tavern, good seafood. *Konoba Adriatik,* in the heart of old city beneath the *Slavija* hotel. National dishes. *Lijepa Dalmacija,* Hektorovićeva bb, just southeast of old town. Local specialties. *MAK* in ultramodern Koteks shopping center east of old town. *Sarajevo,* in old town. Bosnian specialties.

Trogir. Superb little medieval town. 800 meters (half-a-mile) north, on the coastal highway, is *Motel Trogir* (M), 85 rooms. 1½ km. (one mile) farther on is *Jadran* (I), 152 rooms; 3 km. beyond is *Medena* (M), 663 rooms, pool (closed July–Aug.) and *Medena Apartments* (M), 261 rooms. Sports facilities.

Tučepi. Popular resort near Makarska. All the hotels are on the west of the resort by pebble beaches and linked by a shore path. Tennis and other sports facilities are shared. *Alga* (M), 370 rooms; open-air pool. *Jadran* and annex (M), 170 rooms, at upper end of price range. *Neptun* and annexes (M), 300 rooms, disco. Also *Afrodita* self-catering apartments.

Restaurants. *Kaštelet* (M), in 18th-century fort near Alga. *Gusari* (M), private.

Zaostrog. *Dalmacija* (M), 68 rooms, at lower end of category. Own beach.

Živogošće. Small resort south of Makarska. *Nimfa* (M), 350 rooms; disco, indoor pool, tennis. Above pebble beach, a short stroll from village.

THE MAIN ISLANDS

Brač

Bol. Attractive resort on mountainous shore in south of island. *Bretanide* (E), 260 rooms; in complex attractively designed to resemble Dalmatian village, open-air pool. The closest to the superb beach of Zlatni Rat. *Elaphusa* and pavilions (E), 324 rooms; indoor pool, nightclub. Tennis and other sports amenities available to guests of other hotels. Next to *Borak*. *Bijela Kuča* (M) and pavilions, 210 rooms, tennis. By stoney beaches at east end of village, near monastery. *Borak* (M), 148 rooms, at upper end of category; open-air pool. About 1½ km. (a mile) from village; also 95 self-catering apartments. *Kaštil* (M), 32 rooms, some (I), in renovated old building on waterfront. Also 56 self-catering apartments in new blocks.

Supetar. Attractive capital of island, surrounded by vineyards. *Kaktus* (E), 95 rooms plus apartments, some (M); open-air pool, tennis. Tourist settlement, a little outside town.

Hvar

Hvar. The island's delightful capital. *Palace* (E), 75 rooms, some (M); indoor pool. By harbor and with charming Renaissance loggia. *Adriatic* (M), 63 rooms; by harbor. Indoor, roof-top pool. *Amfora* (M), 380 rooms; indoor Olympic pool (closed in high season), own beach, sports hall. A pleasant shore-side stroll from center. *Dalmacija* (M), 73 rooms, at lower end of its category. Overlooking sea, beach, a short stroll from center. *Delfin* (M), 55 rooms, also at lower end of range; by harbor. *Sirena* (M), 158 rooms; tennis. By quiet cove three km. (two miles) from center. *Slavija* (M), 52 rooms; à la carte meals only. Behind venerable facade, by harbor and ferry landing.

Jelsa. Charming small port and beach resort. *Fontana* (M), 176 rooms; open-air pool. By rocky beach, a short stroll from village. *Jadran* (M), 143 rooms; overlooking sea, nearer village. *Mina* (M), 204 rooms; indoor pool, tennis. Above rocky and coarse sand beaches, a short stroll from village.

Stari Grad. Historic old town and inlet. All hotels are about 1½ km. (one mile) from village. *Adriatic* (M), 94 rooms; by beach, nearby sports facilities. *Arkada* (M), 279 rooms; open-air and indoor pools, sports hall, tennis, disco. *Helios* (I), 214 rooms; bathing area with restaurant, nearby sports facilities.

Vrboska. Delightful small port near Jelsa. *Adriatic* (M), 179 rooms. About 15 minutes' walk by shore path from village, or 10 minutes by boat, to Jelsa. Pebble and rock beach, sports facilities.

Korčula

Korčula. Lovely capital of the island of the same name. *Liburna* (E), 100 rooms, pool, sports facilities. New, on shore, a short walk from town. *Bon Repos* (M), 300 rooms and apartments, open-air pool, sports facilities. 2.5 km. (1½ miles) from town. *Korčula* (M), 26 rooms, at upper end of its category. This renovated hotel is the only one in the old town. Good value. *Marko Polo* (M), 110 rooms, also at top end of range; pool, sports facilities. Well run, a little closer to town. *Park* (M), 161 rooms, at the bottom of its category; sports facilities. Next to Marko Polo.

Restaurants. All moderately priced are *Adio Mare,* in the old town, specializing in old Korčula and Venetian dishes; *Gradski Podrum,* in the old town, medieval setting with open-air terrace; *Peter Kanavelić,* in the old town, Dalmatian fish specialties; *Planjak,* in the old town, top favorite with the locals for its home cooking, with seashore pergola.

Lumbarda. Quiet coastal village a few kilometers from Korčula; season Apr.–Oct. *Lumbarda* (M), with nearby annexes *Borik* and *Lovor,* is excellent if you want the quiet life.

Vela Luka. Charming coastal village in island's north. *Adria* (M), 125 rooms; pool. *Poseidon* (M), 182 rooms. Beach, indoor pool (closed in summer).

Restaurant. *Sunce* can be recommended for its pleasant atmosphere.

Pelješac Peninsula

Orebić. Marvelous views across to Korčula. Season Apr.–Oct. All (M) with own beach are: *Bellevue* and annex, 170 rooms. *Orsan,* 106 rooms. *Rathaneum,* 190 rooms, completely renovated. All a short walk from town. Sports facilities.

Šolta

Maslinica. Season May–Oct. *Avlija* (I), 47 rooms without bath. Houses in Baroque manor in small fishing village.

Nečujam. On a lovely bay, renowned for skindiving and fishing; season May–Oct. *Nečujam Tourist Settlement* (I), self-catering apartments with restaurant and sports facilities.

HOW TO GET AROUND. To visit the entire coast of Central Dalmatia presents no great problem, thanks to the scenic, if often narrow and crowded, Adriatic Coastal Road. However, to visit anything like all the islands by boat would take a long time, but after all most people go to the coast to enjoy themselves on the beach. Perhaps the best solution is to settle in the coastal or island resort of your choice, and then make a few excursions.

Most of the fast coastal vessels, operating from Rijeka, call at Zadar, Split, Hvar and Korčula. Regular car-and-passenger ferries or hydrofoils operate from Zadar, Split, and several other coastal centers to all the main islands. It is an intensive network, especially in summer, and you will need the latest detailed schedules, available from Yugoslav National Tourist Offices abroad, Jadrolinija offices or main travel bureaux. Pag (southern tip) and Murter are connected to the mainland by bridges.

Split is a major road and rail center, about halfway between Trieste and Titograd. There are no railway services along the coast, but mainline connections from Zadar, Split and Kardeljevo. to Zagreb, Belgrade and other points inland.

Zadar airport is used mainly by domestic and international charter services; Split handles many international as well as domestic routes.

SPORTS. Water sports of all kinds are popular along the Dalmatian coast—facilities for water skiing and, increasingly, wind surfing exist in many resorts.

In most places the shore is stony or pebbly, but in many resorts cemented areas have been created which are excellent for both swimming and sunbathing. A number of secluded beaches are reserved for nudist bathing. Quite a few hotels have swimming pools, and these avoid the Adriatic's only real snag—the sea urchins, usually confined to the rockier stretches. Otherwise the water is almost always gloriously crystal clear and a joy to bathe in; exceptions are a few of the more shallow bays which collect some flotsam when the wind is in the wrong direction.

Local and international regattas take place during the season at Split, Zadar and numerous other venues of less importance. Sail and auxiliary motorboats, also canoes, can be hired from a number of resorts—enquiries should be made at local tourist offices or travel firms. Note also the marinas operated by ACY (see page 26). Flotilla sailing arrangements are marketed ex-U.K. Tennis courts and mini-golf are widely available.

FISHING. Because of the deeply-indented coastline, and the large number of islands, this part of the Adriatic is particularly interesting to fishermen, and only a meter or two down you can see beautiful shells, giant sponges and strangely shaped coral, where shoals of fish dart to and fro. In the less frequented places fishing becomes quite an adventure.

Some travel firms organize fishing trips, veritable expeditions lasting one or several days. These trips usually take place in the Kornat archipelago, and are for 20–30 persons at the time. Fishingboats, sailboats or motorboats—you can take your pick. All the necessary equipment is provided and an expert goes along to direct the uninitiated. Smaller boats, carrying about 6–14 people, are also available. There is sometimes also a special restaurant boat—if you can tear yourself away from rod and line.

However, such excursions are for the real enthusiast; most people prefer to settle in the place of their choice, either beach resort or village, and do their fishing from there. In that case you have to go to the local travel firms or tourist office, and obtain a permit for underwater or ordinary fishing. These are idyllic waters for underwater sport, but make sure you know about local restrictions. Special regulations, for example, are in force in the national park area of the Kornat islands, and fishing is forbidden in port areas or marine reserves at the mouth of a number of rivers.

MUSEUMS. In Zadar. The Ethnographic Museum, Narodni trg, features some lovely examples of the folk art of northern Dalmatia.

Archeological Museum opposite St. Donat's Church is the home of regional antiquities: prehistoric, Roman, and "old Croatian" objects, including magnificent silver and gold antiquities; a marvelous collection.

Sacral Art. Permanent exhibition in St. Maria, next to Archeological Museum.

In Split

Archeological Museum, Zrinjsko-Frankopanska 13. Interesting collection of Roman and other antiquities.

Cathedral Treasury. Rich collection of sacred objects including gospels from the seventh to eighth century.

City Museum, Papalićeva 5. In fine old Papalić Palace. Excellent displays of historical and art exhibits, which should now have re-opened after lengthy restoration.

Croat Antiquities Museum, Ognjena Price bb. Imposing building on Marjan peninsula displaying objects from the Slav pagan period onward.

Ethnographic Museum, Narodni trg. Housed in the fine Old Town Hall.

Maritime Museum in the Gripe Fortress, part of the massive Venetian fortifications, east of the old town.

Meštrović Gallery, Moše Pijade 46, on the Marjan peninsula. Extensive exhibition of sculptures by this famous artist in his former home. In nearby Kaštelet is a collection of Meštrović's woodcarvings.

Underground Halls, entered from Titova obala 20. Well-preserved and fascinating copy of the floor plan of Diocletian's Palace.

SHOPPING. Visitors to Dalmatia will find plenty of interesting and original things to buy. Lace, for example, has been a great specialty of the island of Pag for centuries. However, you will find not only locally made articles, but also many items produced in other regions, such as the coffee grinders and Turkish coffee sets of Bosnia, and some of the fine crystal produced in the factories of Slovenia and Croatia. Leather suitcases, even if somewhat more expensive than a few years ago, remain popular with buyers because of their beautiful finish and still reasonable price. The great Maraska distilleries at Zadar provide a vast and inexpensive choice of liqueurs in decorative bottles. Shops stay open late in summer and street artists also often add to the animated evening scene.

USEFUL ADDRESSES. Every town and resort has a tourist information office. The three main ones are: Šibenik Tourist Association, 1X1 Divizije bb, Šibenik; Split Tourist Bureau, Titova obala 12, Split; and

Zadar Tourist Office, Omladinska, Zadar. The main travel agency in this area is Dalmacijaturist (head office: Titova obala 5, Split). This and other travel firms have branches in many resorts and organize excursions, make reservations, etc.

SOUTHERN DALMATIA

The World of Dubrovnik

The little town of Dubrovnik stands supreme in Southern Dalmatia—it is the most striking point on the entire coast, outstanding not only by Yugoslavian standards but also in comparison with any town and its environs in the whole of Europe. Its setting is magnificent, its mellow walls and buildings—despite earthquake and fire over the centuries—form a wonderfully harmonious whole, and its facilities are varied and of a very high standard—fine ingredients indeed for a holiday choice.

The city was laid out after a strict geometric plan, but the impression of this classical rigidity is softened by the predominance of Renaissance buildings. The extraordinary harmony is due partly to the white marble of which the entire town is built, and partly to its homogeneous architecture. The result is that Dubrovnik is still today wholly medieval, and the walls which were unbreached for 1,000 years remain unchanged and intact.

Early in the seventh century, Slav tribesmen sacked the once-Greek, and later Roman, town of Epidaurus, a site now occupied by the small town of Cavtat. The surviving citizens of Epidaurus fled north to build a new city on a small rocky island below the slopes of Mount Srd. Strong walls were built, and as it grew in importance the town was called successively Lausa, Rausium, Ragusium and Ragusa.

On the mainland opposite the island, a Slav settlement called Dubrovnik grew up on the fringe of the oak forests—*dubrava* meaning "oak woods." By the 12th century the narrow creek which separated the two towns was filled up, so that Ragusa and Dubrovnik became one, and in 1205 the united town threw off the overlordship of Byzantium and recognized Venice as the paramount Dalmatian power.

The chief citizen was the Rector, elected each month, who shared the management of the city's business with the Grand Council and the Senate. Most of the military and naval commands were held by members of the nobility (of Roman or Byzantine origin) while the increasingly prosperous middle-class were mostly Slavs. At first Latin was the official language, but the use of Croat soon became general.

The rulers of the Republic were primarily concerned with the promotion of maritime business (the word "argosy," by the way, being a corruption of Ragusa), and the laws governing the citizens were unusually liberal for the period. By the use of farsighted diplomacy Ragusa gradually rose to become one of the greatest maritime and commercial ports of the Mediterranean, with a fleet of as many as 2,000 ships.

After the defeat of Venice in 1358 Dubrovnik decided to place herself under the protection of the Hungarian-Croatian kings, but when the Turks overran Hungary the city sought the protection of the Sultan, paying him a yearly tribute. Later the aid of Spain and the Holy Roman Empire was enlisted for the same purpose, namely to ensure the continued independence of the city.

The conduct of the Republic may strike us as Machiavellian, but it was successful in enabling the city to develop rapidly and to extend its influence to the mouth of the River Neretva in the north and to the Bay of Kotor in the south. Consistent with its policy of deserting its overlords as soon as their power began to decline, Ragusa followed the Turkish defeat in central Europe in 1684 by associating itself with the Habsburgs. So by means of cunning diplomacy and opportunism unceasingly exercised, Dubrovnik remained mistress of her own destiny.

However, following the great earthquake of 1667, the decline began, and in the same way as her great rival Venice, Dubrovnik was occupied by foreign troops for the first time in her history. In 1808 Napoleon's General Marmont decreed the end of the Republic. When he in turn had surrendered to a couple of Austrian battalions, the Congress of Vienna awarded the city to Austria, and it remained a Habsburg possession until 1918.

Despite the passing of so many centuries, the memory of the greatest days of Ragusa-Dubrovnik is evident in the matchless beauty of its buildings and its liberal institutions, and in the cultural preeminence of its citizens. As early as 1347 Ragusa possessed a Home for the Aged, and the slave traffic was abolished in 1416—more than four centuries before many of the more "advanced" Western nations. Torture was prohibited in the 15th century, and there were a number of endowed schools which offered to all an education far in advance of the general standards of the time.

Peter Bošković made an excellent translation of the works of Molière and Corneille, and while in Paris, was an intimate of the Encyclopedists. His brother Roger became a distinguished astronomer and mathematician, living for many years in London and being elected a member of the Royal Society. Still, even before the time of these distinguished intellectuals, Ragusa had a copious literature of its own, from the 15th century. This was written in Latin to begin with, but soon replaced by "Ragusian Slav"—a language in use until the beginning of the last century, at a time when the

Illyrian Movement for the union of the southern Slavs was striving to awake national consciousness of their great historical heritage.

Southward to Dubrovnik

It takes some two hours by boat from Korčula, and rather less than an hour from Trstenik on the Pelješac peninsula to reach the thickly wooded island of Mljet. It is quite different from most of its neighbors, not only because of its rich vegetation, but also due to its freshwater lakes. On a tiny island in Veliko Jezero ("Big Lake"), the hotel Melita, housed in a 12th-century Benedictine monastery, makes an excellent and peaceful base from which to explore. Mljet has one peculiar claim to fame in that it is the only place in Europe where you may find the mongoose roaming about at liberty. One explanation for this is that long ago these little animals were imported from the East to exterminate the snakes with which the island was infested.

Furthermore, it is claimed that one of the island's snakes bit St. Paul (without doing him any harm) when the apostle was shipwrecked on what was then called Melita while he was on his way to appear before Caesar, and to meet his martyrdom in Rome. Malta, which in those days was also called Melita, disputes this putative honor.

The waters round Mljet are particularly well stocked with fish, and the island is consequently a great favorite with fishermen, though you must bring your own equipment. It's also very popular with discerning foreign yachtsmen. The chief village is Babino Polje, and the main port is Polače.

The Dubrovnik boat passes between the coast and the three islands of Šipan, Lopud and Koločep. The first is completely covered, almost to the shore, with dense forest, Šipanska Luka being the "capital." There are a number of elegant mansions here, among them the summer homes of rich merchants and sea captains of Dubrovnik.

Lopud is a bathing resort set among pine woods and olive groves, attractively placed and with several fine, gently sloping beaches. It's also the most interesting of the islands with an excellent local museum and fine paintings in the Franciscan monastery church. Koločep, less than eight km. (five miles) from Dubrovnik, is small and thickly grown, but has several good beaches and a number of old churches.

These three small islands are well worth mentioning because of their nearness to Dubrovnik. Most of the large travel firms operate boat excursions to them, and regular steamer services and modern hotels are available if you want an offshore stay.

Along the *Magistrala* southward to Dubrovnik the scenery appears, if anything, even more striking. Following the coast opposite the long peninsula of Pelješac, you will reach the point at which the peninsula juts out from the mainland, and from here there is an attractive detour of some eight km. (five miles) to the strikingly picturesque fortified village of Ston, once the second city of the Republic of Ragusa, whose salt-pans are still being worked. In fact it's made up of two villages, Mali Ston and Veliki Ston, linked across the intervening hill of Pozvizd by an imposing line of medieval defense walls, still largely intact. The surroundings are scattered with pre-Romanesque churches and chapels, largely in ruins, but the tiny 11th-century Church of St. Michael is worth seeking out for its frescos. It's on a hill dominating the plain. In Veliki Ston itself are the Gothic

Chancellery of the Republic, Bishop's Palace and the Franciscan monastery.

Slano lies at the head of a deep inlet, whose waters are serene and sheltered. Here, where a few years ago there was nothing but a tiny decaying village, a fine modern holiday resort has grown up. The only place of real interest between here and Dubrovnik is Trsteno, where there are two enormous plane trees reputed to be 1,000 years old. Trsteno also has a botanical garden, once the grounds of a patrician house where the poet Byron was a guest.

The road continues along the right bank of the Dubrovnik or Ombla river. This appears to be a large inlet of the sea but is, in fact, the River Trebišnjica, which rises far inland, wanders along the *karst* plateau, then suddenly disappears into a swallow-hole, to reemerge at the base of a 400-m. (1,300-ft.) cliff about five km. (three miles) from the sea. The point where it reappears is a magnificent sight, especially in springtime when the cliff is covered with the wild iris *(Iris dalmatica)* which were the ancestors of many of our modern garden-varieties, and with fragrant herbs, like thyme, sage, and lavender. A fine patrician house in the village of Komolac, overlooking the river, is now part of Dubrovnik Marina, a mecca for the boating fraternity with restaurant and other sports facilities. The situation is splendid. But many visitors who knew this district as it was will regret the surge of modern buildings which now overlook a large area of the Ombla's shores.

The main Adriatic Highway bypasses Dubrovnik; if you're heading into town you will soon come to the industrial harbor area of Gruž, a Dubrovnik suburb and not an especially attractive introduction to one of the world's most beautiful fortified cities. Here, too, new buildings are rising quickly. A complex one-way traffic system helps to ease bottlenecks, but motorists will still find themselves in a slow procession at the height of the season.

Exploring Dubrovnik

In 1667 Dubrovnik suffered the worst of several earthquakes throughout its history. The effects of the 1979 quake, centered on Montenegro, were far less devastating, but nevertheless caused much structural damage. A long-term plan of restoration is in progress, and although much has been achieved, some major buildings may be closed and there will be scaffolding around for some time. Discoveries made during the restoration are causing experts to rethink the city's early history.

Such natural disasters notwithstanding, Dubrovnik remains an entrancing place, witness to the artistic skills and technical craftsmanship of bygone centuries. Your best plan is to begin with a circuit of the city's undamaged medieval walls (remembering that they close at 7 P.M., earlier in the winter). There's no great distance involved, as the old town was extraordinarily compact. The walls were designed principally by Michelozzi of Florence and George of Dalmatia, and include five great bastions: the Lovrjenac fort and the Minčeta, Bokar, Revelin, and Sveti Ivan towers.

Entrance to the old city is restricted to two heavily protected gates at Ploče, close to the old port on the east, and Pile on the west, and from either of these you can gain access to the walls themselves. If you have only time to go half way round, or are feeling lazy, follow the route on

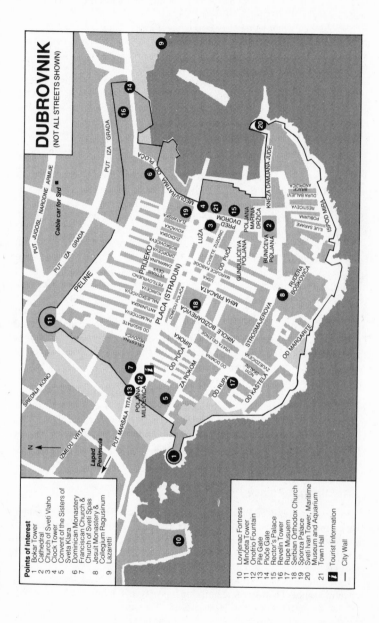

DUBROVNIK
(NOT ALL STREETS SHOWN)

Points of interest

1. Bokar Tower
2. Cathedral
3. Church of Sveti Vlaho
4. Clock Tower
5. Convent of the Sisters of Sveta Klara
6. Dominican Monastery
7. Franciscan Church & Church of Sveti Spas
8. Jesuit Monastery & Collegium Ragusinum
9. Lazareti
10. Lovrijenac Fortress
11. Minčeta Tower
12. Onofrio Fountain
13. Pile Gate
14. Ploče Gate
15. Rector's Palace
16. Revelin Tower
17. Rupe Musuem
18. Serbian Orthodox Church
19. Sponza Palace
20. Sveti Ivan Tower, Maritime Museum and Aquarium
21. Town Hall

ℹ Tourist Information

— City Wall

the landward side; it gives by far the best views over the city. A small fee is charged. Incidentally, no private wheeled traffic is permitted within the walls.

The old city's main thoroughfare is the Placa—known by some locals as "Stradun"—which crosses it from one side to the other, and runs along what was once the narrow channel separating Ragusa on its island from Slav Dubrovnik on the mainland. It is here that you will find the principal buildings, though there are of course countless narrow medieval streets leading off it which the visitor will find very well worth exploring. One of these narrow streets, Prijeko, runs parallel with Placa to the north and has always had a number of restaurants. On a recent visit we found there are now so many hotly competing with each other to draw in the passing crowd that, in our opinion, it is best avoided in the evenings if you're looking for a quiet place.

Crossing from west to east, you will soon see the Onofrio Fountain built in the 15th century (at the time of the installation of the city's fresh water supply), which was designed by the Neapolitan Onofrio de la Cava. Behind the fountain is the Convent of the Sisters of Sveta Klara, dating from 1290. Here Europe's first hospice for homeless children was opened in 1432.

Opposite there is the Renaissance-style façade of the Church of Sveti Spas, St. Saviour, designed by the Andrijić brothers after the great earthquake of 1520. Not far away stands an imposing 14th-century Franciscan church, with a remarkable Gothic porch carved by the brothers Petrović in 1498. Inside there is a 15th-century painting of Sveti Vlaho holding a model of the city. Sveti Vlaho, or St. Blaise, is Dubrovnik's patron saint and you will find statues of him dotted about the town and walls, his hand raised in blessing. Attached to the church is a lovely cloister, the work of Miho de Bar. The capital of each one of the cloister columns is ornamented by a different group of grinning or grimacing faces, half nightmare, half humorous, and wholly arresting in their originality.

Leading off the cloister is an interesting little museum, part of which is devoted to the pharmacy which the Franciscans founded here in the 14th century. Some of the old equipment is easily recognizable. The museum also features old manuscripts, paintings and church reliquaries. At the entrance to the monastery, incidentally, a present-day pharmacy, furnished in the old style, carries on the centuries-old tradition.

The Sponza Palace

At the other end of Placa you will see the 30-m.-high (100 ft.) Clock Tower built in 1445 (recently rebuilt) standing in the center of a small but beautiful square. Nearby is the Sponza Palace, Gothic in style with Renaissance elements. It was built by the architect Miličević in the 16th century.

The main façade is ornamented with an external gallery supported by graceful arches. This very fine building has played a major part in the city's life—as Ragusa's Customs House, State Treasury, a bank, and a grain warehouse. Today the upper floors contain the archives of the old Republic—7,000 tomes and over 100,000 other documents from the 11th century onwards, including signed statements from almost every European ruler over the centuries confirming or granting privileges to this tiny city-state.

The Archives are only open to scholars, but an exhibition of a selection of documents may be reinstated once restoration work is complete.

The 18th-century Baroque Church of Sveti Vlaho is immediately opposite the Sponza Palace. It replaced the 14th-century church that was destroyed by fire. The only object that escaped the flames was the silver statue of the saint, holding a model of the city, which today stands on the High Altar of the later church. You can see how little the city plan has changed from that of 500 years ago. Every year, on February 3, the statue is paraded through the streets as part of a major celebration.

In the little open square in front of Sveti Vlaho is an attractive fountain, also "Roland's Column," placed there in 1418, from which the Town Crier broadcast decisions of the Senate. The Republic's flag was flown here on public holidays. A local legend, pleasant even if improbable, is that the column and the city's constitution were given to the young Republic by Roland, the nephew of Charlemagne.

The Rector's Palace

The most remarkable building in Dubrovnik is the Rector's Palace, now re-opened after restoration. Built in the 12th century, it was subsequently so severely damaged in several earthquakes that in the 15th century the three architects Onofrio de la Cava, Michelozzi, and George of Dalmatia were charged with the work of designing the present building. It shows a combination of late Gothic and early Renaissance styles. The center of the façade is supported by five massive pillars, each crowned with its capital. In the courtyard there is a bust of a rich 17th-century shipowner, Miho Pracat, who contributed generously to state funds and was the only citizen of his time to be honored with a statue.

On the first floor of the palace are the large rooms where in the days of the Republic the Great Council and the Senate held their meetings, and also the Rector's work-room. One of the Laws of Ragusa was that the Rector might not leave the confines of the palace during his month of office. Deprived of all family and social distractions, it was thought, he would be forced to get on with his job. The Ragusans were obviously fully aware of their own frailties, as the same insistence on hard work is echoed in the inscription over the entrance to the meeting place of the Grand Council, which reads *Obliti privatorum publica curate* or "Forget private affairs, and get on with public matters."

Halfway between the Clock Tower and the Rector's Palace is the Town Hall, containing the municipal theater, which occupies the site of the 14th-century Palace of the Grand Council, destroyed by fire in 1816. The ground floor accommodates a large and popular café. Here the city's war galleys were once stored.

Close to the Rector's Palace is Dubrovnik's imposing Baroque Cathedral, which stands on the site of its pre-1667 earthquake Romanesque predecessor. Restoration, following the 1979 quake, has revealed foundations from Byzantine times; a section of these can be seen to the right of the main entrance. The Cathedral has valuable church ornaments and paintings by late Renaissance and Baroque masters. Its modern altar seems rather out of keeping with these, though it is backed by a fine painting attributed to Titian.

Innumerable other treasures are to be found among the maze of narrow streets. You could begin from the open-air morning market on Gundulić Square near the Cathedral, and climb the steps up to the Jesuit Monastery and, next to it, the Collegium Ragusinum, Dubrovnik's ancient Learned Academy. Or, if you follow Puča Street from the market, you will soon come to the little Orthodox church and, in the building next door, discover a fine collection of icons. Heading up into the alleyways behind the Sponza Palace near Ploče Gate, you will find the Dominican Monastery, with very beautiful cloisters, a rich treasury of incunabula, and paintings (including a Titian). Next to the Monastery is the Sebastian Gallery, with changing exhibitions of modern art. Indeed, the old streets of the city are now peppered with art studios, boutiques, and restaurants, most of them privately run.

Just outside the walls near Ploče Gate are the *lazaretti* where, in the Middle Ages, travelers waited for permission to enter the city, and where if they were merchants they stored their trade-goods. These have now been converted into a complex of shops, tavern, disco, and galleries.

Mercifully Dubrovnik completely escaped physical damage in World War II, though the citizens still recall the day when the Germans, the Italians looking on, drove out 200 members of the city's Jewish colony, not one of whom has ever been seen or heard of again.

Just off-shore from the old city is the lovely green island of Lokrum, a favorite place for bathing, with regular boat services. It is also a protected nature reserve, and a fitting setting for botanical gardens and the Natural History Museum. Richard the Lionheart is reputed to have been shipwrecked here on his way back from the Crusades.

Dubrovnik's Summer Festival

Among Dubrovnik's sobriquets is "The Slav Athens," and throughout her long history she has deliberately maintained her cultural traditions. Accordingly, in 1950 she initiated her annual Summer Festival; now every year from 10th July to 25th August an intensive program of concerts, plays, operettas, involving many internationally known guest artists, takes place against the backdrop of some of the city's most beautiful historic buildings. You may be slightly shaken to hear Hamlet, Prince of Denmark, discoursing in Serbo-Croat, but at least the background of the Lovrjenac fortress makes a highly-satisfactory Elsinore.

One word of warning: Dubrovnik's total hotel capacity is considerable, but there is still a summer shortage of top-class accommodations. Note, too, that many of the resort's hotels are on the pleasant Lapad peninsula some distance from the walled town, though linked with it by frequent bus services. If you want to be within strolling distance of the old city, make sure you choose your hotel accordingly.

Farewell to Dubrovnik

There are magnificent views back to the walled city as you head off towards Montenegro, passing above a string of pleasant resorts such as Kupari, Srebreno, Mlini, and Plat. Beyond these, the next fork in the road, on the right, leads to Cavtat, which is one of the most strikingly attractive villages on the Dalmatian coast. It is set among pines in the heart of a bay, and its narrow streets run parallel to each other as they climb steeply from the shore. Each house has its own little garden with orange and lemon trees. One of the best views of Cavtat (the Epidamnus or Epidaurus of the ancients, whose surviving inhabitants fled to Dubrovnik in the seventh century following a destructive Avar raid) may be obtained from beside the cypress-guarded tomb of the Račić family, the work of Meštrović, which stands on a small promontory within sound of the waves. A resort-area has developed a little way from Cavtat, in a spot where there is a fine sheltered beach.

The way now lies along the fertile Konavli Valley, where ethnologists claim to be able to detect the classic features of Graeco-Roman Epidaurus in the handsome peasant girls. About ten km. (six miles) from Cavtat (from *civitas*—"township") is the village of Čilipi, which you should visit on a Sunday morning if possible when the people wear their particularly attractive traditional costume. Unfortunately, the men are tending to abandon these reminders of a colorful past. With a busy international airport now dominating their village, this is perhaps understandable.

Next comes Gruda, famous for its wines, and the entrance to the bare Sutorina valley. Soon there are unforgettable views as you cross into Montenegro and descend upon the majestic Gulf of Kotor, the Boka Kotorska.

PRACTICAL INFORMATION FOR
DUBROVNIK AND VICINITY

HOW TO GET THERE. By plane. You can reach Dubrovnik from London, Paris, Rome, Vienna and other major European cities by direct or connecting flights throughout the year. In season, there are direct flights from many additional cities.

By boat. The express boats from Rijeka stop at Dubrovnik, some continuing to Bar (Montenegro), and Corfu and Igoumenitsa in Greece. There are also regular additional links with Corfu and Patras and the Italian ports of Ancona and Bari.

By train. There is no direct mainline rail link with Dubrovnik, so take the through train from Belgrade or Zagreb to Kardeljevo on the coast from where there is a bus on to Dubrovnik (journey time 2 hrs.).

By bus. Regular buses serve the whole of the coast and provide links with major inland cities. Most travel agents operate regular all-in tours between main inland cities and Dubrovnik, lasting two or more days.

WHEN TO GO. The best times to go to Dubrovnik are between the start of April and the end of June, and during September and October. These are the most pleasant periods of the year; generally the weather is ideal and you avoid the July and August crowds. On the other hand, you would miss the Summer Festival, which begins on the 10th July each year, continuing until 25th August.

During the entire six weeks the public can watch one or more performances each day. There is a succession of operas, ballets, plays, concerts, and evenings of folklore music and dances. Yugoslav and foreign artists and ensembles take part. The performances by groups specializing in folk dances and music have a sparkling vitality and fascinating color. Lovely old buildings and other parts of the town serve as backdrop for the festival.

HOTELS AND RESTAURANTS. The city of Dubrovnik contains many excellent hotels, but if you plan on going during the high season—which coincides with the famous festival—it is highly advisable to book well in advance, as the place is packed. Even in the "shoulder" months of May/June and September, hotels are often full. However, an increasing number of them now open year round.

Other accommodations include guest houses and private households—check with the local Tourist Information Center (see Useful Addresses end of this chapter).

The restaurants we have listed below are additional of course to those in the hotels and represent but a selection from the numerous establishments that have sprung up of late.

Cavtat. Old village and summer resort in a beautiful bay, 17 km. (10½ miles) southeast of Dubrovnik, notable for water sports. *Croatia* (L), 480 rooms. Indoor and outdoor pools, tennis, casino, nightclub. Above rock and pebble beach, a short distance from village. *Albatros* (E), 246 rooms. About 1½ km. (one mile) from town; disco, open-air and indoor pools. Nearby is *Epidaurus* (M), 328 rooms. Older, but well-modernized. Closer to town is *Cavtat* (M), 109 rooms. *Makedonia* (M), 84 rooms; recently renovated, near center. *Supetar* (M), 39 rooms. By the town's small harbor. All are by or near rock and pebble beaches.

Dubrovnik. There is actually only one hotel *in* the old town: *Dubravka* (M), 22 rooms, a few with bath.

Newest and plushest is the *Belvedere* (L), over 200 rooms; several restaurants, nightclub, open-air and indoor pools, sports hall, bathing areas, and superb views. It is 1½ km. (one mile) east of the walled city, with regular boat service in high season.

If you want to be within strolling distance of the city, choose somewhere in either the Ploče or Pile district near the walls: *Argentina* (E), 155 rooms, some (M); and *Villa Dubrovnik* (E), 56 rooms. Both in Ploče district, each with swimming pool, and own section of artificial beach of rocks and paving stones. On the Pile side of the walls, the grand old *Imperial* (E), 108 rooms, casino, retains an aura of more old-fashioned elegance in the palatial style of 1910, but no beach. Good service, now renovated and enlarged, but choose a room away from the terrace and its noisy music.

About three km. (two miles) from the city walls and rapidly reached by frequent bus service is the peninsula district of Lapad, dominated by Petka mountain. Here there is a large number of hotels, often with their own lovely gardens, in a marvelously peaceful setting with plenty of sports facilities. Fringing a deep bay in the peninsula is a series of accommodations of various categories. On a headland, for example, is *Dubrovnik Palace* (E), 325 rooms; indoor and open-air pools, tennis; nightclub; generally very popular. Nearby is the smaller *Splendid* (M), 61 rooms, set in a small pinewood beside its own artificial beach. A peaceful and pleasant spot.

Several hotels grouped near or above the public beach of Sumratin in this bay are *Kompas* (E), 130 rooms; indoor and open-air pools; *Park* (E),

225 rooms; open-air and indoor pools, nightclub; and *Sumratin* (M), 70 rooms. The nearby beach inevitably gets crowded, so if you are in this area check your hotel has its own pool. Otherwise there is bathing off the rocks in various parts of Lapad, though the area is becoming increasingly built-up.

On the farthest part of the peninsula is the Babin Kuk development comprising a number of hotels set by or near a tastefully designed shopping precinct with boutiques, galleries, restaurants and taverns, and extensive sports facilities. Among the hotels sharing these facilities are *Dubrovnik President* (L), 169 rooms; an impressive structure soaring up from its own bathing area and served by funicular-type lifts. Nightclub, open-air and indoor pools. Nearby the *Argosy, Plakir* and *Tirena,* all (E) with open-air and indoor pools, are linked by the attractive shopping precinct. Newest, with similar facilities, is the *Minčeta,* a short distance away. In the same area, *Neptun* (M) has 210 rooms; open-air pool, nightclub; bathing area with rocks.

In a delightfully tranquil spot about ten km. (six miles) from town, Dubrovnik Marina at **Komolac** features *Dvorac Sorkočević* (M), a restored patrician house with a few rooms.

Restaurants and Cafés. Most of the following are in the old town, unless otherwise specified, and most are private. *Amfora* (E), at Gruž Harbor. *Domino* (E), Od Domina 3, excellent steak house. *Piccolo Mondo* (E), Zamanjina 8, fish specialties. *Prijeko* (E), Prijeko 14, intimate atmosphere, local and fish specialties; heavily tourist-oriented. *Ragusa II* (E), Zamanjina 12, again local and fish specialties; also heavily tourist-oriented. *Ankora* (M), Siroka 1, Dalmatian and fish specialties. *Dubravka* (M), Brsalje 1, near Pile Gate with tables set under shady trees. *Jadran* (M), P. Miličevića 1. Atmospheric setting in cloisters of former monastery. *Wanda* (M), Prijeko 8, fish and other local specialties.

Farther afield but worth the journey are *Gostiona Oaza* at Gruda, about 25 km. (15 miles) east of Dubrovnik; *Konavoski Dvori,* in a renovated watermill at the mouth of the river Ljuta, about 35 km. (20 miles) east; and *Soline,* by the sea at Zaton, about 15 km. (nine miles) west. All serve local specialties.

Koločep. Unspoilt island near Dubrovnik; season Apr. to Oct. *Villas Koločep* (M), 110 rooms with central restaurant, near sandy beach. Regular boat service to Dubrovnik.

Lopud. Wooded island near Dubrovnik; season Apr. to Oct. *Grand* (M), 100 rooms; sandy beach. *Lafodia* (M), 196 rooms; pebble beach. *Dubrava-Pracat* (I), 94 rooms; in the village near the sandy beach. Boat service to Dubrovnik.

Mlini. Pleasant coastal hamlet in fertile area, 12 km. (7½ miles) from Dubrovnik. *Astarea* (M), 221 rooms; indoor pool, nightclub. Good service. Above pebble beach. *Mlini* (M), 93 rooms; in the village; friendly and efficient if a little noisy. Near pebble beach.

Mljet. Delightful wooded island, part of which is a national park. *Melita* (M), on an islet in a lake of the national park, and housed in a Benedictine monastery founded in the 12th century—an idyllic spot.

In the coastal village of **Pomena,** *Odisej* (M), 160 rooms, overlooks the attractive bay, near rocky beach.

Orašac. *Soderini Holiday Village,* major new development 20 km. (12 miles) north of Dubrovnik with self-catering apartments, and full entertainment and sports facilities. Over 400 apartments, two open-air pools, tennis, water sports facilities, disco.

Plat. Hamlet beyond Mlini. *Ambassador* (M), 300 rooms; indoor and open-air pools, tennis, disco. Perched on steep hill-side above small beach. A little isolated but near the airport. *Plat* (M), 346 rooms; indoor and open-air pools, disco. Near rock and pebble beach.

Šipan. Unspoilt island near Dubrovnik; season Apr. to Oct. *Šipan* (I), 90 rooms; short walk from sandy beach. Boat service to Dubrovnik.

Srebreno. Near Mlini and Dubrovnik; season Apr. to Oct. *Orlando* (M), 275 rooms. (M) and (I) villa annexes. Near pebble and shingle beach, tennis.

Ston. Astonishing little walled town at southern end of Pelješac peninsula. *Ston* (I), 22 rooms, some with bath.

Restaurant. Seafood aficionados are recommended to try the attractive *Koruna* eaterie.

HOW TO GET AROUND. Half or full day excursions take in all the main beauty spots and points of interest along the nearby coast, on the islands and inland. Don't miss the opportunity to see something of the interior, which is culturally as well as scenically so different (see chapters on Bosnia-Hercegovina and Montenegro).

By boat. There are regular local services and excursion trips to the islands of Koločep, Lopud and Šipan, as well as hydrofoils to Korčula and Mljet. In summer, a frequent service by motorboat links Dubrovnik with the nature reserve island of Lokrum, and there are other motorboat services to nearby resorts such as Cavtat.

By bus. There are excellent regular buses running up and down the coast and inland to Mostar, Sarajevo, Titograd, Ohrid, Belgrade and beyond. Local buses also link the port of Gruž, Lapad and Dubrovnik with each other.

By cable car. There is a cable car you can take to the top of Srdj mountain, where the view is guaranteed fabulous.

SPORTS. The emphasis of course is on the aquatic variety, with a number of hotels having their own beaches. Of several public beaches, the largest is the Sumratin at Lapad, which has a restaurant; elsewhere in Lapad you can bathe off the rocks, though this district has been developed in recent years. The beach of Ploče, near the Excelsior, also has a restaurant. At Pile, at the foot of the Lovrijenac fortress, is a rather narrow creek; if you can find the postern gate behind the Bishop's Palace, you can dive into 6–9 m. (20–30 ft.) of water from the rocks below it. Farther south, at Srebreno, Mlni and Cavtat, the bathing is better and less crowded, and there is good rock bathing on the island (and nature reserve) of Lokrum. (There are also several nudist beaches in the area.)

Water skiing and wind surfing facilities are offered by a number of hotels, notably in Lapad and at Cavtat. For fishing and skin diving, apply to the Tourist Information Center or to the fishing association (Orhan) at Lapad for the latest regulations.

Yachts can be hired, together with crew, from Orsan Yacht Club at Lapad. Yacht services are also available at the Dubrovnik Marina, Komolac, on the Ombla (Dubrovnik) river. Flotilla sailing arrangements are marketed ex-U.K.

MUSEUMS. In Dubrovnik. The Cathedral Treasury contains fine gold and silver reliquaries, including the skull of St. Blaise in the form of a Byzantine crown.

The Cultural and Historical Museum is a part of the Rector's Palace, and its exhibits give a picture of life in Dubrovnik from the early days up to the downfall of the Republic, particularly the 18th and 19th centuries. There are vases and porcelains, and a gallery of mainly Italian paintings brought home by sailors of the town.

The Ethnographical Museum, Maritime Museum and the **Aquarium** are each excellent of their kind. All in the fortress of St. John.

The Franciscan and Dominican Libraries contain ancient manuscripts, early incunabula, books and pictures. The Franciscan monastery additionally has an interesting small museum featuring its ancient pharmacy and some fine art treasures.

The Icon Collection is on Puča St., next to the Serbian Orthodox Church.

The Rupe Granary is an historical monument of the 15th-century and features a permanent exhibition of Yugoslav folk art.

The State Archives, in the Sponza Palace, house a priceless collection of historical documents from the year 1022 up to the present day. It includes agreements and guarantees signed by most of the heads of state of the great powers over the centuries. This may be closed for restoration, so check.

SHOPPING. There are plenty of shops in the Placa in Dubrovnik, and any number of boutiques in the side streets where you will find a wide range of articles, often in very good taste: leather goods, trinkets and carved-wood souvenirs, filigree, lace, handwoven textiles and other handicrafts. Prices may be slightly higher than elsewhere but not prohibitive. *Kuča Moda* on Puča Street has tasteful if expensive fashions. Original paintings and prints from the *Sebastian Gallery* by the Dominican Monastery might well become collectors' items.

USEFUL ADDRESSES. There is now a British Consulate housed in the same building as Atlas (the main travel agency in the area) at Pile 1. Many of the other major travel firms have branches here and provide full services. The Tourist Information Center is at P. Miličevića 1, at the Pile end of Placa in the old city of Dubrovnik. The head office for the Dubrovnik Summer Festival is od Sigurate 1, YU-50000, Dubrovnik (tel. 27996/7).

NIGHTLIFE. Most of the principal hotels in Dubrovnik have a night-club or restaurant with music. Otherwise, a popular spot is the *Labirint* open-air bar, surrounded by ramparts, near the Ploče portal. The *Lazaretti,* former city quarantine quarters built in the 17th century just outside the same Ploče portal, have been adapted as a leisure area that includes a disco and tavern. There are casinos at the *Belvedere, Imperial,* and *Libertas* hotels.

Frequent and excellent performances of national dances and songs are given by the Lindo folklore ensemble in Fort Revlin.

MONTENEGRO

The Unconquered Land

Anyone who knows Yugoslavia will know too the Yugoslavs' passion for freedom. Nowhere does this passion burn more fiercely and determinedly than in Montenegro. In all the region's history it has never been wholly subjugated—not the inland portions at any rate. And from Roman times these extraordinarily gentle, outstandingly hospitable heroes have been renowned for their valor.

Britain's greatest Liberal statesman William Gladstone, thundering in the House of Commons against the iniquities of Turkish oppression, said of the Montenegrins, "Those are men who, when asked to pay tribute offer stones. These are the men who dress the cowards into women's clothes, and whose wives, when need requires, boldly get hold of the gun."

Their independence lasted for 500 stormy years, and the national spirit of freedom remains unchanged, even though the Turks have gone forever, and even though this tiny mountain land is today no more than the smallest of the six federal republics.

Hemmed in by Bosnia-Hercegovina, the Dalmatian coast of Croatia, Serbia and Albania, Montenegro is the smallest republic not only in area but also in population, with a mere 580,000 inhabitants. The interior is dominated by the rugged Black Mountains that led the Venetians to give the whole province the name of Montenegro, which the Yugoslavs have translated literally as Crna Gora. Farther north are the Durmitor, Bjelašica, Komovi and Proketije ranges, each with at least a few green valleys and studded with beautiful lakes.

The especial charm of Montenegro is of something wild, yet warmly human, and there is no lack of surprises. Waterlily-ringed Lake Scutari or Skadar (Skadarsko Jezero), for instance, is not quite what you expect to see among majestically gaunt mountains. Many green Alpine valleys are equally unexpected. And, in further contrast, there is the magical 130-km. (80-mile) stretch of coast, so tragically hit by an earthquake in April 1979. Over 90 lives were lost in this tragedy which did incalculable damage to the region's economic life and cultural treasures. It will take many years to make good all the damage, but much has already been achieved, including the restoration of full tourist facilities in all the resorts and, stretching from the truly magnificent Gulf of Kotor—among the most remarkable landscapes of Europe—to the Albanian border, the coast has some of Yugoslavia's very finest beaches.

The inhabitants are as remarkable as the country in which they live. Their history is one of unceasing struggle ever since the foundation of the medieval Serb state of which they were originally citizens. While they are peaceful shepherds by choice the Montenegrins in times of war are terrifying fighters—as they showed very clearly in World War II—and have their own strongly individualistic mentality, which defies change. Some of them find it difficult to cope with the complexities of present-day life, and they detest compromise. Fiercely independent, influenced by the harsh conditions of their surroundings, they have something in common with the Highland Scots—mountaineers, and (in their absence only) a favorite subject for wry humor among their neighbors. This strong sense of independence also makes the Montenegrins a little unpredictable, so don't be too surprised if things don't always go according to schedule! But beneath their bluff exteriors, these people are extremely generous and warmhearted.

The Troubled Past

Montenegro's history is closely linked with that of Serbia, whose first ruling dynasty, the Nemanjas, was originally a noble Montenegrin family. Under the name of Zeta, a semi-independent Montenegro came within the sphere of influence of its northern neighbor, which between 1184 and 1389 was the leading Balkan power. Then, following the Turkish victory at the Battle of Kosovo, the Ottoman domination of southeastern Europe began. Serbia shrank northward and finally disappeared. Though isolated, Montenegro continued to resist, and despite numerous campaigns the Turks never wholly pacified the country.

Late in the 15th century Ivan Crnojević, chief of an important Montenegrin clan, left Žabljak, a fortified islet on Lake Skadar, to move farther away from Turkish pressure, and established himself in Cetinje, making it his capital.

Gradually, Crnojević obtained support from Montenegrin tribes sufficient to form a truly independent principality, which thanks to the heroism of these tough mountain people and the inaccessibility of the whole region, successfully defended itself not only against the Turks, but also against Venice and the Austrian Empire.

From the beginning of the 16th century, the country was governed by Orthodox Bishop-Princes, the family of Petrović-Njegoš particularly distinguishing itself in this office. For a while Montenegro was supported by

Russia, but at the close of the Napoleonic Wars Russia opposed the unification of the coast and the Gulf of Kotor with Montenegro, and the tiny
country perforce remained isolated.

Petar II, who reigned from 1830 until 1850, was the ablest of all Montenegro's priestly rulers, and introduced a number of reforms into his still
very backward country. He used to say of himself, "I am a prince among
the barbarians and a barbarian among the princes," which seems to suggest that not only was he an astute leader but he also possessed a sense
of humor.

After a successful campaign against the Turks, Montenegro at last won
a corridor to the Adriatic in 1878, at Bar and Ulcinj, by driving out the
Turkish occupiers. Austria, however, retained the northern coast till the
end of World War I. In 1910, Nicolas I declared himself King but, with
the creation of united Yugoslavia in 1918, retired to Paris, where he died
in 1921.

The Gulf of Kotor

If your approach to Montenegro is from the north by the coastal road
from Dubrovnik, you are not likely quickly to forget your first impressions
of it. After crossing the "border" at the top of the Nagumanac Pass, you
descend into the bare Sutorina valley and so to one of the most striking
and unexpected features of the Yugoslavian coast, the Gulf of Kotor. This
extraordinary arm of the sea probing into a seemingly impenetrable barrier
of mountains consists of two main bays, separated by a strait only 300
m. (330 yards) wide, and subdivided into many smaller bays. The inner-
most point of this deep, mountain-ringed inlet is some 30 km. (20 miles)
from the open sea. The Gulf begins peacefully enough with normal rocky
hill-sides sloping down to the sea. But as you progress farther and farther
inland along its shores, you find yourself traveling by a curving road suspended a little above sea-level on a steep mountainside that soars away
out of sight.

The history of the Gulf of Kotor is closely linked with that of Venice,
whose territory it was until Napoleon's abolition of the maritime Republic.
The ports of this region sent many great sailors to serve Venice, whose
art and architecture are still everywhere apparent.

While the inland parts of Montenegro were never conquered by Turkish
invaders, the coast was only partly recovered in 1878, when the Great
Powers assigned the northern portion to Austria. In recent years the Republic of Montenegro has made strenuous efforts to develop tourism in
the region. Some think the efforts made have been too successful in regions
such as Budva and the coast immediately to the south. But happily the
Gulf of Kotor has acquired nothing to spoil it.

Our first visit is to Igalo, near the Montenegrin "frontier," a spa whose
mud is renowned for its curative properties. Nearby is the outer Bay of
Topla, where two peninsulas almost close the only outlet to the sea. The
small island of Mamula looks like a ship at anchor from here. On our right,
is the Oštri Rt—the pointed cape upon the edge of which is perched the
village of Prevlaka, with Luštica just beside it. In Topla church there are
several ancient and precious icons.

Herceg-Novi and Beyond

Herceg-Novi, below 1,500-m.-high (5,000 ft.) Mount Orjen, was founded in 1382 by King Tvrtko I of Bosnia with the dual objectives of giving his country an outlet to the sea, and of ensuring a supply of salt. The town was totally destroyed by the Turks at the end of the 16th century, who then rebuilt and fortified it. The Venetians took it two centuries later, and held it until its brief seizure by Napoleon. It was under Austrian rule until 1918.

The main square has a Turkish clocktower and the fountain of Karadža Bey, and the city is crowned by fortifications in three styles—Turkish, Venetian and Austrian. The Orthodox Church, although relatively new, is built in the medieval Byzantine style discussed in the chapter on Serbia. The Botanical Gardens are memorable for tropical and subtropical plants. Indeed, Herceg-Novi is a place of flowers, not least during the Mimosa Festival which lasts several weeks from January to March; the highlight is the special day of the Mimosa Harvest, usually in February, when the blossoms are gathered from tens of thousands of shrubs and there is a procession through the town. Another attractive feature of the resort is the 6½-km. (four-mile) path along the shore to Igalo, with plenty of small restaurants along the way.

From Herceg-Novi there is a pleasant full-day excursion from the Španjola Fort to 1,430-m.-high (4,700 ft.) Mount Radostak. From the summit there is a tremendous view across the Bay of Kotor, wild yet beautiful. 16 km. (ten miles) from Herceg-Novi, on the slopes of the Subra Mountains, there is excellent skiing to be had as late as the month of May. Après-ski could be to bathe in the warm waters of the Adriatic.

A footpath connects Herceg-Novi with the Monastery of Savina, restored in 1839. In the little 11th-century church nearby, there are some remarkable frescos. The monastery is named after the first head of the Serbian-Orthodox Church, St. Sava Nemanja, of the medieval Serbian royal house. The monastery library is of exceptional beauty and value, possessing among many other treasures a collection of manuscripts of church and monastic rules known as the *Savinska Krmčija,* dating from the 13th century and considered unique. The monastery was damaged in the earthquake, but can be visited.

In the days when the sailors of the Bay of Kotor were famous for their long and daring voyages, it was their habit, on their return, to salute the monastery with a salvo of cannon, to which the reply was a peal of the monastery bells.

The coast road now descends to the little Bay of Meljine, and beyond Zelenika we pass the picturesque Kumbor channel.

The straits grow steadily narrower, until barely 300 m. (330 yards) separates us from the great out-thrust of the second of the main peninsulas that so forthrightly divide the Gulf into three or four great saltwater bays. In the Middle Ages the men of the Boka used to stretch great chains across the narrowest point in times of war, to prevent enemy ships from penetrating to the inner bays. Nowadays you can cross it by ferry boat from Kamenari to Lepetane, which will save time (if there isn't a long line) but means you will miss the most dramatically beautiful shores of the inner bays.

Once past the narrows beyond Kamenari our road turns away sharply westward through Kostanjica to Morinj, with its magnificent view five km. (three miles) across the bay to Risan, passing on the way the waterfall of Sopot, which pours out of a hole in the cliff below the road.

Risan is a pleasant little village, and it is still proudly conscious of its past. In the third century it was already an important Illyrian city. After the Roman conquest, it was here that Teuta, Illyria's last Queen, took refuge. When the remorseless enemy once more caught up with her, she drowned herself in the limpid waters of the bay rather than become their prisoner. The village still possesses some Roman mosaics, of which the most remarkable is that of Hypnos, god of sleep. You'll find this behind protective railings on the left as you turn into the village, off the main road on the minor road to Nikšić. Much of the town's commercial property once came from the guides it provided to escort caravans into the interior of the country and back.

Indeed, a network of rugged minor roads winds into the Krivošije region dominated by Mount Orjen, offering some splendid mountain scenery with glimpses of the blue waters of the bays far below. The inhabitants of the Krivošije are peaceable shepherds who, in time of war, become particularly ferocious soldiers. In the 19th century they refused conscription into the Austrian army. A force of 20,000 trained troops was dispatched by Vienna to break their defiance, and succeeded in surrounding them, but was then forced to retreat in face of intrepid sharpshooters. During World War II the local resistance was probably the most ruthless of any in occupied Yugoslavia.

Back on the *Magistrala,* past the Monastery of Banja, you will see the two small islands of St. George (Sveti Juraj) and Our Lady of Škrpjelo, either of which can be reached by boat in ten minutes from the next little town, Perast. St. George has a sad air, with tall cypress trees marking the sailors' burial ground beside the renovated Benedictine chapel. The island inspired Böcklin's well-known painting, *The Isle of the Dead* (which in its turn was the inspiration for Rachmaninov's hauntingly melancholy music of the same name).

The other island was originally little more than a reef, but the sailors of Boka brought great stones to the place, which they piled upon the rock until they had accumulated enough to provide the foundations for a rather austere looking church, appropriately named Our Lady of the Rocks, which soon became a popular place of pilgrimage. The interior and its adjoining museum are in marked contrast however, containing a number of fine 17th-century paintings by the local master Kokolja, and many gifts, including hundreds of silver votive tablets, from grateful sailors to their patron saint. There are still Dominican nuns in residence who will show you around this wonderfully peaceful place. Two popular feasts are held here every year, on 22nd July, and 15th August, when in addition to a procession of garlanded fishing boats, there is folk dancing in the local peasant costumes, and various country sports and games are held.

The Boka has always produced the best seafarers of the Adriatic, and the cream of these came from Perast. They founded the earliest maritime fraternity both of that sea and also of the Mediterranean. Their Common Law was already in force by A.D. 809, though this was revised and its statutes codified in 1463. Perast gave Venice some of her greatest admirals and sailors, and on the recommendation of the Venetians, Peter the Great sent 60 young Russian noblemen to the Naval School of Perast founded in 1698. In time, they provided the nucleus for the first Russian fleet in the Baltic which, under the command of Matija Zmajević, three times inflicted defeat upon the Swedes ruling those waters.

However, Perast's past is not solely a tale of naval victories. The Turks launched repeated land campaigns against it, but always in vain, their most crushing defeat being in 1654 when Mehmed Rizvanajić, the Bosnian Moslem convert leader of the Turkish forces, was killed in battle. His prayer carpet may be seen in the Church of St. Nicolas, which also contains some wonderful church robes and ornaments worked by pious country-women, and an exquisite Renaissance crucifix.

Perast is a splendid little town full of 17th- and 18th-century Baroque palaces, but was sadly very badly damaged by the 1979 earthquake. However, the whole place is a protected historic monument and will undoubtedly be restored. The finest building is the Palača Bujović, once the residence of a Venetian captain, now the town museum (closed for restoration). The eclipse of this once-powerful and prosperous city began with the Napoleonic Wars, when embattled British and French squadrons repeatedly disrupted the normal life of the Adriatic with fire and blockade. The coming of steamships sealed the fate of the ancient port, whose past glories can be recalled now only in the Maritime Museum of Kotor.

The farthest of the bays is the Bay of Kotor. East of Perast is Orahovac and, above it, the little church of St. George, said to have been of great importance in the time of the Nemanjić kings, but since much altered. At this point you can turn off to follow a shore-side road south through Dobrota. This is the collective name of a group of villages containing many Venetian-style houses and churches from the period when this section of the Gulf prospered as a merchant shipping center. Again, many were damaged in the 1979 earthquake, but this shore-side road makes a more attractive approach to Kotor than does the main road.

Medieval Kotor

The arrival at Kotor, some 16 km. (ten miles) by road from Perast, is even more exciting if you catch your first glimpse of the extraordinary water-maze from the sea. You will feel that you have come somehow to the World's End when you reach this inmost recess of this inland sea. The town itself, surrounded by formidable medieval ramparts, would be striking anywhere. What makes it seem almost unearthly is its setting at the very end of a long, narrow bay immediately backed by the almost-sheer, pale, 1,749-m.-high (5,738 ft.) wall of Mount Lovčen.

The medieval Serbian Nemanja Kings were quick to realize the immense strategic importance of this almost hidden port, and awarded it a number of special privileges. Later the Venetians did the same, granting the town semi-independence. In 1807 it was occupied by Napoleon's General Gauthier. Encouraged by the English, the Montenegrins and the people of Boka united, rose up against the French and besieged Kotor. Gauthier seized part of the cathedral treasure and minted silver coins with it to buy food for his troops, and some of these numismatic rarities are on view in the Maritime Museum. On one side they bear an N with an Imperial Crown and the motto *Dieu protège la France*—which, by 1813, was very necessary indeed. On the other are the words, *Cattaro en état de siège*—

1813. The French surrendered in January 1814, but at the Congress of Vienna the Russians successfully opposed the promised unification of the Gulf region with Montenegro, and the whole coast became Austrian.

Alas, this remarkable little town was among the worst hit by the 1979 earthquake and it will be some years before it is restored to its former glory. The situation concerning its most important monuments is constantly changing so it is wise to consult the Tourist Information office on arrival. One of the first buildings to be restored, however, was the unique Maritime Museum, already mentioned. It is housed in the Grgurin Palace and gives a very complete idea of the seagoing activities of the Boka region. The Seamen's Guild of Kotor is one of the oldest in Europe, its records going back to A.D. 809. The most interesting building in Kotor is unquestionably its 12th-century Romanesque-style Cathedral of St. Tryphon. This also suffered badly in the earthquake, and is likely to be closed until 1995; interestingly, restoration work has revealed traces of an earlier basilica. There is a legend that Kotor bought its patron saint with gold. Apparently in A.D. 890 a ship in difficulties sought refuge in the Boka with a cargo of sacred relics for sale in Europe (one of the biggest exports from the Near East at that time), including the head of a Byzantine saint by the name of Tryphon, who had suffered martyrdom by decapitation. The inhabitants of Kotor, who had for some time been feeling the lack of a patron saint of their own, bought the head and other relics of the saint for 300 pieces of gold. The third of February is the anniversary of this strange transaction, and every year it is celebrated with an important fair. The people wear their folk costumes, and there is peasant dancing and other festivities.

The cathedral was built in the 12th century on the foundations of a ninth-century church, and is dominated by its two Renaissance towers, which were added following an earlier earthquake which had almost totally destroyed the town. The ciborium, or baldachin, a kind of sculptured stone canopy over the high altar, is one of a number of such structures in Yugoslavia. The reliefs carved upon it recount the life story of the saint. There are countless other objects of great historic and artistic value in the cathedral and its treasury.

Other interesting churches in Kotor were closed after the earthquake, but most will re-open as restoration progresses. One that has re-opened is the small Orthodox basilica of St. Luke, built in the 12th century in Byzantine style, and containing innumerable icons, some of great value; another is 13th-century St. Mary, built in a style reminiscent of the Serbian monasteries. Here you will find another great work of art, formerly in the cathedral: a silver panel in bas-relief (1440) by John of Basle, a wandering artist whose condition of chronic bigamy carried him all the way to Kotor by way of escape. As far as civil architecture is concerned, there are the patrician homes of the Bysanti, Prima and Drago families. The City Tower was built in 1602 over the ancient "Turris Torturae," or Torture Tower, the clock being added as a peace offering from the French invaders in 1807. This overlooks the spacious main square of Oktobarske Revolucije, just within the main Sea Gate (1555), the town's social center and an excellent setting for local festivities.

An excursion from Kotor is to the Vrmac Peninsula northwest of the city, perhaps leaving the coast road at Prčanj to climb Mount Vrmac, from which you can see Dobrota across the water. Although only 760-m.-high (2,500 ft.), Mount Vrmac was a landmark familiar to countless great medi-

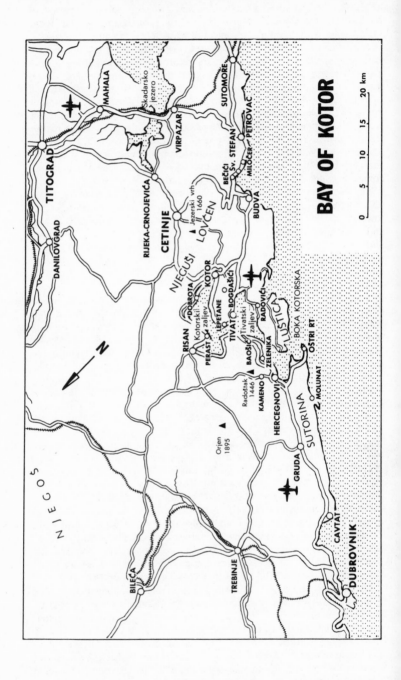

BAY OF KOTOR

0   5   10   15   20 km

eval sailors—the welcome sign that yet another dangerous voyage had been safely accomplished. One of the last of these sailors was Ivo Visin, who sailed away in 1852 in a locally-built ship to make a circumnavigation of the globe. Prčanj reached the peak of its prosperity in the 18th century, and there are a number of fine baroque houses of the period there, also a large neo-Renaissance church well adorned with paintings and sculptures.

Rounding the northern tip of the peninsula, where the gap separating it from the opposing coastline is so narrow that strong swimmers have swum it despite the current, you come to Lepetane (the name coming from the Italian *le putane* for the ladies of easy virtue who flourished here) set among tall palms and flowering shrubs. In this obviously attractive spot, the Venetian Republic established a sort of glorified brothel to give a welcome to sailors visiting the ports of the Boka.

The circuit of the peninsula from Kotor and back is only some 32 km. (20 miles), and about halfway round, in the southwest, is the industrial town and port of Tivat, which has an airport. It's a popular tourist center, and there is a big open-air summer stage. Just north of Tivat, at Lastva and Pržno, are a number of good bathing beaches. Just south of it, near the base of the peninsula, are three small islands, one of which is an important tourist-settlement.

After Kotor the *Magistrala* bypasses both these peninsulas and climbs to Trojica, from which there is a magnificent view of the Budva and Kotor bays. The old fortifications here remind us that this was the frontier between Venice and later Austria, and the tiny independent principality of Montenegro. It was here that Napoleon's General—later Marshal— Marmont had discussions with the Prince Bishop Petar I in 1807, in an unsuccessful effort to bring Montenegro in on the French side.

Trojica, six km. (four miles) south of Kotor, is the meeting place of no less than five roads, and one of them (the renowned Serpentine) eventually leads to Lovčen and the 19th-century Montenegrin capital of Cetinje, to be described later.

Budva and Beyond

The *Magistrala* continues from Trojica 20 km. (12 miles) south to Budva, where there are more beaches than can be found on much of the Dalmatian coast to the north. This area was badly hit by the 1979 earthquake, and most older and many modern buildings were damaged or destroyed. All the tourist amenities have been re-established and expanded, the damaged walls restored and the charming old town re-opened to visitors. The first glimpse of Budva bay is unforgettable: steep, scrub-covered mountains slope down to a beach-fringed shore, and there at the northern end of the bay stands Budva itself.

The old town is delightful. Built within 15th-century walls on a tongue of land thrust into the southern Adriatic, with a history going back to Phoenician times, it also possesses the remains of an ancient Greek cemetery. When the Roman Empire split in two, Budva was a frontier-town between the halves, ruled respectively from Rome and Constantinople. It was Venetian for four centuries, and it was the architects of the maritime Republic who gave it its present appearance. During the recent restoration, every stone was numbered in order that the original should be faithfully recreated. There are a number of old churches, including the tiny church of St. Mary, originally part of a medieval monastery, now sheltering an archeological collection. Nearby you can see traces of an ancient basilica. Part of the walls now house an artists' colony and the whole place makes a magnificent back-drop for cultural performances of all kinds in the summer. The so-called "mosaic beach" of nearby Bečići is acknowledged to be one of the best on the Montenegrin coast, so that it ranks among the first half dozen in Yugoslavia. Budva and its surroundings have become one of the biggest tourist-centers of the coast, with a marked degree of sophistication.

9½ km. (six miles) by road south of Budva (five by sea) is the quite enchanting little village of Sveti Stefan. Originally it was an island, but is now connected to the mainland by an artificial causeway. In 1945 this charming old settlement was virtually deserted. Becoming aware of its potential, the Montenegrins built an original tourist-complex comprising the whole village. Sveti Stefan's bathing beaches are the fringes of the narrow causeway linking the town with the mainland. It once possessed powerful fortifications to withstand Turkish raids from their advanced base at Ulcinj only 65 km. (40 miles) to the south, but war and neglect slowly reduced the little town to a decorative ruin which has been expertly restored, each cottage being beautifully transformed into a self-contained apartment, making this a showpiece of the tourist industry.

On the mainland, north of Sveti Stefan, is Miločer, once the summer palace of the royal family, now a hotel and a particularly peaceful spot. Above Miločer is the tiny Monastery of Praskavica, containing some interesting frescos. A number of large hotels have been built in this once remote and peaceful region.

As you travel farther south, through olive groves and delightful coastal scenery, you are actually on a long and quite narrow bridge of land that separates the sea from the freshwater Lake Scutari. It is only 24 km. (15 miles) as the crow flies from the coast to the lake, but the mountain range of Rumija climbing sharply at your left hand to a height of 1,578 m. (5,177 ft.), keeps the two worlds apart, though linked by an excellent road from Petrovac on the coast to Titograd.

Petrovac is only ten km. (six miles) south of Sveti Stefan but, before we reach it, we skirt the great crag of Skoči Devojka—"maiden's leap"— so called because of the legend that a local beauty, pursued by lustful Turks, leaped from there to her death in the sea far below, rather than suffer a fate that is popularly supposed to be worse than death. Petrovac, surrounded by vineyards and crowned by a crumbling fortress, has become a very popular holiday resort, now restored after the earthquake. Its Roman mosaics prove that it has survived through 20 stormy centuries. Its fine sandy beach is crowded enough during the summer.

18 km. (11 miles) farther on is Sutomore, another modern resort, completely rebuilt since the earthquake; but pause on the way to glance at the Gradište Monastery which has three churches and 17th-century frescos. Two great fortresses, Haj and Nehaj built by the Turks, stand up gauntly against the skyline, just before Sutomore. Some of the inhabitants of the region, known as *Spič*, still wear their attractive peasant costumes.

Beyond Sutomore the *Magistrala* leads to Bar, the terminal point of a spectacular railway linking Belgrade with the extreme south coast of Yugoslavia. This line was completed in the 1970s and is an outstanding feat of engineering, for it penetrates apparently impregnable mountains on its way, in the process passing through dozens of tunnels and across scores of bridges. Apart from being a remarkable achievement, it also provides a scenically unforgettable, if slow, journey.

Bar is a major and growing port, connected by ferry across the Adriatic with Bari in Italy. Inland from Bar lie the remains of Stari Bar immediately below the highest peak of the Rumija Mountains and the ruins of its Turkish fortress, an area particularly badly hit by the earthquake. The ruins remind us that it was finally seized by the Montenegrins after many fierce skirmishes only as recently as 1878 (seen through the eyes of eternity, that is!). The remains of Stari Bar are quite extensive, with several ruined churches, a medieval palace and aqueduct—all set amidst a tangle of shrubs and wild flowers. Below these remains, the present Stari Bar had a certain picturesque and disheveled charm prior to the earthquake, but will really have no place on tourist itineraries for some time to come.

From Bar the *Magistrala* continues for 30½ km. (19 miles) to its southern terminal at Ulcinj, and into a different world—a world of mosques and minarets and Ottoman corsairs. It was in 1571 that the Sultan Suleiman II based pirates in Ulcinj, with orders to harass Venetian shipping in the Adriatic wherever they might find it. They arrived accompanied by their negro servants, a few of whose descendants are in evidence here, the only colored Yugoslavs in existence. These settler pirates soon began to act entirely on their own account and for their own benefit, without thinking too closely which ships they attacked.

Ulcinj has a bustling market, at its best on Tuesdays and Fridays. Of its colorful past it has rather little to show except some crumbling fortifications, and a fortress castle, occupied until recently by various Albanian families. Part of it has been adapted as tourist accommodations. The original occupants obviously did not feel strongly about the conservation of archeological remains, as they cheerfully employed stones bearing Roman and Greek inscriptions for current domestic needs such as blocking up a drafty window, or as the hearthstone for their cooking. The 1979 earthquake was felt particularly strongly here, too, but most of the restoration work has been completed, and the main tourist area of Velika Plaža ("Long Beach") was very little affected. This lies about four km. (2½ miles) south of the town, with a number of modern hotels set beside a huge beach. The gray silky sands here are radioactive and said to produce remarkable results among those suffering from rheumatic complaints, so it is quite common to see visitors burrowing hollows in the beach in which to lie covered up to their necks in sand.

A few kilometers farther south you come to the River Bojana, the border with Albania. On the island of Ada in the river is a particularly well-equipped nudist center.

Exploring Inland Montenegro

Even in a country as strikingly beautiful as Yugoslavia, inland Montenegro stands out. It is not only the sheer beauty and variety of the scenery and the friendly welcome given by the local people that remain in the mind: there is something, too, in the very atmosphere of this strange, quiet region of remote, towering mountains, lowering gorges, and green valleys, that suggests peace in a land which has rarely known it till recent years.

Cetinje

Our first stop in inland Montenegro is the curious little former capital, Cetinje, with the embassies and official residences built by the Great Powers little more than a century ago, when Montenegro's independence was formally recognized. There is a good road from Budva, but the route we shall take climbs the mountainside from the former Montenegrin-Austrian frontier-post at Trojica (which we have already called at on our way along the coast), high above Kotor.

This latter road, known as the "Serpentine" because of its innumerable hairpin bends, is one of the most spectacular in Europe, and affords breathtaking views from what feels like the side of a precipice. It's also a very narrow road, so if you are nervous of heights you would do better to keep to the main road from Budva. Not far from the top we come to the fertile fields of Njeguši, birthplace of Montenegro's great poet-ruler, Petar II Petrović-Njegoš: his house is now a museum. From here, it is only a short and comparatively easy run into the old capital of Cetinje, but the journey is a tiring hour or more in a good car, and much longer by bus.

Cetinje lies in a fertile bowl of the bare *karst* limestone mountains, snow-bound for four or five months of the year. Today, it is quite a modern small city, but interesting both for its fine site surrounded by mountains and its historical associations. It was founded in 1484 by Ivan Crnojević as better suited for defense against increasing Turkish pressure. His successor, Juraj, had the country's first printing press brought from Venice in 1494, and it was employed in an Orthodox monastery built by Ivan, in producing religious works of various kinds. The first book printed in a Yugoslav language may be seen here. This monastery was the residence of the Prince-Bishops who ruled the country from the 16th century, though it was repeatedly devastated in Turkish raids on the city. The present building dates from 1785. Close beside the monastery is the sinister round Tablja Tower, where in those fierce days (up to less than a century ago) the Montenegrins used to expose the heads of the Turks they had slain.

Cetinje, too, was badly devastated in the 1979 earthquake, but most of its important historic sights, such as the Biljarda Palace and the former house of King Nicolas described below, have been restored. The graceful Biljarda Palace adjoins the monastery and was built in the mid-19th century to be a more appropriate residence for Montenegro's rulers; it now contains the Njegoš Museum and, adjoining it, a giant detailed relief map of Montenegro, illustrating the towering peaks and deep valleys of this fascinating land. The Biljarda (Billiard Table) took its name from the trouble attendant on bringing up from the coast a quarter-size billiard table (still on view) when the palace was built. Close to the Biljarda the former house of King Nicolas, now the State Museum, is preserved almost as it was when occupied by the monarch who reigned for 58 years until his abdication in 1918. Among the exhibits are links with both the American President Roosevelt and the British Royal Family. Also near the Biljarda, the former Parliament now housing the History Museum and Art Gallery (it may still be closed for restoration), is worth a visit. Check, too, on the current whereabouts of numismatic and philatelic collections if you're an enthusiast in either, for the currency and stamps produced by independent Montenegro are now much prized. Scattered through the city are other large houses which served mainly as foreign embassies in the days of Montenegro's independence.

From Cetinje, a modern road leads in about 19 km. (12 miles) almost to the summit of 1,749-m. (5,738-ft.) Mt. Lovćen, now topped by an imposing mausoleum to Montenegro's most famous leader Petar II Petrović-Njegoš. Make sure the monument is open (normally 8 A.M. to 6 P.M.) before you start the beautiful but long, winding drive. When you get there, there are still about 450 steps to climb to reach the mausoleum itself, designed by Meštrović. Though only 38 when he died in 1850, Njegoš accomplished much for his small country. As Prince-Bishop he persuaded the turbulent tribal chiefs to introduce fair taxation and a codified set of laws based upon common right. As a poet his reputation is worldwide.

There is a story that well illustrates his, and his people's, fierce pride. When he was in Rome he was offered the chains of St. Peter to hold. The monk who was acting as his guide asked him why he did not kiss them in the usual way of a pilgrim and he replied, "No Montenegrin will ever kiss a chain!" His great epic poem, *The Mountain Wreath,* is a hymn to liberty that is still acknowledged as unequaled in the poetry of what is now Yugoslavia.

From the mausoleum there is a stunning view. To the northwest is the intricate outline of the Kotorska Gulf, and northeast the chain of the Durmitor Mountains. Eastward lies the stony wilderness of Montenegro, with Cetinje at its heart, while southeast is the vast, waterlily-ringed Lake of Skadar, with Albania beyond. Southwest you can see the blue of the Adriatic and, on clear days, the faint line of the Italian coast on the horizon—all in one of the most romantic and magnificent views in Europe.

When we have looked round Cetinje, we can continue along the modern road that leads to Titograd, the Republic's more accessible modern capital. This route climbs out of Cetinje's fertile valley over bare mountains, and then drops into a wild valley. The road bypasses the remarkable and remarkably colorful village of Rijeka Crnojevića. It's a sort of tiny rural Venice, with brilliantly painted little boats on the river's backwaters as it flows toward Lake Skadar. The boats really are used for fishing: their colors are traditional. The river is spanned by two stone bridges, mellowed by the years and perfect in proportion.

As you travel this road, you look out across pools and marshes along Lake Skadar's shallow edge, where waterlilies grow in great clusters. In May, when they're in bloom, the colors of the flowers, their dark green leaves, the lake's blue and green water, the stony white mountainsides and a brilliantly clear blue sky make it impossible to pass by without stopping to gaze at the remarkable scene. But this lake is historic as well as scenically lovely, lying as it did in the heart of the medieval lands of Zeta. Thus, depending on which road you take to approach it, you will glimpse islets crowned by venerable churches or pass the massive walls of ancient fortresses.

Another modern road links Cetinje to the coast near Budva. This winding route passes through 32 km. (20 miles) of monotonously arid, near-desert mountain stretches alternating with small patches of fertile land. The road eventually zigzags down the side of the mountains facing the sea, to give magnificent views of the coast. If your object is merely to get to the coast—say on a circular tour from Budva or some other coastal resort—this is a useful route. But don't follow it just as a short cut and do yourself the disfavor of leaving the Serpentine out of your itinerary. It's almost worth coming to Yugoslavia just to experience this road and to see the strange sight of large coaches and cars creeping like beetles down a perpendicular mountain wall.

From Petrovac to Titograd

Following this modern road, with the railway never far away, we climb past the northwestern shoulder of the Rumija Mountains, among numerous ruined forts, which bear mute but unmistakable witness to the battles that once swept to and fro across these remote lands. When you reach the top of the Sutorman Pass you should stop to take a last look at the Bay of Bar and the Montenegrin coast before rounding countless hairpin bends to Virpazar. There is a pleasant local-style hotel and restaurant in Virpazar, which also has some attractive old houses, and offers possibilities of boating excursions and fishing on the lake. From here, you cross Lake Skadar on a long causeway and a few kilometers farther on enter Titograd.

Ptolemy mentions a town in this area in the second century by its Roman name of Dioclea. The earliest Slav immigrants settled here and gave the town the name of Podgorica, which it retained until 1944, when it was almost completely destroyed.

Rebuilt and renamed Titograd, it is the capital, cultural, economic and political center of Montenegro: a modern city with some striking architecture. But despite the war damage there is still something of old Podgorica to be seen, notably the castle fortress of the Nemanjić, the medieval kings of Serbia, which stands at the confluence of the rivers Zeta and Morača. Also there are the old Ljubić Mosque, the small tenth-century Church of St. George, the old Clock Tower and various Turkish houses. There are some fragments of Roman water conduits to be seen, and on the banks of the Zeta, the substantial remains of what was once Dioclea—now Duklja—with its forum, baths, temples and early churches.

Montenegro's Mountain Heart

The Durmitor Mountains afford some of the most magnificent scenery in Yugoslavia, and have been made a National Park. In many ways this region provides a striking contrast with some of the bare mountainsides to be seen not very far away. It is also quite different from the coast. Here you can see vast flowering fields, grazing herds of fat cattle, pine forests, deep canyons, and unexpected mountain lakes.

The road we will follow runs northwest from Titograd, through Danilovgrad. Just short of Bogetići, you will suddenly see among the cliffs the twin monasteries of Ostrog, reached by a branch road to the right, just over 1½ km. (one mile) beyond Bogetići.

Next comes Nikšić, 56 km. (35 miles) from Titograd, which, although today wholly industrial, is not lacking in interest. It was founded as Anagastum by the Romans, of which traces are still visible together with the ruins of "the Emperor's" bridge. Near the Church of Sveti Petar is another of the strange graveyards of the 16th-century heretic sect of the Bogomils.

Some 70 km. (45 miles) north of Nikšić and west of Žabljak (from the latter by a scenically magnificent but atrocious road) is Plužine in the Piva valley, where there is a newly built mountain settlement. The old town has been submerged under the artificial lake created for the hydroelectric power plant of Mratinje, but the well-preserved 16th-century Piva monastery has been reconstructed a few kilometers south of the town.

It is only well beyond Nikšić that the countryside assumes the wild beauty of the Durmitor Mountains, and for this you should take the right-hand road from Nikšić to Šavnik, a run of another spectacular 45 km. (28 miles). The town of Šavnik is divided by the deep gorge of the River Komarnica, from the banks of which there is excellent fishing. From the valley we now climb to the Sinjajevina plateau, 2,180 m. (7,150 ft.) above sea level. Once again the road plunges down over 915 m. (3,000 ft.) before we reach Novakovići, where we take the left fork to Žabljak, itself 1,370 m. (4,500 ft.) high, and a popular base for excursions into the mountains that almost surround the little town.

Here there are several hotels, including the recent Jezera, as well as private accommodations and a good camp site. The setting is idyllic and there are marvelous excursion possibilities, by road, on foot or on horseback. Great mountains and deep canyons are the special features of these landscapes, the canyons including the magnificent Tara tumbling beneath towering rock cliffs reaching up to well over 915 m. Three- or four-day raft trips can be arranged along the Tara (through Montenegroturist); camping along the way with equipment and food provided, it is an unforgettable experience. Winter is also a good time for Žabljak, which now has reasonable skiing facilities.

The famous Black Lake is only three kilometers (two miles) away, hidden in a deep pine forest beneath the mass of Mount Medvjed (Bear Mountain). A path winds its picturesque way through the forest to Lake Zminje and the Durmitor Hotel, from which there is a majestic view of the great peaks of Sljeme, Savin Kuk, Bogaz and, highest of them all, Bobotuv Kuk, 2,500 m. (8,200 ft.) above sea level.

The road from Žabljak to Plevlja, 74 km. (46 miles) away and the northernmost town in Montenegro, crosses the spectacular 163-m.-high (536 ft.) viaduct that spans the River Tara, the scene of dramatic Partisan activities during World War II. It then climbs once more through Kosanica to Odžak. Among Plevlja's numerous mosques that of Hussein Bey is outstanding. The Monastery of the Trinity, built in the 16th century, is just outside the town.

An attractive alternative road back to Titograd from Žabljak follows part of the magnificent Tara river to Mojkovac and Kolašin—a matter of some 160 km. (100 miles) by road. The gorges are among the most extraordinary sights of their kind in Yugoslavia—and it is a country of many gorges—rising almost sheer to over 915 m. above the river bed.

Kolašin, just off the main route, is on a ringroad that completely encircles the National Park on the Bjelašica Mountains, where there are a number of delightful lakes—Lake Biograd, 1,190 m. (3,900 ft.) above sea level, being the most attractive of them all. This is the center of the National Park, which is also developing winter sports facilities.

Kolašin itself is a small town dominated by a Turkish fortress. From Kolašin southward the main highway rises to cross a high ridge, then plunges spectacularly down into the valley of the Morača River. 26 km. (16 miles) from Kolašin you reach the astonishingly well-preserved Morača Monastery, founded in 1252 by Prince Stefan of the Nemanja dynasty, rebuilt in 1574. Morača's interior is completely covered with frescos, including traces of one portraying Elijah in the wilderness which dates from 1252. Most of the others date from the 16th and 17th centuries, and are rather traditional in style. South of the monastery you continue for about 40 km. (25 miles) along the Morača river gorge, yet another among Yugoslavia's innumerable scenic highlights.

Kolašin also serves as the gateway to little known eastern Montenegro, via the steep mountain road which leads over the 1,585-m. (5,200-ft.) Trešnjevik Pass to the village of Andrijevica, a good center for hunting and fishing trips. To the south stand the Komovi Mountains, rising to over 2,450 m. (8,000 ft.), and forming the frontier between Montenegro and Albania. Most tourists, however, avoid this adventurous route by following the wide, well-surfaced modern road round the Bjelašica Mountains' northern slopes to Ivangrad. From here another road runs eastwards through Rožaj to Peć or to Titova Mitrovica, north of Priština, both in Serbia's Kosovo region, described in our chapter on Serbia.

From Andrijevica we suggest two excursions. The first is north for some 20 km. (12 miles) to the 13th-century Monastery of Djurdjevi Stupovi, close to Ivangrad—not to be confused with the ruined monastery of the same name near Novi Pazar in Serbia. The second is for those who like magnificent scenery and fishing, and takes you south from Andrijevica, through Murino, to Plav, a small mountain resort by a lake in which, believe it or not, the trout often weigh up to ten kilo. (22 lb.).

The last halt before the Albanian frontier is the little oriental town of Gusinje, where in any case the road comes to an end. It is famous for peasant costumes and folk dancing.

It is from Murino that the road leading over the 1,830-m. (6,000-ft.) Čakor pass into Kosovo begins. It was over this terrifying road, covered at the time in deep snow, that the Serbian army—their king at their head—retreated in 1915 from the Austrians all the way into Albania. Scores of men slipped to their deaths from the icy rock-ledges along which they had to struggle—there was no road in 1915—and 1000s more died when they dropped exhausted and tried to sleep in the snow. The Čakor is Yugoslavia's highest pass and the road over it is rugged but scenically magnificent. Its summit marks the boundary between Montenegro and Serbia.

PRACTICAL INFORMATION FOR MONTENEGRO

HOW TO GET THERE. By plane. Many visitors reach Montenegrin resorts via Dubrovnik airport. There are also daily services between Belgrade–Titograd and Belgrade–Tivat.

By train. There is a spectacular route through rugged mountain ranges from Belgrade to the port of Bar. It's a slow journey, but well worth it.

By boat. Some of the express boats from Rijeka come as far as Bar, some continuing to Greece; Bar is also linked by ferry with Bari in Italy.

By bus. Regular services link towns and resorts with the rest of the coast and the interior.

WHEN TO GO. Like the adjoining coast of southern Dalmatia, Montenegro's has a long season, and it is best if possible to avoid the hottest, most crowded months of July and August. Winter can be pleasant and prices are very reasonable then. Inland Montenegro is a place in which to visit the mountains, and to enjoy a remarkable but little known range of monuments and museums. In summer the alpine climate of the Durmitor Mountains offers hot days followed by delightfully cool and refreshing nights, one of the region's greatest attractions. There is also a developing winter sports season, the main center being Žabljak. There is plenty of entertainment of all kinds along the coast throughout the summer. Budva's City Theater cultural program is in July and August.

HOTELS AND RESTAURANTS. There has been a rash of hotel development along the coast, not all of it beautiful, but providing good amenities against a usually fabulous backdrop of profuse vegetation and soaring peaks. Greater attention is now being given to self-catering facilities, while accommodations in private houses are also available in a number of resorts (enquire through Montenegroturist).

Except at a few centers, hotel accommodations in inland Montenegro are still relatively scarce, and often simple. However, establishments in categories (E) and (M) will have all or many rooms with bath or shower, and provided you are prepared to manage without a few luxuries for a night or two, you will find the others quite adequate for a short-term stay.

Apart from those within the main hotels, the choice of restaurants is fairly limited. One regional specialty you might like to try, if you can get it, is a whole sheep cooked in a vast cauldron filled with milk. It's an excellent gala dish, particularly if cooked over charcoal in the open air.

Andrijevica. On the road to Kosovo. *Komovi* (M), 45 rooms.

Bijelo Polje. *Sandžak* (M), 82 rooms, at lower end of price range.

Biogradsko Jezero (Lake Biograd). *Biogradsko Jezero* (I), 15 rooms.

Budva. Popular resort with old walled town and several beaches of coarse sand or stones. *Avala* (E), just outside the walls, has been rebuilt and is ultramodern, 220 rooms, indoor and open-air pools, nightclub; also some villas (M). *Mogren* (M), next door to Avala, 49 rooms, at top end of the scale.

A major new holiday center (M), at the top end of its category, recreates a charming, small-village atmosphere by the more extensive pebbly beach of **Slovenska Plaža,** a few minutes' walk away, 700 rooms, two open-air pools, and a wide range of sports and entertainment. A little farther on, by the large beach of **Bečići** (a few kilometers south of the old town) is a complex of hotels set in pleasant gardens, with swimming pools and varied sports facilities, beside extensive beach of pebbles and coarse sand: *Bellevue* (M), 310 rooms; *Mediteran* (M), 220 rooms; *Merkur* (M), 260 rooms; *Montenegro* (M), 350 rooms; and *Splendid* (M), 190 rooms. All at upper end of price range.

Restaurants. The *Vidikovac* on the main road offers a marvelous view overlooking the old town. Otherwise, *Sunce* in town near the harbor, and *Jadran,* by the marina.

Cetinje. The intriguing former capital of Montenegro. *Grand* (M), 200 rooms, at upper end of its price range; indoor pool, disco, in the Castle Park. New.

Restaurant. *Gradska Kafana,* fairly basic but with terrace and dancing. Well-placed for visiting the monuments.

Herceg-Novi. Attractive resort with splendid gardens set steeply on slopes by Bay of Kotor. *Plaža* (E), 320 rooms. Rebuilt hotel with indoor pool (closed in high season), mini-golf, nightclub, shops; rises like a massive glasshouse from the shore (stony and paved bathing beach). *Topla* (M), pavilion-type villas on terraces by the sea, tennis. *Rent-a-Villa* near the town center is a modern complex of self-catering accommodations. Private rooms also available in town.

At **Njivice,** reached by motorboat across the bay in about seven minutes: *Riviera* (M), over 200 rooms in several pavilions above pebbly beach, tennis, disco. Guests may share the facilities of other hotels in the town. Njivice lies a little beyond neighboring **Igalo,** where *Igalo* and *Tamaris* are both large (M)s, with pools and all facilities. (The Institute of Physiotherapy and Rehabilitation at Igalo offers cures through radioactive water and mud, but the resort lacks the charm of Herceg-Novi).

Restaurants. The following are all recommended: *Glicinia,* with terrace; *Gradski Restoran,* with shady terrace; and *Škver,* for fish specialties.

Kolašin. *Bjelašica* (M), 145 rooms. Reconstructed.

Kotor. Fabulous situation on inner Bay of Kotor. *Fjord* (M), 160 rooms, indoor and open-air pools, tennis. New about 500 m. or yards from old town on shore side. *Vardar* (M), 35 rooms. Renovated traditional hotel right in the old town.

Miločer. Peaceful small resort linked with Sveti Stefan and with beaches of coarse sand. *Maestral* (L), 160 rooms, some (E), indoor and open-air pools. *Miločer* (M), housed in the former summer residence of the Yugoslav royal family. Small, gracious, and with fine terrace restaurant; very quiet in extensive grounds which also contain the *Villa Miločer* (L), 60 rooms, some (E), in four villas, indoor pool in low season.

Mojkovac. Useful and attractive transit point near the Tara River in the heart of the interior. *Mojkovac* (I), 35 rooms. Modern.

Nikšić. A handy stop-off point en route to the Durmitor Mountains. *Onogošt* (M), 180 rooms, at lower end of its category.

Petrovac. Pleasant resort just off the main road with good facilities. *Pallas* (E), 180 rooms, pool. Newly rebuilt, near beach of coarse sand. *Castellastva* (M), 175 rooms, tennis, short stroll from beach. Friendly atmosphere. *Oliva Villas* (M), 110 rooms, tennis. *Rivijera* (M), 80 rooms, tennis.

About five km. (three miles) to the north: *As* (E), 180 rooms, indoor and open-air pools, sports facilities, disco. In splendid isolation by shingle beach linked by one-mile shore path to Petrovac.

Rožaje. An embryo winter sports center in the mountains near the South Serbia border. *Motel Turjak* (M), 13 rooms. *Rožaje* (M), 38 rooms.

Sutomore. Attractive small coastal village, almost entirely rebuilt, with beach of coarse sand and stones (also waterfront). *Nikšić* (M) and *Sozina* (M), the former new, are both near the waterfront.

Just south of the village, by the larger beach, is the *Zlatna Obala* (M), a complex of hotels terraced by narrow shingle and sand beach, including *Juzno More* and *Korali,* 870 rooms, indoor pool, tennis. Direct access to the main road which passes above the resort.

Sveti Stefan. A former fishing village within medieval fortifications on a tiny island linked to the coast and Miločer by a modern causeway; now converted into 110 apartments of a luxury holiday village. With open-air pool, casino, nightclub, sports center, open-air theater; utterly charming.

Titograd. The entirely rebuilt capital of Montenegro. *Crna Gora* (M), 130 rooms. Modernized. *Podgorica* (I), 60 rooms. Situated on the bank of the River Morača, with its restaurant terrace overlooking the Nemanja fortress. Attractive stone building. *Zlatica* (I), 64 rooms.

Restaurant. *Mareza,* 9½ km. (six miles) from the town on the Cetinje road, specializes in fish and has its own fish tanks to prove it. *Ribnica,* good national dishes.

Tivat. Resort and small port on the Bay of Kotor, now also the site of an international airport. Indifferent beach. *Palma* (E), 21 rooms, some (M). *Mimoza* (I), 69 rooms. In the town overlooking palm-fringed waterfront.

Toward neighboring **Lastva** is *Tivat* (M), 26 rooms.

Ulcinj. The southernmost seaside resort in Yugoslavia, close to the Albanian border. Much post-earthquake restoration has taken place in this appealing town stacked around a bay and sandy beach. There is a distinct oriental atmosphere to the place and several naturist complexes in the vicinity. *Galeb* (E), 173 rooms, now reconstructed, with indoor pool, and *Mediteran* (I), 244 rooms, are both in the town. About 1½ km. (one mile) out is *Albatros* (E), 75 rooms, some (M); indoor pool. Three private beaches, one reserved for nudists.

Around four km. (2½ miles) south of town is the 12.5-km.-long (eight miles) Velika Plaža ("Long Beach") of very fine, gently shelving sands, Yugoslavia's most extensive. Here there is the *Bellevue* (M), 370 rooms, sports facilities. Beach-side restaurant. *Grand-Hotel Lido* (M), 52 rooms and many bungalows, nightclub; at the top end of its category. Great location on the edge of the sands. *Olympic* (M), 130 rooms, nightclub, sports facilities. Latest is the *Otrant* hotel and apartments complex (M), by the beach with sports center; at the top of this category's price range.

16 km. (ten miles) to the south is the large and splendid *Ada Naturist Complex* (E) and (M), set on an island in the River Bojana forming the border with Albania. Offers a wide range of water sports and riding facilities.

Restaurants. There are several small pleasant private restaurants, among them *Stijena,* set in the rocks overlooking the Bay of Ulcinj from the south.

Žabljak. Mountain resort at around 1,370 m. (4,500 ft.) in spectacular setting among the highest peaks of the Durmitor range. *Planinka* (M), 150 rooms. *Jezera* (M), 103 rooms, indoor pool. *Žabljak* (M), 31 rooms, some (I).

HOW TO GET AROUND. By coach. There is a farflung network of coach services operating from Titograd's bus station. You can reach any sizeable town in Yugoslavia within 24 hours of leaving the Montenegrin capital.

Montenegroturist and the other main travel firms run a full range of excursions, and will make all your bookings and reservations.

By car. All major roads are surfaced, but narrow, and because of Montenegro's mountainous nature they are very winding. The main axes lead northward from Petrovac on the coast road across the northern edge of Lake Skadar, via Titograd and Bijelo Polje to Titovo Užice in Serbia; with a lateral connection from south of Bijelo Polje to Kosovo. A rugged branch road parallel and south of this route climbs the spectacular Čakor pass and descends to Peč.

SPORTS. Hunting and fishing are at their best in northern Montenegro. There are a number of state-run hunting preserves—for permission apply to the Secretariat for Agriculture in Titograd. The best fishing is in the rivers Lim and Tara, and their tributaries the Morača and Piva; also in the upper reaches of the Zeta near Nikšić. Biograd Lake near Kolašin, Black Lake near Žabljak, and the other neighboring glacial lakes are excellent for trout. Permits for fishing are granted at the Town Hall of the nearest town or village.

Spectacular rafting trips (usually three to four days, with camping equipment) through the Tara river gorges are arranged by Montenegroturist. Also, water skiing and wind surfing, notably in Budva (Bečići), Sveti Stefan and Ada (near Ulcinj).

USEFUL ADDRESSES. Montenegroturist are to be found in the majority of resorts. Their principal office is in the town of Budva. Most resorts have a local Tourist Information office, though the actual information dispensed is rather limited.

BOSNIA-HERCEGOVINA

Approaching the Orient

The domes and slender minarets scattered across the landscapes of Bosnia and Hercegovina lend them an oriental air, hardly to be wondered at when you recall that they formed part of the Ottoman Empire for no less than four centuries.

The Turkish heritage is evident not only in the architecture. A good many of the present-day inhabitants have also kept the faith of their former masters, although there are, and always were, numerous Christian districts and enclaves. The Moslems built their houses in the Turkish style, with balconies and interior gardens or patios. The older centers of their townships are crowded closely round the mosque and public fountain, with narrow, winding, haphazard alleys typical of all old oriental towns. The Christian villages, on the other hand, have wider streets. Their houses are far more spaced out. There are also a large number of modern towns that have been built since World War II, to replace others destroyed during the fighting.

Despite the harsh and rocky aspect of its treeless hilltops, the province of Hercegovina, in the south nearest the coast, is not inhospitable, for there are green mountain hollows *(polje),* and its rainfall and high sunshine record allow parts of it to produce excellent wine and three crops of tobacco in a single year. In addition there are everywhere disciplined ranks of olive groves and sturdy fig trees to testify to the fertility of this rough-looking soil.

There is no lack of distraction if you decide to spend a few days in this part of the country, among some of the most striking scenery in all Yugoslavia—but it is not a place in which to try to force the pace. Although the main routes are good, you will find secondary roads vary from adequate to poor.

Both Bosnia and Hercegovina afford magnificent scenery and fascinating towns. They also provide good rock climbing and mountaineering, and no shortage of well-equipped refuges and chalets to serve as bases for such activities. The forests which cover the lower slopes are rich in game such as chamois, deer, bear and wild boar, not to mention a great variety of partridge, pheasant and other game birds. The rivers are teeming with trout, and trips can be made by raft or kayak down the moderately easy but exciting rapids of the Drina Gorge, and other reaches of the mountain rivers.

In certain parts of the Republic, you will come across large and curiously carved tombs, placed there in the Middle Ages by the religious sect of the Bogomils who inhabited these remote places during periods of persecution.

The capital of the combined provinces of Bosnia-Hercegovina is the picturesquely situated city of Sarajevo, architecturally a blend of East and West, though Hercegovina's principal town is Mostar, farther south. The town's historic core is largely Turkish in appearance, with houses and mosques clustering upstream from its famous Turkish bridge.

Away to the northeast is Travnik, the home of the Turkish Vizirs or Governors of Bosnia for 150 years. Other interesting towns include Jajce at the junction of the rivers Vrbas and Pliva. The rivers meet at a dramatic waterfall below the ruined castle captured by the Turks after many attempts in 1528. Banja Luka is one of the few other large towns, and is largely Western-looking, despite its many minarets. Everywhere in this little-known corner of Yugoslavia you will be captivated by reminders of its Roman, Islamic and Christian past.

A Brief Historic Background

During the sixth century there was a massive influx of Slav tribes from the northeast into what is today Yugoslavia. They were early converted to Christianity, and sovereignty over them was a matter of long-drawn-out dispute between Rome and Byzantium. After a time the western area, made up of Slovenia and Croatia, became Catholic (though employing the Slav Liturgy), while Serbia and Macedonia in the east favored the Orthodox religion. The dividing line of this marked difference in religious development therefore ran directly through Bosnia.

The Slav tribes were ruled by patriarchal chieftains *(pleme)*. Bosnia, at least during the tenth and 11th centuries, fell within the Serbian sphere of influence. Later it was one of the founder members of the little semi-independent state of Duklja, which was to become Montenegro. By the 12th century, Bosnia had allied itself with the Hungarian-Croat monarchy, which upon becoming wholly Hungarian, extended its frontiers into the mountainous south. The province was given the status of a duchy—Hercegovina deriving from the Hungarian word *herceg,* meaning "duke."

In 1463, the Turks under Sultan Mohammed II occupied the country and converted many to Islam—there are still, today, well over a million

Moslems in the province—especially members of the schismatic Bogomil sect. The Bogomils followed the ascetic beliefs and dualism of the Manichees, a fourth-century Christian heresy prevalent in this region during the late Roman Empire, colored by the desire for a national church. They maintained connections with the forerunners of the Reformation in Western Europe—the Albigensians or Cathars (the Pure Ones) of northern Italy and southern France. But that is about all we know for certain, except that their western cousins lived very simple lives that demanded much more self-sacrifice than the official religions.

The Bosnian chieftains adopted the Moslem faith and continued to wield wide administrative powers. Their example was slowly followed by many of the common folk.

The Turks had come to stay for over four centuries, and it was not until 1875 that Bosnia raised the standard of revolt, abetted by Serbia and Montenegro. The Great Powers were engaged in the struggle to gain influence in the Balkan Peninsula, and Bosnia's fight for independence was discussed by Bismarck and Disraeli during the Congress of Berlin in 1878. Britain, France, Russia, Prussia and Italy, however, destroyed the hopes of the Bosnian patriots by doing no more than changing their masters from Constantinople to Vienna. Bosnia fought on for three months to prevent the completion of Austro-Hungarian occupation, but matters became still worse when the Emperor Franz Josef annexed both Bosnia and Hercegovina to make them part of the Habsburg Empire in 1908.

This produced increased tension between the Entente Cordiale and members of the Triple Alliance.

In Bosnia, university students formed themselves into a secret society called *Mlada Bosna* (Young Bosnia). One of its members was Gavrilo Princip, who in 1914 assassinated Archduke Franz Ferdinand, heir to the throne of Austria-Hungary, during his state visit to Sarajevo—launching a series of events which led to World War I.

Austria accused Serbia of complicity in the assassination, and the four years of death and destruction that was World War I followed. With the demise of the Austro-Hungarian Empire, Bosnia and Hercegovina became a province of the new Kingdom of Yugoslavia. During World War II it was one of Tito's principal partisan strongholds.

Yugoslavia's stormy past does much to explain the varieties of religions to be found within its frontiers. There is a misleading habit of classifying Moslems as "Turks." Actually, much of the Turkish population voluntarily returned to Turkey as the power of the Ottoman Empire declined. The present inhabitants of Bosnia and Hercegovina, Christian and Moslem, are mainly Slavs.

Exploring Bosnia-Hercegovina

If you have chosen Sarajevo as your destination in this region, leave the *autoput* near Okučani to cross the River Sava which marks the boundary between Bosnia and Croatia. After a run of some 60 km. (38 miles) you will reach Bosnia's second town of Banja Luka, rebuilt after a severe earthquake in 1969. There is an Old Town and a New Town divided by the river, but the latter has not much to show the casual visitor. The town's most remarkable building is the 16th-century mosque of Ferhad Pasha Sokolović, erected with the 30,000 ducats which the Turks received from the Austrian General Auersperg by way of ransom for his son. The Sahat-Kula (Clock Tower) is also of interest. 35 km. (22 miles) southeast along the Vrbanja River, Kotor Varoš lies below an impressive castle that long withstood the Turks. The main road to Jajce closely follows the Vrbas River south through increasingly striking scenery, winding round the edge of precipices and diving through tunnels as it passes rocky peaks, crowned by ruined medieval strongholds. The first town after Banja Luka is Jajce, where early in the 15th century Hrvoje Vukčić Hrvatinić, Duke of Split and Governor of Bosnia, built a great fortress on the site of a still earlier building. Excavations within the walled town and its surroundings have uncovered traces of Roman villas; just outside the walls, not far from the *Turist Hotel,* you can see a fine bas-relief of the god Mithras from a temple that must once have stood there.

It's well worth a stroll through the steep narrow alleys of the old walled town. With its mosques, medieval fortifications and typically oriental houses and streets, it has great charm, and you cannot fail to notice the 30-m.-tall (100 ft.) belfry of St. Luke, which was built early in the 15th century in an amalgam of the Gothic and Romanesque styles. When the church was converted into a mosque the bell-tower served as a minaret. The so-called Catacombs are also of interest: a two-level subterranean mausoleum from the 15th century with unusual bas-reliefs. You will need to get the keys for both this and the Mithras temple from the Tourist Office. Beneath the town walls, the river Pliva tumbles over a great fall into the Vrbas.

Since early in the 15th century Jajce has played an important rôle in the country's history. It was here that the Turks executed Bosnia's last king, Stjepan Tomašević, in 1461. His remains are buried in the small Franciscan Church. It was in Jajce, in 1943, that the Partisans met under the very noses of the Germans and worked out the constitution of the new Yugoslavia when—not if—the war was won.

There are several attractive excursions to be made from Jajce, notably to Jezero along the artificial lakes formed by the river Pliva just west of Jajce. After a few kilometers you pass some ancient and charming water-mills beside a small waterfall. A little further, there's a good modern hotel set above the lake. Šivopo, 11 km. (seven miles) upstream from Jezero, preserves several bas-reliefs from its Roman past.

Back on the main road for Sarajevo, the next main point of interest after about another 75 km. (46 miles) of grand scenic driving, is Travnik, at the foot of Mount Vlašić, where the Turkish Vizirs, or Governors, of Bosnia ruled from 1700 until 1852. Once a busy seat of government, immortalized in Ivo Andrić's novel *The Bosnian Story,* is today a sleepy, predominantly Moslem little town, of which the old quarter is wholly Turkish in appearance. A new quarter was created at the beginning of the present century following a serious fire. Some of the fortifications built by the Bosnian King Tvrtko II may still be recognized, and the tombs of the Consuls of Travnik, the Colored Mosque and the still older Mosque of Hadji Ali Beg (with Bosnia's only sundial) and the Turkish cemetery are all of great interest. So is the house, typical of its period, in which Andrić himself was born in 1892; it's now a museum.

Beyond Travnik, you soon reach the Bosna valley through which in ancient times a caravan route linked Sarajevo with central Europe. The present railroad follows this old trail north to join the main rail route from

Zagreb to Belgrade, the entire 240 km. (150 miles) having been laid immediately after the war by volunteer bands of Yugoslav youth, helped by student delegations from 42 different nations.

Of the two minor roads branching south off the Zagreb–Belgrade *autoput,* farther east, the one starting at Slavonski Brod and connected to
Bosanski Brod by a bridge is preferable. Both roads leave the plain of the
Sava to converge on the Bosna Valley, which leads into the heart of the
country, which is itself dotted with attractive little towns, guarded by the
crumbling walls of medieval fortresses. The roads meet about 20 km. (12½
miles) north of Doboj, near which are the remains of a large Roman camp.

Continuing south, Maglaj is perched on the side of a cliff, with a well-
preserved medieval castle and ancient houses huddled round the Kuršumli
Džamija (Mosque). Farther up the valley is the medieval village of
Vranduk, with its magnificent castle.

South of Vranduk the main road by-passes Zenica and is joined a few
kilometers further on by the road from Travnik. Beyond Kajanj, a minor
road to the left leads in 9 km. (5½ miles) to Kraljeva Sutjeska, once the
medieval capital of Bosnian kings, with ruins of a castle and of the palace,
as well as the Franciscan monastery dating from 1340, which contains
priceless manuscripts. Next, the industrial town of Visoko was an important trading center in the Middle Ages and for a time the residence of Bosnian rulers. There are several monuments from those and Turkish times.
Soon after this, we begin the approaches to Sarajevo.

Sarajevo, Heart of Bosnia

Sarajevo, a city of nearly 500,000 people, is known to everyone as the
setting for the events that led to World War I. Today it is a city of many
differing aspects. In the old center you feel that you are in the middle of
the Orient. The mosques, the craftmen's little shops, the narrow streets
and cobbled lanes suggest an Eastern country. A few of the buildings left
over from Habsburg rule, however, indicate curious attempts to mingle
East and West. Then, when you travel out to Sarajevo's suburbs, you find
yourself among the squared-off modern apartments and public buildings
that might be found almost anywhere. More recently the city has expanded enormously with districts of high-rise and other modern architecture
and, of course, achieved international renown as the venue of the 1984
Winter Olympics. These meant the construction of a number of fine installations, such as the great stadiums of Skenderlija and Zetra, and the Olympic Village.

The name "Sarajevo" is of Turkish origin, deriving from *Saraj Ovasi,*
or "Field round the Governor's Palace," though it has been an inhabited
site from time immemorial, as is proved by the Neolithic remains and the
ruins of Roman baths. After the diminution of the power of Byzantium,
Slav tribes established themselves here, but it was under the Turks in the
15th century that the town first became important. Despite present developments and large-scale Austro-Hungarian building during the last century, the older part of Sarajevo retains its secretive and oriental character.
Under the Sultans it became one of the most active military and administrative centers in the Ottoman Empire, and the 16th century, coinciding
with further Turkish expansion, was the city's Golden Age. The great
builder of Sarajevo was Gazi Husref Bey, who was its governor from 1521

until 1541, and he brought fine taste as well as great energy to his task, so that by the 17th century the city possessed a number of palaces and public baths, and 73 mosques.

This period of expansion and prosperity was followed by one of disaster. Sarajevo was captured in 1697 by Prince Eugene of Savoy, fighting in the service of Austria. His troops did great damage, and deported or conscripted many of the inhabitants, so that it was not for a long time that the city regained anything of its former animation and beauty. Under pressure from the Western Powers, the Turks introduced a number of reforms in 1850, which encouraged the city's recovery, and the Austrians, when they took control of Bosnia in 1878, began extensive plans for its modernization.

Exploring Sarajevo

The old town, with its narrow streets bordered by oriental-style houses, is perched on the steep slopes of the Miljacka Valley, and the new quarter has spread across the plateau of Sarajevsko Polje, situated at the mouth of a fortified gorge at a height of over 490 meters (1,600 ft.). The whole is encircled by mountains gradually dropping down into small hills, upon which are laid out the many delightful Turkish-style gardens for which the city is famous.

Undoubtedly one of the most interesting quarters of Sarajevo is that of Baščaršija, the Oriental-style bazaar threaded by a maze of narrow alleys between tiny shops with double-shuttered doors behind which craftsmen and merchants are often one and the same. Among them are *aščinica* serving spicey local specialties, as well as a growing number of café–discos with their all-too-familiar blare. These narrow ways—where you'll find excellent buys in leather, copper and silver and lovely hand-woven carpets—converge on the open area of Baščaršija proper, dominated by Baščaršija Mosque.

Farther on you will come to the Brusa Bezistan, built in 1551, where the carpets, silks and brocades were stored to await the departure of the next caravan for the north, and now housing displays of Bosnian folk costumes and crafts. These caravans always stopped at Moriča Han, which was one of the oldest caravanserais in the Balkans, and which has been restored as a restaurant after a recent fire. *Hans,* though now often ruined, may still be seen throughout Anatolia, Syria, Iraq and Persia. Some were often little more than sheltered stopping-places for man and beast, set about a day's march of 30–40 km. (20–25 miles) apart for 100s, sometimes 1000s, of kilometers along main caravan trade routes. Some, however, are quite elaborate.

It was the energetic Gazi Husref Bey who built among other things the magnificent Begova Džamija (Mosque of the Bey) in 1530, which you will see from Sarači (Saddlers') Street in the Baščaršija district. It has exquisite Persian carpets and prayer rugs, as well as one of the earliest-known copies of the Koran. After his death a tomb was erected for Gazi Husref by the mosque, where he is buried beside his greatest friend, Murat Bey Tardić, a Christian converted to Islam, and subsequently Governor of the province. This is the only mosque from which the call to prayer goes out "live" rather than by means of a tape recording. It also has a special railed-off area for visitors, so you will not need to remove your shoes before entering as you should for most other mosques. Unless they are obviously open to non-Moslems, check first whether you may enter—usually you will be welcome.

Close beside the mosque is the Clock Tower, or Sahat-Kula, upon the face of which the hours of prayer are marked in Arabic numerals. Inside the gates is the fountain whose waters are used for the ritual ablutions demanded by Islamic law as a preliminary to prayer.

If you turn west from this courtyard into Mudželiti Street, you will come to the *Imaret,* built at the same period to provide food for poor students. Here, too, is Musafirhana, a hostel in which any poor traveler had the right to claim free bed and board for three days. The great bakery of the Imaret of Sarajevo is still intact. Another reminder of the golden days of Turkish rule is the Kuršumli Medresa, a theological High School facing the mosque, with finely worked doors and windows. Inside, the building is divided into 12 separate classrooms. Its tall chimneys are designed to resemble minarets.

There are so many remarkable mosques to be seen in Sarajevo that a full list would make lengthy reading, but two more at least must be mentioned. The first is the Mosque of Ali Pasha, and the second the Mosque of the Emperor (Careva Džamija). The Ali Pasha Mosque, built in 1560 a mile or so west of Baščaršija, is small but beautifully proportioned—an outstanding example of 16th-century Turkish architecture. In the mosque garden are the tombs of two Moslem patriots, Sumbul and Mutelević, executed by the Austrians. The Emperor's Mosque, across the River Miljacka from Baščaršija, was built by the Sultan Suleiman in 1566 on the site of an earlier mosque destroyed in 1480 by Bosnian Christians. Next door is Husref Bey's Library. Founded in 1537, it contains a magnificent collection of illuminated manuscripts almost unique in the perfection of their lettering and binding.

Other points of interest include the pseudo-oriental building intended by the Austrians to serve as the Town Hall, and the strange little Orthodox Church reconstructed when the Turks were in occupation, with a wall that hid those who visited it from view. Its little treasury contains 14th-century manuscripts, various valuable reliquaries and some beautiful icons. It also has a magnificent iconostasis. Not far away is a very good Jewish Museum, featuring a copy of a 14th-century Haggadah (the original is in the National Museum). Svrzo's House up a nearby street illustrates the life-style of an 18th-century Moslem family in an original family house.

Opposite Princip Bridge, on the wall of the Young Bosnia Museum, is a commemorative plaque marking the spot from which the young Gavrilo Princip fired those fateful shots at the Austrian Archduke, that sparked off World War I. The museum records this fateful event with documents, photographs and maps.

Try and make time to stroll through the picturesque residential quarters of Kováci and Vratnik, which climb the steep slopes above Baščaršija.

From the walls of the ancient fortress that crowns Bentbaša you will see what were the homes of the Turkish aristocracy of four centuries ago. Even better, admire the view across the city while drinking a very thick, very black, very strong Turkish coffee on the terrace of a *kafana.* On the hill facing you are the white stones of the Turkish cemetery of Alifakovac. The more important graves, those of civic dignitaries and highly-placed

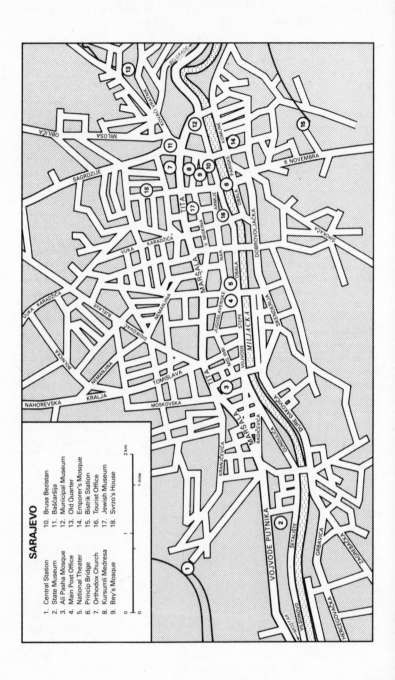

SARAJEVO

1. Central Station
2. State Museum
3. Ali Pasha Mosque
4. Main Post Office
5. National Theater
6. Princip Bridge
7. Orthodox Church
8. Kursumli Medresa
9. Bey's Mosque
10. Brusa Bezistan
11. Baščaršija
12. Municipal Museum
13. Old Quarter
14. Emporer's Mosque
15. Bistrik Station
16. Tourist Office
17. Jewish Museum
18. Svrzo's House

families, are roofed with stone canopies to distinguish them from the simple graves of their subjects.

Sitting there as it grows dark, with the swifts screaming overhead as they seek out a late supper, you may well feel that you are a very long way indeed from Times Square or Piccadilly Circus.

Allow some time, too, to explore the surrounding mountains: Trebević (accessible by car from Sarajevo), Jahorina, Igman, Bjelašnica, scene of many of the 1984 Winter Olympics events, and Treskavica a little farther afield. They offer good accommodation and, if you have your own transport, offer an attractive alternative to staying in the city itself. The fine modern park-like War Memorial on Vrace on the way to Trebević is well worth a halt. A couple of attractive small resorts a short drive away are Kiseljak to the northwest and Pale to the southeast of Sarajevo.

The Road to Mostar

Both the railway and the road from Sarajevo to Kardeljevo run through the thermal spa of Ilidža in which the ill-fated Archduke Franz Ferdinand spent the night before his assassination. It's a popular excursion point, linked by a regular tram service with Sarajevo. From there, three km. (two miles) along a sideroad, are Vrelo Bosna, the several sources of the River Bosna, with horse-drawn carriages available to cover the distance. It's an extraordinarily pleasant spot at the foot of Mount Igman, where woods and water combine to make the place seem cool, even in summer. Road and rail turn south through the Ivan pass (through tunnels), and you then come into the beautiful sheltered valley of the Neretva, with superb views, passing through many small tunnels and crossing great viaducts.

In this short distance the whole character of the country has changed dramatically, and the climate from temperate to almost subtropical. Here you are in a land of tobacco plantations set among fig, almond and olive trees.

Konjic is a charming little town set under the shadow of the great mountains, and despite damage during World War II it still retains something of its former wholly-oriental character. Some 21 km. (13 miles) from Konjic, near Borci, the lake Boračko Jezero lends green charm to otherwise rather arid scenery.

We now enter the district of Jablanica (also the name of the artificial lake we have been following for many miles) which is a center for hunting trips in the Prenj Mountains and the surrounding forests. The great hydroelectric dam retains the waters of three rivers.

Beyond the town of Jablanica, over whose bridge Tito led 4,000 wounded partisans to safety (there is a museum to the battle near the bridge), the scenery becomes austere but impressive, until once over the pass, the valley again widens to bring us at last to Mostar. On the way you pass more recently built dams and their attendant lakes whose waters are also being exploited for recreational purposes.

Mostar's Mosques and Minarets

Mostar (*most:* bridge) is the provincial capital of Hercegovina. Despite high-rise blocks on the outskirts, the view of the town is still dramatic. The countless thin pencils of its minarets, backed by wild and rocky mountains, lend the old town an enchanted air.

The single-span, hump-backed bridge over the Neretva was built by the Turks in 1556, and is one of the most famous and delightful civic works in the whole of Yugoslavia. Local youths prove their manhood by diving or jumping from the highest point into the swift green waters below, and every 4th July there is a competition dedicated to this feat.

Probably Mostar's most attractive mosque is Karadjoz Beg's from the 16th century, which is graceful architecturally and has a richly decorated interior, with carpets presented by many Moslem heads of state. Also worth seeing is the History and Ethnographic Museum near the old bridge. It contains an attractive model of the old town with sound and light effects, and is housed in Inad Mosque.

Up on the hill there's an old and unusual Orthodox Church featuring a special grille behind which women were screened from the sight of the male worshippers in the same way as they are in a mosque; unfortunately it is usually closed to visitors. Also well worth visiting are two houses typifying the architectural styles of the Turkish period. Biščević House, which dates from the 17th century, has a good ethnographic collection. The 16th-century Kajtaz House gives an excellent picture of the life of a wealthy Moslem family in days gone by.

In the middle of so much that is old, it is sobering to note that Mostar's memorial to the dead of World War II must be one of the most striking and moving constructions in the whole of Europe. It is not something you stand and look at, for to see it you have to walk through its stone-flanked lanes and symbolic little artificial gorges.

There are a number of attractive excursions from Mostar. One is to the nearby village of Blagaj, where the River Buna emerges suddenly from the base of majestic cliffs after running underground for nearly 20 km. (12½ miles). Overlooking this dramatic spot is a 17th-century Dervish Monastery. High up on the slopes above still stand the ruins of the great fortress of Stjepangrad, built by Herceg (Duke) Stjepan Kosača on the site of the impregnable Roman city of Bone. Blagaj is the original home of the Žilavka grape, and produces the best heavy white Žilavka wine and Blatina red wine.

The latest draw in these parts is the village of Medjugorje, about 30 km. (21 miles) southwest of Mostar. This remote place was unknown until 1981 when visions of the Virgin Mary appeared to some local schoolchildren. Today, tens of thousands of believers and sightseers from all over the world have transformed this tiny spot into a center of pilgrimage. There is a new church, with a mass held every hour, and a vast number of new houses offer accommodation. Visits to the "children"—now young adults—can be arranged. Some find it an uplifting place; others regret the rising commercialization.

From Mostar along the valley of the Neretva, both road and railway are flanked by cliffs rising to well over 915 m. (3,000 ft.). The 16th-century Žitomislić monastery near here has some precious icons. About 30 km. (20 miles) south of Mostar you will see the fortified village of Počitelj. It is set on the banks of the river and was for many centuries a Turkish frontier post. This picturesque spot, abounding in delightful cherry trees, has been painstakingly restored stone-by-stone. It has become an active artists' colony of international standing, with a number of charming restaurants and accommodations in the village houses.

Soon after, a road to the right leads across the Neretva to Čapljina, near which (about a mile away) are the impressive remains of the 4th-century fortified Roman villa of Mogorjelo. A little further south, the main road passes near the fringes of Hutovo Blato, a major marshland area famed for its fishing and wild fowl hunting. Beyond Metković, you enter the wide watery Neretva delta, now largely irrigated to provide fertile land for fruit and vegetable crops, and very soon you get your first unforgettable view of the Dalmatian coast, the Adriatic, and its chain of islands.

An alternative route from Mostar to the coast is the newly built road from Tasovčići via Stolac, Ljubinje and Trebinje. At Radimlja, just before Stolac, there is a remarkable Bogomil cemetery with its typical, strangely-carved tombs. Stolac itself is a fascinating little town whose roots go deep into prehistory. The old part of the town straggles along the Bregava river below the great ruins of fortifications, and there are a number of lovely houses and even ancient watermills still fulfilling their original purpose. Traces of Illyrian settlement have been found nearby, giving rise to the curious claim by a Mexican scholar that here, rather than in Asia Minor, is the true site of Homer's Troy—a claim not surprisingly dismissed by archeologists. Popovo Polje, the region some 40 km. (25 miles) beyond Stolac, is an interesting spot. In winter, this plain used to become a shallow lake fed by subterranean streams which forced their way to the surface through a number of craters. Hydroelectric projects along the Trebišnjica river have changed this, though irrigation is planned to keep the plain the green, fertile place it had always been as a result of regular flooding. At Zavala, you will find an old monastery with some very distinctive 17th-century frescos. The road continues to Trebinje, a small town famous for its tobacco, called *trebinjac,* and also a popular excursion center from the coast. Market days on Saturdays are fun.

If Turkish architecture interests you, you should certainly make it a point to see Begova Kuća (the Bey's house) and the Mosque of Osman Pasha at Trebinje. The fine, seven-arched, 76-m.-long (250 ft.) Turkish bridge, Arslanagića Most, has been reconstructed about 800 m. (half a mile) from its original site before the damming of the Trebišnjica river. Fishermen should note that California trout are plentiful in the upper Trebišnjica during the months of July and August. It is an odd river, as it disappears underground in the Popovo Polje to reemerge close to Dubrovnik, as the Ombla, described in our chapter on Southern Dalmatia.

Wild Grandeur

Trebinje is only 32 km. (20 miles) northeast of Dubrovnik, on the scenically lovely road inland, roughly along first the border of Hercegovina with Montenegro, then of Bosnia with Serbia. The 16th-century frescos of Dobrićevo monastery have been preserved, even though it had to be moved and painstakingly reerected when the Bilećko Lake was created. Round Bileća, where the Turkish invaders suffered in 1388 their first defeat, are 1000s of Bogomil tombs.

After some kilometers through forbidding Karst, there is a dramatic change to luxuriant vegetation at Gacko, due to the presence of innumerable little streams. Tjentište on the River Sutjeska lies in a National Park framed by Bosnia's highest mountains. Beside excursions to Europe's only virgin forest, at Perućica, the 72-m. (240-ft.) Skakavac Waterfall and the seven glacier lakes of the Zelengora Mountains, Tjentište offers unusually extensive athletics facilities and an artificial lake for watersports. This wild area, incidentally, was the scene of the fiercest fighting between the Partisans and occupying forces in World War II, during which Tito was wounded and a British officer killed. A museum, a great memorial and many other monuments commemorate these events.

Foča, at the confluence of the Cehotina and Drina rivers, was the seat of the Turkish Sandžak Begs of Hercegovina, and is thus endowed with fine buildings, outstanding among them the remarkable Aladža (Colored) Mosque. From June through August Foča is the center of rafting on the Drina (see also the Tara, p. 157). Newly-felled tree trunks from the endless forests are lashed together for a thrilling journey over the rapids of the fast-flowing currents in an evocation of past times. More modern, but no less exciting, are the kayak regattas.

The road crosses and recrosses the Drina on its way northeast between Bosnia and Serbia, through the apple and plum orchards of the Goražde district. A few kilometers away is one of the most ancient of all the Orthodox churches of Bosnia-Hercegovina, that of St. Juragi. It was built in 1454, when the region was still part of Serbia, by Herceg Stjepan Kosača. It was later to house Serbia's first printing press which, from 1519, produced missals and prayerbooks in the Cyrillic script.

However you reach Višegrad you will pass through some of the most beautiful mountain scenery in central Bosnia, and the town itself is no anticlimax. It was once a great Turkish stronghold, and in the 16th century, Mehmed Pasha Sokolović, Vizir of Bosnia, commissioned (in 1571) Turkey's greatest architect, Sinan, to span the Drina. The monumental 11-arched bridge, 165 m. (180 yards) long, inspired Ivo Andrić's Nobel Prize-winning novel *Bridge over the Drina.*

Beyond Višegrad, the main road climbs away from the Drina into yet more mountains and soon crosses into Serbia.

PRACTICAL INFORMATION FOR
BOSNIA-HERCEGOVINA

HOW TO GET THERE. By plane. There are many services linking Sarajevo and Mostar with Belgrade, Dubrovnik, and Zagreb, with connections to other centers.

By train. Trains link Kardeljevo on the coast via Mostar and Sarajevo with Zagreb and Belgrade.

By bus. Regular express buses link all the main centers with the rest of the country.

WHEN TO GO. The mountains of Bosnia attract many winter visitors, as the area for snow sports is extensive and the terrain relatively easy. Facilities in the surroundings of Sarajevo, site of the 1984 Winter Olympics, are of top standard. Owing to the mountainous and thickly wooded nature of the province, summer is usually pleasant in Bosnia (though Sarajevo can be very stuffy). On the other hand, in the plains of Hercegovina it can be unpleasantly hot. The best time for Bosnia-Hercegovina as a whole is late April and May through June, and Sept. to early Oct.

If you are staying on the Dalmatian coast do not fail to set aside two or three days to see something of the exotic hinterland—it is well worth exploring at any time of the year.

HOTELS AND RESTAURANTS. There are very few (E) hotels in Bosnia-Hercegovina, but those in the (M) price range are generally reliable, and the more modern (I)s will be adequate. We would suggest, however, that you try to avoid accommodations in the lowest category. Every hotel listed here has all or at least some rooms with bath or shower, unless otherwise stated. Most are open year-round. Private accommodations are available in all main centers.

There are now a number of good hotels as well as mountain refuges and alpine inns in the Bosnian mountains, notably at Bjelašnica, Prenj, Romanija, Trebević, Treskavica, Vlašić and Zelengora. Numerous camping sites are also to be found in the area.

Food and Drink. Most Bosnian food specialties are of partly Turkish origin, and thus exclude pork. *Musaka* is fresh meat minced and roasted in an oven with egg-plant and covered, before cooking, with Béchamel sauce; *kapama* consists of mutton cooked together with spinach and green onions and served with a yogurt sauce; and *kalija* is a mixture of finely chopped cabbage and mutton prepared after the manner of pot-au-feu. Bosnian *lonac* is a ragout of the vegetables currently in season, while *sarma* is minced beef rolled in a leaf of cabbage or vine.

For those who like their dessert to be sweet, the Turkish specialties of Bosnia will be most appreciated. *Baklava* is a wafered pastry containing nuts and covered with syrup. *Kadaif* is a pastry cut into thin strips and, as always, covered with syrup. *Lokum* is our childhood friend, Turkish Delight, *alva* is better known to us as halva or hulva. Stewed fruits are called *rošaf* or *zerde*.

Yugoslavia's best white wine comes from Mostar, and is called *Žilavka*. *Blatina* is a pleasant red Bordeaux type. Žilavka, like Traminer, Riesling, Sylvaner and other well-known wines, is actually the name of the grape, so wine made anywhere from Žilavka grapes can use the name. Much is of extremely poor quality, but the original is superb; it comes from the village of Blagaj and is labeled accordingly.

Banja Luka. *Bosna* (M), 150 rooms. Central. *Motel International* (I), 68 rooms. About five km. (three miles) on main road to north.

Bihać. 35 km. (22 miles) from the Plitvice Lakes. Popular fishing center. *Ada* (M), 86 rooms. *Park* (M), 110 rooms.

Bjelašnica. Mountain resort near Sarajevo, developed for 1984 Olympics. *Famos* (E), 52 rooms, some (M), near chairlift.

Foča. *Zelengora* (M), 87 rooms. On the banks of the River Čehotina, with a natural bathing beach, terrace and garden.

Goražde. *Gradina* (M), 56 rooms.

Igman. Mountain resort area near Sarajevo, developed for 1984 Olympics. *Igman* (M), fine mountain forest setting, 24 km. from Sarajevo; indoor pool, sports hall, disco.

Ilidža. Spa a few kilometers out of Sarajevo. In a lovely park are five tastefully reconstructed hotels in the (M) range: *Bosna, Hercegovina, Jadran* and *Srbija,* all restored traditional style. The more modern *Terme* has a pool. *Stojčevac* (M), in quiet park about 2 km. away. 57 rooms, tennis. These make excellent alternatives to those actually in Sarajevo, particularly if you have your own transport, though there are frequent and inexpensive connections with the city by tram. Other accommodations in Ilidža include an autocamp, complete with bungalows.

Jablanica. *Jablanica* (I), 45 rooms.
Restaurant. If traveling between Sarajevo and Mostar, stop for lunch at one of a number of road-side restaurants along this stretch where your lamb roasts on a water-powered spit.

Jahorina. Part of the splendid 1984 Winter Olympics venue near Sarajevo. *Bistrica* (M), 164 rooms, pool. *Jahorina* (M), 135 rooms, at lower end of its category. *Košuta* (M), 62 rooms. Young travelers will find inexpensive accommodations at the three youth hotels.

Jajce. *Jajce* (M), 75 rooms, indoor pool, modern. A few km. west overlooking lake. *Plivska Jezera* (I), 32 rooms, 18 chalets. Out of town, on the lakeside. *Turist* (I), 40 rooms. In town.

Kiseljak. Spa near Sarajevo. *Dalmacija* (M), 113 rooms, at lower end of price range.

Konjic. Starting point for the Prenj mountains. *Motel Konjic* (I), 32 rooms.

Medjugorje. Pilgrimage village, about 30 km. (21 miles) from Mostar. *Kompas-APRO Hotel Village* (M), 100 rooms.

Mostar. *Bristol* (M), 56 rooms, and *Neretva* (M), 40 rooms, Moorish-style, face each other across the Neretva river, but some rooms are noisy. *Ruža* (M), 75 rooms, Recent hotel a short stroll from the famous bridge and the old part of town. Also campsite and chalets at **Buna,** a few km. south.
Restaurants. *Aščinica Balkan* is the place to go for oriental-style home cooking; unpretentious, in the town center. The very-tourist-oriented *Labrint* has a terrace overlooking the river. *Stari Most* is near the old bridge. All (M).

Mrkonjić-Grad. *Krajina* (M), 39 rooms. *Motel Balkan* (M), 24 rooms.

Pale. 16 km. (ten miles) from Sarajevo. Starting point for excursions to Jahorina and Romanija mountains. *Koran* (M), 42 rooms. Pool. *Panorama* (M), 59 rooms.

Počitelj. Well-known artists' colony. Accommodations available in various houses in the village.

Restaurant. Charming old *Han* (inn) has been restored as an attractive restaurant. Also private restaurants.

Stolac. Interesting small town on alternative route to the coast. *Bregava* (M), 25 rooms.

Tjentište. In a wild and beautiful national park. *Mladost* (I), 41 rooms. *Sutjeska* (I), 50 rooms.

Trebinje. 26 km. (16 miles) from Dubrovnik. *Leotar* (M), 110 rooms.

Tuzla. *Tuzla* (E), 223 rooms, pool, nightclub.

Višegrad. *Bikavac* (M), 44 rooms. *Vilina Vlas* (M), 68 rooms. Pool.

Zenica. *International* (M), 62 rooms, at top end of range. *Metalurg* (I), 73 rooms.

Zvornik. *Drina* (I), 72 rooms.

HOW TO GET AROUND. By car. Main roads, though often winding and narrow, are good to adequate, and the scenery is mostly superb. The main highway ascends along the Neretva north from the coast at Metković through Mostar to Jablanica, then strikes east to Sarajevo, from which there are three connections with the Zagreb-Belgrade *autoput*. The shortest is due north to Županja; the second passes through Zvornik to Belgrade; and the third, running through Jajce and Banja Luka, joins the *autoput* much nearer Zagreb. The branch from Jajce to Bihać and on to Karlovac in Croatia is a quieter route to Zagreb, which can also be reached via Banja Luka. The Dubrovnik–Belgrade road via Trebinje, Foča, along the Drina to Višegrad, where it turns east to Titova Užice in Serbia, is perhaps the loveliest. Filling stations are adequate.

By bus. An excellent network of bus services radiates from the modern bus station at Sarajevo.

By train. A main line links Doboj, Zenica, Sarajevo, Mostar to the coast.

SPORTS. The winter variety inevitably predominates, with the choice of Sarajevo as the venue for the 1984 Winter Olympics. This has given a tremendous boost to facilities available in the nearby mountains, making it one of the top areas outside traditional Alpine skiing haunts. The resorts of Jahorina and Bjelašnica are particularly well-developed for downhill skiing, with several ski-lifts, and Igman for cross-country skiing. Buses provide regular links between the city and the skiing grounds for those who prefer to stay in the town.

The huge areas of forest in Bosnia-Hercegovina make it one of Europe's most varied natural preserves for hunting. Here hunters may come across brown bear grown to the size of small grizzly, not to mention wolves. Wild boar, bear, red deer, fox, and wild cat are all plentiful, and in the Maglić, Zelengora and Prenj mountains there are herds of chamois. You will find developed sites in all hunting zones, and most provide accommodations, with electricity, running water, and bathroom facilities. Mountain refuges, though simpler, are also well-equipped. Guidebeaters with dogs, saddle horses and row-boats are available. Arrangements for hunting can be made through the local travel agency, Unis Turist.

There are few more exciting or romantic experiences than to make the descent by kayak from Šćepan Polje on the Tara, via Foča to Goražde on the Drina. Between Foča and Goražde, you can also do it by raft. Other suitable rivers kayaking are the Neretva, Una and Vrbas. Advance details are not easy to obtain, but the best sources of information are the Foča Tourist Office or Unis Turist, Moše Pijade 2, Foča.

FISHING. The numerous fast-flowing mountain rivers of Bosnia-Hercegovina provide excellent fishing, with no less than 18 different varieties of fish being caught in the Drina alone, and everywhere there is an abundance of trout, salmon, and grayling.

Rivers Una, Vrbas, Neretva, Drina and their tributaries offer splendid possibilities, as do the glacial lakes in the Treskavica and Zelengora area. Bihać, Martin Brod, Ključ, Jajce, Mostar, Buna, Foča, Zvornik and Tjentište are among the important centers. Permits are obtainable from tourist offices and some hotels, but you must bring your own equipment.

SHOPPING. You will find a variety of interesting and original things to buy as souvenirs in Bosnia. The oriental handicraftsmen in the souks of Sarajevo produce attractive metalwork, and everyday household utensils in beautifully carved wood make an appealing and useful gift. If you are interested in hand-loomed carpets, embodying traditional peasant designs, then you can examine them without obligation to buy at one of the numerous shops specializing in rugs and carpets. Colorful Turkish slippers with knitted stocking tops are another specialty of the area.

USEFUL ADDRESSES. Every town possesses a Tourist Information office and at least one travel agency. The main agency in Bosnia is Unis Turist, whose head office is at Vase Miskina 16, Sarajevo.

PRACTICAL INFORMATION FOR SARAJEVO

HOTELS. Preparations for the 1984 Winter Olympics included a sharp boost in hotel accommodations. Generally speaking, most visitors in the past have been transient, a situation which the tourist organizations are anxious to change—and certainly, longer stays are justified in this fascinating and beautiful region. In addition to those listed below, there are guesthouses (bookings through local travel agencies), and plenty of private accommodations (handled by Unis Turist). The following have all or some rooms with bath or shower, unless otherwise stated.

Expensive

Holiday Inn, Vojvode putnika 6a, close to the rail station and some distance from the old town. 330 rooms. Pool, shopping arcade; all top facilities.

Moderate

Beograd, Slobodana Principa 9. 75 rooms; central, good service.

Evropa, 225 rooms. Service is a bit erratic but they've been accommodating travelers for about 100 years now. Just round the corner from the lively Baščaršija (bazaar) area; has a pleasant garden restaurant.

National, Obala Pariške komune 5. 73 rooms. Across the river from the center. At the lower end of this price category.

Inexpensive

Central, Zrinjskog 8. 39 rooms. Adequate and centrally placed.

RESTAURANTS. Three with lots of atmosphere in the Baščaršija district are *Daira,* Halači 5, in a charmingly converted complex of 17th-century Turkish storehouses; *Morića Han,* Sarači bb, formerly an old inn; and *Aeroplan,* Saraći 3. All serve Bosnian specialties. *Magnum,* Kranjčevića 18, is near the rail station. *Una,* P. Bakovića 8, is intimate and central. The *Dalmacija,* Maršala Tita 45, specializes in fish; pleasant garden. *Kula,* at Butmir out near the airport, has a beautiful situation, good food, and very reasonable prices. *Lovački Rog,* Nicole Tesle 24, is another moderate place. Two self-service restaurants for the budget-minded, both central, are *Bosna* and *Marin Dvor* (latter also has waiter-service section), at respectively Maršala Tita 36 and 1.

Otherwise, there are numerous small private eateries and food bars where you can get national or local specialties, *čevapčići, burek,* etc., as quick and inexpensive meals.

There is dancing in the *Plavi Podrum* restaurant in the Evropa hotel (see above). There are innumerable discos packed with the young, many small coffee bars, and the more sophisticated *Hamam-bar,* the latter attractively adapted from a 16th-century Turkish bath at Maršala Tita 55.

MUSEUMS. The Jewish Museum, Maršala Tita 98. Housed in an old synagogue and excellent of its kind.

The Municipal Museum, Remzije Omanovića 31. Contains objects dating back to the Iron Age, utensils employed in Turkish medicine, a reproduction of a Turkish barber shop—also vestments, tools and harnesses dating from Turkish times, icons and frescos.

The Museum of Young Bosnia, Vojvode Stepe Obala 36. The theme is the revolutionary student group whose activities sparked off World War I. On the pavement outside are the footprints marking the spot from which the fatal shots were fired that killed Archduke Franz Ferdinand.

Orthodox Church, Maršala Tita 106. Houses a rich collection of Orthodox artefacts.

The State Museum, 7 Vojvode Putnika St. (not far from rail station). One wing contains prehistoric, Greek, Roman and medieval objects; another a truly remarkable ethnographic collection, including reproductions of Bosnian peasant houses and feudal Turkish-period dwellings. In the gardens of the museum are a number of the unique burial steles of the Bogomils.

Svrzo's House, Jovana Kršića 6. A typical house from the Turkish period; several rooms are fully furnished with 17th-century articles.

ENTERTAINMENT. The National Theater on Vojvode Stepe Obala, also features opera and ballet. Performances at the several other theaters in Sarajevo are in Serbo-Croat of course, but the Puppet Theater might be of more general interest. In summer, folkloric evenings of good standard are common—details from the Tourist Information Center. There are also a number of concert halls and art galleries.

USEFUL ADDRESSES. The Tourist Information Center is at Jugoslovenske Armije 50. All the larger Yugoslav travel agents have offices in Sarajevo; the principal Bosnian one is Unis Turist, Vase Miskina 16.

The main post office is at Obala V. Stepe 8. The First Aid Center (Hitna Pomoć) is at ugao Ž. Jošila i Darovalaca krvi.

INLAND SLOVENIA

An Alpine Land

This region is much like Alpine Austria, though only half its size. Set between Austria and Italy, it is the obvious entry to Yugoslavia for any visitor coming from the north or west by road or rail. It is a land of excellent hill-walking and good climbing. Its mountain roads are of good quality.

Slovenia's northern borders are the abrupt peaks of the Karavanke Mountains. The Julian Alps lie in the northwest, and to the east the mountains gradually descend to the great Hungarian plain. In the southwest lies the Adriatic, and the southern limits are marked by the Croatian hills. The white limestone mountains of Slovenia are dominated by majestic Mount Triglav (Three Heads) which rises to a height of 2,863 meters (9,393 ft.). There are several fairly easy climbing routes to the peak. Old Three Heads watches over the province—one looking to the past, one to the present and the third to the future, or so say the peasants of Slovenia.

There are many charming lakes both in the mountains and amid the thickly wooded valleys, most famous of them all being Lake Bled, with its castle and the high mountain valley of the Seven Lakes of Triglav nearby. Waterfalls and twisting little trout streams break up the landscape, and here it is easy to realize how Slovenia alone in bygone years furnished enough hydroelectric power for the needs of the greater part of the country.

The mountains in the east and south of the province did not provide such a good defensive barrier as those in the west and north, but at the time of the Turkish invasions they formed the boundaries of the Christian world, as you will realize from the profusion of castles and fortified churches.

The level uplands are characterized by a number of shallow basins in which soil has collected, where the peasants cultivate their smallholdings. The region has other, rather special characteristics, chief among them the famous Postojna Caves, which experts consider one of the most extraordinary underground curiosities in Europe—a series of halls pillared with stalactites and stalagmites, that continue for over 19 km. (12 miles).

Until recently, Slovenia was—and in some aspects still is—more advanced than the other five Republics, because of its contact with the West in those centuries when Turkey ruled much of the rest of Yugoslavia. Its capital, Ljubljana, differs little in architecture from such capitals as Vienna or Budapest. The countryside resembles neighboring Austria. The snowy peaks, the wooden-tiled chalets clinging to the mountainsides, the long sloping green fields, the gardens bright with roses, geraniums, carnations and dahlias, unmistakably recall the Austrian Alps.

However, the illusion, strong though it is, soon vanishes when you meet the inhabitants, whose way of life is Alpine, but whose main language is Slav. Older folk speak German, or along the coast many speak Italian, but English is also widely understood.

Slovenia's History

Someone who knew his subject once remarked: "Geography is the key to history." Lying along the easiest route to and from the Adriatic, Slovenia witnessed the Romans marching north (and had Roman legions quartered on it in the second century), and later the Germans and Huns pushing south toward the Mediterranean. Local tribes put up a long and fierce resistance to the Romans, but once the Pax Romana was established the country became one of the richest colonies of the Empire. However, as the power of Rome waned in the fourth century the Germanic hordes swept into the Balkans and were followed by the Slovenes who took possession of the mountainous east, replacing the Celto-Romans whom they found there.

After a period of political uncertainty, Slovenia became a frontier province of Charlemagne's great empire, later to pass for over 1,000 years under Austrian rule, fighting for the Habsburgs against the Turks. While many of the other southern Slavs were overrun by Turkey, Slovenia remained an Austrian province. Neglected by absentee landlords, the Slovenes' sense of national identity developed very slowly.

The first Slovene books of Primož Trubar were published in 1551, but it was not until the introduction of reforms by Joseph II at the end of the 18th century, and the Napoleonic occupation of 1809–13, that the Slovene literary Renaissance developed.

Napoleon recreated the Roman province of Illyria, and the Slovene language was revived, but once the French interlude ended Austrian hegemony was reestablished. However, the Illyrian Movement had by now drawn up a truly nationalistic program that inspired both Slovene and Croat literature to their full flowering, defying the Habsburg determination to Germanize the country.

Slovenia was annexed by Hitler and Mussolini in World War II. Many of her young men fought in the anti-Axis guerrilla units.

Exploring Slovenia

Visitors coming to Slovenia from Austria mostly cross by the nearly 1,070-m.-high (3,500 ft.) Koren (Wurzen) Pass—one of the most popular routes through the Karavanke barrier. After the frontier the road begins to descend to the upper Sava valley. A new road tunnel is under construction, which will make the crossing even simpler; its exit will be near Jesenice, some distance east of the Wurzen pass. Farther east still the Ljubelj tunnel on the Klagenfurt–Ljubljana road already saves traffic some mountain-climbing.

If Slovenia is entered from Italy by way of the town of Tarvisio, the first Yugoslav village will be Rateče, which is almost at the exact point where the frontiers of Yugoslavia, Italy and Austria meet. Only a little farther on is Planica, with one of the best ski-jumps to be found anywhere in Europe.

Returning to our road along the upper reaches of the River Sava, we wind along a narrow, mountain-bordered valley, through scenery wholly typical of the Karavanke and Julian Alps, soon reaching the village of Podkoren and, next, Kranjska Gora, an attractive village and extremely popular winter sports resort, at a height of some 800 m. (2,630 ft.), but surrounded by some of the highest peaks. From here there is a secondary but magnificent road over the Vršič Pass (1,611 m./5,285 ft.) linking with the Tarvisio road by means of the beautiful Soča valley.

On the way up Vršič, you pass a small wooden church built in memory of the 400 prisoners of war who died in an avalanche while building this road in the winter of 1915–16. There are also a number of mountain hotels and refuges along the way. As you descend from the pass, you'll find many reminders of major World War I battles, for this was the setting for the bitterly contested Soča front in 1915–17. You will also pass the lovely Botanical Gardens Alpinum Juliana, with every variety of flower native to these *karst* regions. The road eventually descends to Bovec (see below).

Continuing from Kransjka Gora towards Ljubljana, you soon reach Gozd Martuljek, from whence you can look across the great mountain mass of Martuljek. The Martuljek Waterfall at the foot of 2,475-m. (8,125-ft.) Mount Spik is another local attraction.

If you are tempted to take a closer look at Mount Triglav after reaching Mojstrana, there is a narrow road that turns off to the right for a distance of some 13 km. (eight miles). Within five km. (three miles) of leaving Mojstrana, you will see the impressive 50-m. (160-ft.) Peričnik Waterfall. Near the end of the valley, under the northern flanks of Triglav, is the small mountain hut of Aljažev Dom, set at a height of 1,005 m. (3,300 ft.) above sea-level, an acknowledged headquarters for both Yugoslav and foreign mountain climbers. From there two tracks set out for the 2,863-m. (9,393-ft.) summit. On the way you can rest, or stop the night, at another refuge (open only in summer) at a height of 2,380 m. (7,800 ft.). For less experienced mountaineers, the Škrlatica ascent from Aljažev Dom is relatively straightforward.

Returning again to the Sava, the road takes us past the great metalworking town of Jesenice. From there we follow the railway that leads to within a few kilometers of the romantic and world-renowned Lake of Bled.

Towards Istria

If you have entered Yugoslavia by the Predel Pass from Tarvisio, Italy, you will soon pass through the village of Log pod Mangrtom and descend the Koritnica valley, joining the Soča valley (see above) near Bovec.

The Predel Pass, originally a Roman military road to the north, was also the route taken by the Lombards when they in their turn invaded the fertile plains of northern Italy. It then became the "Amber Caravan Route" of the Middle Ages which later served to link Trieste with the great cities of central Europe. Naturally enough the road is lined with old fortifications that last served Austria in delaying Napoleon's advance toward Vienna.

Bovec is an expanding resort as are several centers along this lovely valley: ideal centers for walkers and climbers, and not least for canoe and kayak enthusiasts in the swift waters of the Soča and its tributaries. All this area, incidentally, is dotted with cemetaries and memorials to the Soča battlefront of World War I.

Beyond Bovec the main road continues to follow the River Soča, giving us a delightful glimpse of the 60-m. (195-ft.) Boka Waterfall.

At Kobarid the road from the Udine-Robič Pass comes in from the west, and we pass the 2,275-m. (7,465-ft.) mass of Mount Krn on our left. Some distance further, you can leave the main road, crossing the River Soča, to Tolmin. This is another small summer resort, and only four km. (2½ miles) farther to the south the rivers Soča and Idrija meet. Here a dam has been built to create a charming little lake, in which bathing is permitted. Needless to say, the whole area is famous for the excellence of its fishing and, more humble but still not to be despised, the most delicious sheep's milk cheeses.

If you stay on the main road, you continue along the Soča to the frontier town of Nova Gorica, near which very good white wine is produced. From here it's an easy run of about 50 km. (31 miles) to join the main Ljubljana coast road, only a short distance from the famous Postojna caves. If you want to explore more of the interior, though, we suggest that from Most na Soči, a few kilometers south of Tolmin, you take the road up the Idrija valley through Idrija, and eventually to the Postojna Caves. An alternative but much rougher route would be via Čepovan to Vipava, taking in the Teran vineyards and the winter sports center of Lokve.

Alternatively, if you are heading for Ljubljana, a few kilometers from Most na Soči you can take a minor road running east along the beautiful Bača valley toward the Slovene capital.

Between Grahovo and Podbrdo you will have plenty of opportunities to admire the peaks of Črna Prst and Porezen, both of which, incidentally, can be reached by easy paths. This remote region was one of the principal hideouts of the Slovene underground during World War II. After climbing a pass our route descends to Železniki, formerly famous for its excellent ironwork. From here you have the choice of continuing through Škofija Loka to Ljubljana or turning north over minor roads to the major attractions of lakes Bled and Bohinj. Skofja Loka is a charming little medieval town, with a baroque castle which is now the regional museum. From here it is only another 20 km. (13 miles) to Ljubljana.

At Most na Soči we are already in the *karst* area—a rugged, rough, broken kind of limestone—and the river is flanked by plateaux over 915 m. (3,000 ft.) above sea-level. From here we now take the main alternative route already mentioned, through Kanal to Nova Gorica, a summer resort with a full-size swimming pool and a number of good camping sites.

If you spend a little time there you may visit the Franciscan Monastery of Kostanjevica, perched on a neighboring hill and pay your respects to the memory of the last of the Bourbon kings of France who, after fleeing from the Revolution of 1830, spent his declining years in England where he surprised his hosts by his passion for shooting sparrows. In due course, this became the last resting place of King Charles X, brother-in-law of France's ill-fated Marie Antoinette.

Of Wine and Lippizaners

The limestone soil in this region supports vines of excellent quality and, if you take the lesser road via Sežana to the main Trieste–Ljubljana road, you will pass through communities whose livelihood depends on the vines of Teran.

One such place is Štanjel, built of the local stone and perched, for defense, on top of a hill. Another is Sežana itself, popular with visitors because of its huge park containing exotically scented plants, and a third, Lipica, just south of Sežana and very close to the Italian border. It was in Lipica that the Lippizaner breed of white (called "gray") horses originated, and where they first received their training. The establishment was founded by Austrian Archduke Charles in 1580, and it was originally from here that all the horses came that took part in the intricate, ballet-like maneuvers of the Spanish School of Riding in Vienna. The stud farm had difficulty in starting again after the last war, but there are now nearly 300 excellent horses in the stud book. There are two good hotels here, and conducted tours of the stud can be arranged, with twice daily displays of the Spanish Riding School in summer. Some of these superb steeds are available for hire and seven-day riding courses are arranged. There are, of course, stud farms in Austria and Hungary.

From nearby Divača, if you are a caving enthusiast, you should take the opportunity to visit the Caves of Skocjan, less commercialized than the more famous ones at Postojna and thus even more profoundly primeval in character. From Divača we continue along the main road to Kozina, and soon are rewarded by our first view of the Gulf of Trieste.

Bled and Its Castle

Bled has become one of Yugoslavia's best-known tourist attractions, and rightly so. The resort has excellent amenities for sports and entertainment of all kinds, and the setting is glorious. A rare facility is the golf course (18 holes) magnificently situated above the River Sava gorge: guest players are welcome, and indeed golfing holidays here are becoming popular.

When you reach the lake itself, 460 m. (1,500 ft.) above sea-level, you have only to lift your head to get an impressive view of the whole mass of the Julian Alps, backed by Triglav. In the foreground, set in the wooded hills, the still waters of the lake reflect a stately castle at the summit of a steep cliff. In the middle of the lake there is a romantic little island, with an ancient church (rich baroque interior) close to the shore, which can be visited by gondola-like boats.

Legend has it that Živa, the Slav goddess of love and life, made this island her home. In Christian times it became a place of pilgrimage, as it still is today, seven centuries later, though it is no longer used for religious purposes. The local people will assure you that any wish expressed while the bells are ringing will be granted and, as you will hear, visitors are allowed to ring the bell while making their wishes.

The island itself has only the church and a café, but along the shores of the 1½-km.-long (one mile) lake there are numerous first-rate hotels, in one of which there are a large number of trout from the lake swimming about in an aquarium, happily unconscious that they are on the menu.

Bled was founded at the time of Charlemagne, but remained nothing more than a feudal stronghold for nearly 1,000 years, and it was only with the advent of modern transport facilities that it suddenly became an internationally famous tourist resort. It was the favorite home of the Regent Prince Paul of Yugoslavia during the years before World War II, and the late Marshal Tito observed the precedent by spending several weeks each summer in his villa there (now it's a hotel). Probably because of deep hot thermal springs the temperature of the lake in summer is around 68°F. despite the Alpine streams feeding it.

From the fortified castle set on the top of a bluff that rises vertically from the edge of the water, you get dramatic views across the lake and mountains. The castle was founded in the 11th century, though rebuilt many times and today includes a museum containing some indifferent paintings and a most terrifyingly malevolent carved wooden devil. In another part you will find the restaurant, famous for its smoked ham.

The Country Round Bled

One exciting local excursion is to the Vintgar gorges and waterfalls. Another is to the plateau of Pokljuka, returning via the Savica Falls, Bohinj Lake and its nearby summer resort of Bohinjska Bistrica. Or you can do the 30 km. (18 miles) from Bled to Bohinj direct, through the lovely narrow valley of the Sava Bohinjska. Lake Bohinj lies silent beneath the peaks of the Julian Alps, but there are a few pleasant hotels on or not far from its shores—it is an ideal place for anyone really wishing for peace, much wilder than Bled, but with freshwater swimming, boating, and interesting walks or climbing excursions into the mountains available. Bled and Bohinj are starting points for mountain trips in the Triglav reservation.

About five km. (three miles) beyond the end of Bohinj Lake, the road culminates near a hotel and fish restaurant, and a short walk brings you up to where the waters of the Savica make a tremendous leap over a 60-m. (195-ft.) fall. This is the source of the River Sava, which grows into an important tributary of the Danube. From here you can continue via the Seven Lakes to some of the highest Julian peaks, if you have the stamina and are properly equipped.

The Roads to Ljubljana

Ljubljana, the center and capital of Slovenia, is a university town of some 330,000 inhabitants. It is also an important center for coach and rail communications, and its airport receives visitors from many countries.

Coming from Klagenfurt by car you may enter by the 1,356-m. (4,453-ft.) Karavanke Mountains through the Ljubelj (Loibl) tunnel. The very good road descends in a series of loops and bypasses the old city of Tržič on its way to Ljubljana.

There is another more interesting route which begins east of Klagenfurt and passes through Eisenkappel to climb the 1,218-m.-high (3,996 ft.) Seeberg Pass to enter Yugoslavia.

This leads you through the attractive little winter-sports resort of Jezersko, a good starting point for several of the Karavanke peaks. The descent, always steep, leads through a narrow valley, and after passing Kranj, rejoins the main Ljubljana highway.

If you approach Ljubljana from Bled, the road runs southeast bypassing the 17th-century town of Radovljica (fascinating beehive-art museum), which lies on a terrace at the meeting place of the rivers Sava Bohinjka and Sava Dolinka. From here you will have a tremendous view of the Karavanke and Julian Alps, and it is only some 40 km. (25 miles) to Ljubljana.

Ljubljana, Slovenia's Capital

Ljubljana was founded by the Romans with the name of Aemona, though the only significant trace of their presence is a wall and complex of foundations, including mosaics and central-heating system, in the Mirje district of the city. The original town was destroyed by the barbarian hordes that swept out of Asia in the fifth century, and reconstructed by the Slavs with the name of Luvigana. Later it became the capital of the Duchy of Carniola and is known in German as Laibach.

Nearly 2,000 years old, Ljubljana is one of the most ancient cities in Yugoslavia, but in appearance it is wholly central European and not Balkan. The city lies on both sides of the River Ljubljanica and is in a position of unusual strategic importance, since is commands the "Ljubljana Gap" through the mountains.

Exploring Ljubljana

The most attractive part of the city is the old quarter on either bank of the Ljubljanica river, right at the foot of the castle-dominated hill. This is an area where a lot of open-air entertainment takes place in summer. At one point the river is spanned by the unusual triple bridge of Tromostovje, while on either bank there are pleasant riverside walks. In this district developed the medieval town, largely reshaped in the 17th and 18th centuries, thus accounting for its predominately baroque appearance today.

Its focal point is Mestni trg, dominated by the baroque town hall (Rotovz) and with a fountain representing three Slovene rivers by Franc Robba, an 18th-century sculptor whose work is to be found in several churches, including the cathedral. The latter also features fine ceilings by Quaglio. Near the cathedral are the Episcopal Court and Seminary, the former most attractively arranged round a courtyard with three stories of arcaded balconies successively built in the 16th–18th centuries; Napoleon stayed here briefly during his campaigns to recreate Illyria, when he was greeted as a great liberator.

Pleasant, if steep, walks lead up to the castle from whose tower you get a marvelous view of not only the city and its many bridges, but also the tremendous backdrop of the Julian Alps. Much of the castle is closed for restoration, but part of it has been adapted in unusual modern style for official marriage ceremonies on certain days of the week, and can be visited when these are not in progress. There is also an attractive coffee house.

The modern center of the city lies a few blocks west of the river, the mini-skyscraper of the Nebotičnik building providing a landmark on the main avenue of Titova cesta. Further west still, at the foot of the park on Tivoli hill, are the main cultural buildings: museums, galleries, opera house. A pedestrian way through the city center links Tivoli Hill with Tromostovje, passing near most of the main sights. Don't miss the National Museum on trg Herojev, whose treasures include the Vače bronze urn from the sixth century B.C. Neighboring it to the south is one of the latest additions to the Ljubljana scene: Cankarjev dom, an ultramodern complex of congress and concert halls, with adjoining shopping mall and high-rise blocks. Open spaces have been adapted as a kind of modern "forum," with one or two original Roman stones in evidence.

Finally, one of Ljubljana's great attractions is undoubtedly its opera; another is its International Summer Festival which extends from late June through August. Main venue for this is the interesting complex of Križanke, adapted in the 1930s by the architect Jože Plečnik from an old monastery.

To the Kamnik Alps

There is a delightful excursion by car north from Ljubljana which will show you the best of the Kamnik Alps in one day. After crossing the Sava River, drive about 23 km. (14 miles) to the town of Kamnik, set amid rich and smiling uplands. It is a quaint little place beneath the ruins of the old castle of Stari Grad and the romantic-looking little fortress of Mali Grad, with its curious three-story chapel. The large number of other old castles in the neighborhood clearly shows the great military importance attached to this road in medieval times.

Continuing north, we keep company with the little River Kamniška Bistrica for the five km. (three miles) to Stahovica, and there turn left. We climb from the narrow valley, parallel with the series of rapids and falls that carry the river from the heights, until we come to the mountain refuge of Dom pri Kamniška Bistrici, which is named after the small river that rises nearby. From the little inn there is a majestic view of the Kamnik Alps, dominated by 2,484-m. (8,147-ft.) Mount Grintavec and Mount Ojstrica (2,329 m./7,638 ft.).

From here we return to the fork in the road and turn east, over the 902-m. high (2960 ft.) Črnivec Pass and down to Gornji Grad, a popular mountain resort surrounded by deep forests facing the highest ridge of the Kamnik Alps. 6½ km. (four miles) brings you to Radmirje, where you turn left to Ljubno and Luče, a matter of another 12 km. (7½ miles). Both nestle beneath the mountains in the valley of Savinja. The road follows the winding channel of the river through the Robanov Kot valley, of glacial origin, cut into the base of Mount Ojstrica.

Following the Logarska Dolina (valley), the road struggles on through scenery of ever-increasing grandeur, reminiscent of the famous *Cirque de Gavarnie* near Pau in the central Pyrenees. Here, beside the source of the River Savinja, are various hotels and inns, and in the surrounding mountains climbers' refuges and shelters, for it is a popular center for all kinds of excursions by foot.

In the Path of the Roman Legions

Celje lies almost due east and 76 km. (47 miles) from Ljubljana. The road between the two towns was taken by the Roman legionaries as they thrust toward the plains of what is now Hungary and the banks of the mighty Danube. It is a smiling, undulating countryside through Trojane and Vransko to Šempeter, only a few kilometers from Celje, and it is there that important archeological discoveries have been made in the ruins of what was once the thriving second-century Roman city of Claudia Celeia. Of exceptional interest is the open-air collection of Roman funerary memorials from the second and third centuries.

Celje itself was seriously damaged during World War II, but still retains something of the medieval charm it had when the Counts of Celje made it the capital of their domain. Of special note is the lovely Gothic Chapel of Our Lady of Sorrows in the abbey church of St. Daniel. The Old County Hall (Stara Grofija) is another fine building, this time in late Renaissance style with a double-tiered arcade. It contains the Regional Museum and features a magnificient early 17th-century ceiling in the main hall.

Other interesting sights of Celje include the Minorite Church of St. Mary. You can also drive (or walk) up to the ruins of the ancient castle that dominates the whole town and houses a small restaurant with a mighty view.

Celje on E57, halfway between Ljubljana and Maribor, with the spa Dobrna to the north, is the starting point for roads leading either south along the valley of the Savinja or to the east. The former leads to Laško, where a castle perched on the conical hill of Hom has a fairy-tale air, and thence to the popular spa of Rimske Toplice. Almost next door is Zidani Most, where the Savinja joins the River Sava, and if we follow the river southeast, we shall soon be on the main road to Zagreb, a total run of 106 km. (66 miles).

Some 26 km. (16 miles) before Zagreb, we pass near Čateške Toplice, another spa with radioactive water at a constant temperature of 131°F. Almost the last glimpse of Slovenia before crossing into Croatia is of the Castle of Mokrice on our right.

Should you take the route east of Celje, you soon have the choice of detours to two more of Slovenia's spas, both particularly well-equipped: Rogaška Slatina and Atomske Toplice, in very agreeable scenery. The road through the former could provide a longer alternative route to the main road to Maribor. The route via Atomske Toplice, on the other hand, continues into Croatia taking in such sightseeing high spots as Tito's birthplace at Kumrovec on the way to Zagreb (see Inland Croatia).

Maribor and the Pohorje Mountains

There are two other main roads from Austria which will bring you to Maribor, second only to Ljubljana among the cities of Slovenia.

The first is east from Klagenfurt, through Völkermarkt to the frontier beyond Lavamünd, after which the first Yugoslav village is Dravograd in the valley of the River Drava. Following the winding course of the river on its way to join the Danube, we pass through pleasant rustic scenery where the centuries seem to have wrought few changes even though, paradoxically, rapid industrialization is taking place. On our right the Pohorje Hills can be seen, the last gentle foothills of the Alps, sweeping down between partially wooded slopes.

It is some 14½ km. (nine miles) from Dravograd to Muta, with its tiny medieval church, and another four km. (2½ miles) to Radlje ob Dravi. Here steep, forest-clad cliffs close in above the valley, but fall away before we come to Fala, one of the main centers for trips into the Pohorje. The Drava is interrupted by several hydro-electric dams and their attendant lakes; one of them, Brestrnica, on the outskirts of Maribor, well-equipped with recreational facilities.

The second route from Austria covers the 71 km. (44 miles) from Graz to Maribor, passing Leibnitz and the Yugoslav frontier village of Šentilj. From there it is less than 16 km. (ten miles) through the Slovenske Gorice hills to Maribor, a city of 130,000 inhabitants. Maribor is the economic and cultural center of the northeast of Slovenia (Lower Styria), though its fame outside Yugoslavia is chiefly for its splendid apples. The district is virtually one vast apple orchard—and a sight beyond description when all the trees are in blossom.

Maribor was founded in the 11th century, though there is evidence of prehistoric settlements in the neighborhood. It was a Christian outpost and bastion, built to stem the repeated tides of Turkish conquest that swept into central Europe and which twice threatened the walls of Vienna itself.

There is a monumental pillar which commemorates the Great Plague of 1643, which followed the ravages of the Thirty Years War. The 16th-century Town Hall is unusual because of its Renaissance balcony, and the Audience Chamber has interesting baroque ornamentation. Near here is a small, charming square, formerly the Jewish quarter, with an old synagogue (later a church, then warehouse) and tower, both now used for exhibitions. This peaceful spot becomes the setting for a lively mixed market on Saturdays in summer. From this point you can look down over the town walls on to the waterfront and a pentagonal water tower in Renaissance style. In earlier times, tolls were imposed here on the rafts that used the river as a means of transport. The buildings along this waterfront, which had fallen into some disrepair, are now being restored and developed to accommodate small shops and restaurants. For an attractive view of it and the town piled up behind, cross the old bridge over the Drava to the other bank.

Two other major buildings in town are the Cathedral (rebuilt in Gothic in the 15th century, with Baroque chapels added later) and the impressive castle (with Renaissance and Baroque elements grafted onto its original Gothic core). Some of its halls are now used as the regional museum, and that reserved for archeological exhibits contains a good collection of Celtic and Roman antiquities, while elsewhere there are some beautiful wood carvings and a magnificent display of medieval arms and armor. Not far from the center of town, a fine park slopes up between vine-covered hillocks to provide pleasant walks through woods and alongside fish ponds.

Excursions from Maribor

Maribor is an excellent center for all manner of excursions, not least into the lovely Pohorje mountains that extend for some 60 km. (37 miles) to the west—ideal for walking in summer and skiing in winter. Indeed a system of ski lifts is planned that will eventually make it possible to travel by ski up and down these heights from Maribor to Slovenj Gradec. By road, it's about 20–30 km. (12–20 miles) into the hills, but 5 km. (3 miles) from town is the lower station of a cable car which gets you up pretty smartly to well over 1,000 meters.

In contrast there are some delightful excursions into the wine-growing hill district of Slovenske Gorice to the north of the Drava. A marked Wine Road is being developed through the by-ways, linking unspoilt villages and such famous centers as Ormož, Jeruzalem, Ljutomer and Radgona, where you can sample and buy the local vintages. A map of this route should be available by now, including a list of the names and addresses of producers, some of whose wines are without doubt among the best in Yugoslavia. At Murska Sobota, the character of the country changes. With the long balanced wooden arms standing high above the wells, and the gipsy orchestras that play on every important occasion (including funerals), the atmosphere becomes very much like that of the villages of the Hungarian *puszta* or Great Plain, of which this region is an extension.

The small medieval town of Ptuj lies 25 km. (15 miles) to the southeast of Maribor, a charming wine-growing center with its roots in Roman times when it was Poetovium. Relics from that era are the ruins of two interesting Temples of Mithras, the Persian sun-god, neither of them easy to find as they are in the outskirts 2 or 3 km. from the center. Look for a sign *"Mitraju."* The core of the town is very compact, huddled by the Drava below an imposing hill-top castle, its narrow streets crowded with old secular and religious buildings with Gothic, Renaissance and Baroque features, and several incorporating Roman stonework. One of them, the Dominican monastery, is now the Archeological Museum. In the center, between the old town hall and the interesting Priory Church (Gothic pews and fine high altar) a second century tombstone forms the Orpheus Pillar, used as a pillory in the Middle Ages.

The castle itself houses the collections of the families who once owned it—among them the Leslie family from Scotland who served as mercenary generals in the Austrian army and occupied the castle until 1802. The views from the walls are well worth the short steep climb if you haven't a car.

You can combine sightseeing and accommodations if you stay in the Castle of Štatenberg, today the Grad Statenberg Hotel, as all the original installations have been kept intact, though of course modern adjuncts have been added for the comfort of the 20th-century visitor. The frescos in the Hall of the Equerries are extremely fine.

Another 15th-century castle that has been turned into an attractive hotel is that of Borl, east of Ptuj on one of the roads to Varaždin in Croatia. The terrace of its restaurant affords a peaceful view across the valley of the Drava to green pastures and rich vineyards.

Toward the Sunny Adriatic

A favorite itinerary for visitors to Ljubljana is southwestward to the shores of the Adriatic. E63/E70 widens and becomes a toll-highway for over half the distance, and it is just off this road that you find Postojna and its famous caves in the heart of a fascinating *karst* area characterized by extraordinary underground formations and disappearing rivers. There are good accommodations right by the most famous caves of Postojna if you want to explore the region at greater leisure.

The Postojna Caves are among the largest and in some respects the most extraordinary in the world, being no less than 19 km. (12 miles) long, of which the first seven km. (4½ miles) are easily accessible and illuminated by electric light. As the distances are so great there is a miniature railway that carries you through a representative three km. (two miles) with the minimum effort, and from its "terminus" you will be led by a guide on a figure-of-eight circuit after which you emerge once more into the light of day. But do not lose the guide, or you may disappear forever into this fantastic world of stalactites and stalagmites that have been growing for a million years in a darkness that has only quite recently been disturbed by man.

It is a predilection of all guides to underground grottos to find resemblances between the formations of blind nature and something within human experience. If you cannot accept them for what they are, tremendously strange and impressive forms, then there are the "Cathedral," "the Concert Hall, " "Paradise Grotto," "the Great Ball Room" (with rock clusters that might be giant chandeliers), all strangely-colored, glittering and slightly warped, as though seen in some waking dream. There is the stalagmite like a monkey or a cockerel, or the leaning tower of Pisa, and no doubt if your imagination is vivid enough, like the Brooklyn Bridge or Winston Churchill! Fantasy aside, however, probably the most impressive hall is the first to be visited, called the "Grotto of Mount Calvary."

Entirely in keeping with the strangeness of this underground world are the snake-like creatures, the size of a pencil, called Proteus Anguineus, which may be examined—we will not say admired—in a floodlit aquarium in the "Great Hall," next door to a small picture-postcard shop and post office. Eyeless and colorless because of countless centuries of life in total darkness, the proteus is both fish and mammal. It is a biological conundrum, and can live for up to 60 years.

Parts of the Postojna Caves are blackened and scorched by fire. During the Axis occupation of World War II, the German High Command decided to use this perfect bomb-proof shelter for the storage of a great part of their reserves of gasoline and oil. Slovenian guerrillas discovered this, and making use of an unmapped entrance unknown to the enemy, a small band of them entered secretly to rig up a time-bomb, with the result that 10,000 tons of strategically vital fuel went up in smoke.

The River Pivka and the Postojna Caves end abruptly, to reappear some kilometers farther north as the Unec River and the Planinska Jama Caves.

Around 24 km. (15 miles) north and then east of Postojna, near the village of Cerknica, is another curiosity of nature, the disappearing Cerkniško Jezero. In winter it is some 26 km. (16 miles) long by 1½ km. (a mile) wide, but in summer it drains away through fissures in the limestone bed of the lake, and the peasants harvest the thick grass that grows there.

Not far from Cerknica is the national park of the Rakova Dolina valley, in beautiful scenery. Close by the Križna Jama Caves, near to Stari Trg, can only be reached by boat, and with the assistance of a guide. This grotto is several kilometers long and contains no less than 22 small lakes.

The entire area is riddled with caves and grottos, some of them barely explored, so that any visitor will find even a short excursion an adventure. We have already mentioned the Škocjan Caves close to Divača, which although smaller than those of Postojna, are of an even wilder beauty, and echo ceaselessly to the sound of great waterfalls. The caves in the region of Kras provide valuable material to expeditions by teams of professional speleologists.

The short Slovene section of the Adriatic coast is described in our chapter on Istria.

From Ljubljana to Zagreb

The main link between Slovenia and Croatia and Serbia is the 160 km. (100 miles) or so of road between Ljubljana and Zagreb, which is designated an *autoput* or express highway; but it carries a great weight of traffic and should be traveled with caution. This cuts across fertile, agreeable country, with small churches and chapels perched on the top of its low hills. The road runs southeast through marshes that mark the extent of what, long ago, was a great lake.

If you are more interested in seeing something of the district through which you are traveling rather than in reaching your destination by the shortest possible route, then we would advise you to turn off and follow the valley of the Krka. The river bursts from the mouth of a cave, then flows below numerous impressive medieval castles. Some miles before Novo Mesto, a turning off this road leads to the well-equipped spa of Dolenjske Toplice.

Novo Mesto, capital of Lower Carniola, is built on a steep promontory worn from the rock by the action of the river. The Church of St. Nicholas contains a *St. Nicholas* by Tintoretto. The Franciscan monastery is interesting. To the north is yet another spa, Šmarješke Toplice.

As we continue east, the powerful walls of the Castle of Otočec, rising from the shores of a small island in the River Krka, come as an agreeable surprise even in this land of ancient fortresses. It has been restored and adapted as a well-equipped hotel. Farther along the Krka valley road is the typical Lower Carniolian town of Kostanjevica, built upon another island in the Krka. It is now a major cultural center with several of its historic buildings, including the nearby Cistercian abbey church, providing settings for art exhibitions.

21 km. (13 miles) east from Kostanjevica we reach the highway to Zagreb, and soon leave Slovenia.

PRACTICAL INFORMATION FOR SLOVENIA

HOW TO GET THERE. By plane. Ljubljana is linked by air with the major cities of Yugoslavia and with many cities in Europe, including London.

By train. The Slovenian capital lies on the route of main expresses running between various countries. The through rail route links Ljubljana also to Zagreb, Belgrade, Niš and Skopje.

By bus. Buses from Ljubljana go to major towns throughout Slovenia and beyond.

WHEN TO GO. There are two separate tourist seasons in Slovenia, the winter for skiing, etc., and the summer, to be spent either by the sea or in the mountains. Winter sports begin at Christmas and continue until mid-April, and the summer holiday season is from early June until the end of September or mid-October. Here is a list of annual events which may help you to make your choice.

March (second half). International Skiing Competitions (slalom and giant slalom), Vitranc Cup at Kransjka Gora.

June (mid). International Jazz Festival, Ljubljana. **(Late)** Traditional wedding festivities for couples from several countries, Ljubljana.

July (end). Peasant Wedding, Bohinj; folklore event.

July (mid)–August (end). Ljubljana Festival, with open-air performances of opera, ballet and symphony concerts.

August (mid). Peasant Wedding, Bled; folklore event.

August (end). Ljubljana International Wine Fair begins.

September (mid). Maribor: Merry Autumn (market, folklore and exhibitions).

HOTELS AND RESTAURANTS. Most Slovenia hotels listed here are open year-round; unless otherwise stated, all have rooms with bath or shower. Note that Slovenia is also well-provided with privately run guest houses (look for the sign *gostilna*), as well as private accommodations. In addition, farmhouse accommodations are now widely available and a special booklet from Kompas travel agency (see Useful Addresses) gives full details.

Food and Drink. Slovene cooking reveals the influence of Austria, and this is particularly evident in the delicious pastries and cakes. *Štruklji* is a Slovene specialty made of a dough of buckwheat or other flour, with layers of cheese. You can also get a *Wiener schnitzel* or *escalope Viennoise* (Dunaiski Zrezek) the equal of any to be had in an Austrian restaurant. Similarly, the famous sausages of Kranjska are unmistakably Germanic, and are called *kranjske klobase*. In northern Slovenia, the influence is more Hungarian, as is clear from such dishes as chicken fried in breadcrumbs *(pohovano pile)* and the "gipsy roast" called *cigansko pečenje,* flavored with garlic.

Slovenia is fortunate with her wines, which are among the best in the country. The red *Teran,* grown not far from Trieste, was appreciated by the Romans nearly 2,000 years ago. Those who prefer white wines should try Slovenia's *Ljutomer* or *Jeruzalem*. *Radgona* is excellent, whether still or sparkling. "Vin ordinaire" in Slovenia is never bottled; it is a powerful rosé known as *cviček*. It is very cheap and is served in every little roadside inn or tavern, drawn straight from the cask.

Bled. A delightful lakeside resort in the Julian Alps. *Villa Bled* (L), 30 rooms, some (E), own beach. Former summer residence of President Tito, with lovely grounds, tennis, free use of pool at Grand Hotel Toplice, and free green fees at Bled Golf Course. *Golf* (E), 150 rooms. Modern, central, with indoor and open-air pools, saunas, sports facilities and garden terrace. *Grand Hotel Toplice* (E), 121 rooms. Grand, top-class old-style hotel by lake with indoor and open-air pools, own beach, extensive keep-fit facilities, saunas, bridge room. *Jelovica* (M), 146 rooms. Short stroll from lake shore, garden, championship skittle alley. *Krim* (M), 127 rooms. On main street. *Kompas* (M), 92 rooms, near center. *Lovec* (M), 72 rooms, near center. *Park* (M), 217 rooms, at upper end of its category. Modern, near lake—very central; rooftop pool, several bars, disco, nearby Kazina dance hall.

Bohinj. A pleasant resort in the Julian Alps. *Bellevue* (M), 22 rooms, plus annex. Near small shopping center, 1 km. from lake. *Jezero* (M), 31 rooms, about 70 m. above lake. Recently renovated. *Kompas* (M), 55 rooms, nightclub. In parkland, 100 m. above lake. *Ski Hotel* (M), 40 rooms, some baths, at lower end of its category. *Zlatorog* (M), 43 rooms, at top end of its category. At far end of lake on the shore, indoor pool, sauna. On Vogel plateau, about 1,000 m. (3,280 ft.) above lake.

Bovec. A mountain resort in the Julian Alps and Trenta Valley. *Kanin* (M), 130 rooms. Sauna, indoor pool. *Alp Hotel* (I), 60 rooms.

Celje. Historic center roughly equidistant from Maribor, Ljubljana and Zagreb. *Celeia* (M), 84 rooms. *Evropa* (M), 110 rooms. *Merx* (M), 26 rooms, open-air pool.

Dolenjske Toplice. *Zdraviliški Dom* (M), 53 rooms, indoor and open-air pools.

Gozd Martuljek. Pretty hamlet near Kransjska Gora. *Špik* (M), newly renovated, 98 rooms, tennis, disco.

Kobarid. *Matajur* (M), 36 rooms, at bottom of its category. On the main square.

Kranjska Gora. Summer mountain resort and winter sports center. *Kompas* (M), 155 rooms, first-class; indoor pool, tennis, nightclub. *Alpina* (M), 101 rooms, nightclub. Comfortable Alpine style, short walk above village. *Larix* (M), 130 rooms, indoor pool, disco. *Lek* (M), 75 rooms, indoor pool, tennis, short walk from center. *Prisank* (M), 65 rooms, friendly inn-style.

Lipica. Original home of the famous Lippizaner horses; riding courses available. *Klub* (M), 102 rooms. *Maestoso* (M), 84 rooms, indoor pool. Both at top end of their category.

Ljubelj. Near Yugoslav entrance to Alpine road tunnel link with Austria. Two-stage chair lift; fine skiing and walking. *Kompas* (M), 36 rooms.

Ljutomer. *Jeruzalem* (I), 43 rooms.

Maribor. Historic town and excellent center for excursions to the Pohorje mountain region nearby. No truly first-class accommodations. *Habakuk* (M), 40 rooms. By lower station of cable car, 5 km. (3 miles) from town. *Orel* (M), 150 rooms, very central. *Turist* (M), 130 rooms. *Zamorec* (I), 36 rooms without bath, very central. *Motel Jezero* (M), 15 rooms, 7 km. (4 miles) out, by lake, on Dragograd road. *Motel Pesnica* (M), 5 km. (3 miles) out towards Šentilj pass.

Restaurants. *Hugo* (E), good private restaurant a little out of town. *Pec* (M), also private, a little out of town, attractive national décor. *Pri treh Ribnikih* (M), excellent national dishes. Located in town park. *Vernik* (M), award-winning private restaurant, a little out of town. *Center* (I), self-service, central.

Mariborsko Pohorje. Winter sports center near Maribor. *Areh-Sport Hotel* (M–I), 25 rooms. *Bellevue* (I), 51 rooms.

Most Na Soči. In the Julian Alps. *Kompas* (M), 24 rooms. At the lower end of the scale.

Murska Sobota. Near the Hungarian border. *Diana* (M), 103 rooms. *Zvezda* (I), 34 rooms.

Nova Gorica. Near the Italian frontier. *Park* (M), 105 rooms, at the top of its category.

Novo Mesto. *Metropol* (M), 47 rooms. *Pri Vodnjaku* (I).

Otočec. *Grad Otočec* (E), 21 rooms, some (M). Annex with 90 rooms. A charming castle on an island in the Krka River, now converted into hotel accommodations. Pool. Situated 400 m. (¼ mile) off the *autoput* between Ljubljana and Zagreb. *Motel Otočec* (I), 40 rooms, 24 bungalows, indoor pool. Actually on the *autoput*.

Podvin-Radovljica. Stopover near Bled. *Grad Podvin* (M), 33 rooms. Pools.

Pokljuka. Mountain plateau hotel near Bled. *Šport* (I), 39 rooms.

Postojna. Europe's largest caves, with fantastic stalactites and stalagmites, and an internal railroad. *Jama* (E), 143 rooms, some (M); pool. *Kras* (E), 54 rooms, some (M). *Motel Proteus* (M), 155 rooms, some (I). On Ljubljana–Trieste highway.

Ptuj. Historic and wine-growing center. *Poetovio* (I), and annex, 43 rooms, some with bath.

Radenci. Spa. *Radin* (E), 300 rooms, some (M), top-class. Indoor and open-air pools and sports facilities.

Radovljica. Southeast of Bled, starting point for canoeists on the River Sava. *Grajski Dvor* (M), 76 rooms. Pool. On the road to Ljubljana.

Rogaška Slatina. One of Yugoslavia's best-known thermal spas. *Donat* (E), 150 rooms, indoor and open-air pools and annex. *Sava* (E), 256 rooms, top-class; indoor pool. *Soca* (M), 55 rooms. *Styria* (M), 64 rooms.

Slovenj Gradec. Mountain resort. *Kompas* (E), 63 rooms, some (M), open-air pool. *Pohorje* (M), 26 rooms.

Šmarješke Toplice. Thermal spa in Eastern Slovenia. *Krka* (M), 111 rooms. Indoor and open-air pools.

Štatenberg. *Grad Štatenberg* (M), 30 rooms, a few with bath. In a former castle.

Tolmin. *Krn* (I), 54 rooms.

Vršič Pass. Leading from Kranjska Gora to Trenta Valley. *Tičarjev Dom* (M), 70 beds. Modern, situated at top of the pass. There are several other mountain inns in the area, each set among fine scenery.

SPORTS. Slovenia is Yugoslavia's best winter sports area, largely because the various resorts are relatively accessible, well-organized, well-served with hotels—*and* charges are reasonable. The Olympic ski-jump is at Rateče Planica. There are chair and ski lifts at Kranjska Gora to the choicest slopes of Vitranc Mountain, also a great number of inns and mountain cabins where everyone is very helpful. The Pokljuka Plateau, 1,200–1,585 m. (3,900–5,200 ft.) above sea-level, affords perfect conditions for beginners. In Bohinj there are ski lifts to extensive *pistes* on Vogel and Komna plateaux (1,370–1,645 m./4,500–5,400 ft.). Others from Kamniška Bistrica to Velika Planina. In the Pohorje Mountains, near Maribor, the terrain is easier—and prices lower.

In summer months climbing and mountaineering attract many visitors, the principal centers being Kranjska Gora, the valley of the Trenta, Bohinj, Bled, Kamnik, Jezersko and Solčava. The last stages of the European Footpath, E6, from the Baltic to the Adriatic passes through Slovenia, crossing the Pohorje Mountains, then continuing east of Ljubljana and over Snežnik Mountain to reach the coast west of Rijeka.

There is a fine golf course (18 holes) about 1½ km. (a mile) from Bled, situated above the River Sava gorge, with splendid views of the mountains. Season is from mid-April to mid-October, and equipment may be hired—green and caddies' fees are reasonable.

Swimming and boating are popular on the lakes, particularly rowing on Lake Bled (no motor boats allowed). For kayak enthusiasts Slovenia offers marvelous opportunities: on the Soca river from Žužemberk, on the

River Krka, through a countryside dotted with ancient castles, or from the junction of the two rivers Sava to the frontiers of Croatia.

PRACTICAL INFORMATION FOR LJUBLJANA

HOTELS. Apart from the hotels listed below, Ljubljana has a good selection of inns and guest houses, as well as student hostels—details from the Tourist Information Center. Camp sites are: Autocamp Ježica, Titova 260, four km. (2½ miles) from center, and Camp Dragočajna, Zbiljsko jezero, on the lake shore, 18 km. (11 miles) north of the town.

The following have all or some rooms with bath or shower unless otherwise stated.

Deluxe

Holiday Inn, Miklošičeva 3. 132 rooms. Central, with all amenities, including pool.

Expensive

Kompas, Miklošičeva 9. 61 rooms, some (M). Central, nearest to rail station.

Slon, Titova 10. 185 rooms, some (M), nightclub. Rooms overlooking main street can be noisy. Good national restaurant.

Moderate

Gostilna Pri Mraku, Rimska 4. 27 rooms. Inn. Good value.
Turist, Dalmatinova 13. 192 rooms, some (E).
Union, Miklošičeva 1. 270 rooms, some (E).

Inexpensive

Motel Kompas Medno, on the Kranj road, 9½ km. (six miles) north. 42 rooms.
Motel Tikveš, Draga. 14 rooms.
Park, Tabor 9. 90 rooms, a little out of center. Good value.

Several student hostels, open to visitors of all ages, offer extremely low-priced, good-value accommodations in summer. They include: *Dijaški dom Ivana Cankarja,* Poljanska 26–28; *Dom Učenev Tabor,* Vidovolanska 7; *FSPN-Študenski dom,* Kardeljeva pl. 5; but check with the Tourist Information Center.

RESTAURANTS. In addition to the listed hotels, Ljubljana has numerous restaurants, many of which are extremely attractive and with good service. *Ljubljanski Dvor* (E), Dvorni trg. By the river, with terrace, separate lower-priced pizzeria. *Rotovž* (E), Mestni trg. In the heart of the old town. *Mrak* (M), Rimska 4. A short stroll from the center, unpretentious. *Na Brinju* (M), Vodovodna 4. Excellent food, small summer garden, out of center. *Pod Rožnikom* (M), Cesta na Rožnik 18. Near Tivoli Park, with large garden and Serbian specialties. *Kresnica* (I), Rolovićeva 8. Out of center. *Triglav* (I), Miklošičeva. Central, includes self-service section.

The Ilirija, Lev and Slon hotels all have nightclubs, and there are several discos.

The town has a good selection of cafés where you can drink coffee and eat huge cream cakes in the best central European manner. Two are in the Lev and Slon hotels. Self-service restaurants include *Emona, Triglav* and *Maximarket.*

HOW TO GET AROUND. Kompas and other Ljubljana travel agents organize circular tours that visit the Julian Alps, the Kamnik Alps, the Logar Valley (Logarska Dolina), and the caves and grotto country around Postojna.

MUSEUMS. International Center of Graphic Arts, Pod turnom 3.

Modern Art Gallery, Cankarjeva 15. Also arranges major international Biennale of Graphic Art (in years with uneven numbers).

The National Gallery, Cankarjeva 20, contains the best works of the particularly prolific Baroque school of Slovene artists.

The National Museum, Trg Herojev 1, has one ethnographic and one archeological section. Its greatest treasure is almost certainly the Vače Situle, a bronze urn discovered in Vače in Slovenia. Dating from the fifth century B.C., it is a wonderful example of Illyrian workmanship of the best period, and illustrates the high degree of civilization attained by the original inhabitants before Roman, or even Greek, influences had made themselves felt.

The National and University Library, Turjaška 1, includes first editions of all books printed in Slovene, also a number of interesting incunabula.

THEATERS. Most of the summer is taken up by the Ljubljana Summer Festival, with performances at Križanke, Trg francoske revolucije 2, and other historic settings. The main concert hall is the Slovenian Philharmonic Hall, Trg Osvobodite 9, while the Opera House is in Župančičeva and is well worth visiting for performances of a high quality. The ultramodern complex of Cankarjev dom, Trg revolucije 2, is equipped for congress and cultural events of all kinds.

USEFUL ADDRESSES. The Tourist Information Center is at Titova 11. The offices of the main Slovene travel agencies include: Kompas, Miklošičeva 11 or Titova cesta 12, and Globtour, Maximarket, Trg revolucije 1. Other main Yugoslav travel firms also have offices in the center of town. Ljubljana Airport is at Brnik near Kranj, 40 minutes from the town. Auto-Moto Zveza Slovenije is the principal motoring organization, and is at Titova 138. The main post office is at Cigaletova 15. First Aid Service, Boboričeva (urgenti blok) and Zaloška 25; 24-hour pharmacy, Prešernov trg 5.

INLAND CROATIA

Prosperity, Hills and Plains

Inland Croatia is very different from its great length of coast. While the latter is stony and fierce and elemental, tree-clad in Istria but bare and glaring over the rest of its length, Croatia inland is a region of rolling hills, fertile rivers and rich plains. We can distinguish five main sub-areas: the Zagorje hill area; the Gorski Kotar; the hills and valleys stretching south from Zagreb to Karlovac, the Plitvice Lakes and the Lika Valley; and the flat plain of Slavonia.

Varaždin, to the north, is the heart of Zagorje. Between the rivers Drava and Sava, east from the latter, lie the fertile plains of Slavonia that spread away unbroken to the banks of the Danube. Zagorje and Slavonia together make up northern Croatia. Between them and the long limestone ridge of the Velebit, which lies between inland Croatia and the Adriatic, the Gorski Kotar is east and northeast of Rijeka, pierced by the road to Karlovac. The Plitvice Lakes and the Lika, as it is usually called, occupy the south, having a common border with the Republic of Bosnia-Hercegovina.

The Historical Background

What is the modern province of Croatia was colonized by the Romans and formed part of the Pannonian province of the Empire, a vast territory stretching to the present Hungarian border. The arrival of the Croats, members of the great family of Slavic peoples, occurred over the sixth and seventh centuries. Established between the rivers Sava and Drava, the

Croats were still subject to the Avars (who had conquered them before their arrival in their new home), and remained so until they liberated themselves in the middle of the eighth century.

The following years saw the gradual fusion and unification of the various Croat tribes, until in the year 924 they created their own kingdom. Though Catholics, the Croats adopted the Slav liturgy fought for by Bishop Gregory of Nin. Their greatest kings were Tomislav, Petar, Krešimir and Zvonimir. Later, the Croat nation associated itself with the Magyar Kingdom, recognizing the royal house of Hungary as their overlord.

In 1527 the Turks occupied Hungary, and the Croats therefore transferred their allegiance to Austria. Throughout this alliance with—and subservience to—Vienna, the nobility were all-powerful, and there were repeated unsuccessful peasant revolts against their dominance, that of Matija Gubec in 1573 being suppressed with particular ferocity. Others that followed met the same fate, nor did the revival of the Croat-Magyar union in 1779 remove feudal injustice.

The Prussian defeat of Austria in the war of 1866 brought about great changes, among them the creation of the dual monarchy of Austria-Hungary. Austria took the overlordship of Slovenia and Dalmatia, while Hungary obtained control of Croatia, to which she granted autonomy in 1868. Under this arrangement, Croatia directed her own internal political affairs, including education. She was also allotted a certain number of seats in the Budapest Parliament. These concessions increased the determination of Croatia to achieve full independence, and her aims found expression in the Illyrian Movement, whose objective was that of the union of all southern Slav peoples. However, various pan-Slav attempts to realize this end failed to produce positive results, the long-awaited opportunity presenting itself only with the collapse of the Austro-Hungarian monarchy in 1918. The map of the Balkan peninsula was redrawn at the conclusion of World War I, and Croatia became an integral part of the new Kingdom of the Serbs, Croats and Slovenes.

Between the two world wars, certain Croat pretensions brought about the formation of an extreme nationalist political party under Ante Pavelić, which degenerated into the Fascist movement known as the *ustaše,* more concerned with killing Serbs and Jews—if necessary with the aid of Axis troops—than with the struggle for independence.

The assassination of King Alexander and the French Foreign Minister Louis Barthou during the former's official visit to Marseilles was the work of the *ustaše,* which seized power after the occupation of the country by German and Italian troops in 1941. The reality of an "independent" Croatia rapidly vanished, however. It became a mere puppet state.

After 1944 Croatia took its rightful place in the federation of Yugoslav Republics and struggled, like all the country's other regions, toward a viable economic existence. Partly through large tourist revenue from its coast, the Republic soon began to outstrip the rest of the country in prosperity—and new trouble began. Many Croats objected to being compelled to contribute funds for the economic development of non-Croatian backward areas (which was an essential provision of the new, increasingly decentralized Constitution adopted in the early 1970s) and voices were raised in favor of secession from the Federation, specifically permitted by the new Constitution. It required the personal intervention of President Tito, himself a Croat, to stop nationalist separatism.

Zagreb, Capital of Croatia

Zagreb's 1,000,000 inhabitants live on the fringe of a rich and fertile plain where maize, wheat, orchards and vines are cultivated under the lee of the wooded heights of Zagrebačka Gora.

The second city of Yugoslavia, Zagreb is in effect a second capital of the country. It has an intense cultural life of its own, and vies with Belgrade in the profusion of its concerts, theatrical performances of all kinds and literary and artistic exhibitions, including folklore festivals.

Exploring Zagreb

The city's attractive center is surrounded by a rapidly growing belt of undistinguished and indistinguishable suburbs. Even in the center there are striking contrasts between the lower town, with the spacious avenues and flower-filled gardens which divide up the districts of commercial and cultural institutions, and the two ancient quarters of the upper town, Kaptol and Grič. Here you will find the palaces of the former nobility, and such churches as have survived the city's two major earthquakes and one disastrous fire.

Zagreb is a main road, rail and air junction, and is unmistakably busy and prosperous, with its two famous International Trade Fairs (Spring and Autumn) among the world's largest and most important. Unless they are of specific interest to you, however, it is wise to avoid Zagreb at these times when accommodations are virtually impossible to find. If you are in search of the past, then remember that within half an hour's journey from all the bustle of Zagreb main station, you can still find ancient villages largely untouched by the passage of the centuries.

Zagreb—meaning "behind the hill"—claims to be the year-round cultural capital of Yugoslavia. Its theaters, Opera House and various orchestras are justly famous. Here, too, is the headquarters of the Yugoslav Academy of Arts and Sciences, and the university attracts the most talented among the youth of the nation. Zagreb's art galleries are particularly rich and many of the exhibitions are outstanding.

Centuries ago Zagreb comprised two neighboring but separate towns, one secular and the other religious. Perched on the summit of a hill, the former dominated the latter as it did the whole valley. In the 13th century it was named Gradec, meaning "fortress," and was walled to protect the citizens against the Tartars. The other town, named Kaptol or Chapter House, was also fortified in the 16th century, at the time of the great Turkish drive to the Danubian plain, though as it happened the enemy never came within 65 km. (40 miles) of the town. The separation of the two towns continued until the time of the Napoleonic Wars, and it was only in the 19th century that new building at last united them into the single city of Zagreb.

The lower town is centered around Ilica, the main street that crosses it for a distance of some 4 km. (2½ miles). It is full of shops and cafés, and leads you to the center, the recently renovated Trg Republike— Republic Square. Apart from trams, this square and part of Ilica is closed to traffic. From there you should climb Radićeva Street and Strossmayer Promenade to the quarter of the upper town known as Gornji Grad. This route affords fine views.

HUKOVIC

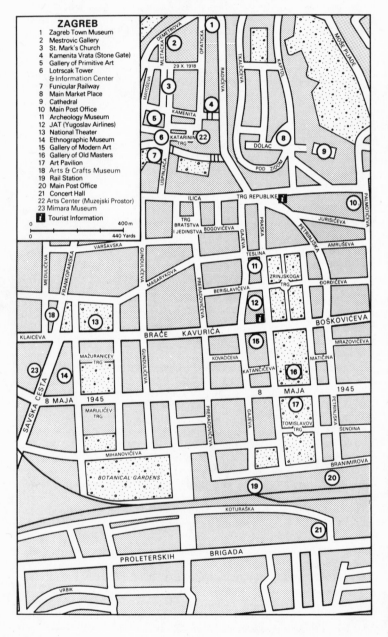

ZAGREB
1 Zagreb Town Museum
2 Mestrovic Gallery
3 St. Mark's Church
4 Kamenita Vrata (Stone Gate)
5 Gallery of Primitive Art
6 Lotrscak Tower
&Information Center
7 Funicular Railway
8 Main Market Place
9 Cathedral
10 Main Post Office
11 Archeology Museum
12 JAT (Yugoslav Airlines)
13 National Theater
14 Ethnographic Museum
15 Gallery of Modern Art
16 Gallery of Old Masters
17 Art Pavilion
18 Arts & Crafts Museum
19 Rail Station
20 Main Post Office
21 Concert Hall
22 Arts Center (Muzejski Prostor)
23 Mimara Museum
i Tourist Information

0   400 m
0   440 Yards

Alternative ways up are by Radićeva Street and the Kamenita vrata, the ancient Stone Gate (where, legend has it, a devastating fire was miraculously halted); accordingly a small shrine was incorporated into the ancient stonework, and became a favorite place of pilgrimage for those seeking consolation, as evidenced by the countless little plaques inscribed with *"hvala"* (thank you), including one in English.

You can also reach the upper town the effortless way by the venerable and much-loved funicular which takes you up from Ilica street in under a minute and puts you down opposite Lotrščak Tower, or Little Gate, which is the entrance to the fortress of Gradec. In memory of the days when all the gates of the fortress were closed against the perils of the coming night, a bell is still rung every evening at the hour of sunset. And at noon each day (except in August) a canon is fired.

Lotrščak Tower now houses a small museum and computerized information center not only on the cultural events of Zagreb but the whole of Europe! You can climb the tower for splendid views. Beyond it you will see two churches.

The first was built in the 17th century as a monastery dedicated to St. Catherine, the second, built in the center of Radićev trg (Radić Square) is the Church of St. Mark the Evangelist, its roof brilliant with red, white and blue tiles depicting the emblems of Croatia (on the left) and Zagreb. It was in front of St. Mark's that Matija Gubec was executed after the defeat of his peasant revolt in 1573.

The interior of St. Mark has been decorated by the best modern Yugoslav artists, including the sculptor, the late Ivan Meštrović, who spent the last years of his life in the United States. The modern frescos by Jozo Kljaković and various other works of art blend quite harmoniously with the 14th-century Gothic sanctuary. Do not miss the painting in the unfinished chapel, of King Tomislav holding his first Council of State in the tenth century. Some of the city's most interesting museums are in the upper town and one of the loveliest is the Arts Center in the 17th-century former Jesuit monastery, near St. Catherine's church. The exhibitions change frequently here, and the theme may be anything from ancient Chinese culture to the life of Tito—but it is worth going whatever the subject. Open-air concerts are held in the atrium on summer evenings. You will find several other worthwhile museums listed in the Practical Information section on Zagreb, but one you should make every effort to see is the Mimara Museum in the Lower Town, whose priceless art treasures are said to be among the most valuable one-man collections in the world, and referred to locally as the Yugoslav Louvre.

The slightly out-of-date elegance of Gornji Grad has a certain charm, but Kaptol as a whole is disappointing. The Catholic Cathedral of St. Stephen is imposing, but has little of interest to offer except, perhaps, the inscription of the Ten Commandments on the north wall, written in 12th-century Glagolitic characters.

A pleasant local custom is for the townspeople to take a morning walk, more often than not a few turns of the cathedral building. Among the chattering throng you will recognize the peasants who have come in from the neighboring villages. Very near the cathedral, too, is the bustling and colorful open-air market of Dolac, doing business seven days a week.

Zagreb has comfortable hotels, restaurants and cafés to suit most tastes and pockets. In addition, its many parks and gardens are beautifully kept.

Some of them are immense, like the parks of Tuškanac and Maksimir, the latter including Zagreb's zoo.

This is not only a city worth a visit on its own account, it is also a first-rate center for excursions, particularly to the hills of Medvednica. Many visitors like to climb to the highest point, Mount Sljeme (also accessible by cable car), from the slopes of which there are unforgettable views across the city of Zagreb, as well as the scenic River Sava valley. A short excursion west of the city is to Samobor, a pleasant little place built astride a stream and backed by more hills. It is famous for its crystal factory (visits by arrangement only) and its excellent local wine.

Zagorje

A most picturesque district lies beyond the Medvednica hills and is known as Zagorje, more or less meaning "the land beyond the mountains." Varaždin in the north of the region (75 km.—47 miles—from Zagreb) is full of interest. Recently celebrating its 800th anniversary, the little town sits close to the Drava river, its ancient core—much of it a pedestrian precinct—threaded by narrow streets along which you can easily distinguish some of the Baroque palaces of the former aristocratic and wealthy, with their ornate balconies and entrances. The castle, now a historical museum, lies near the center in a small park surrounded by grassy ramparts. A short walk away is the very unusual cemetery, its massive hedges trimmed and shaped round some extraordinarily ornate memorials to the long departed.

If you are traveling between Varaždin and Zagreb, you can choose from a number of routes, preferably avoiding the most direct and obvious along the main road. We suggest you take to the by-ways, bearing in mind some of the highlights mentioned below, losing yourself amongst the wooded heights that are interspersed with rolling open stretches of farmland or patterned with narrow strips of vineyards, so characteristic of the Zagorje. These minor roads are well surfaced and link villages that still seem quite remote from the world. Along them you are likely to encounter horse- or ox-drawn traffic (though now largely replaced by the ubiquitous tractor) or scatter a flock of geese. Hay and maize are stacked up to dry in cottage yards; and at the top of each steep stretch of vineyard you'll note the little house or *klet,* many of them now taking on the status of a weekend cottage.

Often the hills are crowned by a crumbling castle, or there are interesting churches to seek out. In the eastern part of the region, Belec, for instance, has two—one from the 13th century, the other an amazing extravaganza of Baroque and Rococo, built by a countess who had had a vision. Among the castles, that of Trakošćan in the north of the region is a highlight—rebuilt in the 19th century, but with a delightful setting perched above a wood-fringed lake, with a modern hotel nearby. The castle museum has a particularly good collection of weapons from over four centuries.

If you take a southeasterly direction over the Ivanščica hills you will eventually cross the Krapina valley and reach Marija Bistrica, whose church with a 15th-century Black Madonna is a major place of pilgrimage. From here a beautiful minor road leads over the Medvednica heights to Zagreb.

The western part of the Zagorje is more easily visited on minor routes to Zagreb from Maribor in Slovenia. It includes Krapina where the remains of Paleolithic man (now on exhibit in Zagreb) were discovered in a nearby grotto which can be visited. Krapina was the birthplace of Ljudevit Gaj, a founder of the Illyrian Movement in the early 19th century, and it also has an ecclesiastical gem, the early Baroque church of St. Mary of Jerusalem on the nearby hill of Trški Vrh.

In the rolling countryside to the west are several castles, among them the picturesque ruins of Veliki Tabor and the well restored Baroque castle of Miljana. But the highlight of this area for all Yugoslavs and many foreigners is the once remote village of Kumrovec. Here the late President Tito was born in a humble home and here he went to school. The village, which is largely in typical Zagorje style, has been reconstructed or restored. His birthplace, the barn in which he played as a child, the school, his later residence, and several other attractive old houses, can all be visited, and a modern Memorial Home provides a meeting place and inexpensive accommodations. In the courtyard of his birthplace is a fine statue of Yugoslavia's great leader by Augustinčić, a disciple of Meštrović.

If you have approached Kumrovec from Zagreb via the attractive Sutla valley, you will have passed through the magnificent Zelenjak Gorge, near Klanjec. In this dramatic place, a small monument is dedicated to the Croat national anthem written by Antun Mihanović who was inspired here to write it. Klanjec itself was the home town of Augustinčić and there is a gallery of his beautiful sculptures.

Finally, we should mention some of Zagorje's famous thermal spas, which might provide an attractive alternative to the city for accommodations if you have your own transport. Quite near Kumrovec is Tuheljske Toplice which features a major new sports and recreation center. Known since Roman times (their Aquae Vivae) is Krapinske Toplice a few miles to the northeast. Closer to Zagreb is Stubičke Toplice. All offer excellent facilities for open-air and indoor bathing.

Gorski Kotar

Leading southwest from Zagreb to the sea is the E65, a toll motorway for its first 53 km. (33 miles). This takes it as far as Karlovac, a flourishing town at the confluence of the Korana and Kupa rivers. Karlovac was once one of the Christian world's bastions against the Turks and today its 16th-century fortress is still impressive. It's also at the heart of a region laced by speedy little rivers, ideal for fishing and kayaking.

The town is an important crossroads. To the northeast, back along the minor road to Zagreb, is Jastrebarsko, still dominated by its 15th-century castle. To the south is Slunj Castle, where Napoleon billeted his troops and, beyond Slunj, are the Plitvice Lakes.

West from Karlovac and only a few kilometers inland from Rijeka is the wildly picturesque district of Gorski Kotar. Separated from the Adriatic coast by the hills inland from Rijeka, the heights of Gorski Kotar are everywhere thickly covered with silent forests of pine, though there are frequent grassy clearings. Lower down, the land is gashed by countless ravines, with fast-running streams.

Some of the peaks in this area, such as Risnjak and Sniješnik (or Snežnik), reach a height of nearly 1,525 m. (5,000 ft.). They are popular with ski enthusiasts, who can indulge in their favorite pastime well into the month of May, when bathing in the neighboring Adriatic is already possible.

One of the most attractive places in Gorski Kotar is the waterfall of Zeleni Vir, near to the town of Skrad, which hurls itself, with the noise of thunder, from a height of almost 90 m. (300 ft.). There is an unusually interesting grotto on the fringe of a neighboring lake.

We have mentioned only in passing that winter sports facilities are available in the heights of the Gorski Kotar. One of the most popular centers for skiing is the little town of Delnice, set between mountains and forests, and at Platak regular ski-competitions are held every season. Incidentally, if winter sports are not in your line, it may be worth remembering that the River Kupa, a tributary of the Sava, is not far away, and is a favorite with fishermen.

Delnice is conveniently central, and from it you can easily reach the various other sporting centers and beauty spots of the Gorski Kotar. An area of rocky hillsides, deep gorges and forests of giant pines is to be found near Lokve, and is strikingly beautiful in its wild grandeur. You should try to visit the 1,370-m. (4,500-ft.) Mount Bitoroj if you can. Its ascent is definitely worthwhile.

From Delnice, the shortest run to the shores of the Adriatic is via Fužine, a village attractively positioned beside a pine-fringed lake. However, the road is still only partly paved and you would do better to continue along the E65 which leads all the way to Rijeka, Yugoslavia's principal port, and widens into a motorway as it nears the coast.

The Plitvice Lakes and Lika Valley

These 16 lakes are among the greatest tourist attractions in Yugoslavia. Each is on a different level, and the water cascades from one to the other in a series of extraordinarily beautiful falls, gleaming and making rainbows of spray in the sunshine. Scenically speaking, the serene and romantic countryside round the lakes is, though relatively little known, one of the most beautiful districts in Europe. Today it has been declared a National Park to preserve it from thoughtless commercial exploitation. You will need to leave your car at one of the large parking lots at either entrance to the Park, where you will also pay the entrance fee and can collect all information. There are excellent accommodations, sightseeing vehicles and excursion boats on the largest lake (Kozjak). Better still is the network of paths and walkways offering many miles of unforgettable walks.

In this remote place, each season of the year has its special enchantment. In the spring, the melting of the heavy snows of a Balkan winter fill to the brim the higher lakes, creating a tremendous flow to the lower ones. In the summer, this thunderous series of waterfalls gradually quietens, and the special charm of autumn is that the utterly still surface of each lake perfectly mirrors every shade and leaf of the shores. Even the harshness of winter seems softened when the immaculate white of the snow is reflected in those quiet waters, and summer and winter alike there is the music of the falls between lake and lake. Their beauty aside, the Plitvice Lakes abound in fish and that gourmet's delight, freshwater crayfish.

You will probably notice the gigantic waterweeds and vegetation of all kinds that grow around the innumerable falls with such exuberance. Some of the trees in the surrounding forests are more than 50 m. (160 ft.) tall.

Near the village of Ljeskovac, two little streams unite to form the River Matica, which less than 1½ km. (a mile) farther on flows into the highest of the Plitvice Lakes, Prošće. This vast expanse of water is at a height of well over 610 m. (2,000 ft.) above sea-level, and flows into a far smaller lake which in turn supplies a third no less than 13 m. (42 ft.) below it. Next comes a group of four, connected by a whole series of magnificent cascades, and so, step by step, the chain descends to the third largest, and quite the bluest of the 16, Lake Galovac, which is at a height of 580 m. (1,900 ft.).

Past the last houses of Velika Poljana, Lake Kozjak narrows toward a mountainous canyon. From far off you can hear the roar of the great waterfall by which the upper lakes thunder down into Lake Kaluderovac, 530 m. (1,650 ft.) above sea-level. At the heart of the current the water is still the deepest blue in color, though the edges of the stream are dark gray.

There are a number of caves, one of which may be reached by a series of rough steps cut in rock for the purpose. From the head of these falls there is a magnificent view across the lower lakes.

The water from the last lake of all flows into a remarkable natural dam at the foot of the magnificent fall known as "watersmeet." From there it forms the little River Plitvice which gathers momentum for another series of cascades which together fall nearly another 70 m. (230 ft.). Various terraces provided for the visitor make it possible to appreciate the extraordinary sight of the sun shining with every color of the spectrum through the curtain of falling water which is to form the River Korana.

From here the Korana river follows a tortuous course northwards to join the Kupa at Karlovac, mentioned earlier. The region to the west of it, between the two main Karlovac–Rijeka and Karlovac–Plitvice roads, is another remote area—very beautiful indeed and particularly worth the attention of canoeists and kayakists or fishermen for it is laced by a network of exquisite little rivers like the Dobra and the Mrežnica. A main center in this area is Ogulin.

Continue along the main coast-bound road from the Plitvice Lakes and you come into a region called the Lika. Most of it lies in fact in the valley of the River Lika which runs parallel with the coast. Tiny Gospić is the area's main town, but though fertile, it is not a part of Yugoslavia that offers very special attractions, apart from the views from roads leading in and out of the area.

From Gospić, you can reach the coast either by the more direct route to Karlobag, or first follow the Lika valley south. Either way you must cross the mighty 80-km. (50-mile) long Velebit ridge which encloses the Lika on its seaward side; the huge 1,525-m.-high (5,000 ft.) mountain range gives the valley a very different climate from that of the coast. In October it is possible for the Lika to lie under ten cm. (four in.) of snow while people are still bathing and complaining of the heat a bare 30 or 40 km. (20–25 miles) away. The Velebit also provides superb views of the Kvarner Gulf and all its islands—once you have crossed one of the passes at the top of its ridge. Rab, the nearest of the islands, seems to be within a stone's throw, though it is in fact some 25 km. (15 miles) distant.

The road at the Lika's southern exit takes you over the magnificent Alan (or Halan) Pass, with the town of Obrovac at its southern approach. The Alan affords stupendous views from whichever side you approach. If you come from Obrovac toward the Lika you have the experience of crossing suddenly from a bare landscape to one filled with forests. If you travel southward you climb up out of the thick trees and suddenly see, spreading for kilometer after kilometer below you, the enormous and unforested sweep of the Velebit's southern end continuing all the way down to Obrovac.

It is also worth noting that a different southward-leading side road from Plitvice takes you quickly into a mountain area previously accessible only to the tough and determined, but now popular with both mountaineers and Yugoslav summer tourists. Its focal point is the little town of Udbina, where you can find modest lodgings. It lies east of the Lika Valley.

Slavonia

The final part of inland Croatia that we must consider is the region called Slavonia. Unlike the rest, it is flat—or very nearly so.

The province is really of greater economic interest than it is in terms of tourist attraction. It stretches from Zagreb to Belgrade, and is watered by both the rivers Drava and Sava, and crossed by the *autoput* linking the two capital cities. The land here is extremely fertile, with rich grasslands, vines and oak forests. Despite its industrialization, Slavonia is not without its attractions, notably at Daruvar, the *Aquae Balissae* of the Romans, and at Lipik, set in the romantically beautiful Pakra Valley. The two towns are only 26 km. (16 miles) apart on the road that runs from the *autoput* at Okučani.

Daruvar and Lipik are thermal spas, their waters leaving the spring at a temperature of 142°F, and containing a high concentration of iodine. Fortunately, or unfortunately, according to your point of view, oil has been found locally, and the exploitation of the wells during the next few years seems certain. Of the many fortifications built along the River Drava during the Middle Ages, few have survived. Among those that have is the fortress at Djurdjevac.

Another 160 km. (100 miles) east is the industrial city of Osijek, Slavonia's greatest manufacturing center. It is situated on the banks of the Drava, and its history goes back to Roman times. South of Osijek and only 21 km. (13 miles) north of the Zagreb–Belgrade highway is the town of Djakovo, which grew round an elegant 18th-century castle, and was once the home of the priest Strossmayer, one of the champions of Yugoslavia's 19th-century renaissance, and founder of the Academy of Arts and Sciences in the Croat capital. Today Djakovo is the seat of a bishopric. A traditional folklore event "Djakovo Embroidery" takes place here in July.

Despite its present peaceful air, Slavonia was the scene of many great battles in the past. Conquered by the Turks early in the 16th-century, the region remained under Ottoman domination for a century and a half. The Habsburgs subsequently fortified the whole of the province against the threat of further Turkish invasion. To achieve Croat cooperation, they were granted various special privileges, among them the right of soldiers to possess their own land, and exemption from all feudal taxes. Like the men of the Swiss Confederation, these peasant soldiers organized themselves so that they could muster many thousands of men at a few hours' notice, and their bravery and efficiency soon became famous throughout Europe. This military régime was maintained until toward the end of the last century. It is an amusing historical digression to recall that the members of a cavalry regiment of these soldiers in the service of Louis XIV of France were the inventors of the necktie. They wore a kind of white handkerchief round their necks, a fashion which was copied by the courtiers of Versailles—the French word *cravate* being a corruption of *croate* (*hrvat* in Serbo-Croat).

PRACTICAL INFORMATION FOR
INLAND CROATIA

WHEN TO GO. Remember that on the edge of the central European plains, it can be very hot in summer and cold in winter. Spring and fall are lovely times for the countryside at its best; summer and winter in the extensive mountain areas offer good open-air opportunities. The major events on the inland Croatian calendar take place in Zagreb and are listed in the Practical Information section for that city.

HOTELS AND RESTAURANTS. In the selection of accommodations below, where no dates are indicated it means the establishment is open the year round. Those listed have all or some rooms with bath or shower unless otherwise stated. Croatia is also well provided with privately run guest houses or pensions (look for the sign *gostionica*), as well as private accommodations.

Food and Drink. Croatian cooking is simple, tasty, and slightly sharp. It is not especially original, resembling central European cuisine in general. You can order just about anywhere such Balkan specialties as breaded chicken (*pohovano pile*) and gipsy roast (*cigansko pečenje*), both particularly good. The latter dish has a little garlic in it. As for pastries, Croatia is justly proud of its *štrudla,* a flaky crust with cherries (*sa trešnjama*), apples (*sa jabukama*) or cottage cheese, which is delicious if eaten when still warm—but watch out for your digestion. Noodles (*rezanci*) are eaten as dessert with chopped walnuts or poppy-seed, or with white pot-cheese and sugar. Cakes are typically central European—excellent. Whipped cream is used freely.

Light Croatian wines include *Žumberak* and *Moslavina.*

Delnice. Mountain resort. *Delnice* (M), 43 rooms, nightclub.

Jastrebarsko. *Jaska* (M), 50 rooms.

Karlovac. *Korana* (M), 192 rooms, nightclub. Terrace on the bank of the Korana River. At **Duga Resa,** 6½ km. (four miles) west of Karlovac, on the road toward Rijeka, is *Motel Roganac* (M). 11 rooms.

Krapinske Toplice. Spa. *Toplice* (M), 164 rooms; indoor and open-air pools. At the lower end of its category.

Kumrovec. The late President Tito's birthplace. *Spomin Dom* (Memorial Home) (M), 62 rooms, sports ground.

Marija Bistrica. Pilgrimage town near Zagreb. *Kaj* (I), 40 rooms, night-club.

Nova Gradiška. *Slaven* (M), 34 rooms. On the *autoput, Motel Turist* (I), 16 rooms.

Osijek. Good stopover in the northeastern section. *Central* (E), 36 rooms, some (M). *Osijek* (E), 182 rooms, some (M).

Plitvice Lakes (Plitvička Jezera). Magnificent situation with sports center. *Jezero* (E), 250 rooms. Sauna, indoor pool, tennis. *Plitvice* (E), 70 rooms. *Bellevue* (M), 90 rooms.

Samobor. *Šmidhen* (M), 60 rooms. Splendid pools for all ages, night-club.

Slavonski Brod. Conveniently located halfway along the *autoput* between Zagreb and Belgrade. *Brod* (M), 78 rooms. *Motel Marsonia* (M), 63 rooms. On the *autoput. Park* (M), 49 rooms. In the town. All representing good value for their category.

Slunj. In the narrow valley of the Korana River. *Park* (M), 14 rooms.

Stubičke Toplice. Spa. *Matija Gubec* (I), 36 rooms, indoor and open-air pools.

Trakošćan. *Trakošćan* (M), 50 rooms; at lower end of its price range. Modern and near lovely castle in the Zagorje.

Tuheljske Toplice. *Mihanović* (M), 178 rooms; indoor and open-air pools. In new recreation and sports center.

Varaždin. *Turist* (M), 85 rooms.

Županja. On the *autoput* between Zagreb and Belgrade. *Motel Rastovica* (M), 50 rooms, at lower end of price range.

SPORTS. If you are interested in kayaking, spend some time on the Kupa, Korana and Mrežnica rivers, set in wonderful woodland scenery. Canoeing and kayaking trips on these rivers are arranged from Karlovac. The Croat Krka can be reached from Knin, where you can also start the descent of the Cetina, as far as Šibenik. These rivers additionally provide excellent fishing.

Inland Croatia has tremendous hunting reserves, especially in Slavonia. The main quarry are deer and wild boar. Game birds also abound. Hunting in Croatia, one of the best grounds in Europe, is very well organized and offers all facilities to the amateur.

PRACTICAL INFORMATION FOR ZAGREB

HOW TO GET THERE. By plane. Zagreb is covered by the international air routes and can be reached direct from London, Paris, Amsterdam, Zürich and other cities. In summer, the city has air connections with all Yugoslav tourist centers that have airports.

By train. Of the numerous through trains stopping at Zagreb, many continue on to Belgrade, Niš and Skopje, or to towns on the coast such as Rijeka, Zadar, Šibenik and Split.

By car. The *autoput* (E70) connecting Ljubljana via Zagreb with Belgrade goes through the Slavonia region for a stretch of nearly 300 km. (190 miles), before entering Serbia. Zagreb can be bypassed by E70 which is a turnpike for over half the distance to Belgrade. There is also a turnpike from Zagreb to Karlovac, where E65 continues to Rijeka. Good roads now link the interior and the coast across various mountain passes. The usual access from Croatia to Bosnia-Hercegovina is from various branches off the *autoput* farther east. North of Zagreb, E65–E71 leads to Varaždin and Budapest.

By bus. Regular bus services connect Zagreb with all main centers.

WHEN TO GO. April or September is the time to choose if you are interested in major international trade fairs (described later); and either month is also a good time for the surrounding countryside. Cultural events are year-round, with the emphasis on open-air and street entertainments in the summer months, especially during the Summer in Zagreb festival from late-June to mid-September. The International Review of Original Folklore in the last week of July is of particular note. In addition, during alternate years (odd numbers) the International Festival of Contemporary Music takes place in April and (even numbers) the World Animated Cartoon Festival in May–June. Otherwise, like all big cities, Zagreb has plenty to offer at any time.

HOTELS. A major restoration program has had a salutory effect on the city's accommodations, though there is often still a great shortage. The hotels listed below have all or most rooms with bath or shower unless otherwise stated.

Deluxe

Esplanade, Mihanovićeva 1, opposite main rail station. 235 rooms. An imposing turn–of–the–century building, modernized; nightclub, casino and dancing on the terrace in summer—which can make some rooms noisy. One of the restaurants is in regional style. Though classified as A—it lacks a pool—this is one of Yugoslavia's best hotels and one of the chain of Leading Hotels of the World.

Inter-Continental Zagreb, Kršnjavoga 1. 457 rooms. Restaurants include one in national style; also casino, nightclub, indoor pool.

Holiday Inn, Ljubljanska avenija. 163 rooms, nightclub. New, near *autoput* in west part of city.

Laguna, Kranjčevićeva 29. 347 rooms. A little out of center.

Palace, Strossmayerov trg 10, near main rail station. 124 rooms. Some (M) accommodations.

Moderate

Beograd, Petrinjska 71. 130 rooms. Central. Some (I) accommodations.

Dubrovnik, Gajeva 1. 279 rooms. Recently renovated; very central, overlooking Republic Square. Amusement arcade. Some (E) accommodations.

Inexpensive

"I" Industrogradnja, Remetinečka 106. 219 rooms. New, near *autoput* and close to Zagreb Fair exhibition grounds.

Jadran, Vlaška 50. 48 rooms. Near the Cathedral. Some (M) accommodations.

Panorama, Trg športova 9. 320 rooms. Near Sports Palace in west part of city. Some (M) accommodations.

Park, Ivanićgradska 52. 145 rooms. New, quiet location in east part of city.

Motels and Pensions

Dvorac Brezovica (I), 28 rooms. First class pension and elegant restaurant in old castle (bungalows). Out of town.

Plitvice Motel (M), 140 beds, good national restaurant, several snack bars. About 15 km. (9 miles) from center to southwest, on main *autoput.*

Šumski dvor (I), Prekrizje. 9 rooms. A pension and attractive restaurant in a quiet and attractive district on the outskirts of the city.

Zagreb Motel (I), Dubrovačka aleja. 51 rooms. South of river Sava, near Fair grounds.

Camp site. The best is by the Plitvice Motel, see above.

Youth and budget accommodations. *Omladinski hostel* (youth only), Petrjinska 77. Central, near main railway station. In summer, student rooms and dormitories are available as very inexpensive accommodations for tourists (no age restriction), most completely renewed and with excellent facilities. Check with the Tourist Information Center or Youth Tourist Center (see Useful Addresses).

Private accommodations. Can be booked through travel agencies (see Useful Addresses).

RESTAURANTS. There is a wide choice of places to eat in Zagreb, covering the whole price spectrum; those below are but a small selection. Additionally, there are any number of self-service restaurants, milk bars and snack bars. Four good ones among the latter are *Corso,* Gundulićeva 2; *Medulić,* Medulićeva 2 (best in town for vegetarians); *Mosor,* Juričićeva 2 and *Splendid,* Zrinjevac Square 15. All four are central. For quick and cheap snacks, look for *čevapi u somunu* (selling *čevapčići* with bread) or *buregdžinica* (for tasty Bosnian pastries known as *burek*), especially near market places; also, at *Stari fijaker,* Mesnička 6.

There are also any number of coffee shops; two central ones, recently renovated, are *Gradska Kafana* and the *Dubrovnik Hotel* coffee shop, both on Republic Square.

The following restaurants all qualify as Moderate, though naturally if you choose the most expensive dishes in some of them, you will cross the boundary into the Expensive range.

Dubravkin put, on the road of the same name. A lovely situation among woods near the city.

Gradski podrum, A. Cesarca 2. One of the city's best known eating places, elegant and central, on a corner of Republic Square.

Harmica, Radićeva 3. Tiny snack bar near Republic Square, specializing in mushroom dishes.

Kaptolska klet, Kaptol 5. Central and good.

Korčula, N. Tesle 17. Specializes in fish and Dalmatian dishes. Central.

Lovački rog, Ilica 14. Central, game specialties. Oldest restaurant in town.

Okrugljak, Mlinovi 28. A little out of the center, but in a pleasant setting. There is an open-air section in the garden.

Plavi Podrum, Gajeva 10, by Republic Square. Zagreb cuisine, popular with the young.

Pod mirnim krovovima, Fijanova 7. Lamb-on-the-spit here is particularly good; also freshwater fish.

Šestinski lagvić, Šestine. Rustic décor and lovely hillside situation to the north of town.

Split, Ilica 19. Fish and Dalmatian specialties. Very central.

Starogradski podrum, Ćirilometodska 5, in the Upper Town. In the cellars of the old city hall; specialties include dishes from early 19th-century recipe book.

HOW TO GET AROUND. By bus/tram. There is a good network of trams serving the center, and there are buses out to the suburbs. The price is the same regardless of distance, and you can change as often as you like while traveling in the same direction, including from tram to bus, within a time limit of 1 hour. Tickets can be bought on boarding the vehicle from the conductor.

By coach. Generalturist and other travel firms in Zagreb run comfortable coach excursions to such tourist areas as the Plitvice Lakes and Dubrovnik.

By cable car. There is a cable car from the Gračani district (trams 14 and 21 from the city center) to the top of Medvednica Mountain (summit, Sljeme). The lower and upper levels of Zagreb are connected by a venerable funicular in less than a minute, saving you a short but steep haul.

Note. Car parking in the center of Zagreb is a major problem and best avoided if possible.

SPORTS. There are facilities for swimming, sailing, and wind surfing at Jarun Recreation Center by an artificial lake in the suburbs, and water skiing at Čiče lake near the airport. In Zagreb itself, you can swim in the pool at Mladost, by the River Sava. The hosting of Universiade, the World University Games, in Zagreb in 1987 gave a major boost to a variety of sports grounds and amenities, especially swimming pools and tennis courts.

From a spectator point-of-view, football is the favorite, as elsewhere in Yugoslavia. The first clubs in Zagreb were organized in 1903, and the Dinamo stadium, where big international matches are played, seats 60,000 persons.

Winter sports are practiced on beautiful Mount Sljeme, Zagreb's natural playground rising to the north of the city. It is reached by cable car to Medvednica from the Gračani district in about 25 minutes.

The area also offers excellent hiking.

MUSEUMS AND ART GALLERIES. These are usually open six days a week, with Monday the common day of closure; Sunday is mostly mornings only. The following is a selection of the most important, but there are many others, especially art galleries.

Archeological Museum, Zrinjski Sq. 19. From pre-history to the 19th century. Fine coin collection.

Art Center, Jezuitski trg. Beautifully arranged changing exhibits displayed in the magnificent buildings of a former Jesuit monastery in the Upper Town. Worth visiting for the building alone.

Arts and Crafts Museum, Maršala Tita Sq. 10. Furniture, musical instruments, textiles, clothing, and handicrafts—all from the 15th century to modern times.

Ethnographic Museum, Mažuranić Sq. 14. Admirable collection of folk costumes, crafts, instruments and other artefacts; also interiors of peasant homes.

Gallery of Primitive Art, Cirilometodska 3. Memorable display of foreign and especially Yugoslav naïve painters, many of international repute.

Meštrović Gallery, Mletačka 8. Sculptures and drawings by Ivan Meštrović, most famed of Yugoslav sculptors.

Mimara Museum, Roosoveltova trg. Some of the fabulous treasures of the private art collector Mimara, a reclusive figure who died in 1987. Items include 5,000-year-old Egyptian, Greek, Persian and Celtic treasures and rare Old Masters and French Impressionist paintings.

Modern Gallery, Braće Kavurića 1. Croatian art over the past 150 years.

Strossmayer Gallery of Old Masters, Zrinski Sq. 11. Yugoslavia's largest gallery of Old Masters, including Italian, Flemish, Spanish and Dutch schools from the 14th to 19th centuries.

Zagreb Town Museum, Opatička 20. Excellent displays showing the development of the city through the ages.

ENTERTAINMENT. Your best bet is to get the latest calendar of events from the Tourist Information Center. There is a lively program of summer happenings throughout the city, but especially in the attractive settings of the old Upper Town, with music, drama and folklore performances taking place in courtyards and old buildings, or often in the open air. In late July, an International Folklore Festival unfolds in the streets and squares of the city. Markos Fair is a two-week event in summer and autumn in the old town.

Zagreb has a number of theaters (and many theater groups), though these do present most visitors with a language problem. Music, however, has no barriers. There is opera and ballet at the excellent National Croat Theater, and at the Conservatory of Music you can hear the Croat Symphony Orchestra or the Zagreb Soloists, an internationally known chamber music ensemble. There are also top-class performances in the modern Concert Palace (Vatroslav Lisinski). Musicals, rock, operas, etc., are the specialties of the Komedija at 9 Kaptol. Organ recitals are given in the Cathedral. Open-air concerts take place in the atrium of the Arts Center (former Jesuit monastery) in the Upper Town.

MARKETS AND SHOPS. Zagreb has 15 open-air market places where fresh food, household goods, textiles and souvenirs can be bought seven days a week—and where prices for handicrafts are likely to be substantially lower than in the popular coastal resorts. The biggest and most colorful market is at Dolac, which is very central, opposite cathedral. Many shops are open until 8 P.M. (9 P.M. in summer) and some throughout the weekend.

TRADE FAIRS. Zagreb, as has already been mentioned, is the setting for one of the world's oldest trade fairs, which takes place in the well-laid-out fairgrounds just to the south of the River Sava. The two principal events are the Spring Fair (consumer goods) in April and the Autumn Fair (science and technology) in September, but many specialized shows continue almost throughout the year. The Autumn Fair also marks the beginning of a month of cultural and sporting events.

USEFUL ADDRESSES. Consulate: U.S., Braće Kavurića 2. Tourist Information Center, Trg Republike 11 and Zrinjevac 14 (Lower Town) and Lotrščak Tower (Upper Town). Travel agencies: Atlas, Zrinjevac 17; Croatiaturist, Tomislav Sq. 17 and at bus terminal, Drižćeva; Dalmacija-turist, Zrinjevac 16; Generalturist, Zrinjevac 18, also several other branches; Kompas, Gajeva 6; Putnik, Preobraženska 6; Turist Biro TD Gorjni Grad (Upper Town), Kemenita 15; Youth Tourist Center, Petrinjska 73. Motoring: Auto-moto savez Hrvatske touring service, Draškovićeva 25. Main post offices: Jurišićeva 13, Zagreb 1; and Branimirova 4, Zagreb 11. Central pharmacy: Trg Republike 3.

NIGHTLIFE. The *Inter-Continental* hotel has a casino and dancing in its top-floor Opera restaurant. There is also dancing on the open-air terrace of the *Esplanade* hotel in summer, and at the *Ritz Cabaret* nightclub, Petrinjska 4. (See Hotels section for other addresses.) The Esplanade also has *The Diamond Club* in the basement. Several clubs provide disco music and a convivial atmosphere till midnight or later; the Tourist Information Center or your hotel porter can give you the latest position. Two open-air clubs in summer are *Studenski Centar* and *Scena,* both popular meeting places for the young. Others include *Kulušić, Lapidarij, Number One* and *Saloon*—the first one with many visiting bands and a theater stage.

SERBIA

Hub of the Modern State

Despite considerable tourist attractions, the Socialist Republic of Serbia is still given relatively little attention by travelers. Nevertheless, Serbia has both attractive scenery and historic towns and buildings, dating from medieval times, the period of Turkish occupation and the independent state.

Anyone who has ever seen the towering Iron Gates of the River Danube will know why they have been called one of the greatest natural wonders of all Europe. Elsewhere, too, rivers through the ages have worn deep gorges through living rock. You cannot fail to be impressed by the Gornjak Gorges in the east, by the Rugovo Gorge in the west or those of the Ibar in the center. In addition, there are a number of excellent thermal spas.

In the remotest fastnesses you will come unexpectedly upon beautiful medieval Serbian churches and monasteries, many with polychrome brick and stone exteriors, and often containing exquisite frescos that reveal the influences of the Renaissance at work here long before the movement reached its first flowering in Italy. Now restored or undergoing much-needed restoration after many years of neglect, the priceless artistic treasures that these churches have guarded for so many centuries are now becoming better-known to the outside world.

History

Archaeological excavations are uncovering some remarkable prehistoric sites that show a very advanced level of culture in the Danube basin between 2500 and 3000 B.C. Several of these are near Belgrade. In Roman times, Serbia formed part of the provinces of Lower Pannonia and Moesia, and comprised the basins of the rivers Morava, Ibar and Upper Vardar. When the Empire was divided it came under the rule of Byzantium. But by the seventh century the Slavs had penetrated this far and established their own rule.

The new state almost replaced Byzantium as the dominant power in the Balkans when Serbian Tsar Dušan, in 1349, promulgated his famous Code of Common Law—the most important document of the medieval Slav state. But at his death there was a serious deterioration in the situation, and the Golden Age ended at the great Battle of Kosovo in 1389, when a much larger Turkish force was victorious. During the next two centuries unceasing warfare drastically reduced the population, and the gradually weakening military power of the Ottoman Empire only served to make things worse, with the provincial governments of the Pashas becoming increasingly arbitrary and oppressive in their efforts to maintain control. There was a series of popular uprisings during the 17th century against the provincial government of the Turks, which had in the supervening years become more and more tyrannical. They were crushed with ferocious violence, leading to the two Serb migrations across the Danube and the Sava in 1690 and 1739.

At the order of the Pasha Pasvan Oglu, a cruel massacre of the leading Serbs was carried out in 1804. A national revolt of protest led to the capture of Belgrade by Karageorge, the ancestor of the Karageorgević dynasty. Karageorge was elected the national leader, but unfortunately rivalries between the leaders of the revolt made it possible for the Turks to reoccupy Belgrade. In 1815, Miloš Obrenović led a second insurrection, and then, before the Turks had time to mass sufficient forces against him, imposed on them an agreement under the terms of which Serbia received autonomy.

In 1867, bowing to international pressure, the Turkish garrisons gradually withdrew from the few fortified towns still in their possession, and ten years later Serbia achieved full independence, again adding to her territory at the expense of Turkey. In 1882 Serbia elected an Obrenović king. When his descendant was assassinated in 1903, the Karageorgević house was restored, ruling until 1941.

In 1912 Serbia, Montenegro, Greece and Bulgaria formed an alliance to expel the last remaining Turks from the Balkan peninsula. This led to the two Balkan Wars that troubled the years just prior to the outbreak of World War I, when notable Serbian successes made a strong impression upon those future Yugoslavs still under foreign rule. The growing power of Serbia was a hindrance to Habsburg plans for further expansion, and when Gavrilo Princip assassinated the heir to the 84-year-old Emperor Franz Joseph of Austro-Hungary at Sarajevo in June 1914, Vienna was not slow to send an ultimatum. What the Emperor meant to be a "preventive war" against Serbia rapidly expanded into a world war, that was to destroy the Habsburg Empire itself, together with so much else.

Serbia was already exhausted by her rôle in the Balkan Wars, but before she was crushed by her still mighty enemy, she earned the admiration of the world for the fierce courage with which her soldiers fought on the long and bitter retreat across the mountains of Albania to Corfu, where, thanks to her allies, they could safely reequip.

The Treaty of Versailles recognized the new Kingdom of the Serbs, Croats and Slovenes, but the Kingdom was weakened by internal dissension and outside pressure. Her people's decision in 1941 to remain loyal to the Allies cost her nearly a million dead before she finally regained her independence.

Today, Serbia has lost the position of political preeminence she held between the wars, when the overwhelming majority of important appointments in every branch of public life went almost automatically to Serbs. But this is not so much a loss for Serbia as a gain for the whole country: all the Republics now stand on an equal footing. Belgrade, in particular, now has the advantage of being not only the capital of Serbia, but also a truly federal center for the whole of Yugoslavia.

Serbia also has within its boundaries two autonomous zones with large national minorities. In the north, the Vojvodina, Yugoslavia's granary, has an important Hungarian element. In the southwest, the area formerly called Kosmet and now Kosovo (*Kosovo i Metohija* is the full title) is inhabited largely by Albanians, of whose current troubles there will be more later.

Belgrade, the Capital

Under the present régime of six federated Republics, Serbia has very largely lost the leadership that was hers in the years between the two world wars, but which had been the cause of much friction (for example, of the country's 169 generals in 1939, all but three were Serbs). However, she remains the heart of the country, and the capital city of Belgrade (Beograd) is here, which phoenix-like has risen from its ashes to become one of Europe's modern capitals.

Since Herodotus first mentioned it 25 centuries ago the city has been repeatedly destroyed—the price it has had to pay for its strategic position, spread out as it is on hills commanding at the junction of the rivers Sava and Danube, a crossroads between the West and the Orient, and the gateway to central Europe. However, Belgrade today has relatively little to show of her stormy past, almost the only ancient complex still in existence being the great fortress Kalemegdan, which dominates the Vojvodina Plain.

The Celts founded the first settlement here, which had become a fortified town by the fourth century B.C. The Romans occupied it some 300 years later and named it Singidunum, but the Huns razed it in the fifth century, and it was abandoned for over 100 years, when the Emperor Justinian ordered it to be rebuilt. A period of prosperity followed, until the Slavs overran the city in the seventh century and gave it its present name.

The city is briefly mentioned in connection with the Crusades of the 11th century, and it then appears as the capital of the first Serbia under King Dragutin. 300 years later, in 1521, it was captured by the Turks. However, being right in the path of the perpetual ebb and flow of the Christian crusade against the penetration of Islam into Europe, Belgrade was repeatedly burned, sacked and almost destroyed, and suffered again heavily in the reprisals for the Serb uprisings against the Turks at the beginning of the 19th century. When in 1867 the last Turkish Governor handed over the keys of the city to Prince Michael of Serbia, it was at last free to develop into the political, economic and cultural capital of the new Serbia.

Since that Palm Sunday in 1941, when 300 Nazi bombers killed 25,000 people in one morning, Belgrade has grown again to a city of 1,500,000 people, with broad avenues, modern, airy houses and vast blocks of apartments that crowd upon the occasional pre-war survivor, and the carefully tended parks, so that it once more justifies its name made up from *belo* (white) and *grad* (town). There is acceptable and even occasionally interesting architecture of the 1970s and '80s among the abortive high-rise experiments of the 1950s. But the city is still suffering acutely from growing pains, as the building program cannot keep pace with the demands of the expanding population. Nevertheless, the modernization and improvement of amenities of all kinds continue to change the face of Belgrade annually.

Exploring Belgrade

The great fortress of Kalemegdan is the city's most notable historic complex. Its superimposed Celtic, Roman, Turkish, Austrian and Serbian construction make it a mute history of Belgrade's troubled life over some 2,000 years. Most of the surviving buildings date from the times of Turkish rule or subsequent Serbian independence.

From the center of the city, Knez Mihailova street (now a pedestrian precinct) leads to the hilly park crowned by the fortifications of Gornji Grad, the highest point of Kalemegdan. Crenellated walls and creeper-covered turrets give the old citadel a romantic air and, from its terraces, there are stunning views of the confluence of two great rivers, the Sava and the Danube, as well as the city spread at your feet. According to the experts, the present upper fortifications are built partly on the site of a Roman *castrum* dating from the times of the Flavian Emperors.

The boundaries of Kalemegdan and its park encompass a number of significant monuments from its long history. One group includes the King's Gate and Roman Well (mis-named for it dates from the 18th century, but still interesting). Close by is the soaring sculpture *Monument to the Victor*, one of Ivan Meštrović's best known works, and a short distance away the early 18th-century tomb of a Turkish grand vizier. In the same area is one of Yugoslavia's best museums for history buffs; don't be put off by its name—the Military Museum—for it provides an excellent overall view of the checkered fortunes of Yugoslav territory before and particularly since the coming of the South Slavs.

Another interesting group of buildings is close to the Kalemegdan Terrace restaurant and includes the medieval Zindan Gate and towers, Jakšić Tower and Ružica church, originally a powder warehouse from the 18th century. From here paths lead down via Charles VI Gate and a cannon foundry to the octagonal Nebojša Tower down by the Danube. In other parts of the park are a zoo and an exhibition pavilion of contemporary Yugoslav art and sculpture.

From Kalemegdan a short stroll will bring you to the Serbian Orthodox Cathedral of Belgrade, dedicated to the Archangel Michael, built between

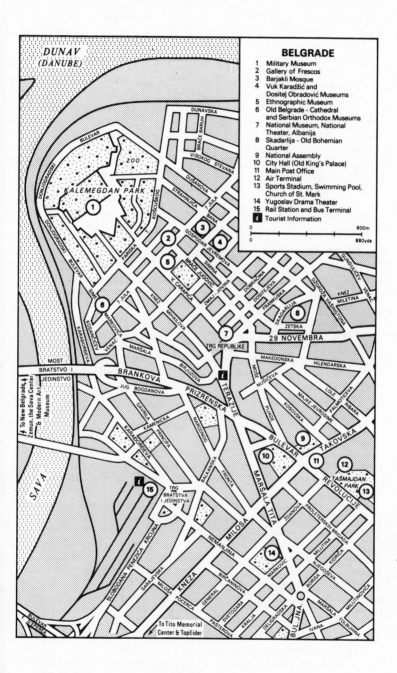

BELGRADE

1 Military Museum
2 Gallery of Frescos
3 Barjakli Mosque
4 Vuk Karadžić and
  Dositej Obradović Museums
5 Ethnographic Museum
6 Old Belgrade - Cathedral
  and Serbian Orthodox Museums
7 National Museum, National
  Theater, Albanija
8 Skadarlija - Old Bohemian
  Quarter
9 National Assembly
10 City Hall (Old King's Palace)
11 Main Post Office
12 Air Terminal
13 Sports Stadium, Swimming Pool,
  Church of St. Mark
14 Yugoslav Drama Theater
15 Rail Station and Bus Terminal
i Tourist Information

1836 and 1845. The cathedral's architecture is neoclassical with a baroque tower. The church contains the tombs of several Serbian princes; just outside its main entrance are the graves of the two great Serbian educators, Vuk Karadžić and Dositej Obradović. Across the street from the cathedral is the Patriarchate of the Serbian Orthodox Church.

Most of the exquisite frescos that are to be seen in the widely scattered monasteries of Serbia, Macedonia and Montenegro are in somewhat remote places, so for visitors on a tight schedule it is a big advantage to find good reproductions of some of the best in the special Fresco Art Gallery of Belgrade. The originals date from the 13th up to the 15th century. Many have been exhibited in the West.

Not far away is the Bajrakli Džamija, the Mosque of the Flag, so called because in Turkish times it used to fly a signal flag to show the moment when the *imams* of the other mosques should make their five daily calls to prayer to the faithful. This mosque and much of Kalemegdan Fortress are the only relics of Turkish occupation—really quite remarkable when you think that less than two centuries ago Belgrade was a thoroughly typical town of provincial Turkey.

Most of what you see today is either from the late 19th or 20th centuries. You can get a general impression of the city center by the following itinerary. Start in Trg Republike, or Republic Square, where you will find the National Museum (well worth visiting). Opposite is the National Theater, where there is an opera season each year. Not far from here is the narrow cobbled street called Skadarlija, a favorite haunt of the Bohemian set in the 19th century. It has now been restored to provide a very popular dining-out area, as well as being animated by various forms of street entertainment during the summer months. There are several crowded, lively restaurants with good folk music. Back on Republic Square, past the building called Albanija, you will come to the nerve center of the capital, the street called Terazije. Here two main streets meet, and we follow the Bulevar Revolucije which is 6½ km. (four miles) long. It brings us soon to the impressive Parliament House, or, more properly now, the Federal Assembly Building. Then we come to the Tašmajdan Park, and glimpse the Church of Sveti Marko (St. Mark): it is a copy of the church at Gračanica. Here lie the bodies of King Alexander and Queen Draga, brutally murdered by the followers of the Karageorge faction in 1903, when the Obrenović line was exterminated. The former Royal Palace, incidentally, is not far from here; it stands in the former royal gardens, facing Parliament House.

Surrounded by lovely gardens in the peaceful Dedinje district, just south of the center, is a museum complex of significance to all those interested in Yugoslavia's modern history. This is the Josip Broz Tito Memorial Center featuring the late President Tito's residence, in its original state, and several museums devoted to various aspects of his life and times. But the building which draws most visitors from all over Yugoslavia and, indeed, the world, is the garden house or House of Flowers where Tito spent so many hours and in which he now lies surrounded by banks of flowers and guarded by the young men of his Special Guard.

Across the Sava River from the main part of Belgrade, on land which before World War II was swampy and desolate, a vast expanse of modern buildings, collectively known as Novi Beograd ("New Belgrade") has been built. According to the plans which have been drawn, Novi Beograd will grow to accommodate a population of a quarter million. Aside from its high-rise residential areas, Novi Beograd is also the site of a number of government and cultural institutions. One of its most imposing structures is the 24-story headquarters of the Central Committee of the Federal Executive Council. The Modern Art Museum, on the bank of the Sava River, adds a contemporary esthetic touch to Novi Beograd's neat appearance. So does the impressive Sava Center, a huge congress and concert hall complex with the Belgrade-Intercontinental Hotel adjoining it. It has already provided the venue for many major international gatherings. From here, a riverside promenade is well on the way to completion, linking the Sava Center along the banks of the Sava and Danube with the ancient little town of Zemun, now virtually a suburb of Belgrade.

The most popular local excursion is to 520-m.-high (1,700 ft.) Mount Avala, 20 km. (12 miles) south of the city, in the hilly, forested region called the Šumadija. On the summit of Avala the Monument to an Unknown Soldier was built in 1938. The memorial is of dark polished granite and is especially notable for its sculptured figures of eight women symbolizing the eight nationalities of Yugoslavia. It is the work of Yugoslavia's famous sculptor, Ivan Meštrović.

Not far from the monument stands a 200-m.-high (660 ft.) tower, topped by the principal radio and television antennae for the Belgrade area. Resting on a tripod base, the tower has, halfway up, a restaurant and observation platform, which offers visitors a magnificent view of the surrounding region.

East from Belgrade

After the Danube has been augmented by the Sava at Belgrade it becomes Europe's greatest river. It then flows for some 105 km. (65 miles) through the fertile Serbian plain, after which for the next 210 km. (130 miles) or so, it marks the Yugoslav-Romanian frontier. During the last stage of this part of its course it runs through the tremendous gorge that it has worn through the living rock, known as the Iron Gates, one of the most famous stretches of river in the world. The roads to the Iron Gates are not all in very good condition, and in any case they don't follow the river completely through the most interesting parts of the gorge. Therefore, by far the best way to see the Iron Gates is from the river itself. You can make a one-day excursion from Belgrade as far as Kladovo by hydrofoil. There is a road bridge across the dam which considerably shortens the journey to most parts of Romania.

Exploring the Danube Valley below Belgrade

From Belgrade to Smederevo, the Danube flows lazily past numerous low-lying islands, and along the banks the vines still grow that give us the *smederevka* wine, which has been produced for the past 2,000 years. The immense fortress of Smederevo is one of the most imposing military constructions of the Middle Ages. It was built by Prince Djuradj Branković in about 1420, and was destined to change hands many times in the succeeding centuries. Its original form was triangular, and even today its five-m.-thick (17 ft.) walls and fortified towers convey a tremendous sense of ancient power and durability—despite massive damage caused in 1941 when explosives stored there by the Germans inexplicably blew up.

Soon the River Morava flows into the mighty Danube, which wends its way through a countryside where roads are still very poor. Further on is Kostolac, a small town today but an important base for the Danubian fleet in Roman times, when it was called Viminatium.

Shortly before reaching the Romanian frontier on the left bank, we pass the 15th-century Turkish fortress of Ram.

The entrance into the gorge was defended in the old days by the fortress of Golubac, which now stands deserted but still impressive, its ancient turrets crowning the crest of a hill against the skyline. Golubac was built upon the site of the Roman Castrum Calumbarum, and retained its strategic importance for nearly 2,000 years.

From here a road follows the Danube, which has been of imposing width, but at this point a spur of the Carpathian Mountains reaches out and forces it into a channel between rocky cliffs, some bare and some forest-covered. From here on, it is rarely more than 400 m. (¼ mile) wide for the entire 40 km. (25 miles) of the "Little" Djerdap, part of what is virtually a 130-km.-long (80 miles) artificial lake as a result of the building of the Djerdap (Iron Gates) Dam.

Soon we pass the site of one of the most important archeological finds of recent years, known as Lepenski Vir. Here, on the former banks of the river, the remains of one of the oldest and most complete neolithic settlements in the world were found in 1965. To preserve it from the risen waters, it has been transferred to the site of the Roman camp of Thallus which is on higher ground. The substantial remains have been roofed over and there is an excellent museum. Particularly interesting are the strange human heads, carved with primitive stone tools by the community of Danube fishermen who lived here up to 8,000 years ago.

Soon after, the narrow waters widen into lake-like proportions on the approach to Donji Milanovac, beyond which we enter the Kazan—the Cauldron—the "Great" Djerdap. Imprisoned by sheer rock, the Danube is compressed at times into a width of barely 150 m. (500 ft.), between cliffs rising to over 610 m. (2,000 ft.). Innumerable lives were lost over the centuries in these once-turbulent waters that are now deep and mostly calm as they approach the massive Iron Gates dam.

On the right, or Yugoslav, bank was the Roman road that once linked Golubac with Orsova, and which has now disappeared under water. Work was begun on it during the reign of Tiberius. The living rock had to be cut away to a depth of two m. (6½ ft.).

Precisely at the river's narrowest point, graven upon a sheer wall of rock, is the *Tabula Traiana,* or Trajan's Tablet, which commemorates both this extraordinary engineering achievement and the victorious campaign against the Dacians made possible by it. This too has been moved above the risen waters of the Danube and may only be seen by river travelers. Not far beyond the tablet the narrows come to an end and the Danube widens again, separating the opposing Romanian and Serbian towns of Orsova and Tekija.

The river then narrows once again for the approach to the Djerdap Hydroelectric Dam, a joint Yugoslav-Romanian project and the largest scheme of its type in Europe. Regular guided tours of the Dam installations are arranged. Soon after comes Kladovo, the end of our hydrofoil-excursion from Belgrade, where the well-preserved fortress of Fetislam dates from the 16th century. A little beyond Kladovo, facing the old Romanian city of Turnu Severin across the river, you can see part of the massive pillars of Emperor Trajan's bridge over which he led his legions to the conquest of Dacia, as Romania was then called. By the bridge, excavations are currently revealing the presence of a substantial Roman settlement.

If you have done the trip by car, you can continue beside the Danube through the rich Wallachian plain. The local inhabitants, the Vlachs, called *Kučovlasi* in Serbo-Croat, who gave their name to the Romanian principality of Wallachia, speak a dialect even closer to the Latin of their ancestors than the Romanian language. Their costumes, songs and dances further accentuate their difference from the Serbs.

This whole area is relatively seldom seen by visitors. From Prahovo, the farthest point on the Yugoslav Danube, you could return by road through the vineyards of Negotin near the border with Bulgaria, which produce a full-bodied wine like a young Burgundy. Besides the usual museum, an old church, the Bukovo monastery and a Hajduk tomb, Negotin has a Stevan Mokranjac museum, commemorating the locally-born composer. Just southwest of it, at Bor, are the largest copper mines in Europe, of great importance in these days of "strategic metals." Nearby is the pleasant little thermal spa of Brestovačka Banja. For devotees of archeology, a further detour off this circuit is south to Zaječar or, more specifically, to Gamzigrad 11 km. (6½ miles) to its southwest. Here are the quite outstanding remains of a citadel from the late 3rd or early 4th century, and abandoned in the 6th. The excavated ruins are substantial and include some superb mosaics.

From Brestovačka Banja, the way back to Belgrade leads along the valley of the River Mlava to one of the most extraordinary locations in Serbia, the Gornjak Gorge. In deep forests nearby there is a monastery, on the left bank of the river, which dates from the 14th century. The route continues through the town of Petrovac, which lies in the center of a region of rich orchards. We continue on to Požarevac, briefly Prince Miloš' capital, the agricultural center of eastern Serbia, famous for its early fall horseriding competitions. The ruins of the Roman town of Viminacium are near here and have yielded some fascinating finds, especially sarcophagi, for the local museum. From here it is an easy 80-km. (50-mile) run back to Belgrade, and our circuit of this region of Serbia is complete.

South of Belgrade

The tourist wishing to explore Serbia can distinguish four regions on his southward routes from Belgrade. Directly south of the capital is a charming area of wooded hills and rolling farmland known as the Šumadija (*Šuma* in Serbian means "forest"). It is a fertile area, much fought over in the past but now notable mainly for its farming and as an excursion region for the people of Belgrade.

The *Ibar Magistrala* leads south past Avala through the Šumadija, to Kraljevo. Beginning from the city of Kraljevo (which means "Kings' Town"), a valley formed by the Ibar River extends due south. It was this "Valley of the Kings" which constituted the heart of the original independent Kingdom of Serbia (then known as Ras) at the end of the 12th century. And in this valley the earliest Serbian kings built the monasteries which were to give spiritual cohesion to their young nation. This oldest group of Serbian monasteries, identified as the Raška School, holds a place of honor among all the cultural and spiritual achievements of the Serbian people. The Ibar Valley forms our second region.

Our third is made up of what is called the Morava Valley, though the name is a little confusing. At Kraljevo the north-flowing Ibar joins the Western Morava which here flows east. After some 110 km. (70 miles) the Morava joins the Southern Morava (Južna Morava), northbound on a course roughly parallel to the Ibar's, to form the Great Morava (Velika Morava). We treat all three Morava valleys as forming one region, which extends as far south as Niš and the Macedonian frontier. But when art historians talk of the Morava Valley, they are referring only to the Western and Great Morava's regions. Here you can find other examples of early Serbian monasteries and Serb-Byzantine art.

Western travelers of the 19th century, when the Turkish Iron Curtain was being slowly lifted from the Balkans, have stories to tell of their visits to a chain of monasteries and churches hidden away in almost inaccessible mountain country. These extraordinary places, remote and mysterious, are built in a Byzantine style that tends to mix Western influences with those from the East.

Inside them is a great wealth of unique frescos in which the artists broke away from the rigidity of formal Byzantine mosaics, and employed firm yet sweeping lines to portray more ample movement and nobler figures than seen in frescos of this period elsewhere. The final and most highly developed stage of Serbian-Byzantine architecture is to be found in the valley of the Morava River, and is known as the Morava School.

There remains one more important region of Serbia proper. It extends from the Sava River in the north down to the border with Montenegro in the south, and on its western side adjoins Bosnia-Hercegovina; it runs from rich farmlands across deep valleys to dry and sparsely populated hills. We will consider this diversified region as "Western Serbia."

Exploring Šumadija

The *Ibar Magistrala* is the westernmost and scenically most attractive of the three roads leading south from Belgrade. Bypassing Lazarevac, 55 km. (34 miles) south, is an important crossroads, the western (right) branch following the railroad up the Kolubara Valley to Valjevo amidst densely forested mountains, and Divčibare, a resort 997 m. (3,270 ft.) up in the Maljen Mountains, where in late May the White Narcissus Festival is held; the eastern branch leads via the spa of Bukovička Banja—which produces the Knjaz Miloš mineral water and holds the Marble and Harmony Festival July to September in conjunction with an International Sculpture Symposium—to Topola; the *Ibar Magistrala* climbs south over the Rudnik Mountains and through the plum orchards of Gornji Milanovac to Kraljevo, where it is joined by the middle road from Belgrade.

Topola was the home of the leader of the First Serbian Insurrection against the Turks (in 1804), whom the Turks named Karageorge ("Black George"). Karageorge's family home, as well as the village church and school, have been restored.

This First Serbian Insurrection ultimately failed. In spite of this, the Karageorge family reclaimed the leadership of Serbia in 1903 in the course of another political upheaval. From that year onward, a Karageorge was to sit on the throne of Serbia, and ultimately all Yugoslavia, as king.

As the Karageorge family mausoleum, a remarkable church of Venčac marble with a graceful gilt dome was built on the Oplenac hill overlooking Topola. The interior of the church, as well as of the crypt below, is completely covered with stunning mosaics, almost unique in quantity and workmanship. Each is a faithful reproduction of one of the masterpieces of Serbian medieval frescos. Thus a visit to Oplenac is like a summary of a tour to all the greatest of the Serbian monasteries.

From Topola it is a further 42 km. (26 miles) to Kragujevac. The town was the family home of Miloš Obrenović, leader of the Second Insurrection. Following his success against the Turks he made Kragujevac his capital from 1818 to 1842. Interesting examples of Serbian architecture from this period include Sveta Trojica (Holy Trinity) church, and especially the house known as "Amidžin Konak," once belonging to a member of Prince Miloš' train, and now part of the Kragujevac city museum. This is not merely a city of 19th-century history. It occupies a uniquely tragic place in the Serbians' memory of World War II, for it was here that on 21st October 1941, a Nazi punitive expedition shot 7,000 citizens, including 300 secondary school pupils who were taken directly from their classes to the place of execution in the fields of Šumarice. The site has been made into a memorial park through which you can drive along a 7-km. (4-mile) circuit through well-landscaped grounds past the many graves and sculptures commemorating this hideous event. A museum is also devoted to the poignant tragedy. Otherwise Kragujevac is a thriving industrial center, home of Crvena Zastava enterprise, Yugoslavia's main manufacturer of automobiles.

From Kragujevac, a drive of 58 km. (36 miles) will take you to Kalenić monastery, the least accessible of the major monasteries of the Morava School. Kalenić was founded in about 1413 by the nobleman Bogdan, a cupbearer at the court of Prince Stefan Lazarević. The building itself is of alternating layers of dressed stone and brick, incoporating archivolts, rose windows and a wealth of stylized bas relief carving, so that the general effect is of a fusion of oriental and western styles, as is so frequently encountered in these ancient monasteries. It owes its present fine state of preservation to several restorations, during one of which the remarkable frescos were discovered after the removal of the coating of whitewash with which the Turks nearly always treated Christian works of art. Among them are apocryphal scenes from the life of the Virgin Mary and the principal incidents in the life of Christ, a notable one being the Wedding at Cana (note the husband pricking his wife's finger in a symbolic act of blood relationship). The site of the monastery is delightfully tranquil and the place well looked after by cheerful nuns who make excellent *rakija.*

From here you could quite easily link up with either the Ibar or Morava Valley routes described below.

Exploring the Ibar Valley and the Sandzak

At the confluence of the Ibar and the Western Morava rivers, surrounded by the Stolovi and Goć mountain ranges, stands the busy town of Kraljevo, its modern hub the spacious circular Maršala Tita "square." Kraljevo, too, had its day of stark tragedy in October 1941, when nearly 6,000 of its citizens were murdered by the Nazis. A memorial park marks the site of the executions near the rail station. Among its historical monuments, the 19th-century Gospodar Vasin Konak now houses a museum which includes a fresco gallery that gives the visitor an opportunity to become acquainted with the art of the Raška School monasteries before setting out to visit the monasteries themselves.

The closest of them is Žiča which can be reached most directly by taking the first right turn from the road following the Western Morava east from Kraljevo. It quickly brings you to the towering tomato-red walls of Žiča, which has been much restored and is more commercialized than most. The best of the frescos here is the *Last Supper,* though that of the founder, the crowned figure of Stefan Nemanja Prvovenčani, is extremely fine. The remainder are of a later period, and depict 40 martyrs being tortured by the Turks.

The background of Žiča is more interesting than the building itself. Soon after the coronation of Stefan by the Pope, a certain dualism between state and church developed in Ras, core of the new Serb empire. The king's brother, Sava, was a monk and writer, and also emissary to the Greek Patriarch of Nicea. He advised the Patriarch to authorize the establishment of an autonomous Serb Orthodox Church, which would be able to counteract the Latin influence of Rome. Sava himself became the first archbishop of the new church, which established its seat in 1219 in Žiča, where seven medieval Serbian kings were crowned.

The two brothers cooperated successfully in their government of both the spiritual and secular administration of the country, and it was principally the work of these two remarkable men that laid the foundations for the great days of Serbian rule. Žiča became the cradle of the Serbian Orthodox Church. Sava died in 1233, shortly after returning from a pilgrimage to the Holy Land. His hold upon Serb religious sentiment was so strong that even 300 years later the Turks thought it necessary to remove his bones from the Monastery of Mileševa and have them publicly burned in Belgrade. Close beside Žiča is the little Church of St. Peter and St. Paul, with yet more beautiful frescos.

Before leaving the Kraljevo area, it's worth mentioning that about 25 km. (15 miles) east along the same road that follows the Western Morava is Vrnjačka Banja, among the best-known and best-equipped spas in Yugoslavia. It is not too far from here across the valley and into the hills to Ljubostina Monastery, described under the Morava Valley.

For the moment we are concerned with the main road that runs south from Kraljevo along the left bank of the Ibar River and this is the route we must follow to explore the monasteries of this region. Where the valley narrows to form a dramatic gorge, 29 km. (18 miles) from Kraljevo, stand the eight towers of the Maglič fortress perched like an eagle's nest upon a separate spur of the mountains. The first views of it present an even more astonishing sight if you are traveling in the opposite direction. Although the fortress dates from the 15th century, it is still in a pretty good state of repair, but the only way to reach it is by crossing the Ibar (there's a ferry if you can find the ferryman) and even then it is a steep scramble up.

Another 21 km. (13 miles) from Kraljevo is the village of Ušće from which a winding road leads 11 km. (7 miles) up to the village and monastery of Studenica, one of the most famous and loveliest. The monastery, a happy fusion of Byzantine and Romanesque styles in gray-white marble and completely surrounded by walls, is richly ornamented with sculptures. Destroyed and pillaged time and again, Studenica was repeatedly rebuilt. Old prints show that at one time no less than 13 churches and many other buildings stood within its protective walls.

It was established by the first king of Serbia, Stefan Nemanja, whose remains, as well as those of his son, King Stefan the First Crowned, are still venerated in the largest of its three churches, Sveta Bodgorica, dedicated to the Virgin Mary. This contains a number of beautiful frescos, the best of which date from the early 13th century, and are among the very earliest of that monumental style with its new and impressive emphasis on the dignity and strength of man. The procession of the church-fathers, behind the altar, is remarkably well preserved, but the greatest of the frescos is the incomparably moving Crucifixion. This church also displays various interesting treasures, such as gold and silver liturgical vessels, richly illuminated Gospels and copies of a number of Turkish decrees.

The smallest of the three churches is dedicated to St. Nicholas, and likewise dates from about 1190. The third church was built by King Milutin in 1315, and is known as the King's Church. The frescos are mainly dedicated to the life of the Virgin and have a great animation and wealth of detail.

An interesting annual event that has become well-established, with increasing foreign participation, is the two-week Studenica Days (second half of August) in which artists are invited for a free stay in exchange for the donation of the paintings they are expected to create.

14½ km. (nine miles) south of Ušće, a road branches off southeast (left) to the spa of Jošanička Banja, and into the Kopaonik Mountains, where Suvo Rudište is being developed into an important skiing resort. Back on the *Magistrala* the ruins of the Turkish fortress of Brvenik come into view. Here, a side road leads 11 km. (seven miles) west to the Monastery of Gradac, founded by Helen of Anjou, wife of King Uroš. Built in the 13th century, Gradac was abandoned 400 years later at the time of the Turkish invasions. It has been reconstructed in its original form in recent years, its Gothic features probably designed by architects from Helen's homeland.

Continuing south up the Ibar valley, you reach Raška in whose vicinity are the ruins of the Stara and Nova Pavlica churches. From Raška, you can choose between the old and the new roads running parallel southwest up a tributary valley to reach Novi Pazar in about 20 km. (12 miles), in the area called the Sandžak. This is a Turkish word signifying that it was under the jurisdiction of a Bey acting on behalf of the Pasha—in this case the Pasha of Belgrade.

If you choose the old road, you will come to the church of Sts. Peter and Paul, a little gem perched above you on the right a short distance north of Novi Pazar. Dating from the 9th or 10th century, this is one of Yugoslavia's very oldest churches. It is designed in the form of a Greek cross set amid circular walls and is a perfect example of pre-medieval Slav architecture, but is unfortunately the only one still standing. There are, however, a few ruined remains from the same period on the Dalmatian coast. As long ago as the 10th century, the Byzantine Emperor Constantine Porphyrogenitus mentioned in the account of his travels "the curious little churches lost in the forgotten places of my vast empire." If they struck the Emperor as "curious" nearly 1,000 years ago, then this surviving example here near Novi Pazar today is truly extraordinary.

From here you may be drawn by the ruins of another remarkable monastery complex, 4 km. (2½ miles) north of Novi Pazar—those of Djurdjevi Stubovi, another foundation of Stefan Nemanja which was in good repair until damaged in 1912 during the first Balkan War. The two world wars virtually completed its destruction and it has only recently been partially restored. Frescos include a monumental St. George seated on a white horse, and in the little chapel you will find effigies of kings Dragutin and Milutin with their families.

Novi Pazar itself is a fascinating little town. The Turks built it in 1460 and, though it was devastated by a fire started by Serbian insurrectionists in 1809, the atmosphere remains unmistakably oriental. The Altum Alem mosque is a good example of 15th-century Moslem architecture, now part of the regional museum, and in the town center the two-story Amir-Aga inn is a typical example of an 18th-century caravanserai. Even the modern buildings on the main square contrive an Oriental impression, including the very charming hotel whose accommodations are tiered above a fountain that splashes away in the circular reception area.

Try and time your visit to Novi Pazar for a Tuesday when the market is a photographer's paradise, full of color and costumes, with goods ranging from hand-woven carpets and curious contraptions of mysterious purpose to modern T-shirts and garish plastic toys. In the fruit and vegetable section, country folk squat beside their hand-scales and their wares: perhaps a small heap of potatoes, a few lettuces, or bundles of the biggest spring onions you have ever seen. One wonders how far they have traveled for such meagre potential gain. If you can't manage a Tuesday, there is a smaller market on Fridays.

And there is more still to be seen from Novi Pazar, including one of the finest monasteries of all: that of Sopoćani, 16 km. (10 miles) to the southwest up the charming Raška valley. On the way you pass a motel and part of the ruins of Ras, Stefan Nemanja's capital around 1160, from which medieval Serbia got its name of Raška. Far more of ruined Ras lies on the plateau above the valley. But to return to Sopoćani, tucked against the mountains in a setting of unutterable peace: its surviving 13th-century frescos are among the finest in the country and miraculously nearly half of them *have* survived, though the church was roofless for about 200 years. From the vast mural paintings, each person portrayed seems to radiate some inner power. The subjects are from the Gospels—the most strikingly beautiful of them all being the *Ascension* and the *Death of the Virgin*—the infinitely compassionate expression on the face of Christ has immense power. Note, too, the Nativity scene and the woman bringing a towel and water to the Infant Jesus while Mary tests the temperature of the water with her hand. On the north wall there is a painting of the dramatic death scene of Anne Dandolo, the Venetian mother of the founder of the monastery, King Uroš I. The mural paintings of Sopoćani are indeed the work of a master hand.

The Morava Valley

For today's traveler, the Morava Valley is one of the most readily accessible areas of Yugoslavia. The *autoput* (now an excellent toll road) which leads from Belgrade in the direction of Niš and Skopje closely parallels the Morava River and its tributaries for some 370 km. (230 miles). The main railroad to Greece and Istanbul also runs along this valley.

After leaving Belgrade, the road crosses fertile agricultural country. We suggest that you leave the *autoput* at the Požarevac junction for a side-trip of 13 km. (eight miles) over a rather bumpy road to Lozovik, where there is an interesting wooden church built between 1804 and 1831. It is especially distinguished because of the carvings on its portal and ceiling. A little farther on, close to Velika Plana, is the Monastery of Koporin, built in the 15th century, where the building itself is of far less interest than the frescos it contains. Three km. (two miles) west of Velika Plana is the interesting Pokajnica ("Repentance") Monastery. It was built in 1818 by Vujica Vuličević, who took part in the assassination of Karageorge, leader of the First Serbian Insurrection against the Turks.

Returning to the *autoput* and continuing south, you soon reach the Markovac junction, some 103 km. (64 miles) from Belgrade, where you turn off for the Monastery of Manasija, 35 km. (22 miles) off the highway on a side road (through Despotovac), and one of the greatest achievements of the Morava School.

It was founded by Prince Stefan Lazarević and built as a fortress in the 15th century; its massive walls rise sheer above the rapid waters of the River Resava. The mountains that dominate the walls of the defile make a perfect setting for our brief return to the stormy days of the Dark Ages.

The frescos in the Manasija church contain an unusual wealth of detail. They represent the Holy Trinity, and also Prince Stefan, holding a model of the monastery in his hands. Warlike saints in sumptuous vestments brandish their swords, handsome and nobly at ease in their finery.

The slightly older Monastery of Ravanica is the next suggested destination; there is a beautiful route to it from Manasija via Resavica across the mountains, but it is difficult to find and, in parts, extremely rough. So unless you are feeling adventurous, it is probably better to get back to the *autoput* at Ćuprija for an easy 10-km. (6-mile) run to Ravanica in yet another lovely and secluded valley. It was founded by Prince Lazar toward the end of the 14th century, but was abandoned by its monks at the time of the Serb migration into the Vojvodina in 1690. On their return 27 years later, after the Turkish defeat by Prince Eugene of Savoy, they restored the original building.

The first impression is less dramatic than Manasija, for the fortress-like walls are much less complete, but the decorative stone-and-brick work of the church make it one of the best examples of the Morava school and there is rich bas relief ornamentation. Though badly damaged, some fine frescos, especially from the latter half of the 14th century, depict scenes of Christ's miracles and the family of the founder. As a complete contrast, a few kilometers west of Ćuprija, beyond the Morava River and the *autoput,* an unusual art gallery in the town of Svetozarevo offers an excellent opportunity to study the works of Yugoslavia's naïve painters, many of them of international repute.

At the Pojate junction, 170 km. (105 miles) from Belgrade, you may wish to leave the *autoput* toward Kraljevo for another side trip, to two more of the greatest treasures of the Morava School. The first is in Kruševac, 24 km. (15 miles) southwest (right). During the reign of Prince Lazar, the Serbian leader who lost the decisive battle to the Turks at Kosovo Polje in 1389, Kruševac was the capital of Serbia. Some of the ruins of the fortifications which once guarded the hill from which Prince Lazar exercised his rule can still be seen; but, most important, you will see Prince Lazar's small church, known as Lazarica, now fully-restored. Built about 1375, this church exemplifies the original pattern of Morava School construction, after which the various Morava School monasteries were designed in the next several generations.

Carry on from Kruševac, still toward Kraljevo, up the valley of the Western Morava River, to Trstenik, from whence it is five km. (three miles) north to Ljubostinja Convent, set beside a chattering stream in a quiet, thickly wooded vale. Incidentally, the word *manastir* is used in the Serbo-Croat language to mean either a monastery or a convent; so don't be surprised when you are looking for a *manastir* (monastery) to discover that it houses nuns instead of monks. Ljubostinja was endowed by Princess Milica, the wife of Prince Lazar. Following Prince Lazar's death at the Battle of Kosovo Polje, Milica decided to become a nun and chose this place to build the new convent where she would spend the rest of her life. The convent was finished in 1402, and in spite of the historical changes which the passage of centuries have brought about, the visitor can still well appreciate the reasons that influenced Milica's choice of this location. It is a magnificent example of the Morava school and, though built entirely of stone and therefore lacking the brick ornamentation so characteristic of other churches of this period, rich carving forms an intricate stone lacework, giving an astonishing delicacy to the arches and rose windows. The interior of the church is less interesting than it might be, because most of its frescos have been damaged or destroyed in the course of the various waves of destruction which have passed this way. There is one curiosity, however, in that the name of the architect, which in Orthodox monastery construction is usually enveloped in anonymity, is here clearly inscribed on the church threshold.

The Sisters sell their superb carpets, which are hand-made, from the spinning of the yarn from the sheep's wool to the final stitch of decoration, and intricate basketwork, painstakingly woven from reeds gathered nearby. They also produce excellent wine, bought by some of the best hotels in Belgrade. In these Orthodox convents and monasteries matins and vespers are sung in the church every day, and if your schedule coincides, you can find in the chanting of the nuns or monks an extraordinary sense of peace and inspiration.

Ljubostina, of course, can equally well be visited from Kraljevo, described in our Ibar Valley section. But if you are aiming for Niš and Macedonia, you must return to the *autoput* and head south.

Niš

Set on the banks of the River Nišava, the city of Niš has always been an important center of communication between east and west. As a Roman city it was known as Naïssus, and it was here that the Emperor Constantine was born. During the barbarian migrations it was destroyed, to be rebuilt by the Emperor Justinian. It was included in the Serbian state ruled by the Nemanja dynasty toward the end of the 12th century.

The importance of the town declined under the Turks, and prosperity returned to it only when they left in 1877. It was repeatedly bombed during

World War II, since which time it has been rebuilt as a flourishing city of 240,000 inhabitants, making it the second largest city in Serbia proper. Its rôle as a transportation center is still as significant as ever, for it is in Niš that both the main road and rail lines from Western Europe divide into two branches, the one to Thessaloniki and Athens and the other to Sofia and Istanbul.

Today it is a sprawling, dusty industrial city, but it has some interesting relics from the past and, if you are planning a stay here, you would do well to consider accommodations at the nearby spa of Niška Banja (see below).

The most dominant historic monument is the great fortress built by the Turks, just across the Nišava river in the center of town on the site of Roman fortifications, some of whose stonework can be seen in the construction. The massive walls and great gates (the main one ornamented with Arabic characters) are in an excellent state of preservation. The area within is today a public park, incorporating such other relics from Turkish times as a mosque and Turkish bath.

In the Jagodina quarter, not far from the fortress, a sixth-century Byzantine crypt with frescos was discovered not long ago—the means by which the date could be accurately fixed being in the many contemporary coins found around the site. Another interesting local discovery came to light four km. (2½ miles) outside Niš near the little thermal spa of Niška Banja, where at a hamlet called Brzi Brod the remains were found of a luxurious Roman villa with beautiful mosaic floors, gardens with fountains—in fact, every indication of the grace and luxury that had been achieved in this town of Mediana in the fourth century B.C. The site can be visited, but most of the finds from this and many other major archeological sites are to be seen in the excellent Niš Museum.

There are still two more unusual sights to be seen before leaving Niš. The first, on the site of the original town, is the 12th-century monastery of St. Panteleimon, largely rebuilt after the departure of the Turks. The second is the macabre Tower of Skulls (Čele Kula), raised after the Serb revolt of 1809 on the spot where Stefan Sindjelić, realizing that he and his forces could hold out no longer, set fire to the powder magazine and died together with his men and such Turks as had already forced their way into the stronghold. As a warning, so that the Serbs would never again attempt to throw off Turkish dominion, the Pasha of Niš built a tower in which he set the skulls of 952 of the insurgents, that all might see and understand the lesson. The result achieved was the reverse of what the Pasha had intended it to be. Over the years, most of the skulls have been removed or eroded; about 60 remain and the tower is now protected from further depredation by an outer structure.

Beside the Nišava River

The radioactive waters of Niška Banja, located on a hillside just outside Niš, have resulted in the establishment of a small spa and the consequent modernization of the little town, which possesses several good hotels. Excavations in the neighborhood revealed that the Romans also took the waters here. It is a pleasant spot, well placed for visiting Niš itself.

The road turns into E80 east along the Nišava to Bela Palanka and farther on to Pirot, which crouches beneath 1,783-m.-high (5,850 ft.) Mount

Trem. This is a sleepy little town of handicraft workers, despite the fact that it is on the main road linking Western Europe to Istanbul and the East. Between it and the Bulgarian frontier, peaks over 2,135-m. (7,000-ft.) high pile up against the sky.

The pressure of huge flocks of sheep has led to the local production of most attractive rugs. These are made by hand on special looms by the womenfolk, and their designs show kinship with their Greek neighbors and their former Turkish rulers.

Near Dimitrovgrad (formerly Caribrod), almost on the Bulgarian frontier, is the 15th-century Monastery of Poganovo, where the frescos in the chantry are particularly beautiful.

This is the end of the road, if you are not driving the 58 km. (36 miles) on to Sofia, and we return to Niš.

From Niš toward Macedonia

E75 follows the Southern Morava to Leskovac, 45 km. (28 miles) from Niš. About 30 km. (20 miles) west of Leskovac is the interesting Byzantine fortress of Caričingrad (the Empress fort) where excavations have brought to light much valuable information about the Emperor Justinian's city that surrounded it. The ruins of a huge basilica, other smaller churches, shops and living quarters make Caričingrad of exceptional interest, but the outstanding floor mosaics are now covered with sand to preserve them.

Leskovac is industrial, but also possesses ethnographic and archeological museums. There are several dwellings typical of the region which it is possible to visit.

On the main road south, the character of the country changes abruptly as you approach the Grdelica gorge. After 44 km. (27 miles) comes the rather oriental little town of Vladičin Han, bypassed by the main road. Still farther south, Vranje has a fine Turkish bridge, Turkish baths, the palace and harem quarters of Rajif Bey from the late 18th century, now a museum giving a graphic picture of the life of a Turkish Bey 200 years ago.

Northwest of Vranje you may see the ruins of the fortress of Markovo Krale. Marko Kraljević, who ruled in the 14th century, is a great figure in Serbian song and legend because of his private war against the Turks long after his people's great defeat at the Battle of Kosovo. Riding a black stallion which drank nothing but wine, he and his small band of followers harassed and raided the Turks, yet somehow always escaped back to their stronghold—or so the legend claims. Ten km. (six miles) south is the branch road heading east to the 11th-century Prohor Pčinjski Monastery. The monastery was destroyed, but later frescos from the 16th century survive in the church which succeeded it in the 19th century.

Western Serbia

We enter this region from the city of Čačak, northwest of Kraljevo, proceeding up the Western Morava River through the dramatic Ovčar-Kablar gorge, and past various new hydroelectric dams. It is a pleasant countryside, and there are in the immediate vicinity no less than eight well-known monasteries, most of them dating from the period of Turkish domination. They are all rather inaccessible, but stand out vividly white among the thick surrounding woods. At Požega it's worth a short detour along the Moravica Valley to Arilje, with its Raška-School church and remarkable frescos. Among these last the Procession of the Archbishops and the Council of King Stefan Nemanja are not only great masterpieces but also extremely valuable historical records.

Though it is off our present route, it is worth mentioning here that Karan, some 9½ km. (six miles) north of Titovo Užice, can be reached by a short stretch of country road beginning right in Užice. Its small church is one of the most perfect examples of medieval Serbian architecture. Because of the inclusion of certain historic personages portrayed in its frescos, it has been deduced that the church was built in the first years of the 14th century.

Užice (as it was called before it honored President Tito by prefixing the "Titovo") was the political and military center of the resistance movement founded to combat the German-Italian occupation of the country in 1941, and it has a small patriotic museum of souvenirs of those days. The surrounding country is particularly pleasing, and on a height above the River Djetinja you will see the remains of an ancient fortress abandoned by the Turks as late as 1867.

Bajina Bašta on the Drina, 37 km. (23 miles) northwest of Titovo Užice, is the starting point of an exciting excursion across the 1,524-m.-high (5,000 ft.) Tara plateau, which can easily be reached by a road that passes close to the Monastery of Rača. In these high places there are many unusual kinds of flowers and plants, for instance the extremely rare Red Fir trees, a species which was officially classified only in 1875. In winter the slopes of this great plateau provide perfect conditions for skiing, but have not yet been equipped for winter sports enthusiasts.

Going south from Titovo Užice we cross the deep vales of the Zlatibor plateau through the villages of Partizanske Vode and Nova Varoš to Bistrica, from where we circle back north to Priboj. However just before reaching the Monastery of Banja there is the little thermal spa of Pribojska Banja, which dates from the time of St. Sava. There are some fine frescos here. But the place that should not be missed on any account lies south of Bistrica and a few kilometers to the southeast of Prijepolje. This is the monastery of Mileševa, standing majestically beside the River Mileševka.

Mileševa Monastery enjoyed all the special privileges reserved for a royal foundation, and ranks second in the land only to that of Studenica. It was repeatedly profaned and pillaged by the Turks, and its present outward appearance dates but from the last century, when large-scale restoration was made. Internally, however, the frescos are the original works of Dimitrije and other great artists of the time of the foundation of the building in 1235. The special technique of the fresco is brilliantly achieved, the colors warm yet clear, the subjects portrayed with immense vitality. The lines are bold. The angel at the Tomb of Christ, and the Descent from the Cross, are outstanding and among the supreme achievements of medieval Serbian art. Of special interest, too, are portraits of St. Sava, Stefan the First Crowned, and the founder, King Vladislav, holding in his hand a model of Mileševa Church. The mural paintings in the open galleries are also extremely fine, though of much later date, the work of 16th-century artists.

With the visit to Mileševa Monastery, we conclude our explorations of Serbia proper. From Prjepolje the road we were following continues on up the valley of the Lim River into Montenegro.

It remains to describe two further regions very different both from each other and from the Serbia we already know. The Vojvodina and Kosovo are both autonomous, self-administering regions, distinct both politically and culturally from the main part of Serbia.

Exploring the Autonomous Region of Kosovo

Because Kosovo is an area which has repeatedly changed hands in the course of history, it is, like the Vojvodina region, ethnographically very mixed. By far the greatest national group is Albanian or Šjiptar, now forming about 90 percent of the population, a massive change in the balance that was around 50 percent at the end of World War II. Though Albanians and Turkish are official languages in addition to Serbo-Croat, and broadcasting and education are carried on in all three languages, resentment has grown over the years among Šjiptars who claim they have been treated as second-class citizens. For the Serbs, on the other hand, this is the heartland of their medieval independence, abruptly ended by the Battle of Kosovo in 1389, and as such a focal point of the Serb nation's emotions. The Šjiptars are temperamentally and culturally quite different from their Slav compatriots, and among some of them blood ties with their relatives in austere little neighboring Albania run deep, a factor encouraged by the literature in their own language which comes from across the border. A desire for greater independence on the part of an active minority led in the early 1980s to considerable unrest and even violence, and order was only restored by a hasty dispatch of the army. After a period of uneasy calm, tensions escalated once more culminating in demonstrations, strikes and some more violent conflicts in 1988–89. Unrest has again been quelled by the army but, as we go to press, visits to Kosovo are not encouraged.

Should the situation change, without any doubt, in Kosovo you are very soon aware of being in different, at times quite definitely strange territory—and indeed many a Yugoslav, especially from the north or the coast would probably admit to similar feelings. The first clue perhaps lies in the style of the dwellings, quite alien to anything a Serb or Croat would build; most are surrounded by walls traditionally high enough to prevent the outside world from intruding on the close-knit family life being enacted on the other side. The Šjiptars, generally speaking, can leave you with an impression of dourness, even mistrust—though of course there are many exceptions, and if you are their guest their courtesy and hospitality would be hard to match. And there is much that is utterly fascinating in their culture, traditions and costumes, if you can make the necessary adjustment.

It should be mentioned that a great deal of money has gone into modernizing many aspects of life in a region that was, until fairly recent years, somewhat primitive if very picturesque—and in some areas still is. It now has some excellent institutions from industrial and educational ones to some rather grand looking hotels, though service and maintenance do not often live up to outward appearances.

Traditional dress for Šjiptar men features the skull cap (sometimes turban) and home-spun white trousers with brown or black braiding, much in evidence on market days. The women are very often handsome when young and treated with great respect in their homes, but many have had little contact with the outside world until quite recently, and this is still the case in rural areas.

But in the towns, the winds of change have blown hard indeed. Priština, the capital of Kosovo, which was under Turkish rule until 1912, has now almost entirely been rebuilt in modern style, though you can still see some of the Turkish mosques and old houses lying off the main road. The Tzar (Emperor) Mosque was built by Sultan Mehmet II in 1461, in the form of a square surmounted by one large and three small cupolas. The interior is richly decorated. Almost next door is the old *hammam* (Turkish Baths) with its installations completely modernized. Oldest of all the city's mosques is that of Čarši (Taš) erected by Sultan Bayazid immediately after the Battle of Kosovo. The Emindžika is a rare example of Turkish 19th-century architecture.

A few kilometers to the northwest of Priština is that most significant battle site in South Slav history: Kosovo Polje (the Field of Kosovo). It is badly signposted, and there is not a great deal to see, but if you have a feeling for history, you should seek out the few monuments on this vast area of open rolling plain on which the biggest battle—in terms of the numbers engaged—in all medieval Europe was fought between the Serbs and Turks in 1389. A simple Turkish mausoleum marks the tomb of Sultan Murad I, who was killed in the moment of victory. Not far off stands another memorial, the Monument to the Heroes of Kosovo, honoring the Serbs who died here in defense of their nation. Tales of this battle, glorifying Prince Lazar and his outnumbered troops, are still recounted in the chants of the few remaining wandering minstrels.

Not far from the village of Laplije Stavo recent excavations have brought to light remains of an important Roman town. Nearby, standing quite by itself in open country, is a small church with alternating red and white stones used in the construction of its walls.

A more distant excursion to the north of Priština takes us through the industrial town of Titova Mitrovica to the Monastery of Banjska, built of delightfully blended white, red and blue marble, at the orders of King Milutin in the opening years of the 14th century. Inside it houses fabulously rich frescos decorated with gold, which were unfortunately allowed to deteriorate during the Turkish occupation. As with so many other similar foundations, it was transformed into a mosque, with the usual thick white-wash covering the Christian frescos. This has now been removed and the frescos restored.

Ten km. (six miles) southeast of Priština is one of the most striking of all Serb medieval buildings, the Monastery of Gračanica. Its church is in the compact form of a Greek cross with powerful, polychrome walls. It is a typical "five-cupola" building, in which four small domes surround the large central dome, but one of particularly complex yet harmonious design. The narthex at the entry into the basilica contains the portraits of King Milutin of the Nemanja dynasty, though the subjects of the other frescos are drawn from apocryphal religious literature and poetry. One can only describe them as epic paintings.

The little town of Lipljan, 18 km. (11 miles) south of Priština, was once the Roman Ulpiana. Later it was the frontier post between medieval Serbia and the Byzantine Empire, and under the Turks an important halt on the caravan-route linking Niš and Skadar (Scutari, on the Albanian side of the frontier with Montenegro). The battered, humble little church was built on Roman foundations in the 17th century.

13 km. (eight miles) beyond Lipljan, at Štimlje, we take the right fork of the road through Sava Reka southwestward of Prizren, one of the most fascinating cities in Yugoslavia, only some 18 km. (11 miles) from the Albanian frontier.

Prizren was already a prosperous town in Byzantine times, and the coin of the medieval Serb state was minted here. The Turks captured it in 1454, the year after the fall of Byzantium, and left it only in 1912. Prizren is still an important market town, and retains much of its oriental appearance. The fortress of Kaljaja dominates its mountain setting. Make a point of seeing the splendid view from its walls.

The River Bistrica flows into Prizren from the south, and leaves it by way of a dramatic gorge, and to follow its course is a favorite Sunday walk with the citizens. Because of the river, Prizren is a city of fountains, and these lend a special charm to its ancient squares and strangely attractive streets. The hub of the place is the Mosque of Sinan Pasha, built in 1615 of masonry from the Monastery of the Holy Archangel. The Church of Our Lady of Ljeviška, built at the order of King Milutin in 1307, was converted into a mosque, and it was not until 1950 that the covering plaster was removed from nearly 460 sq. m. (500 sq. yards) of magnificent medieval frescos. They are particularly notable for their free composition, their clever handling of detail and the charm of the portraits included in them.

Fine gold and silver filigree work has always been, and still is today, a specialist art of Prizren, and it is probable that many similar articles that you see offered for sale in Belgrade or Opatija were made here. Every Wednesday, which is market day, the play of color from the beautiful metalwork exposed for sale in the streets is a delight to the eye. South of the town one of the loftiest mountain ranges in the country piles up magnificently to mark the border with Macedonia. These are the Šar-Planina Mountains, the highest point, some 32 km. (20 miles) away, being "Titov Vrh" (Mount Tito), nearly 2,750 m. (9,000 ft.) above sea-level.

Church Land

We now turn away to the northwest of the Kosovo region; this is called the *Metohija*, a word meaning "church land"; in the Middle Ages, the land here was the sole property of the Serbian Orthodox Church. We pass through another Moslem town famous for its filigree work, Djakovica, which is only 39 km. (24 miles) from Prizren, and keep on for a further 21 km. (13 miles) to Dečani. Here we take a mountain road to the left, along savage gorges and through magnificent mountain and forest scenery, to arrive at the Monastery of Visoki Dečani set beside the River Dečanska Bistrica.

In 1335 a Franciscan friar named Vid of Kotor was ordered by King Stefan Uroš III (nicknamed *Dečanski* because of the monastery's construction) to build this Orthodox church. The style that he chose incorporates certain Western elements into its fundamentally Byzantine structure. Its lively polychrome exterior, high soaring lines and magnificent interior frescos make it one of the most impressive of all Serbia's striking monastery churches. Once inside, among ascending pillars, you will be struck by the fact that it is a much larger building than it appears from a distance. The frescos were executed by artists from the shores of the Adriatic, one of them, called Srdja, having signed his work.

The themes illustrated in the Visoki Dečani Monastery are not solely religious. They also portray the way of life, the costumes, customs, morals and manners of the people of Serbia in the 14th century. There is also a veritable portrait gallery of all the Serbian kings. The scale of these wall paintings is such that there are no less than a thousand figures included in the Last Judgment alone. However, the Church Calendar or Almanac, with every day of the year separately shown, takes up more wall space than anything else. The halos of the saints were not painted, but made from gold dust set in the surface of the wall.

Despite the various wars and pillaging raids that the monastery has suffered through the centuries, the church treasure is still remarkably rich. Outstanding are the ancient parchments and holy books, a series of priceless icons and a great, engraved wooden 14th-century cross.

The Brothers of Visoki Dečani do not possess a guest house, only a rather uncomfortable dormitory. But there is now a quite charming but fairly modest motel a few 100 meters uphill from the monastery. The surrounding pinewoods are cool even in the hottest months of the year. A campsite is attached to the motel. Returning to the main road at Dečani we have a run of only 16 km. (ten miles) to the sizeable town of Peć.

Patriarchal Peć

This town, the capital of the *Metohija,* takes its name from the caves (*pećine*) in the surrounding rocks. The narrow and twisting streets of the Okolj quarter are lined with cavern-like little shops and stalls which never seem to shut, and you will find them surprisingly like the *souks* of North Africa, a likeness heightened by glimpses of numerous mosques and minarets, the open gutters of running water that line each street and by important Turkish potentates' dwellings, with their interior gardens. This is the "Orient" as television would have us know it, even though we are in Europe, and it is in marked contrast with the modern installations of the newer part of town.

The town became important in the 14th century when the Patriarch of the Serbian Church made it his permanent residence. Before that time the Patriarch had lived in the Monastery of Žiča, but this had become too close to the Hungarian war zone. Following their normal practice, the Turks allowed the conquered people to retain their old religion. Their Grand Vizir, Pasha Mehmed Sokolović, nominated his cousin, an Orthodox monk, for the position of Patriarch in 1545.

The Serbs, however, were in no way placated by this move. Successive Patriarchs of Peć became the focal points of all the plots and intrigues that led to the revolts which periodically convulsed the country. On one occasion emissaries were sent to Russia to beg for help against the Turks. Two great uprisings promoted by the Patriarchs failed, and in order to avoid the mass extermination of the population, they led a migration to the Austrian side of the Danube in 1690, and in 1737 settled in the Vojvodina, where the Patriarchate continued more or less in exile. The abbeys and churches they built are in the Fruška Gora region.

The ancient monastery and residence of the Patriarchs is less than 1½ km. (a mile) from the town, not far from the main road leading west to Montenegro. It is a curious building of which the main church, that of the Holy Apostles, dates from the 13th century. No less than four other churches or chapels were built on to the original church at various dates. Most still possess their original frescos, which are especially fine. The outlines of the Patriarchate's original fortified quadrangle can still be made out, as can the foundations of smaller, older chapels. An 18th-century residential block continues to be used by priests and monks. The whole unit, with the churches' fantastic tiled cupolas and the high wooded mountains that look down into the little fortress, enjoys an extraordinarily picturesque setting. Immediately to the west there is the mouth of the gaunt Rugovo Gorge.

The family tree of the Nemanja kings preserved here is a fascinating study in medieval genealogy. In the Treasury the Patriarchate keeps a great number of precious objects, illuminated manuscripts and icons.

The Vojvodina

From Serbia's southern borders with Albania and Montenegro we return once more to the Republic's northern extremities. The plain of Vojvodina, immediately north of Belgrade, is Yugoslavia's granary. Only the extensive wooded heights and hilly vineyards of the Fruška Gora, rising on the southern banks of the Danube in the Novi Sad region, interrupt the green or golden sea of grain or sunflowers that during spring and early summer spreads away endlessly toward the Hungarian and Romanian frontiers.

This remarkably fertile area has in the past been the lure for countless conquerors, and has also known pacific invasion. Various German colonies were brought from Swabia by the kings of Hungary to settle there toward the end of the Middle Ages, and today 50,000 of their descendants are still there. There would be more if, in 1944, many of them had not chosen to retreat with the German Army while others were expelled after the war.

Last century roughly 100,000 Slovaks (racial cousins of the Yugoslavs) were transported from northern Hungary to the Vojvodina, and along the frontier there is a considerable Romanian minority. However, by far the most important ethnic minority in the district is Hungarian. Some are descendants of Magyars who arrived in the ninth century, others were settled there in the days of the Austro-Hungarian Empire. Some Serbs also migrated to the Vojvodina region between the 16th and 18th centuries, seeking so to escape from Turkish repression in Serbia proper.

Some years ago, the Yugoslav Government granted the Vojvodina region internal autonomy, so that all ethnic minorities have their own schools, newspapers, theaters and cultural associations. As a result this part of the country is a fascinating pattern of different customs, costumes and music.

Exploring the Vojvodina

The Autonomous Region of Vojvodina includes three quite distinct parts: roughly speaking, the area north of the Danube and east of the Tisa

River is referred to as the *Banat* (the name, used also in Romanian, means an area ruled by a military governor); the area north of the Danube and west of the Tisa is the *Bačka;* and the segment of the Vojvodina which lies south of the Danube is known as Srem. This multinational melting-pot reflects the long history of social upheavals and population migrations which have crisscrossed the Balkans over the past 2,500 years.

Srem

The visitor from Belgrade generally arrives first in the neighborhood of Srem. This territory has a long history. The Roman settlement of Sirmium, whose remains dating from the early centuries A.D. are now being excavated at the modern city of Sremska Mitrovica, was a fine provincial town with luxurious buildings.

The area between Sremska Mitrovica on the Sava and Novi Sad on the Danube is largely taken up by a section of the Fruška Gora hills. The highest point of this range is 533-m. (1,750-ft.) Mount Crveni Čot. Tucked away in these pleasant wooded hills are numerous historic buildings, such as the 14th-century Tower of Vrdnik and 16 monasteries following the great Serb migration of 1690, when it became a place of refuge for Orthodox priests and monks. The most remarkable of these monasteries are Krušedol, Hopovo, Jazak and Beočin, where there are many precious manuscripts and icons. They are well worth making a special visit to see.

On the Danube side of the Fruška Gora is a string of agricultural villages, including some famous for their vineyards. Some are of major historical importance for the several national groups which have made their home there. Stara Pazova, on the main highway between Belgrade and Novi Sad, for example, is a leading center of Slovakian culture. On festive days, its women and girls wear colorful full skirts and aprons, hand-embroidered and puffed out by a half-dozen starched petticoats.

On the same highway, farther along toward Novi Sad, is the historic town of Sremski Karlovci, where in 1699 the treaty was signed by Turkey abandoning a great part of her European conquests. Soon thereafter, Sremski Karlovci came to be the center of the cultural and political life of the dispossessed Serbian people, since Serbia proper continued under Turkish control. Thus, Sremski Karlovci was the seat of the Patriarchate of the Serbian Orthodox Church, and hence the seat of most Serbian church assemblies of this period; it was the place where Serbian newspapers and books were published; and it was the site (in 1791) of the first Serbian secondary school. The best of the architectural reminders of this period are in baroque style, and include the former Town Hall, cathedral, and Patriarchal Palace. This, considered by some the most imposing 19th-century building in the Vojvodina, houses the charming Patriarchal Chapel.

Novi Sad, the Bačka, and the Banat

Eight km. (five miles) farther on from Sremski Karlovci brings you to Petrovaradin, set in a sudden turn in the course of the Danube and dominated by a great fortress captured by Prince Eugene of Savoy from the Turks in 1716. Later it was to serve as a link in Austria's so-called "military frontier." Built on eleven levels, with 17 km. (11 miles) of underground passages and halls, today it houses museums, a hotel and restaurant. From here there is a memorable view of the capital of the Vojvodina, Novi Sad, a city of over 250,000 inhabitants. It was a great intellectual center during the decisive years of the struggle against the Turks early last century, and the Literary Association called Matica Srpska, formed in 1828, still exists.

The Town Hall is in the main square, facing the Orthodox Church and Bishop's Palace. The Orthodox churches in Novi Sad contain particularly valuable iconostases. Because of the mixed population of the Vojvodina, Novi Sad serves uniquely among the cities of Yugoslavia as a meeting-place of various groups and cultures.

A major center of Slovakian culture in the Bačka is the village of Bačka Petrovac, 34 km. (21 miles) west of Novi Sad. Especially on Sundays during the month of August, you will find yourself caught up in a whirl of bright colors, and strange, half-wild music and dancing.

Srbobran is on the main highway leading into Hungary; from it, it is 67½ km. (42 miles) to Subotica, the last major city before the frontier. This drive will take you across flat country indistinguishable from the *puszta* landscape so typical of Hungary. Subotica's population of 150,000 is predominantly of Hungarian origins. Eight km. (five miles) from the city is Lake Palić, in a vast area of park-like country. Here you will find a hunting museum, and also a small zoo. Sombor to the southwest is another interesting little town, while the Danube area around nearby Apatin is a magnificent natural wilderness for birds and other wild life.

The Banat is less frequented by visitors than the other parts of the Vojvodina. Nevertheless, some of its villages—notably Kovačica and Uzdin—have produced a number of remarkable naïve artists whose work has become known far beyond Yugoslavia's borders. In Kovačica an art gallery displays a selection of these vivid paintings and it is possible, by arrangement, to visit some of the artists' homes. Part of eastern Vojvodina consists of uninviting sand flats. The major city of the Banat is Zrenjanin, but most of the Romanian minority live at Vršac, less than 14½ km. (nine miles) from the Romanian frontier. Vršac has a Bishop's Palace and many of its churches have interesting iconostases. Just over 35 km. (22 miles) to the south is another frontier town called Bela Crkva, justly renowned for its Romanian carnival costumes on high days and holidays.

PRACTICAL INFORMATION FOR SERBIA

WHEN TO GO. Serbia is extremely hot in summer and many parts of it can be very cold indeed in winter. Nevertheless, it is mainly the summer season which attracts visitors. However, the best time to go to Serbia is in spring or autumn. There are growing skiing facilities for winter visitors.

FOOD AND DRINK. Serbia offers a wide variety of exciting dishes—that is, if you can persuade the chef to concentrate on the local recipes. Information on the regional specialties is given in the *Food and Drink* chapter. Many dishes use red peppers and have the highly spiced quality of Oriental cooking. But Serbia is also fish country, and you will find the product of the local rivers cooked in many delightful ways. You may also have your only chance to taste excellent sturgeon (and caviar) fresh from the Danube. Sturgeon is a gastronomic delicacy and is prepared in different ways. Ask for *jesetra* and, to go with it, *Smederevka,* a greenish wine from the vineyards of the Danube, or *Žilavka* (from Hercegovina) which, if genuine, comes from Blagaj and should be so labeled. Soups may be presented either in the accepted Western manner, or as a čorba, common throughout the Balkans—a fish čorba can be a real experience. Chicken (*pile*) is served with bread noodles swimming in the sauce. *Sarma, musaka, čevapčići* and *ražnjiči,* all of them inspired by the Turkish occupation, are also delicious, and the Serbs will be delighted if you try them.

There are a number of local wines, but the beer is very weak. Some of the best wines come from Smederevo, and are drunk cold for preference. *Prokupac* and *Negotinsko* resemble light Burgundies.

The atmosphere in Serbian restaurants is usually very cheerful.

HOW TO GET AROUND. By car. Roads between all major Serbian towns are adequate, if often narrow. However, avoid all those marked green on tourist maps, unless you are prepared for some rough rides. The first part of the main road Zagreb–Belgrade is now a toll highway as far as Novska and widens again 40 km. (25 miles) west of the capital; this road connects to the toll motorway which is now completed to Niš and which is being extended. Take special care on the non-highway sections where the narrowness, combined with considerable traffic, creates some very impatient drivers—and not a few accidents. A scenically rewarding and uncrowded route from Belgrade to Skopje is the *Ibar Magistrala* farther west.

By coach. Comfortable long-distance coaches operate to most destinations. If you take one of the exciting "Monastery Tours" you will find the deluxe vehicles used by the big Yugoslav travel firms give you a very relaxing ride.

SPORTS. In general, the thick forests of Serbia abound in game. Hunting is especially good in the Obed swamps, which are a favorite stopping place for migratory birds, while bear hunting is popular on the slopes of the Šar Planina hills and on the Tara plateau. Fishing is possible in a large variety of rivers.

For those who like swimming, there are numerous lovely beaches along the Danube. And the Ibar lends itself admirably to a descent by kayak. Good winter sports facilities are being expanded in the Kopaonik region.

PRACTICAL INFORMATION FOR BELGRADE

HOW TO GET THERE. By train. All the chief European express trains leaving Paris, Ostend, Basel and Vienna, en route to Athens or Istanbul, go through Belgrade. As behoves the capital, Belgrade is also the hub of Yugoslavia's internal railroad system. The main trans-European line runs from Zagreb to Belgrade, then turns south to Niš, where it divides—one branch going on to Sofia and through Bulgaria, the other continuing south to Skopje, and on through Greece. A more westerly line likewise links Belgrade with Skopje, but in this case via Kraljevo and Priština. From northeastern Europe, there is another international line to Belgrade which goes by way of Suboticn and Novi Sad. There is also a connection between Belgrade and Bar, on the Montenegrin coast through some spectacular scenery. Trains between Bosnia-Hercegovina and Belgrade are very slow and should be avoided if possible.

By plane. Belgrade has air connections with all Western European capitals and also New York, Chicago, Montreal and Toronto. In addition, there are regular flights between every Yugoslav provincial capital and main tourist center and Belgrade, by the national airline, JAT.

By boat. Danube cruise ships from Passau or Vienna call at Belgrade, usually for a few hours.

HOTELS. Economic and political center, seat of all the national government agencies, Belgrade has many visitors but not enough hotels. Therefore it is wise to reserve rooms in advance. If you have any difficulty, the Tourist Information Office in the Pedestrian Underground Passage at the Albanija Skyscraper, Terazije (tel. 635–343), at the railroad station or the airport, will help you find an available room. But note that in low season these three offices close fairly early.

Deluxe

Beograd-Intercontinental, Vladimira Popović 10. 420 rooms. Across the River Sava in Novi (New) Belgrade, adjoining the glossy new Sava Center. Modern accommodations, and very elegant if you don't mind being away from the city center. Indoor pool, health club, tennis, disco.

Jugoslavija, Bulevar Edvarda Kardelja 3. 500 rooms. Across the Sava and nicely placed on the banks of the Danube, but in a rather dull area of apartment blocks. Pool, nightclub, casino.

Metropol, Bulevar Revolucije 69. 206 rooms, nightclub, casino. Smartest hotel in the town center, sumptuous in a slightly old-fashioned way. Excellent food.

Expensive

Excelsior, Kneza Miloša 5. 81 rooms. Across from Tašmajdan Park. Upper end of price range.

Majestic, Obilićev Venac 28. 92 rooms. Central, traditional, some (M) accommodations.

Moskva, Balkanska 1. 140 rooms. The oldest (built 1906), with traditional and modern rooms, though more expensive than 1974 modernization merits. On a busy corner in the city center.

Slavija, Svetog save 1. 332 rooms. Comfortable modern hotel, slightly less central, towards motorway.

Moderate

Kasina, Terazije 25. 96 rooms. Central, but somewhat noisy.

Palace, Topličin Venac 23. 78 rooms. Central. Upper end of price range.

Park, Njegoševa 4. 131 rooms. A short walk from center.

Prag, Narodnog fronta 27. 118 rooms; central, but can be noisy.

Putnik, Palmira Toljatija 9. 118 rooms, across the river Sava, near the Jugoslavija (see above).

Splendid, Dragoslava Jovanovića 5. 50 rooms; no restaurant. Central, quiet location, near Federal Assembly building.

Toplice, 7 Jula 56. 110 rooms; central, the nearest to Kalemegdan, but can be noisy.

Union, Kosovska 11. 74 rooms; central.

Inexpensive

Central, Maršala Tita 10. In the pleasant old "suburb" of Zemun by the Danube.

Grand, Maršala Tita 31, also in Zemun. 21 rooms.

National, Bežanijska kosa bb. 70 rooms. Across the Sava, on the motorway from Zagreb.

Taš, Borisa Kidriča 71. 19 rooms. Small hotel in recreation center by Tašmajdan Park and Metropol. Pools.

Motels. Lipovička Šuma (I), Ibarski put. 20 rooms. On the road to Kraljevo, about 20 km. (12 miles) from city.

Romeo i Julija (I), Ibarski put. 14 rooms. On the road to Kraljevo, about 20 km. (12 miles) from city.

The 1000 Ruža (I), Avalski put. At Avala 14 km. (9 miles) from city.

Camping. National, Bežanijska kosa. With chalets, near National hotel.

Košutnjak, Kneza Višeslava 17. With chalets, quite near Tito Memorial Center.

Youth accommodations. Mladost, Bulevar JNA 56a. Year-round.

Private accommodations. Lasta Travel Agency, Trg bratstva i jedinstva 1A, or enquire at Tourist Information Centers (see Useful Addresses).

RESTAURANTS. In Belgrade, virtually all the hotels have restaurants. In general, however, it is much more fun to go to other restaurants, especially in the evening when musicians and singers create the atmosphere which is peculiar to the city. At many restaurants, the grilled meats, such as the *ražnjići, ćulbaštija,* and *pljeskavica,* are prepared in front of the guests.

Belgrade's restaurants are as varied as you would expect in a capital city and the following is only a selection. Note that some of the most popular ones are in the old Bohemian quarter of Skadarlija, in the center, a lively area for street entertainment in summer. In many cases you can eat quite moderately in the Expensive restaurants by choosing your dishes with care.

Expensive

Arhiv, part of the Metropol hotel (above), overlooking Tašmajdan Park. Excellent atmosphere and old Serbian specialties.

Beogradjanka, Masarikova 2–5, in the Beogradjanka building. Try the stuffed *fricandeau;* also good grills and steaks.

Dunavski cvet, Tadeuša-Košćuška 63. Modern with fine views over the Danube. Folk and popular music.

Dva bela goluba (Two White Doves), 29 novembre 3. Unusual grilled dishes. One of the newest in the Skadarlija quarter. Music.

Dva ribara (Two Fishermen), Narodnog fronta 21. Wide variety of sea and freshwater fish, and crustaceans. Piano music in main room.

Ima dana (There are days), Skadarska 38. Grills and steak specialties. Another old favorite in the Skadarlija quarter. Music.

International Press Center, Knez Mihailova 6/III. Try the mushrooms stuffed with chicken liver, or the lamb in milk.

KPZ Club, Obilićev Venac 27. Specialties include barbecued chicken shashlik.

Peking, Vuka Karadžića 2. Chinese specialties as you would expect. The Guayana duck is memorable.

Romani tar, Terazije 27. Gipsy specialties and music.

Tri šešira (Three Hats), Skadarska 29. Spicey pork and lamb specialties among others. Nostalgic old songs suit the Bohemian atmosphere of this old-established favorite in the Skadarlija quarter.

Ušće, Bulevar ušće bb. Attractive setting near Museum of Modern Art and confluence of rivers Sava and Danube. Music.

Zlatna ladja, Kolarčeva 9. Excellent fish (mainly freshwater) dishes.

Zlatni bokal (Golden Pitcher), Skadarska 27. Serves its own special "Skadarlija supper" in the famous quarter of the same name. Music.

Moderate

Ali Baba, Cara Dušana 128. Oriental decor and specialties in old suburb of Zemun.

Djordje, Šekspirova 29. Attractive private restaurant in quiet residential district.

Dušanov grad, Terazije 4. Good for quick meals right in the center.

Jezero, Ada Ciganlija. Near the bathing beach on Ada Ciganlija island on the Sava river. Good value, sports facilities. Music.

Klub Kniževnika (Writers' Club), Francuska 7. Some of the best food in the city, with an interesting clientele to match. Ignore shabby entrance.

Milošev konak, Topčiderska bb. Interesting building and lovely gardens in pleasant district. Music.

Pri majol'ki, Palmira Toljatija 5. Slovene specialties. In New Belgrade. Music.

Taš, Borisa Kidriča 71. Good veal or pork specialties. In Tašmajdan Park recreation center.

Vuk, Vuka Karadžiča 12. Private restaurant in center; excellent value.

Inexpensive

Atina, Terazije 28. Popular pizzeria. Counter opening on street sells *piroški* (a kind of turnover), excellent for a quick filling snack.

Koloseum, Terazije 40. Another express restaurant, serving fast food, but also Serbian specialties.

Šaran, Kej oslobodenja 53, in the suburb of Zemun. River and lake fish specialties, right on the Danube banks.

Skala, Bežanijska 3. A good bet for vegetarian meals in the old suburb of Zemun.

Venecija, Kej oslobodenja 6, in suburb of Zemun. Fish soups or *paprikaš* (stew), grilled dishes, again overlooking the Danube.

Two good coffee or pastry shops are *Kod spomenika,* Trg Republike 1, and *Moskva Café,* Balkanska 1, both with sidewalk sections. A historic one is *Znak* "?" (The Café of the Question Mark), 7 Jula 6, opposite the Orthodox Cathedral, and typical of Serbian homes of two centuries ago.

HOW TO GET AROUND. To travel about the city of Belgrade, if you do not have your own car, the best bet is to take a trolleybus, streetcar or bus. You can buy a day ticket, valid for an unlimited number of journeys, or a carnet of 12 tickets. For single journeys, it is a little cheaper to buy your ticket in advance from a tobacconist near the bus or tram stop; the ticket must then be punched in the correct machine when you have boarded the vehicle (watch how others do it). To get a taxi, call 4443–443.

EXCURSIONS. A wide range of one-day and longer excursions are arranged to the monasteries and other historic sights described in this chapter. Among day trips, a top attraction is the hydrofoil excursion through the famed Iron Gates traveling along the spectacular defile carved through the mountains by the Danube. Normally, departures from Belgrade are at 6 A.M. with return the same evening, including a two-hour stopover in Kladovo for lunch. However, if there is a delay for any reason the Kladovo stop is canceled, since the hydrofoils must return to Belgrade by sundown. It is therefore advisable to go armed with a few snacks. Another more relaxing alternative is to stay overnight in Kladovo, returning to Belgrade by hydrofoil the next day.

MUSEUMS AND MONUMENTS. Bajrakli Mosque, Gospodar Jevremova 11. Built in the late 17th century; the only survivor of many mosques that once existed.

Cathedral (Serbian Orthodox), K. Sime Markovića. Completed in 1841; beautiful iconostasis.

Ethnographic Museum, Studentski Trg 13, contains national costumes, rugs, and articles in everyday use throughout Yugoslavia. Also models and typical interiors of peasant houses, ancient Slav pottery etc.

Fresco Gallery, Cara Uroša 20, has copies of the finest frescos of the medieval monasteries of Serbia, Macedonia and Montenegro.

Ivo Andrić Memorial Museum, Andrićev venac 8. In the apartment where this Nobel prize-winning author lived and worked.

Jewish Historical Museum, Jula 7, 2nd floor.

Military Museum, Kalemegdan. Presents an excellent survey of Yugoslavia's historic evolution before, but especially after, the arrival of the South Slavs.

Modern Art Museum, on the River Sava in Novi Beograd, has a good display of 20th-century painting and sculpture, with the emphasis on the work of Serbian artists. In addition, it frequently holds special exhibitions of particular interest.

Museum of African Art, Andre Nikolića 14. Fine private collection.

Museum of Applied Arts, Vuka Karadžića 18. Notable exhibits include medieval Serbian jewelry and embroidery.

Museum of the City of Belgrade, Zmaj Jovina 1, depicts the history of the city from prehistoric times. Interesting engravings from 16th–19th centuries.

Museum of the Serbian Orthodox Church, in the Patriarchate, Jula 7, displays some of the best examples of icons, vestments and other art work from Serbian churches.

National Museum, Trg Republike, was founded by Prince Miloš Obrenović. It houses archeological, historical and numismatic collections, as well as a picture gallery. Among the pre-classical material are many vases, statuettes, gold jewelry, and the famous Duplja cart. The antique art section contains Greek and Roman items found on Yugoslav territory. There are gold objects from Trebenište, a late copy of the Athena Parthenos by Phidias, two dancing satyrs from Stobi (all from Macedenia), gold Roman jewelry from Kostolac in Serbia, etc. In the section representing the Middle Ages, besides fragments of frescos from Serbian monasteries, there are superb icons from Ohrid and elsewhere. The Gospel of Miroslav written in 1190 and a 14th-century copy of the Code of Emperor Dušan are the most valuable documents in this collection.

The numismatic section contains unique gold Roman coins, silver pieces of the Byzantine Emperor Nicephorus, etc. Paintings include some fine canvases by Renoir and Degas. The two great Yugoslav sculptors, Meštrović and Rosandić, are also well represented.

Tito Memorial Center, Boticeva 25, south of the city center in the Dedinje residential district. Set in fine gardens, this much-visited complex of buildings covers many aspects of the life and times of Yugoslavia's great leader Josip Broz Tito. Central is the House of Flowers in which his tomb is surrounded by banks of flowers and guarded by the young men of his Special Guard. Other buildings include his Residence, Billiard Pavilion, Hunting Lodge, the Museum of 4th July (concerned with the early days of the Communist Party and national uprising against the Nazis), the Museum of 25th May (a collection of birthday gifts from all over the world), and a Memorial Collection of Tito's personal possessions.

Topčider. This park-like district in the southwest of the city was the chosen site for the court of Prince Miloš Obrenović, and a number of buildings from the 1830s remain from that time, including Prince Miloš's Residence and Topčider Church. The area is a favorite excursion spot for the citizens of Belgrade.

Vuk and Dositej Museum, Gospodar Jevremova 21. Dedicated to two great Serbian writers and educators. The building is of particular interest as an excellent example of 18th-century secular architecture.

ENTERTAINMENT. Belgrade has seven theaters: the leading one is the National Theater, Trg Republike. In addition to its dramatic repertory, this theater possesses a very good opera and ballet company. Otherwise, there are a number of Yugoslav folkdance and folksong groups; one based at Kolora Hall in summer is known as the Kolo Company, and if an opportunity presents itself for you to see their program be sure to take it. The FEST International Film Festival is in February; BITEF, the Belgrade Theater Festival, in September; and BEMUS, Festival of Music, in October.

On summer evenings, Skadarlija, in the city center, is the scene of lively street entertainments. Summer months see open-air concerts in the parks, at Kalemegdan and in the Fresco Gallery. There are also classical concerts in the Zuzorić Art Pavilion, Kalemegdan, and in winter at the Kolorac Hall, Studentski Trg. Many movie houses show French, English or American films, and in summer there are a few outdoor cinemas. The Children's Theater at Trg Republike is justly famous.

SHOPPING. A handy booklet about shopping in Belgrade is available from the Tourist Information Center (see Useful Addresses). Of the major department stores, you can't miss the high-rise block of the Beograd Palace on Maršala Tita, which houses the largest of them all, Beogradjanka. Another big one, Beograd, is at Trg Terazije 15–23, with its drugstore (look for the phonetic spelling *Dragstor*) in the Underground Pedestrian Passage in Nušićeva, open round the clock. Jugoexport is the name to look out for when it comes to exclusive (and expensive!) fashion goods. You'll find women's wear at their salon at Terazie 2; and men's and women's wear at Kolaričeva 1 and Knez Mihailova 10. A chain of handicraft shops known as Narodna Radinost is worth seeking out: at Knez Mihailova 2 and 4, Knez Mihailova 19, and Terazije 45. The Galerija Primenjenih Umetnosti, at Uzun Mirkova 12, has a permanent display of the work of the Association of Applied Artists of Serbia. Leather goods are other recommended good buys, and there are specialist shops for these in Knez Mihailova and Terazije.

The main bookshop in Belgrade is Jugoslovenska Knjiga, at Knez Mihailova 2. Museums can be a valuable source of unusual souvenirs. Try the National Museum, the Fresco Gallery, the Ethnographic Museum, the Museum of Applied Arts, and the Museum of Contemporary Art. Zadruga Pravoslavnog svestenstva, Bulevar Revolucije 26, concentrates on reproductions of icons and jewelry.

There is a number of very lively open-air markets that sell handicrafts from many parts of the country, as well as fresh produce, household goods, clothes—in fact, pretty well everything you can think of. Such markets open daily from 5 A.M., including on Sundays. The principal one is at Zeleni Venac.

NEWSPAPERS. Foreign newspapers and magazines, including most English-language publications common in Western Europe, are sold in the large hotels in Belgrade, also at the Central Railroad Station, and at some kiosks and bookshops in the center of the city. One such kiosk is in the pedestrian subway near the Beograd cinema, another in Knez Mihailova in front of the American Reading Room.

USEFUL ADDRESSES. The Tourist Information Center can be found at the International Airport of Surčin, the Central Station, also in the subway passage at the end of Terazije below the building called Albanija, and in season on main roads into the city. Of the numerous travel agencies in Belgrade, Putnik (the main Serbian travel firm) has its headquarters at Dragoslava Jovanviča 1; Inex is at Trg Republike 5; Kompas, Brankova 9; PKB Beoturs, Bulevar Revolucije 70; Dalmacijaturist, Makedonska 35; and Kvarner Express at Balkanska 8. Naromtravel, specializing in youth travel, is at Knez Mihailova 50. Mladost Turist, Terazije 3, is also a youth travel agency.

Embassies: U.S., Kneza Miloša 50; Canada, Kneza Miloša 75; British, Generala Ždanova 46. Motoring organizations: Auto-moto savez Jugoslavije, Ruzveltova 16; and Auto-moto savez Srbije, Ivana Milutinovića 58. Pharmacies open round the clock: Prvi Maj, Maršala Tita 9; Savski Venac, Nemanjina 2; and Zemun, Maršala Tita 74.

Nightlife. Yugoslavs in general and Belgrade people in particular like to dance. Almost all the good hotels have a bar with dancing, while the former Bohemian quarter of Skadarlija is an especially lively area on summer evenings. There are casinos in the *Metropol*, and *Majestic* hotels and

Beogradjanka, Marikova 5, 6th floor. Nightclubs that can be particularly recommended include that at the *Metropol* hotel and the *Lotos,* Zmaj jovina 4. The *Beograd-Intercontinental* has a disco; in addition, there are many small private ones such as *Amadeus,* Ćirila i Metodija 2A. Among other lively spots with youth appeal are *Disko-Videoteka* at Bežistan, and *Dom omladine* (Youth Center), Makedonska 18.

PRACTICAL INFORMATION FOR SERBIA
OUTSIDE BELGRADE

HOTELS. It should be said that standards of service and maintenance in some centers, especially in Kosovo, do not always meet the expectations that might be aroused by the modernity of the buildings. Note, however, that there are excellent facilities in the many spas and these are well worth considering as alternatives to larger nearby centers or even as bases from which to explore. Village tourism (staying in private households off the beaten track) is developing in a number of small communities.

HOTELS FOR SERBIA EAST OF BELGRADE

Donji Milanovac. By an artificial lake in the Danube defile, well-placed for visiting Lepenski Vir, the Kazan Gorge, and the Iron Gates. *Lepenski Vir* (E), 262 rooms, some (M); pool. On a hill overlooking town; modern.

Golubac. Overlooking the Danube defile. *Golubački Grad* (I), 50 rooms.

Kladovo. Terminus of the hydrofoil excursion through the Iron Gates. *Djerdap* (M), 210 rooms. Modern.

Smederevo. Town with medieval fortress on the Danube. *Smederevo* (M), 128 rooms.

Zaječar. In the Timok Valley. *Srbija* (E).

HOTELS FOR SERBIA SOUTH OF BELGRADE

Aleksinac. *Motel Morava* (I), 104 rooms. On the *autoput.*

Dimitrovgrad. On the Bulgarian frontier. *Motel Dimitrovgrad* (M), 38 rooms.

Kopaonik. Scattered but fast developing winter sports center with a total of over 2,000 beds, good sports and entertainment facilities. *Bačište* (M), 64 rooms, friendly atmosphere, recommended for children. Nearby tennis and riding schools. *Grand Hotel Karavan* (M), 153 rooms. New *Konaci* apartment complex in modern "rustic" style, well-equipped.

Kragujevac. Principal city of Šumadija. *Kragujevac* (M), 109 rooms. *Šumarice* (M), 103 rooms. *Zelengora* (M), 33 rooms.

Kraljevo. Near Žiča Monastery. *Turist* (I), 75 rooms, on main square.

Kruševac. *Rubin* (M), 110 rooms.

Leskovac. Near the ancient city of Caričingrad. *Motel Atina* (I), 40 rooms. Pool. *Beograd* (I), 107 rooms. In the town.

Niš. *Ambassador* (M), 140 rooms. Central. *Niš* (M), 171 rooms; at the top end of its category. Central. *Medijana* motel and camp site with bungalows, 3 km. (2 miles) from center. *Nais* motel (M), 80 rooms, 8 km. (5 miles) from town on *autoput.* Open-air pool; with camp site.
Restaurants. *Stara Srbija* (M), traditional style and specialties. *Zlatni kotlić* (M). Fish and national specialties, pleasant décor.

Niška Banja. Spa 10 km. (6 miles) from Niš. *Ozren,* 96 rooms. New and linked to Radon (see below). *Partizan,* 59 rooms. Modern, pleasant. *Radon,* treatment center built round waterfall. All (M), with some (I) rooms.

Novi Pazar. *Vrbak* (M), 65 rooms. Accommodations attractively tiered round central reception area with fountain. Open-air pool.

Partizanske Vode. *Palisad* (M), 412 rooms. A complex of hotel units and individual cottages, on a ridge of the Zlatibor plateau at an altitude of 960 m. (3,150 ft.). Pool; excellent restaurant, nightclub.

Prokulpje. *Hammeum* (M), 40 rooms.

Ras. Ancient ruins near Novi Pazar. *Motel Ras* (M), recently renovated.

Raška. *Motel Putnik* (I), 40 rooms.

Rudno. Mountain community above Ibar Valley. A developing center for village tourism.

Sopoćani. *Turisticki Dom* (I). Basic (cold water only in rooms), but lovely situation near monastery.

Studenica. *Studenica* (M), 24 rooms. In idyllic mountain valley.

Svetozarevo. Near *autoput* in the Morava valley. *Jagodina* (M), 152 rooms. Indoor pool.

Titovo Užice. *Palas* (E), 44 rooms. *Zlatibor* (E), 150 rooms.

Topola. *Oplenac* (M), 38 rooms. Situated near the Karadjordje mausoleum church in the Oplenac park on a hill overlooking Topola.

Valjevo. *Beli Narcis* (M), 75 rooms.

Velika Plana. *Velika Plana* (M), 36 rooms. Motel on the *autoput.*

Vranje. *Vranje Motel* (E), 64 rooms, some (M). One of the best between Niš and Skopje; on the *autoput.*

Vrnjačka Banja. Serbia's premier spa. Excellent amenities for price, with pools and sports facilities. *Fontana* (E), 228 rooms, some (M). Indoor pool. *Zvezda* (E), 122 rooms, some (M). Indoor pool.

HOTELS FOR KOSOVO

Brezovica. Mountain resort. *Narcis* (M), 120 rooms, pool. *Breza* (I), 40 rooms.

Dečani. *Gja kova* (M), about 1 km. from monastery. New. *Visoki Dečani* (I), 39 rooms. In pine woods above monastery.

Peć. Major center and site of famous monastery. *Metohija* (M), 85 rooms. Newest with attractive architecture on bank of Bistrica river, but standards reported to be well below par. *Korzo* (M), 40 rooms, is lower priced.

Priština. Capital of Kosovo. *Grand Hotel Priština* (E), 370 rooms, some (M). Modern, nightclub. *Kosovski Božur* (M), 120 rooms. The Tourist Information Center is next door.

Prizren. Photogenic oriental city. *Theranda* (I), 90 rooms. *Vlazrimi* (I), 29 rooms. Motel. Restaurant *Maraš* overlooks the river.

HOTELS FOR THE VOJVODINA

Bačka Palanka. Fishing center on the Danube. *Turist* (I), 32 rooms.

Kikinda. *Narvik* (E), 100 rooms. Indoor pool, nightclub.

Novi Sad. Capital city of the Vojvodina. All (E): *Park,* 315 rooms; indoor pool, nightclub. *Putnik,* 86 rooms. Convenient for the city center. *Trdjava Varadin,* 52 rooms. Across the Danube in Petrovaradin Fortress, on a bluff overlooking the river and Novi Sad. Scenic. *Novi Sad.* 124 rooms. *Vojvodina,* 66 rooms. *Auto Camp Ribarsko Ostrovo* (I), 30 rooms, none with shower. Nightclub.
Restaurants include the *Mala Gostiona* inn and *Velika Terasa.*

Sremska Mitrovica. *Sirmium* (M), 54 rooms.

Subotica. *Patria* (M), 200 rooms, some (M). Comfortable. At Palić, *Jezero* (M), 30 rooms, and *Park* (M), 42 rooms. Both pensions.

Zrenjanin. *Vojvodina* (M), 109 rooms.

MACEDONIA

Cradle of Slavdom

It is strange how the name of Macedonia has survived. 23 centuries ago it became the most powerful nation in the world of ancient Greece under Philip and his son, Alexander the Great, and somehow it has conserved its name through 2,000 years of Roman, Byzantine and Turkish occupation, not to mention more recent power politics. Equally miraculous is the survival of Macedonian culture. Not only its language, but many aspects of the Republic's music and folk tradition show marked differences from that of other parts of Yugoslavia. Even certain physical characteristics seem to have withstood the traumas of history; compare the profiles, especially of some of the younger Macedonians, with classical busts of their forefathers in antiquity and you will see what we mean.

Today, as one of the six federal republics of Yugoslavia, the portion of Macedonia lying inside Yugoslavia has recovered something of its independence. It had been a Turkish province until just before World War I, and was little known to the outside world until the 1920s. It is still to a large extent off the main communication lines, so that modern development has started only recently. Progress, however, has been striking, and today you will find excellent modern hotels in a number of towns and resorts, as well as the other organized amenities (excursions, sports facilities, etc.) that go with expanding tourism. Hunting, fishing, spas and winter sports especially are being developed, together with "village" tourism aimed at bringing the visitor into closer contact with the Macedonian way

255

of life. Youth, too, is being given a fair share of consideration, with the construction of more hostels and camp sites.

So, though it is still quite an expedition to reach Macedonia across the full length of Yugoslavia, the effort is well rewarded. Here you will find one of the few remaining corners of Europe where many of the old ways still survive among abrupt mountain ranges of grandiose beauty and fertile valleys given over to the cultivation of tobacco, sunflowers, corn and fruit. In the far south there are three very lovely lakes—Ohrid, Prespa and Dojran—set in more mountains, with gardens and orchards that are alive with nightingales.

Many were the civilizations that lingered in Macedonia until their fortunes declined, so the countryside is steeped in history, especially along the valley of the Vardar and on the shores of Ohrid. The continuing excavations at Heraclea Lyncestis (near Bitola), Lichnidos (Ohrid), Skupi (Skopje), and Stobi (Gradsko) reveal ever more evidence of all the trappings of a sophisticated civilization far back into the Greco-Roman or Roman-Byzantine eras. But above all, this is a stronghold of the Orthodox faith. Once the barbarian invasions came to an end and the Slavs settled here, great changes took place as the people of these new tribes adapted Byzantine culture to meet their own needs and tastes. It is here in Macedonia that you will see some of the earliest and finest examples of an art style expressing a dynamism never before seen in Byzantine art, foreshadowing the "Renaissance" of the 13th and 14th centuries. Then came the Ottoman invasion and over 500 years of Turkish rule. The Orthodox priests and monks withdrew to the remotest mountains and there, in their monastic strongholds, kept the flame of Christianity alight. Nevertheless, evidence of the Islamic culture and religion imported by the Turks is still quite widespread, adding to the fascinating cocktail of Macedonian sights and sounds.

Macedonian folklore, folk arts and crafts are relatively pure and untouched by outside influences, so that the songs, dances, embroidery, carpet-weaving and wood-carving are unequaled in their abundance. The popular dances are a delight to the eye, the most striking being those from the mountainous west of the province.

There are good hotels in all the larger towns and summer resorts, and the roads, now much improved in most of the area, are relatively free of traffic except on main through routes.

Something of its History

The rise of the great Macedonian kingdom began in the fourth century B.C., when both Athens and Sparta had passed their zenith and had exhausted themselves with 30 years of fighting against each other. The Greeks regarded the Macedonians as "barbarians," i.e. people who could not speak proper Greek, and looked down on them accordingly. Nevertheless, by using a mixture of brilliant diplomacy and armed force, Philip II and his son, Alexander the Great, brought the whole of Greece under the control of Macedon.

One secret of their success was the adoption by Philip of the "phalanx," a squad of heavily-armed soldiers carrying strong pikes of different lengths and constituting, in effect, a sort of human tank. At the same time, the Macedonians perfected the employment of lightly-armed troops and cavalry, who could easily outmaneuver military formations of the time. Once all Greece had been brought under Macedonian control, Alexander, universally considered one of the greatest military geniuses of all time, then set out upon his extraordinary conquest of the known world. First he took Asia Minor, then the mighty Persian Empire of Darius. Pressing ever eastward, he next subdued Babylon and continued to the Punjab in India before his homesick troops finally compelled him, much against his will, to turn back. He himself died at the age of 33 without ever seeing his native country again. The generals whom he had left in charge of various provinces seized control for themselves and began to quarrel with each other. After 175 unsettled years, in 146 B.C. Macedonia became a Roman province.

Centuries later, Byzantium tried to check the Slavs' infiltration from the north, but was unable to prevent their settling there, and in the tenth century the newcomers formed themselves into an independent state under Car Samuilo (Tsar Samuel). After several victories over the Byzantines, he added other Slav provinces to his kingdom, whose central portion was what is now Bulgaria. But Byzantium, once fully mobilized, was too powerful for him.

In a terrible battle in 1014, the Byzantine Emperor, Basil II, took 14,000 prisoners, blinded them and sent them back to Samuilo. Stunned by the horror of this monstrous act, Samuilo died soon after, and for a time Byzantine power was assured.

With the expansion of the Serb state under the brilliant Nemanja dynasty, King Dušan occupied Macedonia in the 14th century, but this unification of the two Slav countries was not fully achieved before the Turks made themselves masters of both, staying there for 500 years. It was a period punctuated by rebellion and especially the activities of the *hajduk,* who formed themselves into bands of outlaws or freedom fighters. But for most of the population it was a period of hardship and hopelessness in which the flame of Macedonian culture was kept flickering only in the monastic centers.

Following the growth of nationalistic sentiment in Serbia early in the 19th century, Macedonia began to hope that her long subjection was nearly ended, but her case aroused little support abroad. Her attempts at a national uprising, such as that of Kruševo organized by the Macedonian revolutionary movement known as "VMRO," were mercilessly suppressed. In 1909 there was a state of open warfare for three months, but the insurgents, poorly armed and led, were beaten.

The first Balkan War (1912) liberated Macedonia from the Turks, but the Greeks, Bulgarians and Serbs immediately embarked upon the second Balkan War of 1913. In World War I this unhappy backward province was a theater of operations. The Treaty of Neuilly in 1919 again divided it, the new Yugoslavia being awarded the lion's share, Greece keeping Thessaloniki and its environs, and Bulgaria a small strip in the northeast. In 1941 the Germans presented most of Macedonia to Bulgaria, but the 1919 frontiers were restored in 1945. While the province was probably better-off in the period between the two world wars than she had been under the Turks, the kingdom of Yugoslavia was particularly active in its efforts to bring the region up to date and repair the damage of its long neglect.

However, after World War II, schools were opened for the first time. In them instruction is given in the Macedonian language, which is in many ways different from Serbo-Croat. Macedonia is still in some respects more backward than the northern region of Yugoslavia, but industrialization is going ahead fast, agriculture has been drastically reorganized, and excellent new roads have been built. There remains much to do, but it is significant now that the people are at last free of foreign rule that painters, musicians and writers are very actively asserting the country's highly individual artistic outlook.

Exploring Macedonia

There are two principal routes to the Macedonian capital of Skopje from Belgrade, one via Niš, and the other via Kraljevo and Priština. The first is the faster route, the second more interesting, passing close to several outstanding medieval monasteries referred to in the chapter on Serbia.

By the Niš route you cross the Kumanovo plain just inside Macedonia, where the Serbs in 1912 revenged themselves on the Turks for their enslavement after the defeat of Kosovo over 500 years before, finally destroying the Turkish Balkan Empire. Before reaching the town of Kumanovo, we strongly recommend you should turn east on to E870 (signed Kyustendil in Bulgaria) and after 14 km. (9 miles) turn north for another 4 km. (2½ miles) to visit Sveti Djordje church up a short stretch of rough track in the middle of the village of Staro Nagoričane. Ask one of the villagers for the key. This is one of the less visited and loveliest small churches in Yugoslavia, rebuilt by Serbian King Milutin in 1318. The magnificent frescos by the famous painters Mihailo and Eutihije were damaged to the height of a man during the Balkan Wars, but what remain are quite magnificent, with a glowing clarity and wealth of detail. Note the scenes of *The Passion*—especially the *Flagellation* and the *Last Supper*—and the portraits of King Milutin and his young queen Simonide.

If you are in the mood for another monastery, a by-way from the main road at Kumanovo leads west in 16 km. (10 miles) to Matejče, high in the hills. Reconstructed earlier this century, it dates from the time of King Dušan, and was completed by his widow after his death in the 14th century.

If you come by the road from Priština through Stimlje, you will cross the watershed of the rivers of southern Yugoslavia: everything south of the line flows into the Aegean. Just before entering Macedonia is the oriental-looking little town of Kačanik, and the road then immediately enters the long gorge formed by the Lepenac River, which divides the Šar-Planina Mountains from the Skopska Crna Gora (Black Mountains) that climb to 2,440-m. (8,000-ft.) Mount Ljuboten on your left.

If you have time to take a closer look at the Black Mountains, take the road leading off to the village of Čučer and, above it, the tiny Church of Sveti Nikita (described below). This detour will also give you a glimpse of untouched rural Macedonia.

Skopje City

At the foot of Vodno mountain, the first impression of Macedonia's capital is overwhelmingly one of fast-growing modernity, but don't let this mislead you. The city's roots go back into prehistory, though it was in Roman times that Skupi, as it was then called, first flourished until it was devastated by an earthquake in A.D. 518. Most of the finds from that period are now in Skopje's fine Museum of Macedonia, but part of the original site of Skupi is still being excavated, about 8 km. (5 miles) northwest of the city center.

It was an earthquake that destroyed ancient Skupi and, nearly 1,500 years later, a similar disaster that caused its rebirth as the modern city you see today. In the interim, invaders came and went, a fortified town developed, and the Ottoman Turks ruled for over 500 years. In the 19th century, Skopje became increasingly a center for Macedonian culture and education, a situation consolidated as the capital of the Macedonian Republic in the new Yugoslavia.

Then, on 26th July, 1963, the earthquake struck. The first tremor occurred at 5.17 A.M. (the clock of the ruined railway station still marks the time), followed by others. Over 1,000 citizens lost their lives, and 80% of all the buildings were either ruined or seriously damaged. Within hours help was pouring in from all over the world, and the city was transformed into an international salvage camp. By the fall of 1963, 150,000 people were living in Skopje again, many in tents, before they could gradually be rehoused in the prefabricated lodgings which were arriving from various countries. Since then, rebuilding has continued apace, producing some very fine architecture and practical facilities for the inhabitants, now numbering some 500,000. Skopje today is a thoroughly modern, well-equipped metropolis—and happily many of its historic treasures have survived, albeit in most cases much restored.

The city is naturally divided in two by the winding course of the Vardar river. Above the north bank rise the remains of the old fortified town and, below it, a maze of narrow alleys thread through the Čaršija or Bazaar, by far the most interesting quarter from the visitor's point of view. You can reach it from the modern center on the opposite bank across the charming Stone Bridge, probably dating back to the early 15th century though, of course, repaired many times since.

Not far from this bridge, incidentally, in "modern" Skopje, is the new Trading Center, built on several levels, with shops, restaurants, cafés and offices of all kinds. Interestingly, for some time after it first opened, Skopje's citizens gave it the cold shoulder, preferring the traditional facilities of the Bazaar and market. They have since been won over, though, and it is the Bazaar which now feels the draft. Most visitors, however, will much prefer the color and variety to be found as they wander among the little workshops and boutiques of the Čaršija in which slippers and other leather goods, and items of the gold or silversmith's art, can be bought from the premises on which they are actually made.

On the way into the Bazaar, just across the Stone Bridge, you will pass the Daut Pasha Baths, now an Art Gallery, and in the heart of the Bazaar, the reconstructed Suli Han, now housing the Old Bazaar Museum. Eventually the maze of alleys leads you to the lively market place and, beside it, the largest of Skopje's several mosques, that of Mustapha Pasha from the late 15th century. Not far away crouches the little church of Sveti Spas. You could easily miss it for, following a Turkish decree that no church could rise above the roof tops of their houses, its foundations are well below ground. The present church dates largely from the 19th century, but the treasure for which it must not be missed is the quite breathtaking carving of its iconostasis. Completed after many years in 1824, it is the work of three craftsmen from the region of Galičnik—you will find their self-portraits wielding their tools at a work bench in the far right panel. The main motifs, of course, are all Biblical, interlinked by decorative themes that include figures dressed in local folk costume. One could spend hours unraveling the familiar events. It is a truly majestic achievement.

Also not to be missed is one of the latest additions to the Skopje scene: the new home of the Museum of Macedonia (archeological, ethnological and historical) in a major complex that incorporates the rebuilt Kuršumli han, a magnificent inn originally built in the 16th century and for a time serving as a prison.

Modern Skopje has good, at times strange architecture (not least the Telecommunications Center), including the Cultural Center, Modern Art Museum, Cyril and Methodius University and Cathedral of St. Climent Ohridski.

Skopje Environs

The countryside around Skopje is peppered with evidence of the religious fervor of medieval times. We have selected the four most notable examples.

The first is a "must" whatever else you miss. It is the little hill top church of Sv. Pantelejmon at Nerezi, 7 km. (4 miles) from and almost immediately above the city, on Vodno mountain. Built in the 12th century, it contains some of the most beautiful and best known Byzantine frescos in the country, and among the first to demonstrate a new and powerful humanism. The sorrow on the face of Mary, for example, as she mourns over the body of Christ in *The Lamentation,* is quite remarkable and far removed from the formalism usually associated with Byzantine art. Note, too, the *Bathing of the Infant Christ,* part of a Nativity scene. The views over Skopje and surroundings from up here are superb, and there is a good restaurant next to the church.

Sveti Nikita Monastery, our second suggestion, is about 15 km. (9 miles) north of Skopje, in a remote rural setting in the Skopska Gora hills. Most fresco painters remained anonymous, but the works of Mihailo and Eutihije (see also Nagoričane and Ohrid) from the late 13th and early 14th centuries are often signed and their skill ranks among the highest. You will find them represented here.

Next, Markov Monastery is 17 km. (11 miles) southeast of Skopje. The frescos from the 14th century vary widely in style and skill of execution. Note a rare portrait of the legendary Prince Marko above the south doorway.

Finally, we recommend the Treska gorge, both for its setting and the tiny church of Sv. Andreja at its exit. It lies about 18 km. (11 miles) west of Skopje, down a turning off the road to Tetovo. After passing the village of Matka (another monastery here, but the frescos are shrouded by candle smoke), the narrow road continues up the Treska valley for 1½ km. (1 mile) to the dam. From here you must walk, following a path at the foot of a rock cliff for about 300 meters. It is a lovely, secluded spot (but also a military area, so leave your camera behind) and the little church has some fine 14th-century frescos despite some unattractive modern graffiti—especially *The Agony in the Garden* and the *Last Supper.* If you want, you can follow the path for several kilometers up the canyon.

The Macedonian Circuit

From Skopje, all the most famous and many of the little known treasures of Macedonia can be visited on a circular itinerary, with beautiful Lake Ohrid roughly two-thirds of the way round. You will need to make a few detours, of course, in order to cover everything and, ideally, should allow at least 10 days if you want to enjoy a few days of relaxation on the shores of Ohrid.

If for some reason you are traveling from Skopje to Ohrid in only one direction, we recommend you take the route through Debar, and you will need to follow our description of it in reverse. It is the shorter and more spectacular route, though inevitably you will miss a great deal. If you do not have your own transport, we suggest you divide your time between Skopje (2–4 days) and Ohrid (4–6 days), from either of which excursions can be made to many of the sights we shall describe, though naturally this gives you much less freedom to linger as the mood takes you.

Our itinerary follows a clock-wise circuit and begins with the main road to Greece, running all the way through the Vardar valley.

Towards Greece

After 53 km. (33 miles), Titov Veles on the river's right bank is not without interest, particularly those quarters spread out upon the slopes above the valley, which contain a large number of characteristic Macedonian houses, as well as a good deal of building from the Turkish period. Here, as in Prilep, tobacco is the main crop. True seekers of off-beat places might consider a side trip from Titov Veles northeast to Kočani, the only rice-growing area in Yugoslavia. The two rewards of such an enterprise are unspoilt countryside and villages, and a total lack of fellow tourists.

Another 26 km. (16 miles) down the main road from Titov Veles is Gradsko and, a little farther, where the rivers Vardar and Crna Reka meet, lies the ancient, ruined, yet still impressive Stobi, scattered about the grassy plain of the Vardar valley. It is recorded that Philip V of Macedon built nearby the city of Perseide. It was under the Romans, however, that Stobi prospered from the 1st century A.D. In 386 it became the capital of the Roman province of Macedonia Salutaris, though by then it was the already well established seat of a bishopric. The Goths sacked it in the 5th century and the earthquake of 518 completed the destruction. It is last mentioned in history, briefly, in connection with Samuilo's defeat in 1014.

Stobi once covered a huge area, part of which has been washed away by river floods. But it is still extensive, and what has been revealed by excavations so far gives evidence of a well-organized and well-equipped city. You can get a guide, but unless you are seeking a lot of detail it is probably best to explore alone and let your imagine wander. Most of what you see today is from the 4th and early 5th centuries and includes some of the best and earliest remains of Christian houses in the Mediterranean regions. What will impress the average visitor most, however, are the outstanding mosaics of which there are, in all, several thousand square meters. Remember, though, that these are protected by a covering of sand in the winter—they were just being uncovered on our most recent visit in late April.

The remains of churches are particularly numerous, as well as of palaces (some with swimming pools as well as mosaics), baths (including a reconstructed hypocaust), and a fine amphitheater capable of seating 8,000 spectators.

From Stobi our circular itinerary turns southwest towards Prilep and Bitola, but at this point we suggest the longest of our detours in order to visit Macedonia's least known lake resort, Dojran, on the Greek border. First continue down the main road along the Vardar valley, by-passing Negotino on the way, and in about 34 km. (21 miles) you will enter the highly dramatic gorge of Demir Kapija by means of a long tunnel. The name means "Iron Gate" in Turkish and it is remarkable both naturally and archeologically, for the river Vardar forcing its way between the rocks, here narrows to a mere 50 km. (165 feet) of swift-flowing water.

Demir Kapija was a natural fortress, surrounded on all sides by high hills particularly difficult to scale, and has been used to control the passage of the river and keep watch over the surrounding plains since remotest times, every summit being crowned with some kind of fortification. From any of these you will see all the way from the distant hills in the west to the confluence of the rivers Bašava and Vardar. When the railroad and, later, the road were being constructed, traces of ancient buildings and tombs were uncovered, some of them containing magnificently wrought votive vases. As a result systematic excavations were carried out, which brought to light a number of Greek, Roman and Slav tombs.

The road leads to the Greek border just beyond Gevgelija, but there is little point in going that far. Instead, turn east at Valandovo and follow the signs for Dojran.

Set among low scrub-covered hills at an altitude of only 148 m. (485 feet), this lovely little lake has as yet seen few foreign visitors. It's a situation that is likely to change for a new border crossing into Greece has recently opened near the village of Stari Dojran and, beside it, a new hotel and autocamp. For once there are no historic monuments to seek out. Stari Dojran itself was largely destroyed during World War I; indeed there is a memorial to the British who fell here, now just across the border in Greece. This is an area of fruit and vegetable crops and fishing and, indeed, the professional lake fishermen still practise a unique method of fishing with cormorants, though, alas, you will not see it unless you are there between November and March. Much of the lake shore is fringed with reeds and, tucked in along the edge of them, you will see the fishermen's characteristic reed huts on stilts, each belonging to a syndicate.

Cormorant fishing is a complex operation but, broadly speaking, the birds are used to "herd" the fish in much the same way as a sheep-dog herds its flock. Once driven into the protection of the reed beds, the fish find themselves trapped in fenced-in areas. A score or more of cormorants are captured by each syndicate and used to drive the fish in to progressively smaller enclosures from which they are finally scooped out by the ton.

Other forms of fishing with nets and lines are used during the rest of the year, and summer visitors can hire boats or make arrangements with local fishermen. The bathing is good and the lake waters warm.

Southern Macedonia

From Dojran you will need to retrace your route back to Negotino in order to continue along our circular itinerary. The region round Negotino and Kavadarci 12 km. (7½ miles) to the southwest is the heart of the Tikveš, Macedonia's best wine-producing area. From here the road to Prilep becomes progressively more scenic as it climbs up to the Pletvor Pass (994 m., 3,260 ft.), but its narrowness and curves, combined with the presence of many heavy vehicles, also make it very slow. So be patient—and enjoy the scenery.

Prilep, 48 km. (29 miles) beyond Kavadarci is today a thoroughly modern-looking town, though some old corners and several mosques still stand. Almost the entire population makes its living from tobacco which you will see being planted, harvested and dried in due season.

Just to the northeast of the town are the ruins of the fortress of the redoubtable 14th-century Prince Marko, set on a volcanic rock shaped by nature in form of an elephant's head. Incorporating at least four circuits of walls, it is one of the largest fortresses in the Balkans. On the southern side of the same mountain, the monastery church of Sv. Arhangel Mihailo acquired its present appearance in 1861 but dates back to the 13th century; it now plays host to an international painters' colony each year. You will find this in Varoš, a suburb of Prilep, and the most interesting part of town. It also harbors the churches of Sv. Dimitrije and Sv. Nikola. The latter has noteworthy 13th-century frescos.

Prilep is at the hub of several roads that swoop down on it over the mountains or streak across the fertile tobacco, wheat, poppy and wine growing plains of Prilepsko Polje and Bitolska Polje. It is across these plains that the excellent main road to Bitola (44 km., 27 miles) leads, but at this point we suggest a detour which lengthens this distance to 80 km. (50 miles), taking in much finer scenery and the gorgeous mountain resort of Kruševo, 30 km. (20 miles) west of Prilep. On the way up to it, you may like to turn off along the narrow, winding road of 5 km. (3 miles) up to the monastery of Sv. Spas, much rebuilt but worth visiting for the views alone.

You will see Kruševo long before you reach it, perched high above you in a vivid splash of red roofs and soft colors at 1,250 km. (4,100 ft.) on the slopes of Mount Baba. The origins of Kruševo are at least medieval, but it is the style of its old urban architecture from the 19th and early 20th centuries and the town's lay-out in its mountainous amphitheater that give it such a pleasing and harmonious air. With their jutting upper stories, wood carving and wrought iron work, the houses of Kruševo have enormous charm. Historically, the place was also long a hotbed of resistance against the Turks, and thus it was here that the famous Ilinden Rebellion took place in 1903, whose glorious but all too brief success led to the formation of the Kruševo Republic. It lasted just 12 days before it was smashed in the stark tragedy of mass slaughter. There is a museum to the event and the rather curious spiky globe of the Ilinden Memorial crowns the skyline on one side of town; the views from it over the plains are splendid.

Not surprisingly there is not a mosque to be seen in Kruševo, and none of the churches is older than the 1830s. There are however a number of art galleries and the town is famous for the carpets woven in brilliant colors by its womenfolk in their homes during the winter months. There is also a carpet factory.

An excellent and beautiful road leads down again from Kruševo via Demir Hisar to Bitola, a town which, beneath its rather decrepit surface, has a lot to offer. Its most famous sight is the archeological site of the Greco-Roman settlement of Heraclea Lyncestis, only 2 km. (1¼ miles) from the center, of which more in a moment. But the town itself was immensely important during the Turkish period, at one time second only in size to Salonika in the Balkans. This was in the latter part of the 19th century and it is from those days that some of the fine examples of urban architecture date with their elaborate ornamentation and wrought iron-work (albeit in need of some spit and polish). These were the houses of merchants from which they did business with the distant capitals of western Europe, and you will find some of them along Maršala Tita street in the heart of town.

At one end of this street rise two large 16th-century mosques on either side of the little Dragor river that runs through the town. The best mosque, though, is that of Ajkar-kadi, from the 1560s, and near the reconstructed Bezistan, or covered, market. The old Čaršija or Bazaar quarter, though not comparable to that of Skopje or Sarajevo, is still worth a stroll. In the Orthodox church of Sv. Dimitrije, the iconostasis is another magnificent example of Macedonian craftsmanship of the early 19th century.

But back to Heraclea Lyncestis on the outskirts of town: First of all, the site is well maintained and beautifully situated with its mountainous backdrop. Founded probably by Philip II of Macedon, it reached its main flourishing under the Romans up to the early Christian period. As at Stobi, there are some superb mosaics, true masterpieces of early Christian art. Quite a few, for the moment, are permanently protected by a layer of sand, but an outstanding example from the 5th century can be seen, covering 100 square meters of the narthex of the Large Basilica. It represents the Universe with all forms of life—plants, trees, animals, birds, interlinked by tendrils from a central source of life. There is minute detail and even graphic action, for example in the scene of a leopard tearing at a fallen stag. Other remains include baths and a fine amphitheater, used for gladiatorial contests. Some of the seats are inscribed with the names of their patrons.

By direct road it is only 73 km. (45 miles) from Bitola to Ohrid, but our route will follow a more devious and beautiful route via Lake Prespa. First, though, we suggest a short side trip up a sinuous by-way off the main road into the Pelister National Park, 15 km. (9 miles) west of Bitola. At present, accommodations there are limited to holiday homes for children or the employees of Yugoslav enterprises, but it is a superb area for walking among magnificent coniferous forests rich in plant and wild life. Botanists will find here one of the few habitats of the molica pine and a great variety of plants including rare crocuses. The highest point of the Pelister massif is 2,601 m. (8,532 ft.), and the combination of altitude and pine woods results in a heady cocktail of unpolluted air!

And so to Lake Prespa, only a few kilometers south of the main Bitola–Ohrid road, and wonderfully tranquil, set amid apple orchards and ringed by mountains. At 853 m. (2,798 ft.), it is the highest of Macedonia's three "frontier" lakes, in this case shared with both Albania and Greece. Although so close to Ohrid, it is far less developed and a good choice for those who want a quieter setting within reasonable reach of Ohrid's considerable attractions. Like Ohrid, it is also good for fishing, but rather better known for its bird life—including the pelican which breeds here.

The main tourist facilities are at Oteševo on the northwest shore, from which there is good bathing, wind surfing and boats for hire. From here, too, excursions are arranged across the lake and to the nearby small island of Golem Grad, on which, among traces of several other religious buildings, is an abandoned church with 14th-century frescos. The main town of the area is Resen, about 8 km. (5 miles) north of the lake and best known for its ceramics.

The mountains all around are dotted with monasteries in various states of repair, but the one you should make every effort to see is Kurbinovo, near the village of the same name, above the northeastern shore. You will need to collect the key and caretaker from the first house on the left as you enter the village. A rough road continues up for about 1½ km. (1 mile) to the church by a stream backed by woods, and overlooking a majestic view of lake and mountains. From outside the church does not look very significant, but within, the frescos, dating from 1191, are stunning, with a skill of draughtsmanship which makes robes flow and figures seem almost to be carried on the air; the technique and style are closely related to those of Nerezi. You can hardly miss the dramatic, life-size figure of Christ, expressing strength and compassion. Many other scenes, such as the *Annunciation, Entry into Jerusalem,* and the *Nativity,* are quite remarkable. If you visit Kurbinovo you can be sure you have seen some of the finest frescos in the country—and are among the few to have done so.

Ohrid and its Shores

Lake Prespa is separated from Lake Ohrid by the massif of Galičica. From a few kilometers south of Oteševo another spectacular road twirls up to 1,600 m. (5,250 ft.) and down again to the southeast shore of Lake Ohrid. It provides a magnificent introduction to this most famous of Macedonia's resort areas.

At this point, you will be only about 5 km. (3 miles) from one of the most popular excursion points on these shores: the monastery of Sveti Naum, close to the Albanian border. In addition to its beautiful situation, perched on the lake shore, this is hallowed ground if you are interested in early medieval culture. For though the present church dates from the 17th century, it is on the site of the original one, built by Sveti Naum (see below), and is also his final resting place. The fine iconostasis, dated 1711, is one of very few surviving from that period. Close to the monastery, the leafy source of the Crni Drim—one of the main streams to feed the lake— is a favorite picnic spot.

It is about 30 km. (20 miles) north by road from Sveti Naum to Ohrid, a beautiful drive overlooking the lake most of the way, passing through or near a few scattered communities, including the fishing village and small resort of Peštani, and some of the main hotels a few kilometers south of Ohrid. In summer, a special road "train" links the further hotels with the town itself.

A rash of modern building has changed the outskirts of Ohrid beyond recognition, but happily the old core of this marvelous little town has been carefully protected. So numerous are its churches and other ancient remains that it would be easy to get mental indigestion. We are therefore confining our recommendations to a selection of sights, to which you will undoubtedly add your own discoveries.

Settled by the Illyrians, known to the Greeks (as Lichnidos) and developed by the Romans (who built the Via Egnatia land route linking the Adriatic and Aegean Seas through it), Ohrid became a major religious center early in its history. It was from here that the scholars Sveti Kliment and Sveti Naum (see *Creative Yugoslavia*) undertook their great missionary work to Christianize the early Slav settlers and, from all over the Christian world, pilgrims and scholars came here to study the new Slavonic script, culture and art.

A century or so later, Ohrid became the capital of Samuilo's expanding empire. Later, it was under Byzantine or Serbian rule until the Turkish invasion of the late 14th century. During the following dark times, most of the churches were either turned into mosques or fell into disrepair. A proportion of the frescos were damaged or destroyed, but far more were covered with whitewash, thereby miraculously helping to conserve these extraordinary masterpieces for modern art historians to rediscover.

If you start your tour down by the harbor and work your way up hill, you will, more or less, also be going back in time. Tiny streets thread between the beautiful 19th- and early 20th-century houses so characteristic of Ohrid, their jutting first and second stories all but meeting over your head.

The main thoroughfare is Car Samuil (Tsar Samuel) Street. Almost immediately after following it into the old town through Donja Porta (Lower Gate) you will find the two tiny 14th-century churches of Sv. Nikola Bolnički and Sv. Bogorodica Bolnička, just off on your left. A little farther, on your right, two splendid adjoining 19th-century houses comprise part of the National Museum of Ohrid. Almost immediately, on the left, you come to one of the great ecclesiastic monuments of all Yugoslavia: the Cathedral of Sv. Sofija.

The building and some of its frescos date right back to the 11th century, providing some of the best surviving examples (mainly round the altar) of Byzantine art from that period. In the 14th century the church was enlarged and, from then, dates the superb west façade and more frescos. When Sv. Sofija was turned into a mosque (note the *mimbar,* or pulpit) the frescos were covered with whitewash. The process of rediscovering and preserving them, and restoring the shaky building, has involved the most complex modern techniques; there is no space to describe them here, but an exhibit in the Cathedral's upper galleries gives a graphic demonstration of the rescue operation.

At the top of Car Samuil Street, turn right into Ilindenska, which leads to Gorna Porta (Upper Gate). Before you reach it you will find a recently excavated Roman theater on the left and the way to Sv. Kliment on the right. This marvelous church, completed in 1295, is of quite modest size but had the great distinction of being the only one in which worship was allowed in Turkish times. Thus it became a repository for many of the ecclesiastic treasures from elsewhere. The frescos by that famous pair, Mihailo and Eutihije, are glorious in their execution and glowing colors (glossy 19th-century "restoration" has been largely removed). You can find their names or initials in several places including on the bowl of *The Last Supper.* Among outstanding scenes are *The Lamentation, The Death of the Virgin, Judas's Betrayal* and *The Communion of the Apostles.* Adjoining the church is an exceptional Gallery of Medieval Icons and, close by, the Museum of Slavonic Literacy, a unique collection on the development of early Slavonic writing.

From Sv. Kliment, you can wend your way up to the massive walls of Samuilo's ruined fortress high above the town. From it, paths lead down through woods past the foundations (and mosaics) of a 5th-century church to an ancient complex rather less visited than most, but of great significance. This is the monastery of Sv. Kliment and church of Sv. Pantelejmon, originally built by no less than St. Clement himself in 893 on the site of an earlier church. Later it was enlarged and, later still, in the 17th century, completely obliterated by a mosque whose ruined walls still surround the monastery foundations that have now been excavated. This then was the site of the "university" from which the earliest scholars of the new Slav alphabet went out to spread the message of Christianity, and literacy. It is a wonderfully peaceful spot, perched high on a bluff at the foot of which the tiny fishing community of Kaneo clings to the shore. Our final recommendation is the 13th-century church of Sv. Jovan Kaneo, depicted on almost every brochure of Ohrid, which stands above this little community part way up the bluff, and seemingly suspended over the lake. You can get some marvelous views of it from a boat trip on the lake.

And, of course, boating, bathing and other water sports are the activities which most visitors want to enjoy. Ohrid's amenities are good and expanding. You may even be able to make arrangements to go out with local fishermen though, on the whole, the professionals prefer to concentrate on what they are doing. The alternative is to watch them from a hired boat. In any case, at some time along Ohrid's shores you are likely to encounter the fascinating sight of a fishing syndicate netting in the day's catch the traditional way, a masterly piece of teamwork in action. A good variety of excursions is arranged from the hotels or by local agencies, and the level of folk entertainment is particularly high (see also Practical Information for Macedonia).

For many visitors one of the highlights is a trip of just a few kilometers to the Saturday market at Struga, a small town at the head of the lake astride the Crni Drim as it rushes out of the lake and heads for Albania. The market, which draws country folk in local costume from all around with their rich variety of wares, is among the most colorful in the country. A few kilometers south, near the Albanian border, the monastic complex of Kalište features a small church in a natural cave, and smaller caves that once served as monks' cells.

The Western Route to Skopje

The mountainous nature of Macedonia provides such a ration of magnificent scenery that comparisons are invidious. Yet we venture to suggest that the first part of the return route to Skopje offers among the most spectacular of all. Heading north from Struga, you first follow the Crni Drim river downstream, dammed in several places to create a series of sinuous narrow lakes beneath the mountains that form the border with Albania. The few villages cling precariously to the mountain sides, some with baked-clay houses and slender minarets announcing their predominantly Albanian populations; others typically Macedonian with their square houses of rough and dressed stone.

At Debar (rebuilt after an earthquake in 1967), you are right on the Albanian border. The Crni Drim rushes off across it and the road now turns to follow the Radika river upstream between the towering heights of the Bistra and Korab mountain ranges. The scenery is unceasingly beautiful. About 20 km. (12 miles) north of Debar, almost opposite the village of Rotuše, a small road on the right leads steeply up in about 1 km. (¾ mile) to the extraordinary monastery of Sv. Jovan Bigorski—St. John of the Rocks, aptly named indeed. The views from it are glorious, and the place itself enchanting, with its carved wooden galleries hanging over secretive little inner courtyards. The monastery probably dates from the 11th century, but most of what you see today is from the early 19th, including the huge refectory and the monastery's greatest treasure, the stunning iconostasis in the church, completed in 1835. If you have seen the one in Sveti Spas church in Skopje, you may recognize here the magical skill of the same craftsmen, the Filipovski brothers and Frčkovski from the nearby Galičnik region. In this case you will find their self-portraits in the far left panel. Other themes are from the Old and New Testament, beginning with Adam and Eve, and from the life of St. John.

As the crow flies, Galičnik is very close, but to reach it is rather more complicated, unless you are prepared for a long steep walk. The only way by road is to continue about another 24 km. (15 miles) to Mavrovi Anovi and here turn right for the developing summer resort of Mavrovo by the artificial lake of the same name. It is a pleasant and peaceful spot with a small hotel. From near here begins the narrow winding road which brings you in 12 km. (7½ miles) to Galičnik. The village nowadays is deserted, except in summer when former residents return and many visitors come for its beautiful surroundings, its characteristic 19th-century houses and its famous Wedding Festivities in July. At nearly 1,400 m. (nearly 4,600 ft.), in fact, it is cut off from the rest of the world by snow during the winter months.

Back on the main road you now begin the long descent to Gostivar and the final straight stretch across a plain fed by the upper Vardar river to Tetovo, another tobacco town. Gostivar mainly has a modern look today but, despite its modern center, Tetovo has quite a bit to offer, in addition to its situation at the foot of the Šar Planina mountains, to whose heights it is linked by road and cable car.

Near the center of town an interesting group of buildings includes the 17th-century Colored Mosque, so-called because of the decorative painting on its outer walls. Close by, beside the river, an old *hamam* (baths) is now used as an art gallery. But Tetovo's greatest curiosity is the monastery complex of Sersem Ali Baba (Arabati Baba teke), one-time home of Whirling Dervishes and a particularly well-preserved example of 18th-century Islamic architecture. Several buildings are set amid the monastery gardens, two of them now housing a restaurant and a small hotel, and another the Regional Museum. You will also find a small mosque, a building reserved for dervish rites and the tomb of the founder.

There are now only 40 km. (24 miles) to go before the end of our circular itinerary through Macedonia. It is a pleasant finale over the mountains and twice crossing the Vardar river, on its curving route to Skopje where it all began.

PRACTICAL INFORMATION FOR MACEDONIA

HOW TO GET THERE. By plane. There are frequent air services from Belgrade, Zagreb, and other major Yugoslav cities to Skopje; there is now also an airport at Ohrid, with air connections to Dubrovnik, Skopje etc.
By train or bus. You can reach Skopje from Belgrade by boarding one of the international express trains that travel the length of Yugoslavia on their way to Greece, though you are likely to find accommodations more crowded and less comfortable than on the average luxury long-distance coach. Certain trains from Belgrade operate direct to Bitola, and there are other towns and villages which can be reached more easily from Belgrade by stopping trains (though these are slow) than by coach.

WHEN TO GO. Inland Macedonia has a Continental climate, with cold winters and very hot summers. The southeast, however, toward Gevgelija, enjoys an equable Mediterranean climate. In winter its mountains offer sports conditions which, even if they cannot equal those found in the Slovenian Alps, are still good enough to attract many Yugoslav skiers. In summer the shores of Lakes Ohrid and Prespa are relatively cool, because they are respectively 695 m. (2,280 ft.) and 853 m. (2,798 ft.) above sea-level and surrounded by mountains. Generally speaking, the best seasons are spring and fall.

The Macedonian calendar is full of colorful local events, of which probably the Galičnik Wedding, an outstanding folkloric event featuring old wedding customs, is the most famous. But Macedonia's most important artistic event is the Summer Festival, held each year at Ohrid from mid-July to mid-August, preceded by the Balkan Festival of Original Folk Dances and Songs performed on the open-air stage of the fortress. Toward the end of August is Ohrid's Festival of Old Town Songs and the Evenings of Poetry at Struga, an international event.

HOTELS AND RESTAURANTS. Hotels have been vastly improved in recent years, and there is a far greater realization of visitors' requirements—though standards of service do not always match modernity of style and amenities in the newer establishments. To compensate, prices are lower on the whole, and the local people's innate hospitality will overcome some of the defects you are likely to encounter. The moral of this is simply—don't expect too much. Advance bookings are advisable. All hotels have all or many rooms with bath, unless otherwise stated. Accommodations in private homes are available through some local travel bureaux, notably in Ohrid and Struga. Not the least of the pleasures awaiting you in Macedonia, incidentally, are the performances of folk music and dancing put on by many hotels in the evenings.

Regional dishes we can recommend include *bamnja* (lamb stew with peas), *sarma od vinivog lišća* (vine leaves stuffed with minced meat and rice) and *sarma u jagnjećoj maramici* (eggs and minced lambs' liver). The *čevap* and other grilled meats are generally excellent in Macedonia, as in Serbia. The trout of Ohrid (*belvica*) is a variety of salmon-trout found nowhere else in Europe. *Alva,* made with crushed nuts and honey, makes a wonderful dessert. *Kačkavalj* is a hard cheese, common throughout the Balkans.

In the pastry-cooks' shop you will find a number of Turkish specialties, all very sweet, and the non-alcoholic drink called *boza,* sharp but extremely refreshing, and made from maize flour.

Macedonia produces a number of very palatable wines, mostly red; the best are from the Tikveš district. *Mastika* is an agreeable aperitif.

Bitola. Second largest city in Macedonia. *Epinal* (I), 200 rooms. Modern, central.

Dojran. Lovely, unspoilt lake on Greek border. *Mrdaja* (M), 100 rooms and autocamp right by border. *Stari Dojran* (I), 26 rooms. In Stari Dojran village in which several other hotels (I) are run by Macedonian companies for their workers, but take foreign guests when there are vacancies.

Gevgelija. Principal frontier town between Yugoslavia and Greece. *Jugo* (M), 52 rooms, casino. New. *Motel Vardar* (M), 48 rooms.

Gradsko. Near the Stobi excavations. *Motel Stobi* (M), 20 rooms. On the Titov Veles—Gevgelija road.

Kruševo. Charming hill town. *Montana* (M), 94 rooms, pool. Lovely location overlooking town.

Mavrovi Anovi. On Tetovo-Debar road. *Mavrovo* (I), 28 rooms. Attractive lakeside location, but basic.

Mavrovo. Developing lake resort, 8 km. (5 miles) off main road. *Bistra* (I), 44 rooms. Stands back from southern end of lake against mountains.

Negotino. *Park* (M), 60 rooms. *Autocamp Antigona* (I), 80 rooms without shower. Both by junction with main Titov Veles—Gevgelija road.

Ohrid. (See also Peštani and Struga). Beautifully located and historic lakeside resort. *Grand Hotel Palace* (M), 240 rooms, is near lake and offers the only hotel accommodations in town. Much better are those at Gorica, 5 km. (3 miles) south, managed by the Inex enterprise: *Gorica* (M), 131 rooms, pool, in delightful, peaceful wooded setting above own beach, and *Park* (M), 110 rooms, on shore facing Ohrid across bay. Three km. (2 miles) further south the *Metropol* (E), over 200 rooms, indoor pool (closed in high season), tennis, is the best, but across the road from lakeshore (accessible by underpass). Private accommodations are readily available in town.

Restaurants. *Ohridska Pastrmka,* excellent fish restaurant by harbor— ask for the special Ohrid lake trout cooked the Ohrid way. Also many small private restaurants.

Peštani. On Lake Ohrid, 13 km. (8 miles) south of Ohrid on east shore. *Desaret* (M), 291 rooms. Beach.

Popova Šapka. Winter sports center 18 km. (11 miles) from Tetovo (direct link by cable car). *Popova Šapka* (M), 60 rooms. *Slavija* (M), 55 rooms.

Prespa. Beautiful lake on border with Albania and Greece. In the main resort area of Oteševo on the northwest shore *Oteševo* tourist complex (M), 250 rooms, with hotel accommodations, restaurants, bungalows and camp site. At *Krani,* on the eastern shore, camp site with bungalows.

Struga. Resort on northern shore of Lake Ohrid.
Eurotel (E), the first in Yugoslavia, 325 apartments with self-catering, also restaurant. Excellent water sports and other facilities, shops, but 2 km. (1 mile) east of resort in rather less attractive situation, though on lakeshore. *Drim* (M), 180 rooms, pool, tennis. Spacious domed reception area with garden. On lake shore and near fast flowing Drim river near resort center.

About 8 km. (5 miles) south, near the Albanian border, is the *Biser* (M), 90 rooms, tennis. In charming local style, built into the living rock, adjoining Kalište Monastery. On the lakeshore. The *Izgrev* (M), 200 rooms, and *Skopje* (E), 50 rooms, are nearby.

Tetovo. Starting point for Šar-Planina mountains. *Arabat Baba Teće* (I), small hotel in historic Dervish monastery complex in town. Restaurant serves good lamb specialties.

Titov Veles. *Internacional* (M), 88 rooms. *Makedonija* motel complex (M), 36 rooms, well-equipped. 7 km. (4 miles) from town on Athens road.

HOW TO GET AROUND. By car. Almost all of Macedonia's main routes of necessity pass through deep gorges or over mountains, so that building any road—let alone a fast highway—is a major feat of engineering. Nevertheless, the network of roads linking all main centers and tourist resorts is now good. Many, though, are narrow and this means that on busy through routes you will more than likely be delayed behind a crawling procession of heavy goods vehicles creeping up one side of a pass and down the other side. Patience is probably your most desirable asset in these circumstances. Minor roads vary from good to atrocious.

Filling stations are frequent on the main through road to Greece, and can also be found in each of the main towns through which you are likely to pass—nevertheless, don't miss a chance to fill up your tank, and a spare can of gasoline is a good idea.

By coach. For comfort at a very economical price, the extensive coach network is your best bet. On all long-distance journeys you can, and indeed should, reserve your seat well in advance. Shorter journeys may mean sharing the coach with a multitude of people and, sometimes, animals. It can be fun if you don't mind crowds; the worst factor is usually the heat.

SPORTS. Swimming is possible on beaches fringing Lake Ohrid and Prespa, though lake water tends to be rather cold outside high summer and early fall. Lake Dojran, at the lowest altitude, is the warmest. All three lakes offer good fishing. A special fish-breeding station has been established at Struga, on Lake Ohrid. Boats for lake fishing can be hired by private arrangement from on-the-spot professionals, and information about permits, etc., can be obtained from the local Tourist Offices.

There is an increasingly popular little winter sports resort in Macedonia, Popova Šapka, at 1,783 m. (5,580 ft.) near Tetovo, where, every March, a ski contest known as the Šarplaninski Smuk is held. At Tetovo you board the new cablecar which lifts you in a few minutes to Popova Šapka. There is a halfway station near the village of Lisac from where it's a 90-minute walk. There are many excellent slopes available also on the flanks of 2,601-m.-high (8,532 ft.) Mount Pelister. Mavrovo is another developing winter sports center. The 2,530-m. (8,300-ft.) Solunska Glava, south of Skopje, is ideal for mountain climbing.

Macedonia has two native sports of its own which you should try to see. One is *pelivani,* a kind of Graeco-Roman wrestling, and the other *biška,* which is played on grass and resembles hockey.

SHOPPING. There is a great variety of attractive souvenirs on sale in Macedonia. Embroidery is the richest in Yugoslavia, the ornamental designs employed being of Slav, Byzantine and Turkish origins. Pottery and ceramics generally can be bought more cheaply direct by the tourist in the small towns or villages where they are made, such as Titov Veles and Resen. The Macedonians are past masters in the art of woodcarving, and you will find delightful examples in the shops and markets. In Kruševo, near Prilep, you can buy beautiful hand-made woolen carpets. In Ohrid, unusual pearls are made by a unique process (which remains a well-guarded secret) from fish scales; beware of inexpensive imitations.

USEFUL ADDRESSES. Tourist information *Skopje:* Gradski zid, blok iii, and at the entrance to the Čaršija (Bazaar) near the Stone Bridge; *Ohrid:* Turističko drustvo Biljana, Partizanska (near the bus station). Most travel agencies have branches in Skopje and there are tourist offices in most towns.

PRACTICAL INFORMATION FOR SKOPJE

HOTELS. Accommodations remain a weak spot in Macedonia's otherwise modern capital, though we hear a new international hotel may materialize in the near future. All fall in the Moderate range.

Moderate

Bellevue, 65 rooms. About 8 km. (5 miles) from town on Belgrade road.

Bristol, Maršala Tita bb. 33 rooms, nightclub.

Continental, E. Kardelj bb. 200 rooms. The best, a short stroll from center.

Grand Hotel Skopje, Moša Pijade 2. 180 rooms, disco. Its *Ognjište* cellar restaurant is much to be preferred to the bleak main restaurant. Central and by river Vardar.

Jadran, 27 Mart bb. 23 rooms. Very central.

Panorama, Triglavska bb. 87 rooms. On outskirts, on lower slopes of Vodno mountain.

Tourist Settlement Olympic Village. 176 rooms. Near the Panorama.
Turist, Maršala Tita bb. 80 rooms. Very central.

Camping. Park. By the river in the City Park. The best.
Bellevue. Near Bellevue hotel, above.

Hostels. Youth hostel, Prolet 25, near railway station. Open year-round.
Student hostels (open to all, but summer only): K.J. Pitu, Ivo Ribar-Lola 58, central; and Goce Delčev, Taftalidža, on outskirts.

RESTAURANTS

All the following are Moderate:
Biser, in the Cultural Center.
Ognjište, part of the Grand Hotel Skopje. Folk music.
Pobeda, Gradski blok 1. Good food and central.
Sv. Pantelejmon in the famous monastery at Nerezi, 7 km. (4 miles) from town. Good national specialties and fabulous view over city.
There are many cafés, pastry shops and snack bars in the modern shopping center and the old bazaar quarters.

MUSEUMS AND MONUMENTS. The terrible destruction resulting from the 1963 earthquake has been almost entirely obliterated by extensive building and restoration. Below is a selection of the main sights.
Daut Pasha Baths. Dates from the 15th century, now housing Art Gallery, including collection of Macedonian icons from 14th–19th centuries.
Kale Fortress. On a hill dominating the center of city. The massive walls date from Byzantine times. Today the area is a park.
Kuršumli Han. Formerly an inn and at one time a prison, this ancient structure in the old bazaar quarter has been completely rebuilt since the earthquake. It is now part of the otherwise ultra-modern Museum of Macedonia complex containing several major collections, including the Archeological, Ethnological and History Museums. In summer it is the setting for concerts and drama performances.
Mustapha Pasha Mosque. Dates from the 15th century, but restored after earthquake damage.
Stone Bridge. Though frequently repaired, this famous bridge across the Vardar in the town center retains its original 15th-century appearance.
Suli Han. Completely rebuilt since the earthquake, this interesting complex, originally from the 15th century, is now the home of the Old Bazaar Museum and Academy of Fine Arts.
Sveti Spas Church. The present church dates from the 19th century; its greatest treasure is its iconostasis, the stunning work of the two Filipovski brothers and Makarije Frčkovski, which took several years to complete.

Skopje Environs

Of a considerable number of monuments and monasteries in various states of repair, the following is a recommended selection.
Markov Monastery. 17 km. (11 miles) southeast. Built in 14th century with frescos of varying quality and style. Note the fine portrait of Prince

Marko (Kraljević), historic figure and legendary hero, above the south door.

Skupi. About 8 km. (5 miles) northwest. Ruins of city that preceded Skopje in the 4th–5th centuries A.D. Excavations are still in progress.

Sv. Nikita Monastery. About 15 km. (9 miles) north in the Skopska Gora hills. It features works by the most famous of all fresco painters, Mihailo and Eutihije, from the early 14th century.

Sv. Pantelejmon, at Nerezi, 7 km. (4 miles) southwest. Exquisite monastery church from the 12th century in superb location high above the city. Whatever else, don't miss this one. The frescos in the lower portions of the church date from 1164 and are among the first and best to express human emotions quite absent from earlier Byzantine art. Note especially *The Lamentation* and *The Deposition.*

Treska Gorge and Church of Sv. Andreja, 18 km. (11 miles) west. The approach and setting are lovely with the little church at the canyon entrance, reached by footpath (about 300 m.) from the end of a paved road. Excellent 14th-century frescos. This is a military area, so no photographs. The path can be followed several kilometers deeper into the canyon.

SHOPPING. In Skopje you have a choice between the very modern facilities of the central shopping complex built on several levels (one supermarket stays open round the clock) and the more traditional—and certainly more charming—little shops and workshops of the bazaar quarters and market area. Carpets, leather goods (especially slippers and bags) and jewelry are the main items to look out for, but it is worth comparing prices and quality before you buy. Lowest prices do not always make for the best bargains. Two specialist shops are Kooperativa, M. Gorki 1, and Makedonske rukotvorine, Partizanski odredi 125.

TOURIST VOCABULARY

THE ALPHABETS. Here are the Cyrillic and Latin alphabets, to help you pronounce the place names in Yugoslavia.

А а	A (a)	as in *father*		Н н	(N)(n)	as in	*no*
Б б	B (b)	„ „	*brother*	Њ њ	Nj (ny)	„ „	*news*
В в	V (v)	„ „	*vodka*	О о	O (o)	„ „	*orb*
Г г	G (g)	„ „	*go*	П п	P (p)	„ „	*pop*
Д д	D (d)	„ „	*do*	Р р	R (r)	„ „	*rod*
Ђ ђ	Đ (dj)	„ „	*jump*	С с	S (s)	„ „	*sod*
Е е	E (e)	„ „	*let*	Т т	T (t)	„ „	*too*
Ж ж	Ž (zh)	„ „	*pleasure*	Ћ ћ	Ć (tch)	„ „	*tube*
З з	Z (z)	„ „	*zero*	У у	U (u)	„ „	*room*
И и	I (i)	„ „	*if*	Ф ф	F (f)	„ „	*fa!*
Ј ј	J (y)	„ „	*year*	Х х	H (gh)	„ „	*ach*
К к	K (k)	„ „	*keg*	Ц ц	C (ts)	„ „	*lots*
Л л	L (l)	„ „	*lad*	Ч ч	Č (tch)	„ „	*church*
Љ љ	Lj (ly)	„ „	*million*	Џ џ	Dž (j)	„ „	*John*
М м	M (m)	„ „	*map*	Ш ш	Š (sh)	„ „	*shoe*

PRONUNCIATION. The vowel sounds in the Serbo-Croat languages (the chief languages of Yugoslavia: Serbian is written in the Cyrillic alphabet and Croat in the Latin) are uniform and do not vary from word to word as is the case in English. They are pronounced as follows:

a - as in f*a*ther
e - as in l*e*t
i - as in *i*f

o - as in *o*rb
u - as in r*oo*m

GENERALITIES

Is there anyone who speaks English . . . French . . . German?	Ima li neko koji govori engleski? . . . francuski? . . . nemački?
Yes — no	Da (or) jest — ne
Impossible	Nemoguće
Good day — Good morning	Dobar dan — dobro jutro
Good evening	Dobro veče
Good night	Laku noć
Goodbye — *Au revoir*	Do vidjenja
Mister — Madam — Miss	Gospodin — gospodja — gospodjica
Please — Don't mention it	Molim vas — molim
Excuse me	Izvinite
How are you?	Kako ste?
How do you do (Pleased to meet you)	Milo mi je
I don't understand	Ne razumem
Thank you	Hvala

TRAVELING

I am traveling by car . . . train . . . plane . . . boat	Putujem automobilom . . . vozom . . . avionom . . . parobrodom
Taxi, to the station . . . pier . . . airport	Taksi, na stanicu . . . na pristanište . . . na aerodrom
Porter, take the baggage/luggage	Nosač, iznesite stvari
Where is the filling-station? (gas) (petrol)	Gde je železnička stanica? Gde je benzinska stanica?
When does the train leave for . . . ?	Kada polazi voz za . . . ?
Which is the train for . . . ?	Koji je voz za . . . ?
Which is the road to . . . ?	Koji je put za . . . ?
Where is the ticket-window?	Gde je blagajna?
A first-class ticket, please	Molim vas jednu kartu, prve klase
No smoking (compartment)	Zabranjeno pušiti
Ladies — Men	Zene — Muškarci
Where? — When?	Gde? — kada?
Sleeping-car — Dining-car	Kola za spavanje — restoran
Compartment	Kupe
Entrance — Exit	Ulaz — izlaz
Nothing to declare	Nemam ništa za carinjenje
I am coming for my holidays	Dolazim na godišnji odmor
Nothing	Ništa
Personal use	Za ličnu upotrebu
Must I pay duty?	Treba li da platim carinu?
How much?	Koliko?

ON THE ROAD

Straight ahead	Pravo
To the right — to the left	Desno — levo
Show me the way to . . . please	Molim vas pokažite mi put za
Where is . . . ?	Gde se nalazi?
Stop!	Stoj!
One-way (no entrance)	Ulaz zabranjen
Crossroad	Raskrnica
Danger	Opasnost
Drive slowly!	Vozi lagano!
Look out for the train (railroad crossing)	Pazi na voz

IN TOWN

Will you lead me? take me?	Hoćete li me pratiti?
Street — Square — Place	Ulica — Trg
Where is the bank?	Gde je banka?
Far	Deleko
Quickly	Brzo
Police station	Stanica milicije
Consulate (American, British . . .)	Konzulat (Americki, Britanski . . .)

Theater	Pozorište
At what times does the film start?	Kada počinje bioskop?
Will you dance with me?	Hoćete li da igrate?
Where is the travel office?	Molim vas gde je turistički biro?
Where is the tourist information office?	Gde je turistički informativni biro?

SHOPPING

I would like to buy	Želeo bih da kupim
Show me, please	Molim vas možete li mi pokazati
How much is it?	Šta staje ovo?
It is too expensive	To je skupo
Have you any sandals?	Imate li sandale?
Have you foreign newspapers?	Imate li stranu štampu?
Show me that blouse, please	Pokažite mi onu bluzu
Show me that bag	Pokažite mi onu torbu
Envelopes — writing paper	Koverte — papir za pisanje
Roll of film	Film
Map of the city	Plan grada
Something hand-made	Ručne izrade
Wrap it up, please	Molim vas upakujte mi
Cigarettes, please	Molim vas, cigarete
Matches, please	Dajte mi šibice
Ham	Šunka
Sausage — salami	Kobasica — salama
Sugar	Šećer
Grapes	Grožđe
Apple	Jabuka
Pear	Kruška
Orange	Pomorandža
Bread — Butter	Hleb — puter
Peach	Breskva

AT THE HOTEL

A good hotel	Jedan dobar hotel
Have you a room available?	Imate li slobodnu sobu?
A room with one bed, with two beds	Soba sa jednim krevetom, sa dve kreveta
With bathroom	Sa kupatilom
How much is it per day?	Šta staje dnevno?
A room overlooking the sea	Soba prema moru
For one day, for two days	Za jedan dan, za dva dana
For a week	Za nedelju dana
My name is	Ja se zovem
Here are our papers	Evo vam naših isprava
What is the number of my room?	Koji je broj moje sobe?
The key, please	Molim vas ključ
Where is the chambermaid?	Gde je sobarica?
Breakfast, lunch, supper	Doručak, ručak, večera
The bill, please	Molim vas račun

| I am leaving tomorrow | Ja putujem sutra |

AT THE RESTAURANT

Waiter	Kelner
Where is the restaurant?	Gde je restoran?
I would like to have lunch, dinner	Hoću da ručam, večeram
The menu, please	Molim vas jelovnik
Fixed-price menu	Molim vas meni
Soup	Supa, juha
Bread	Hleb
Hors d'oeuvre	Mešano predjelo
Smoked ham	Dalmatinski pršut
Ham omelet	Omlet sa šukom
Roast chicken — roast duck	Pečeno pile — pečeno patka
Roast pork	Svinjsko pečenje
Veal cutlet	Teleča šnicla
Potatoes	Krompir
Tomato salad	Paradajz salata
Vegetables	Povrće
Cakes	Kolaći, testa
Fruit, Cheese	Voče, Sir
Fish, Eggs	Ribe, Jaja
Serve me on the terrace	Servirajte mi na terasi
Where can I wash my hands?	Gde mogu da operem ruke?
Red wine, white wine	Crno vino, belo vino
Rosé wine	Ružica
Beer — bottled water	Pivo — Mineralna voda
Turkish coffee	Turska kava
Fruit juice	Vocni sok

AT THE BANK — AT THE POST OFFICE

Where is the bank? . . . post office?	Gde je banka? . . . pošta?
I would like to cash a check	Ja želim da promenim ček
I would like to change some money	Ja želim da zamenim novac
Stamps	Poštanske marke
I want to send it by airmail	Hoću da pošaljem avionom
I would like to telephone	Hoću da telefoniram
Postcard — letter	Dopisnica — pismo
Letterbox	Poštansko sanduk
I would like to send a telegram	Hoću da pošaljem telegram

AT THE SERVICE STATION

Service station—Gasoline	Garaža — benzin
Filling station	Benzinska stanica
Oil, please	Molim vas ulje
Change the oil	Promeniti ulje
Look at the tires — a tire	Pregledati gume — guma
Wash the car	Oprati kola

Grease the car	Podmažite kola
The car broke down — I have a flat tire	Imam automobilski defekt — guma mi je pukla
Can you tow it?	Možete-li nas vući?
Spark(ing) plug	Svečica
The brakes	Kočnice *or* bremse
The gear box	Menjać brzine
Carburetor	Karburator
A headlight (headlamp)	Farovi
Starter	Pokretać
Axle	Osovina
Spring	Pero

NUMBERS

1	jedan	8	osam	60	sezdeset
2	dva	9	devet	70	sedamdeset
3	tri	10	deset	100	sto
4	četri	20	dvadeset	200	dve stotine
5	pet	30	trideset	300	tri stotine, etc.
6	šest	40	četrdeset	1000	hiljada
7	sedam	50	pedeset	2000	dve hiljade

Index

GEOGRAPHICAL
The letter H indicates hotels and other accommodations.
The letter R indicates restaurants and other eating facilities.

(The Geographical Index also provides practical information
for each chapter and major cities.)

YUGOSLAVIA ①

② AUSTRIA
③
H U N G A R Y
Slovenia
Ljubljana
Zagreb
⑥
⑦
RUMANIA
Trieste
Istria
Rijeka
Vojvodina
C r o a t i a
BELGRADE
④
Bosnia-Hercegovina
⑤
Ancona
Zadar
D a l m a t i a
S e r b i a
A
D
R
I
A
T
I
C
Split
Sarajevo
⑧
Mostar
Niš
Pescara
Dubrovnik
Monte-negro
Titograd
Pec
Kosovo
Bar
S E A

I T A L Y
N
A
L
B
A
N
I
A
Skopje
Macedonia
Ancona
Bari

CONTENTS

Maps

KEY

〰〰   Motorways

〰   Main roads

—   Other roads

††††   Railways

- - - -   Car ferries

●   Cities

•   Large towns

·   Other towns

✳   Airports

Land over 1,200 feet (Map 1 above only)

Notes

Fodor's Travel Guides

U.S. Guides

Alaska
Arizona
Atlantic City & the
  New Jersey Shore
Boston
California
Cape Cod
Carolinas & the
  Georgia Coast
The Chesapeake Region
Chicago
Colorado
Disney World & the
  Orlando Area

Florida
Hawaii
Las Vegas
Los Angeles, Orange
  County, Palm Springs
Maui
Miami,
  Fort Lauderdale,
  Palm Beach
Michigan, Wisconsin,
  Minnesota
New England
New Mexico
New Orleans

New Orleans (Pocket
  Guide)
New York City
New York City (Pocket
  Guide)
New York State
Pacific North Coast
Philadelphia
The Rockies
San Diego
San Francisco
San Francisco (Pocket
  Guide)
The South

Texas
USA
Virgin Islands
Virginia
Waikiki
Washington, DC

Foreign Guides

Acapulco
Amsterdam
Australia, New Zealand,
  The South Pacific
Austria
Bahamas
Bahamas (Pocket
  Guide)
Baja & the Pacific
  Coast Resorts
Barbados
Beijing, Guangzhou &
  Shanghai
Belgium &
  Luxembourg
Bermuda
Brazil
Britain (Great Travel
  Values)
Budget Europe
Canada
Canada (Great Travel
  Values)
Canada's Atlantic
  Provinces
Cancun, Cozumel,
  Yucatan Peninsula

Caribbean
Caribbean (Great
  Travel Values)
Central America
Eastern Europe
Egypt
Europe
Europe's Great
  Cities
France
France (Great Travel
  Values)
Germany
Germany (Great Travel
  Values)
Great Britain
Greece
The Himalayan
  Countries
Holland
Hong Kong
Hungary
India,
  including Nepal
Ireland
Israel
Italy

Italy (Great Travel
  Values)
Jamaica
Japan
Japan (Great Travel
  Values)
Kenya, Tanzania,
  the Seychelles
Korea
Lisbon
Loire Valley
London
London (Great
  Travel Values)
London (Pocket Guide)
Madrid & Barcelona
Mexico
Mexico City
Montreal &
  Quebec City
Munich
New Zealand
North Africa
Paris
Paris (Pocket Guide)
People's Republic of
  China

Portugal
Rio de Janeiro
The Riviera (Fun on)
Rome
Saint Martin &
  Sint Maarten
Scandinavia
Scandinavian Cities
Scotland
Singapore
South America
South Pacific
Southeast Asia
Soviet Union
Spain
Spain (Great Travel
  Values)
Sweden
Switzerland
Sydney
Tokyo
Toronto
Turkey
Vienna
Yugoslavia

Special-Interest Guides

Health & Fitness
  Vacations
Royalty Watching

Selected Hotels of
  Europe

Selected Resorts and
  Hotels of the U.S.
Shopping in Europe

Skiing in North America
Sunday in New York